Ed Hammond.

Students, University and Society

Students, University and Society

A Comparative Sociological Review

Edited by

MARGARET SCOTFORD ARCHER

HEINEMANN EDUCATIONAL BOOKS

LONDON

Heinemann Educational Books Ltd

LONDON   EDINBURGH   MELBOURNE   TORONTO
AUCKLAND   JOHANNESBURG   SINGAPORE
IBADAN   NAIROBI   HONG KONG   NEW DELHI
KUALA LUMPUR

ISBN 0 435 82375 2

First published 1972

Published by Heinemann Educational Books Ltd
48 Charles Street, London W1X 8AH

Printed in Great Britain by Morrison and Gibb Ltd
London and Edinburgh

Foreword

For a variety of reasons the sociology of education has always appeared one of the least adventurous specialisms within the discipline—it has remained almost to date tightly shackled to its subject matter, reflecting the priorities and preoccupations of educators rather than the theoretical concerns of sociologists. As the crisis developed in higher education throughout the sixties nothing became more obvious than the inability of the sociology of education to provide a framework for the interpretation of events taking place. The reason for this is quite simple—specialists had concentrated upon the analysis of the classroom, the school and social differentials in achievement and interaction, and thus shown a complementary neglect of research about educational systems as such. In other words there was no macrosociology of education, although its development is indispensable to an understanding of the complex interrelations of students, university and society which underpin the crisis.

It was not only the lack of an established theoretical framework or body of research in this field that led to the whole issue rapidly assuming the character of a political and ideological battleground. When academics are themselves occupationally involved in a problem it is only to be expected that they will manifest political and ideological interests and in fact perfectly correct that they should do so. However, what is unacceptable is that the interested statements of professionals should be confused with the disinterested analysis of academics. Yet it is precisely the absence of a clearly defined disciplinary contribution which encourages this confusion. It was one specific aspect of this confusion which gave rise to the present volume. Ideology, by definition, seeks to generalize and one of the major consequences of its international application to the problems of higher education (from whatever point on the political spectrum) was to accentuate universals and minimize cross-cultural differences. The crisis, because of its temporal coincidence in many countries, was seen as unitary. It is to this view that the present symposium is addressed.

Since it was intended to stress the importance of cross-cultural differences in social and educational structure, chapters were commissioned from sociologists with expert knowledge of the society studied, which in most cases is that of their country of origin. Each author is alone responsible for the views advanced in his or her own contribution. However, we all firmly share the conviction that comparative sociology is indispensable to the analysis of such problems and have all attempted to exclude as far as possible our own political affinities from our contributions. How far we have succeeded in this aim is for our readers to judge.

Most of the chapters in this book were first presented as papers in a seminar series at the University of Reading during the academic year 1969–70, under the auspices of the Graduate School of Contemporary European Studies. I would like to express my thanks to the Secretary of the Graduate School, Mrs Patricia Sales, for all her help throughout the series and afterwards when organizing the volume. I am also most grateful to Dr Stuart Woolf, who as Chairman of the Graduate School at the time, was responsible for turning the idea into reality and who has given enormous encouragement at all stages. Finally my warm thanks to Professor Donald MacRae for starting the series off and for the interest he has taken in the whole project.

MARGARET SCOTFORD ARCHER

Table of Contents

List of Contributors

Margaret Scotford ARCHER is Lecturer in Sociology, University of Reading

Colin CROUCH is research student at Nuffield College, Oxford

Toyomasa FUSÉ is Assistant Professor of Sociology, University of Montreal

Salvador GINER is Lecturer in Sociology, University of Reading

Dietrich GOLDSCHMIDT is Director of the Institut für Bildungsforschung of the Max-Planck Gesellschaft, Berlin

Nigel GRANT is Lecturer in Education, University of Edinburgh

Milan HAUNER is Research Fellow, St John's College, Cambridge

Guido MARTINOTTI is Professor of Sociology, University of Milan

Martin TROW is Professor of Sociology, University of California, Berkeley

Michalina VAUGHAN is Senior Lecturer in Sociology, London School of Economics

1. INTRODUCTION

Margaret Scotford Archer

Of the variety of explanations advanced to account for the present disharmony between students, university and society, most fail to take the comparative perspective into account. It is difficult in the copious literature recently devoted to the crisis in higher education[1] to detect any systematic attempt to relate international variations in the form, content and intensity of student unrest to corresponding differences in national university systems and social structures. Frequently, when analysis goes beyond the case-study level, cross-cultural differences are merely tacked on as a kind of peroration after explication of the main theory. This gap in research can perhaps be accounted for by the predominance of two types of approaches to the problem, which, in their very different ways, neglect or minimize international variations in the phenomenon.

On the one hand, the *microscopic* approach, which has both a strong and a weak version, neglects cross-cultural differences. Its strong form involves psychological reductionism in seeking to explain student activism by the social origins, parental child-rearing practices and parental politics of active students, and ignores questions of variation in student goals, and the form and intensity of action. The weaker version could be termed the 'internalist' approach,[2] which pinpoints specific aspects of the student condition—overcrowding, anonymity, low staff-student ratios, etc. as explanatory of student unrest. However, this neglects the historical as well as the comparative perspective, since clearly such conditions do not have an invariant effect. It neglects the importance of social conditions and social change outside higher education, and thus treats universities as isolated social institutions.

On the other hand, the *universalist* approach seeks a general and usually 'externalist' explanation of all historical and contemporary manifestations of the phenomenon. However, such unifying theories as that of the 'conflict of generations'[3] or 'world cultural revolution'[4] neglect the importance of differences in higher education, as well as minimizing cross-cultural variations. In the case of the former, 'to regard the academy as a stage for the playing out of familiar psycho-dramas is to ignore or at least underestimate what the academy may itself contribute to the thematic substance of the play. Most important, a history that coalesces every student movement, here and everywhere, past and present, tends in the end to rob each of its historical character.'[5] In the case of the latter, the same comments apply because of its underlying dependence upon historical idealism.

Thus it follows that any attempt to account for international variations in the form, content and intensity of the crisis in higher education involves an examination of the interrelationships of students, university and society, not an exclusive concentration on one of them. This in turn implies a macro-sociological[6] approach, which outlines the similarities and differences between systems and sub-systems relationships in various countries, which are subsequently related to particular aspects of their respective educational conflicts. In such an examination one would try to chart, classify and account for comparative variations rather than seek an exhaustive explanation of student unrest itself.

The distinction is important because the course and consequences of student politics are determined nationally. There is, as yet, no international student movement, and despite the growing internationalism of symbols, ideas and vocabulary, together with imitation of expressive forms, few signs of cross-national co-ordination (as distinct from solidarity). Even if there were, its orientation, form, content, direction and impact in any country would be mediated by national institutions. The growth of such international iconography and imitative isomorphism among students should not be allowed to obscure the very real cross-cultural differences, which coincide with variations in university and social structure. *The following discussion will be exclusively devoted to bringing together those types of historical and comparative research that have a bearing upon such cross-cultural differences.*

Universities and higher education

Higher educational systems in developed countries are characterized by a diversity of origins and a variety of historical traditions. Despite certain forms of well-documented cross-cultural influence—the German model in American universities, the mutual Franco-Italian influence, and the imprint of the American pattern on the Japanese system— the structural relations linking education to other social institutions generally appear to have changed in response to internal pressures from the national social structure rather than to those emanating from outside, unless conquest or territorial redistribution were involved. In other words, macro-educational change has largely been determined at the national level, although substantive changes have been effected by imitation, diffusion and adaptation of foreign patterns. These structural relations and the systems linkages underpinning them and integrating education with other social institutions are of particular importance, since historically higher education has enjoyed low institutional autonomy and consequently has shown low propensity to initiate change. At the international level, and from the post-feudal period onwards, this has resulted in a diversity of higher educational systems with different structures, goals and values.

Attempts have been made to encompass this variety by pointing to certain universal trends in the structural relations between education and other social institutions, and thus to changes in higher education at the macro-sociological level. A brief discussion of Havighurst's theory will suffice to show the difficulties involved in trying to link educational and institutional change directly. Havighurst[7] distinguishes four different types of relations between social institutions and education, corresponding to evolutionary stages of social development. In the first type, the family controls informal education in simple pre-literate societies. In the second, religion (together with the family, where religion is domestically based) shapes formal education in the theocracy or church-dominated society. In the third type, the emergence of a nation state leads to it taking over responsibility for the educational system. Finally, in the socialist or neo-capitalist society complex structural relations emerge, with the state and the economy jointly dominating education.[8]

There are three main difficulties involved in accepting this sequential account of educational development. Firstly, it assumes that complex structural relationships only characterize the educational systems of advanced economies, and thus implies that simple and complex relations correspond to a pre-industrial post-industrial dichotomy. While it is undeniable that contemporary systems of higher education respond (differentially) to a plurality of demands from the economy, polity, government bureaucracy, army, judiciary and other social institutions, this was also the case with certain pre-industrial systems. Thus the Imperial University of Napoleon was integrated with the political structure—through the use of education for political socialization—with the government bureaucracy and army through training and recruitment, and with the post-revolutionary system of social stratification. Secondly, the historical schema is not applicable to educational change in all countries: in Britain, for example, stages three and four were confounded rather than distinct. Finally, Havighurst incorporates a general statement about educational secularization in making the distinction between stage two and the latter stages, which whilst adequate as a broad description of an overall trend is subject to considerable national variations, as I have indicated elsewhere.[9]

In fact, there appears to be no single deterministic sequence applicable to the historical development of higher education. Even large-scale universal processes like industrialization have had no unitary impact upon educational change. Whilst research has demonstrated associations between stage of economic development and *amount* of educational provision, it has also underlined a lack of relationship between the *type* of education available in countries at the same stage.[10] Decisions about the kind of educational investment (or consumption) to be undertaken with increased wealth depend upon national, and often non-economic priorities. Thus in the pre-World War II period, systems of higher education displayed a plurality of forms, functions and values, and their historical development gave few indications of gradual cross-national convergence: hence the frequency with which those discussing higher education comparatively tend to distinguish the five great university patterns—the German, French, English, American and Russian—sometimes classifying others by reference to them.

However, it is often stated that certain forms of convergence, i.e. movements over time towards a common institutional pattern, are occurring in post-war higher education. The first involves changing structural relations with systems of social stratification, resulting in a growth of educational democratization; the second, changing structural relations with the economic system, leading to greater educational vocationalism, and the third, changing structural relations with the political system, leading to stronger state control over higher education. The concepts of institutional change and convergence must be clearly distinguished in discussing the three aspects. To maintain that higher educational systems are converging towards some point on the 'open closed' dimension, it is necessary to show either that Western Europe has over time narrowed the gap that in the past separated its intake policy from the less élitist practices in both the U.S. and U.S.S.R. or that in the U.S. and U.S.S.R. higher education has become less open over the same period. Absence of comparable sets of data based on the same time-interval for the different countries precludes firm statements on international convergence or divergence. What is clear, however, is that despite the changes taking place in some countries towards democratization, the contemporary differences remain enormous (in Germany children of manual workers represent 4.5 per cent. of students, in Eastern Europe, over 40 per cent.)[11] and indicate very different structural relations between higher education and social stratification. Exactly the same can be said of educational vocationalism —despite any overall increase in the proportion of students taking courses of professional training—when countries employing strict manpower-planning programmes are contrasted with those maintaining open-door admissions policies, and the elective system is coupled with the availability of a wide range of humanistic options.

Finally, statements that there is a general trend towards central direction of education by the state[12] again should not be taken to imply a growing uniformity in relations between polity and university. While it is certainly true that in general governments have come to play the major role in financing higher education, this represents a growing similarity in only one systems linkage. In terms of others—the use of higher education for political socialization or political recruitment —differences, not similarities, predominate.[13]

Furthermore, there are few signs that, even where systems of higher education have responded to similar pressures, they have reacted to them in the same way, thereby increasing cross-cultural uniformity. For instance, similar degrees of 'openness' between national systems can co-exist with widely different educational provisions and practices, and changes on this dimension do not imply corresponding changes in other aspects of the system. Indeed, one of the frequent criticisms of Western European universities is that while they have become somewhat more open, they have retained élitist norms and values, and establishments that embody them. The post-war growth in numerical intake, a near-universal response to birth boom and social demand, also provides a good example of the diversity of substantive provisions to accommodate the same pressure: upgrading of colleges and foundation of new universities (England); expansion of evening and correspondence courses (Soviet Union); new universities and faculties plus overcrowding (France); and so on. Large differences remain between the various countries, both in terms of the structural relations linking higher education to other social institutions and in terms of the specific practices employed where the same systems linkage exists.

It is because of this contemporary and historical variety in higher education that attempts to 'capture' change by juxtaposing ideal types are largely exercises in selective perception. Thus Clark Kerr's[14] description of university development from the collegial community of scholars (with élite intake and internal goal-determination) to the multiversity (with democratic intake and external goal-determination) neglects many past and present patterns. In particular, it omits two equally important types, the Napoleonic (élite intake and external goal determination) and the modern Humanistic (with sub-élite intake and relative autonomy in goal-determination). However, where Kerr is right is not in positing the future universality of the multiversity (a multifunctional institution responding to all external demands by further internal differentiation), but in underlining the plurality of expectations now focused on higher education.

Throughout the twentieth century the perceived relevance of higher education to a variety of goals has increased in all countries. Demand for its products has grown, and competition to determine the type of output has developed accordingly. Furthermore, 'as a differentiated subsystem of the society, it is the source of several different kinds of outputs that in various ways are important in other sectors of the society'.[15] However, different systems have responded in different ways to these multiple external demands and the new systems linkages with other social institutions that they involve. The idea of a multiversity is a very special case of type and method of response. The establishment of a real 'multiversity'[16] would imply a situation in which all external demands and corresponding structural relations were treated as potentially legitimate, and the resolution of forces left to be determined by the buyers' market. This assumes, firstly, the existence of a buyers' market—and yet consumer sovereignty is perhaps the rarest model to be found in contemporary higher education. Secondly, it involves the absence of external imperative control over or internal veto on demands of any kind—i.e. the ways in which certain State universities have excluded theological training and certain faculties have been able to repulse management studies. Finally, and underpinning the previous two points, it assumes no incompatibility or perceived conflict between the various demands that cannot or will not be solved by further differentiation.[17] The multiversity may thus conform to the ideal of classical economics, but it is not a description of contemporary reality, or, it seems, of future world trends in higher education.

The differential responses of such systems to external demands, determined in a variety of ways, has led to different patterns of structural relations between higher education and other social institutions in different countries. Thus universities in some countries are highly responsive to economic requirements while having few systems linkages with the polity, and vice versa in other countries. Of particular importance to the following discussion is the degree of integration of a nation's universities with the respective stratification, economic and political subsystems, as these will profoundly influence student origins, condition and destination. In addition, it is likely that conflict in and over higher education will be centred on the types of structural linkages that should be accepted as legitimate. In Parsons' terms, 'these non-academic value components are sometimes well-integrated with academic values as part of the more general societal integration of values—in the main such integration exists in the health fields—but they are often much involved with social and political conflict, hence with various forms and degrees of opposition to some institutional status quo.'[18] It is not, of course, necessary to accept the 'general integration of values' to take the latter point. Thus the following section will concentrate on an analysis of the relationship between systems of higher education and three other social institutions, to outline some of their implications for the student position *vis-à-vis* the university and the wider society.

University and society

1. Higher education and politics

There are considerable historical variations in the speed with which and degree to which educational systems became integrated with the political structure. The minimal necessary conditions for this to take place involved a political élite desiring educational control and possessing the resources and facilities to replace the provisions of the existing dominant group—in Europe, the Church. The desire to control education more closely depended upon the conviction that greater utility to the State would accrue. In most countries until the late eighteenth century governing élites presented few challenges to clerical domination of education, being relatively satisfied with the output from these institutions and with their independent financial status (with the exception of those with étatist gallican fears of Jesuits promoting ultramontanism through education). Secondly, the State had to devalue the clerical monopoly over educational resources, both physical and human, replacing them by alternative establishments and a new teaching body. A complex series of factors—the prestige of existing universities, opposition from the traditional dominant group and other social groups, difficulties of exercising control, foundation of competing institutions—have influenced the extent to which higher education was integrated with the political structure after clerical control was broken and have thus determined the degree of autonomy of universities from both spheres of influence.

A comparison of modern systems of higher education and their autonomy from the political structure in terms of finance and allocation of income, appointment of academic staff, admission and examination of students, and drawing up of the curricula,[19] indicates that it is only in terms of financing that the State universally intervenes. As far as the other criteria are concerned, there is a very broad relationship between low autonomy and the existence of a highly centralized State. In the centralized continental state, the centralized educational system, which corresponds closely to it, enjoys a different legal status—appointments, admissions and curricula generally being subject to parliamentary legislation and administrative regulation. To the more decentralized and Federal states corresponds the more localized educational system with greater autonomy, at least from national politics. Even in terms of finance, universities in such countries usually have more extensive powers of disposal over their budgets (for example in Great Britain), although provincial control can be important (for example in the U.S.A.).

However, the degree of autonomy of higher education from the polity is not a simple function of the centralized/decentralized structure of both social institutions or of the legal status of universities. There are mediating factors which destroy the simplicity of this 'reflective' relationship between the subsystems. Firstly, as Blondel has argued, there are considerable differences in the degree of *de facto* autonomy possessed by higher educational systems sharing the same formal political constraints. 'These formal powers do not by themselves lead to governmental intervention. Indeed, conversely, the absence of these formal powers is not by itself sufficient to ensure independence.'[20] The degree of prestige attaching to the university and to academics is advanced as a crucial intervening variable, which—where strong—will lessen the use of formal powers, and where weak, as in the anti-intellectual American tradition, will strengthen public controls. Yet it is clear from the experience of the countries of Eastern and Southern Europe, which have had well differentiated intelligentsias, and traditions of awarding the highest prestige to intellectuals and academics, that this has been insufficient to protect the autonomy of the university. Indeed, it appears that in countries where a fair degree of autonomy has prevailed, factors additional to high prestige—some pertaining to the university and others to the polity—have been present.

Secondly, then, as Bereday et al. argue, 'There has always been competition for some of the various services the universities could offer. Consequently in societies where there has existed some balance of power between political groups they have been able to attain autonomy and to preserve their academic freedom . . . The university was protected by institutions which might themselves be in conflict but whose interests were identical in wanting the services the universities could provide and in not wishing them to be subservient to institutions other than their own.'[21] It is when party politics have broken down and the powers of the State strengthened in fascist régimes and post-revolutionary dictatorships that autonomy has been most severely reduced. The particular aspects most affected depend upon the ideology and policy of the régime. For example, the Soviet commitment to educating the new ruling class led to stringent control over admissions, with the introduction of quota and bonus systems to favour applicants from manual backgrounds, whereas Franco's régime relied on the social self-selection of the traditional procedures and concentrated on establishing other types of political control.

The ensuing diversity of structural relations between politics and higher education can best be broken down by specifying the types of systems linkages integrating universities with the polity in various countries. It should be noted, however, that in discussing national systems of education the major trends and characteristics of their component establishments are being stressed, and each will have a range of variation which can only occasionally be touched upon here. Discussion will also be restricted to those linkages of particular importance to undergraduates, omitting some which involve graduates, staff, administration, and research workers to a greater extent. Three major systems linkages and their strength or weakness in any country appear vital to an understanding of how the structural relations between the university and the polity condition, ceteris paribus, expectations of and reactions to the student role. These are:

Political integration: the role of the State in funding establishments of higher education and students, either directly or indirectly, and the influence over university structure and development which this gives;

Political socialization: the use of higher education for conveying political values, and the degree of political freedom allowed students;

Political recruitment: the use of higher education, and in particular of student politics, for recruitment to political careers.

The effect of such linkages on the student condition becomes clear if, for the moment, they are treated simply as factors present or absent. When all three systems linkages are operative, the student is directly subsidized by the State, is expected to manifest ideological orthodoxy and probably to deepen his knowledge of its principles whilst an undergraduate, to accept political limitations on the courses available to him, the way they are presented and the qualifications he receives, and to participate in those kinds of student action and mobilization deemed appropriate. On the other hand, when these linkages are weak or absent, the student is largely making his own investment, will have a less rigorous entry procedure and greater freedom in course selection, will be expected to form his own political opinions and to express them within broad limits and, if interested in a political career, to seek it through external agencies. While crude, this dichotomy serves to indicate that, as Weinberg and Walker have maintained, student movements 'are significantly affected by the existing structural relations between the university and the State and between student politics and the environing political system'.[22] A more detailed examination of the patterning and intensity of systems linkages in different countries is now required to show the marked impact they have on the *form* taken by *institutionalized* student politics.

If these political linkages are considered in isolation, that is, without paying attention to other types of structural relations between higher education and any other social institutions, they are none the less strikingly associated with prevailing forms of institutionalized student organizations. Because of this, they have a further influence over the major types of non-institutionalized student action, since the two kinds of student politics show a high degree of interaction.

It appears that the strength or weakness of each of these linkages has a distinct conditioning influence on institutionalized student politics. When there is a strong *political integration* linkage, and in consequence centralized state control over the ways in which the education budget is distributed and thus over the development of university structure, a parallel form of student organizations tends to evolve. 'This centralisation of authority is likely to have its counterpart in the strong, centralised organization of students at the national level'.[23] This is a joint product of the fact that the condition of students in terms of stipends, facilities, housing and amenities is determined at the national level, and that any problems arising from them cannot be resolved locally. The agency for collective bargaining thus tends to be situated at the same level as the authority structure. Hence when this linkage is weak and the university enjoys greater financial autonomy, while students are not funded centrally, local campus-based 'intramural' organizations predominate and are stronger than national 'intermural' student bodies,[24] the latter concentrating not on collective bargaining, but on welfare and leisure arrangements.

Where higher education is expected to engage in a high degree of *political socialization*, student organizations will tend to be officially established and accredited, to take an active role in party work and to manifest a high degree of ideological orthodoxy. There will be a strong tendency to have a single recognized organization which is subject to frequent purges and official modifications, as the political élite hunts for the maximally useful or minimally harmful formula. Other student bodies will be proscribed or severely restricted, including cultural and religious groups which might lend themselves to counter-politicization, and the official body may be expected to engage in campus policing. Where this linkage is weak or non-existent, student organizations will be non-doctrinaire (even if attached to a political party) and pluralistic (even if a national students' union predominates). These differences thus clearly reflect the role assumed by the political system in the formation, regulation and transmission of political values.

When a large amount of *political recruitment* takes place within the university for party members, workers and future representatives, party branches and clubs are likely to develop. Nationally organized parties which sponsor mobility in this way tend not only to accrue localized support on the campus, but also to be faced by a national student Party organization, unwilling to accept the passive recruitment role, but seeking influence over policy formation. Where this linkage is weak or absent, active students join external political associations, sometimes leaving the university to the apolitical concerns of the institutionalized student organization.

If considered in combination, these three systems linkages show a different patterning of weakness and strength in the various countries here considered. These are related to five distinct types of institutionalized student activity, as the following table, which owes much to Weinberg and Walker's work, shows.

	1	2	3	4	5
Political Integration:	Strong	Strong	Strong	Weak	Weak
Political Socialization:	Strong	Weak	Weak	Weak	Weak
Political Recruitment:	Strong	Strong	Weak	Strong	Weak
Institutionalized student organization	A single official organization	National Union + Political Party Branches	National Students' Union	Political Party Branches	University student Government

The first case, where all three linkages are strong, is typical of the U.S.S.R., of post-war Poland and Czechoslovakia, and of Spain, countries where higher education has been seen as vital to the stability, efficiency and durability of the respective régimes. The Komsomol, Czech Č.S.M., Polish Z.M.P. and Spanish S.E.U.[25] were designed to this end, although their success has depended on the closest political supervision. Post-war Italy falls into the second category, with its high politicization of student associations that reproduced the parliamentary system within the universities, conflicting in the fifties with the national students' union (U.G.I.). Despite the attempts of the latter to keep parties out of the universities, they reasserted their influence during the sixties and led to the emergence of student political factions, which sought influence in both national politics and university government.[26] Thirdly, Japan, France and Sweden are characterized by durable and representative national students' unions. These are intermural associations engaging in collective bargaining on a wide range of issues, although the Scandinavian organizations have taken on more of the character of Trade Unions than either the U.N.E.F. or the Zengakuren. Fourthly, in Britain the political party branches and clubs dominate student politics, although they enjoy different degrees of integration with their parent bodies, and fifthly, student university government is the predominant pattern in the U.S.A., where the student condition is more locally determined, despite recent changes.

Non-institutionalized student action, endorsing norms and values which go beyond those defined by the established agencies that defend student interests, takes a form which is 'likely to be incorporated with, or otherwise linked to, institutionalised forms of activism, perhaps modifying the latter in the process of adaptation'.[27] These relationships can be further specified by analysing the five types of institutionalized organizations in conjunction with the particular forms of student activism that have accompanied them.

(i) *Type I—A single official organization.* Such 'approved organisations are not the product of student initiative, nor are they administered by the students themselves in furtherance of their own interests'.[28] Nevertheless any form of activism taking place outside their framework and in opposition to their values and practices is inextricably linked to them. The exact form taken by such action appears to depend on the degree of political control exercised and the extent to which it makes opposition difficult to organize and maintain. Where this is at its strongest, the major form of non-institutionalized action will be 'indifferentism'—a refusal to join or support the official organization. As Cornell has argued, 'by far the most significant political manifestation by students in communist countries in Eastern Europe is their passive refusal to accept the role delineated for them by the party'.[29] However, while 'indifferentism' involves a recognition that institutionalized agencies cannot be changed nor other bodies founded, there will generally be attempts during a slight 'thaw' to counter-politicize other existing bodies. Film societies, choral or theatrical groups, and writers' and artists' congresses are particularly amenable to this process, as can be religious groups when the Church, denomination or sect is not associated with the political élite. Such activities, however, are easily subject to repression, and in addition represent more of an outlet for expressing affective discontent than for organizing instrumental opposition.

It is because of this that the most effective form of non-institutionalized action seems to involve the *infiltration* of the official organization. As totalitarian régimes have become aware, 'the existence of a separate organisational framework for students may, in time, serve as a channel through which student interests may be aggregated and pressure may be exerted upon decision making organs'.[30] Students in Spain and Eastern Europe have recognized that their bargaining power increases when action is directed to influencing, not by-passing, the official organization. Some type of restructuring of the latter follows successful infiltration. This may either result, as in Spain, in the decline of the official body (S.E.U.) and the creation of associations whose form corresponds more closely to student demands or, as in Eastern Europe, in purges and the creation of new bodies expected to coincide more closely with official requirements. In the latter case the cycle of infiltration and purge is likely to be repeated, as effective non-institutionalized action has few alternatives, apart from the take-over of official organizations.

(ii) *Type II—A national union and political party branches.* This combination of institutionalized student organizations typically appears in formal, but unstable democracies. In post-war Italy the importance of political party branches in the universities was great, owing both to party recruitment and to the significance of political connections for success in other types of careers. However, opposition to the parties and their branches grew, since 'their ideological dogmatism, opportunistic policy, and bureaucratic ossification engendered cynical criticism and deep indifference among the vast majority of students'.[31] Reaction to this involved the foundation of the national students' Union, to minimize party interference and to maximize chances of university reform. The co-existence of both types of institutionalized organization predisposed towards a high politicization of the student body. *Factionalism* became the major form of non-institutionalized activity, as those on the extreme right and left sought to direct the Union against the established parties, while at the same time often using political branches to increase their influence over the Union. It is in this type of situation, which shows some resemblance to the Latin American pattern, that the distinction between institutionalized and non-institutionalized action is the least durable and most unclear. For in the context of national political instability the two kinds of action are in continual flux, and the student factions have greater possibilities of institutionalizing their policies either in political branches or in the national Union.

(iii) *Type III—National Student Unions*. Where such strong centralized organizations have developed, they tend to exert the same kind of influence over non-institutionalized activism as the single official organization. However, because students enjoy great political freedom and because the national union is officially recognized, but not imposed, activists have the possibility both of founding alternative groups and influencing the outlook of the union itself. While the constant splitting and differentiation of *groupuscules* at all points on the political spectrum is characteristic in countries of this kind, these in turn will seek to redirect rather than replace the national union. As in France, 'structurally, because of the centralization of government control over higher education and the consequent importance of the U.N.E.F., the minoritaires desire to radicalize the U.N.E.F. rather than operate as a minority group outside of it'.[32] There is a constant interaction between institutionalized and non-institutionalized action—a fight between the 'majos' and 'minos' to control the French U.N.E.F. and the 'mainstream' and 'anti-mainstream' to dominate the Japanese Zengakuren. Thus *radicalization* is the main form of activism, and whether it emanates from extreme and external political groups or arises out of local conditions (like the 22 March movement at Nanterre) it is quickly assimilated as a *tendance* of the national union. The success of these groups in redirecting institutionalized activity is greatest in times of political crisis—for example the Algerian crisis in France and that of the American Defence Alliance in Japan—but lessening of tension often results in a return to more traditional objectives by the union and intense schismatic reactions from the radicals. A new crisis is required to bring about coalescence and to reinstate the authority of the radicals, and in the interim much of their effort will be devoted to its discovery.

(iv) *Type IV—Political party branches*. The strength of political clubs, closely linked to national parties and the weakness of the national union, have presented two distinct problems for non-institutionalized activism in Britain. The latter has meant that all those seeking radical university reform or social change have been able to achieve has been sporadic, highly localized protests on very specific issues, whose spread has depended on imitation and solidarity, not co-ordination. Secondly, the existence of party branches 'weakens the spontaneous appearance of protest movements—such as the Campaign for Nuclear Disarmament—which are forced to filter their policies through the clubs which function as a damper on the progression towards extremism'.[33] The attempts made to overcome both difficulties have generally involved the joining or founding of national single-issue movements by student activists. Since all of these have opposed the Labour Party's foreign policy—for example on disarmament, South Africa, Vietnam, Biafra—the major form of non-institutionalized action involves *deviation* from a distinct frame of political reference. 'The existence of a politically independent Labour movement is, therefore, one of the crucial factors differentiating student activism in Britain'.[34] So far the Labour Party has contained such activism to the extent that non-institutionalized action has weakened once the national saliency of an issue has declined, as radicals have been unable to consolidate opposition in a durable counter-organization. Thus the future of the student movement is closely linked with the future of the British Left.

(v) *Type V—University student government.* When institutionalized activities of negotiation with university authorities are campus-based, this provides few systematic opportunities for radicalization and offers no prolonged interest to radicals. Activists therefore move out onto the national political scene and join a variety of issue-centred rather than party-sponsored organizations. The major form taken by non-institutionalized action is thus one of *externalization*. The nature of the movement joined and the degree to which it impinges on university concerns determine the intensity with which such activism and localized student government interact. 'Issue movements tend to become involved with campus affairs only when their behaviour, externally oriented, runs up against administration hostility. When campus matters and crises, such as the plight of the Negroes in the urban ghetto, converge, then issue movements take the university administration as their target.'[35] Both civil rights and the draft issue have been of a type whose campus relevance could be stressed, and which could involve the 'campus issue protesters'.[36] However, the impact of activism upon institutionalized student politics will only tend to be as durable as the issue movements themselves, and even with these two lasting cases, new angles of local significance have to be continuously developed to prevent disintegration of the 'alliance'.

To place stress on the different types of structural relations between higher education and the polity as important influences on student activism is not to deny the significance that some have attributed to overall changes in international politics. Lipset's thesis that 1956 represented a watershed in Western political ideology, as anti-totalitarianism, at least for the young, ceased to legitimate foreign policy and justify the domestic situation,[37] is probably a correct diagnosis of a general factor stimulating activism. It is quite compatible with the preceding analysis, which concentrates strictly on formal differences in the expression of activism, not on its causes or content. Whether the basic source of such activism is universal or national, it is maintained that the greater the number of systems linkages between polity and university, the more likely it is to be expressed through the institutionalized organizations, and vice versa. However, even without aiming at exhaustiveness it is necessary, in order to extend the discussion to aspects of student politics beyond the formal, to examine other structural relations of the university beyond that with the polity.

2. Higher education and the economy

As in the case of politics, universities have shown different degrees of responsiveness to the requirements of the economic structure throughout their histories. The prevalent oversimplification, which designates the process of industrialization as bringing about the integration of higher education to the economy, only serves to mask this diversity. Firstly, in taking a restricted definition of the economy, identifying it exclusively with industrial production, those cases are neglected in which the universities prepared their students for the occupational structures of pre-industrial societies. Both the training for clerical roles (of either kind) provided by the feudal universities,[38] and that for bureaucrats, teachers and officers wherever the Napoleonic model took root, are omitted. Secondly, this view tends to assume an immediate adaptive response on behalf of universities to certain universal requirements implicit in the process of industrialization. The case of Britain, whose universities remained unresponsive to the coming of industry, to the threatened loss of economic competitiveness, and still resistant to gearing its expansion to manpower needs in the twentieth century, shows this reaction to be far from automatic. Furthermore, when systems of higher education have responded to economic pressures, they have done so to different degrees and in a variety of ways. Some have accepted the necessity of adapting the universities themselves to the production of scientific and technical manpower, while others have conserved the traditional role of these establishments (often intensifying their non-applied character) and founded other training institutions, which show considerable international variations in prestige.

A comparison of modern higher education systems thus reveals differing degrees of autonomy from the economic structure in terms of inputs, processes and outputs. Low autonomy on these dimensions corresponds to two types of structural relations linking these social institutions. On the one hand, countries engaging in intense economic planning closely co-ordinate educational expansion to manpower needs, gearing educational output to the requirements of the occupational structure. Where this has most markedly occurred there has been a coincidence between the setting of targets for rapid economic growth and the positive repudiation of past traditions of higher education. Without the latter, imperative planning would be resisted by faculties committed to less 'progressive' values and goals. It is significant in this connection that the Soviet Union has had most difficulty in grafting its educational policies on those countries with previously well developed university traditions—Czechoslovakia, Poland and Hungary—and least where such traditions had been less pronounced—Bulgaria and Rumania.[39] On the other hand, low autonomy has also prevailed, at least for a time, when higher education and the economy have been linked together through the free market for professional skills. In this case the university has been characterized by an absence of independent means, enabling it to remain outside the sellers' market, and a weak tradition of value-commitment of a kind antipathetic to it. However, the development of monopoly capitalism coupled with adhesion to egalitarian ideals has increased the autonomy of undergraduate instruction in the U.S.A. from market forces, while leaving that of postgraduate instruction low. It requires, however, an affluent national economy to support this extent of educational inflation before economic needs begin to be met.

Countries whose universities continue to enjoy greater autonomy are those whose economic systems fall somewhere along the continuum between these two types. This broad curvilinear relationship can be depicted in the following diagram.

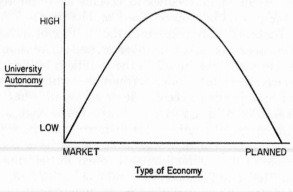

FIG. 1.1

This is not to suggest that such national systems of higher education have remained immune from and unresponsive to economic pressures— merely that their type of reaction has conserved the relative autonomy of universities. For in these countries, characterized not only by growing economic pressures but also by the enduring prestige of the historic universities, the solution had been one of horizontal differentiation, unlike the vertical division of functions practised in the U.S.A. The requirements of technical training as distinct from professional formation have generally been met in special institutes outside the universities. Hans has shown how from the late eighteenth century onwards training in agriculture, veterinary science, mining, engineering and commerce has been provided in technical institutions, owing little to the values, goals, and methods of universities in Germany, France, Sweden, Spain, or Austria.[40] Unless such institutions have been endowed from the start with high prestige, through élite selection of students and their graduation to élite posts—as is the case with the

French Grandes Ecoles—they have rarely been able to overcome the generalized contempt in which the utilitarian values of technical education are held.

This bifurcation within higher education has enabled universities, particularly within western and southern Europe, to retain identification with past traditions and values (or at least with their modern interpretations) and to plead their special status to gain exemption from economic rationalization. This pattern has been least strong in Scandinavia and Japan, where differentiation occurs among universities, rather than between the universities and other forms of higher education. In the former, this coincides with the acceptance of educational planning as an inseparable part of welfare economics and, in the latter, with the foundation of private universities in response to a widening market for technical skills neglected by state institutions. Thus Sweden and Denmark are closer to the Russian end of the continuum and Japan to the other, with the remaining European countries falling in between, together with the contemporary United States.

As in the case of the political structure, a detailed analysis of the particular systems linkages relating universities and the economy is vital to any discussion of the effect different types of structural relations exert on the student condition. Three such linkages are of importance in defining the situation of the undergraduate—the extent to which admissions are geared to *manpower* requirements, courses to *professional training* and graduation to *productivity*. Each of these will be the subject of intranational as well as international variations, and although dominant university trends will be stressed, their importance will depend upon the extent of their predominance in that society.

Where admissions policies are geared to *manpower requirements*, university entrance and expansion will be determined by investment considerations (both economic and social) rather than by social demand, with its heavy consumption component. In no system can the calibration be perfect, owing to imprecision in the calculation of manpower targets and to the near certainty of conflict between different investment priorities. Eastern Europe, which provides the strongest example of this linkage, with its quota of places in each discipline determined in relation to the national plan, has also experienced the latent contradiction between the imperatives of constructing a socialist society and those of developing the socialist economy. However, the rationalizing forces of the latter appear to be prevailing over the former, as admissions policies now put less emphasis on manual origins. Finally, the outstanding feature of higher educational systems whose admissions policies are manipulated in this way is their greater concentration on science and technology and lesser intake for non-applied courses.

Elsewhere in post-war Europe entry to and expansion of universities have been more responsive to social demand than to manpower requirements, despite attempts at indicative educational planning, as for example in the Vth French Plan. Such demand has increased as standards of living have improved, and is intensified as educational prices do not rise for the consumer, thus providing no brake on growing demand.[41] There has been a corresponding growth in the imbalance between social demand and the capacity of systems to cope with it, which has been met, though not rectified, in one of two ways. Where strong traditions of an open-door entry to qualified secondary-school pupils prevail, congestion accompanied by a fall in quality has resulted, with its typical manifestations of crowded lecture theatres, low staff/ student ratios and little possibility of intensive tuition. In the absence of long-established rights to higher education for the appropriately qualified, a tightening of direct rationing procedures using various selection criteria has been used to separate actual from potential consumers.[42] Imbalance is further intensified by a strengthening of democratic values opposing projects to abandon the open-door policy, as in France, and attacking stringent selectivity, as in Britain. Furthermore, this type of admissions policy is closely associated with an unregulated growth in subjects studied, since choice of discipline is relatively unconstrained. It is far from uncommon to find students of the humanities and rapidly developing social sciences outnumbering those admitted to pure and applied science.

Where courses are geared to *professional training* there is a greater degree of functional differentiation and educational diversity at the higher level, both within the university and between it and other establishments. Correspondingly, the condition of students is less uniform and the position of the traditional university less monopolistic of prestige, where the monolithic structure of higher education has been transformed into a pluralistic system whose components do not elicit great disparity of esteem. Where this systems linkage exists most strongly, in Eastern Europe, it appears to have led to a loss by the universities of their hegemony over higher instruction, seven-eighths of students being educated in other institutions at this level in the Soviet Union. Yet the experience of pre-war Japan and the United States seems to indicate that this is not a necessary consequence, as functional differentiation can occur both between universities (in the case of the former) and within them (in the case of the latter). The distinction made in contemporary Sweden between traditional universities and technical universities, which enjoy parity of prestige, as well as the Danish practice of treating degrees as vocational preparation for specific professions, provide similar examples.

Where this linkage is weak, the shift from élite to sub-élite or mass intake has not been paralleled by a change from non-vocational to vocational instruction. With the gradual development towards more open systems in Western and Southern Europe, 'the social philosophy and goals have changed more than the educational system's structures, examinations and practices'.[43] The university has maintained its

pre-eminence over the vast majority of recently established and vocationally oriented institutions. The new inflow of students to the universities is funnelled into the old bottles—the social sciences receiving
the overspill. The speedy development of these latter courses can only
rarely be regarded as functional differentiation *vis-à-vis* the economy,
in view of subsequent employment bottlenecks, especially where rates
of absorption into the teaching profession are low. In consequence a
greater unity characterizes the condition of university students, but at
the same time a wider gap separates them from the experience of those
in other sectors of higher education.

Where *external productivity* is the standard of quality used to assess
degrees, some non-university agency is involved in evaluating output.
The process of evaluation cannot itself be precise, owing to difficulties
in separating marginal net individual, social and economic profits
gained from graduation. Although inadequate in many ways, a very
rough indicator of the standard being employed is the extent to which
particular qualifications are closely linked with entry into specific forms
of employment. This index is mainly deficient because such links may
be conditioned by tradition and other non-rational considerations.
Nevertheless the existence of close links enables external agencies to
monitor quality to some degree, and to preclude its autonomous
determination within the universities themselves. Where this linkage is
strong, calculability for the student is high, both in terms of the career
he will enter and of the relevance of his qualifications to it. The countries
that come closest to exclusive use of this standard are Denmark, where
by law a degree has value only in its special field,[44] and the Soviet
Union. In such countries a high degree of undergraduate specialization
is a corollary of this linkage.

Where this linkage is weak, the 'quality' of education is largely
determined internally in accordance with prevailing academic values.
This in turn will strengthen traditionalism, weaken innovation, lower
calculability of future employment to students, and (economically)
reduce functional specialization. 'The conservatism of faculties has no
ideological or philosophical base. It is a kind of conservatism that
stems almost exclusively from the structure of the university itself'.[45]
At its most extreme, this type of university will function largely for
self-recruitment, the academic content of courses will be boosted and
the pure, not the applied, stressed. It is in precisely these terms that
Bourdieu and Passeron[46] have criticized contemporary French university education, and it is often precisely this internal determination
of quality that is defended by academics in Western Europe under the
blanket term 'autonomy'.

If these systems linkages are again considered in isolation from the
further structural relations the universities maintain with other social
institutions, they appear to profoundly influence the order prevailing
within higher education. When all three linkages are weak, the corres-

ponding autonomy of university from economy renders it a unique type of industry. Buchanan and Devletoglou have argued that 'this is because: (1) those who consume its products do not purchase it; (2) those who produce it do not sell it; and (3) those who finance it do not control it'.[47] The 'order' resulting from market competition will be absent, since the effect of (1) is that demand will tend to exceed supply, of (2) that there will be little effort to meet the demands of consumers, and of (3), equally little attempt to satisfy taxpayers in view of the gulf separating ownership from control. Neither on the other hand will such systems of higher education derive internal order from the mutual integration of economic and educational planning. 'Order' is employed descriptively to denote the existence of a rational relationship between inputs, processes and outputs of higher education; discussion of its desirability lies outside the scope of this analysis, which seeks to highlight only one aspect of its likely consequences.

It has been argued, for each systems linkage in turn, that their weakness or absence increases the irrationality of the student condition by decreasing the calculability attaching to this role. In turn this degree of calculability, derived from the strength or weakness of structural relations between university and the economy, appears to influence both the intensity and content of students' reactions to their position. However, it is clear that variations in this particular type of structural relationship do not in themselves account for recent outbreaks of student unrest, since many of these linkage patterns have existed throughout the twentieth century.

A considerable body of research appears to support the proposition that a direct relationship exists between the calculability of the student condition and the rationality of reactions to it. This has obvious intranational as well as international implications, although the dominant type of reaction in a given country will depend upon the predominant type of student condition. Two studies of different systems of higher education which both show considerable autonomy from the economy help to confirm the effect this has on the experience of students. Marris,[48] studying English students, and Bourdieu and Passeron[49] their French counterparts, insist equally on the vocational aimlessness of students on entry, the absence of perceived relevance of courses studied and their general lack of connection with future activities. Both see the university as responsive neither to the immediate interests of students nor to their future activities. To Marris, the English university falls between the 'automatic' university (on the teaching-machine model) and the 'spontaneous' university (on the interest-guided model), thus cumulating the worst of both worlds—'The worst is to provide a routine academic training by means of relationships whose value lies in their spontaneity. It is at once clumsy and self-deceiving, since it appears to offer an intellectual independence which it continually frustrates.'[50] Bourdieu and Passeron make a similar point when outlining the departure of French universities from the rational model of treating students as professional apprentices, to treat all as apprentice professors, a goal bound to frustrate the vast majority. Thus both studies diagnose this 'inner-directed' academic experience as a consequence of the universities' autonomy.

The impact of this upon students is held to be the same in both systems, and the similarity with which it is expressed in the two studies is striking. To Marris, 'Undergraduates are estranged from their past and their future' and suffer from a 'sense of isolation in a closed, unreal, artificial and irresponsible life'.[51] To Bourdieu and Passeron the same limbo prevails, 'any rational relationships with future expectations being broken, the present becomes a period of fantasy'.[52] Thus low calculability in the student condition, when this temporary state is treated as an end in itself, fosters irrational responses in the absence of goal-directedness. These include both the positively sanctioned reaction of intellectual adventurism, in which studies are treated as an end in themselves, and the negatively sanctioned attempt to transform the student condition by negating the intellectual authority relationships governing it. With equal irrationality in terms of preparation for future active life, the former adapts to the timeless values of academia while the latter seeks to change the values by demoting the academic.

However, these authors are well aware that such tendencies are differentially distributed among the various disciplines—those enrolled in professional training courses, whether in Grandes Ecoles (with physical conditions superior to those of the universities) or technical colleges (with physical conditions inferior to those of universities) are less prone to irrational action of this kind. Such a conclusion is confirmed by the general finding that 'within the university, the professional schools and divisions have been the least turbulent'.[53] It is not that students in more vocationally oriented disciplines have shown universal satisfaction with their condition, but that their reaction has followed the less turbulent pattern of collective bargaining to engineer a more rational relationship between means and ends.

Thus it appears that, contrary to the assertions of certain neo-Marxists, student unrest (as opposed to student reformism) is greatest where there is least integration between university and economy. The difficulties involved in arguing the opposite are nowhere more clear than in Newman's attempt to account for greater activism in English art than technical colleges by claiming that 'the growing importance of art and design in a consumer society has had as its corollary the relative stasis of technology: it is this different relationship between education and production in these two sectors that accounts for divergent experiences.'[54] However, the argument here is *not* that strong relations with the economy preclude student discontent (far from it), merely that they minimize certain irrational reactions due to the indeterminacy of the student condition. This gives rise to a different content of protest, and one fundamentally unamenable to processes of arbitration—as students are usually the first to recognize. Nevertheless, it should be stressed that while the relationship between university and economy is a major influence upon content, other factors intervene to condition the intensity with which such ideas are held and translated into action by students sharing the same condition.

3. Higher education and social stratification

As in the case of the previous types of structural relationships discussed, great danger attaches to any over-emphasis of universal trends in the relationship between systems of higher education and social stratification. In particular, three trends are often over-accentuated and give an exaggerated impression of development towards a common type of structural relationship between the two social institutions. The *first* is that of the change from entry procedures based on social selection towards those culminating in merit selection. Over-emphasis on the change from ascriptive to achievement recruitment for higher education involves exaggeration of the 'closed' nature of historical systems (the Ancient Chinese and the provisions made by the Revolutionary and Napoleonic university), and the 'openness' of modern systems (where Western Germany, France, Italy and Spain admit less than 10 per cent. of students from the working class). The *second* trend is that of the change from a traditionally homogeneous student body to the contemporary heterogeneous aggregate. Emphasis on this shift from community to association, which reflects not only a diversification of the social origins of students but also of academic life-styles, again neglects important historical deviations, particularly the lack of integration due to religious differences (from Anglican and Dissenter controversy in Victorian Oxbridge to the struggle over the separation of Church and State in turn-of-the-century France). As a view of the larger modern universities it also takes insufficient notice of the more differentiated sub-units' departments, clubs, societies, halls of residence, etc. The *third* trend stresses the transition taking place from universities as ante-rooms to élite appointments to their modern role of preparing the majority of students for 'sub-élite' positions in the occupational structure. Of the three, this trend is perhaps the most pronounced, owing to universal increases in student intake, which seem disproportionate to the expansion in élite positions (although it would be difficult to show this statistically). Nevertheless, neither the extent to which traditional universities catered for those who never entered the employment market—and thus acted only as status-confirming agencies—nor the degree to which some contemporary institutions continue to supply certain élite sectors should be forgotten.

It is not suggested that such trends have been wrongly detected, but merely that over-emphasis of them minimizes the diversity of contemporary higher education in these respects. For in fact each trend broadly pinpoints a systems linkage between social stratification and higher education whose patterning appears to vary cross-culturally. Each of these influences the student condition and, it will be argued, the rate of student activism. When expressed exclusively in terms of class stratification, these linkages are: the extent to which university entry represents *class selection*, university enrolment *class membership* and university graduation *class mobility*. The first serves to determine the social composition of the student body, the last the occupational expectations of undergraduates. The second linkage involves the assumption that despite differences in social origins, the transitory occupancy of the role, and the absence of direct relations with production, students can nevertheless constitute a class. While this linkage is mentioned because of the major part it has played in certain interpretations of student activism such as Alain Touraine's,[55] it will not be dwelt upon here because of its dependence upon controversial redefinitions of the class concept.

University entry can reflect *class selection* in two main ways, the one involving social self-selection and the other employing a quota system. On the one hand, the persistence of traditional inequalities in educational opportunity for the different social classes, coupled with a low influence of countervailing egalitarian pressures, has perpetuated the middle-class exclusivity in universities despite their expansion. Thus in spite of numerical growth in places available, applicants from the working class still gain under 10 per cent. of places in France, West Germany, Italy and Spain.[56] While background still plays a crucial role in determining chances of entry to the university, a plurality of institutional arrangements and social pressures towards democratization increase this proportion to 15 per cent. in Sweden, 25 per cent. in Britain and over 35 per cent. in the U.S.A. However, on the other hand, entry conditions can be manipulated in an attempt to more faithfully reflect the national class composition among successful applicants. The use of quota systems and bonus points for candidates from manual backgrounds, while incompletely equilibrating the entry chances of all groups, causes the proportion of places awarded to this class to rise to approximately 40 per cent. in Eastern Europe. The rough percentages quoted here are drawn from national estimates, and their comparability should be treated with extreme caution.

The implications of graduation for *social mobility* vary significantly with changes in university intake and in the occupational structure, *inter alia*. As higher education expands and becomes a more abundant commodity (even if only to restricted groups in the class structure), 'the supply of new top jobs becomes scarcer relative to the number of educated people seeking them'.[57] This means that given an intensified but still 'élitist' recruitment (as in France, Western Germany, Italy and Spain), a large proportion of these middle-class entrants cannot expect social promotion to élite positions on graduation, but will take sub-élite appointments. In Dahrendorf's terms, they will join the 'service' rather than the 'ruling' class,[58] in Touraine's,[59] become technicians rather than technocrats, and in Etzioni's[60] become semi-professionals rather than professionals. This will only mean small-scale social mobility for many and none at all for some. In the case of countries whose twentieth-century expansion in higher education has also been accompanied by its greater democratization, then university graduation represents greater chances of social mobility. For graduates of working-class origin at least, appointment to a sub-élite employment may represent considerable social promotion.

These two factors, social composition of the student body and student mobility expectations, appear to influence the attitudes and actions of a nation's undergraduates. As Bourdieu and Passeron[61] have noted, the social origins of students are influential in bringing about different reactions to the same conditions. If the student role involves low future calculability, it is the bourgeois student who can afford to respond to indeterminacy by various forms of dilettantism. For the working-class student, both the investment made and the potential returns are too great to risk irrational escapism from the means/end aspect of higher education. Their dissatisfaction will tend to be geared towards making instruction more instrumental, while the privileged bourgeois student will seek to make it more affectively satisfying. In other words, in higher education it is those from lower socio-economic backgrounds who display the deferred gratification pattern. However, while the investment made by bourgeois students is less (relative to their parents' means), their potential future rewards are also correspondingly smaller (relative to their parents' occupational position). Consequently, as a group they have less to lose in seeking to redirect the university towards the spontaneous-interest model.

It is factors of this kind that probably underlie the well-documented[62] differential participation rates according to social origins in various forms of student activism. Profiles of activists generally stress their superior social origins, after standardizing for subject studied. Thus it would be expected, *ceteris paribus*, that the more open the higher educational system, the lower the participation in activism—and the greater the concentration on reformism. However, while the systems linkages between university and class stratification do significantly influence participation rates, this does not mean that they determine the intensity of activism. For among other factors, the very expansion of higher education has spelled an absolute increase in students of activist 'orientation', and the accompanying growth in size of universities has increased their concentration. Thus it appears more useful to view class as an intervening variable modifying the form and content of student organization and attitudes rather than having a direct impact upon student activism.

Introduction

Students, university and society

The preceding discussion has stressed the varied patterning of structural relations between higher education and other social institutions (principally the political and economic) in different countries. If these two types of systems linkages are now considered in conjunction, they appear to have a strong influence on the major type of authority exercised in various systems of higher education over their respective undergraduates. In other words, universities represent a series of complex organizations whose authority-type is conditioned by their relationship with the wider social structure. Using Etzioni's[63] typology of the kinds of 'power' characterizing complex organizations, the following table can be constructed for the countries discussed.

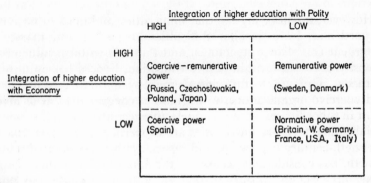

	Integration of higher education with Polity	
	HIGH	LOW
Integration of higher education with Economy — HIGH	Coercive – remunerative power (Russia, Czechoslovakia, Poland, Japan)	Remunerative power (Sweden, Denmark)
Integration of higher education with Economy — LOW	Coercive power (Spain)	Normative power (Britain, W. Germany, France, U.S.A., Italy)

FIG. 1.2

Obviously there can, and in most cases there will be intranational variations in the kind of authority exercised by different institutions because of their dissimilar relations with polity and economy. Furthermore, such a typology also oversimplifies by concentrating on the major aspect of authority, whereas most universities will at least make subordinate or supplementary reference to other criteria. Nevertheless, it represents a useful macrosociological device, providing a preliminary classification of systems of higher education *vis-à-vis* their undergraduate students. It should be noted that since the systems linkages upon which the classification is based concern only undergraduates, its applicability is restricted to them.

Etzioni argues that there are optimal compliance structures where efficiency results when the involvement of participants is[64] congruent with that generated by the organization itself. Ignoring the contentious issue of 'efficiency analysis', this framework is useful simply in pinpointing areas of order and conflict. Positive involvement of the subordinate in the organization depends in part on whether he considers its 'power' as legitimate and in part on its coincidence with his aims. This involvement can take different forms, but organizations have typically used various controls to engineer congruence between type of authority exercised and type of involvement of lower participants. Extending Etzioni's analysis to systems of higher education[65] yields the following congruent/compliance structures for the different authority types—

Predominant kinds of power in Universities	Kinds of student involvement
Normative	Moral
Remunerative	Calculative
Coercive	Alienative
Coercive/Remunerative	Alienative/Calculative

However, it will be argued that universities, and modern universities in particular, have peculiar difficulties in gaining and maintaining congruent compliance structures, and that this in turn influences the intensity of conflict within higher education. Etzioni has outlined two methods, employed to differing degrees by normative, remunerative and coercive organizations, to engineer a congruent form of involvement in subordinates—the use of selective recruitment, and subsequent socialization.[66] Where universities are concerned, it appears that their twentieth-century expansion, and especially their accelerated post-war growth, has considerably weakened the efficacy of both methods. Less stringent selection appears to involve both an absolute and relative increase in entrants who endorse alternative values and seek alternative ends from those of the university. The corresponding increase in scale of universities has made their socialization both less intense and less successful. The extent to which this has resulted in conflict depends upon the type of authority exercised by the university, its respective degrees of reliance on both mechanisms, and the resources which have been made available to reinforce them. While such factors are important in the explanation of cross-cultural differences in (higher) educational conflict, they do not provide a full explanation of student unrest itself. For this would require an understanding of changing values among students and potential undergraduates, which lead them to question the legitimacy of university authority and to seek divergent goals—an action approach as well as structural analysis.

Normative. Systems of higher education in this category have all experienced growing difficulties in gaining *moral* commitment from their students. While it was suggested earlier that the golden days of the academic community of scholars were more conflict-prone than is sometimes admitted, such disruptions (largely on religious questions) mirrored the commitment of the fellows rather than undergraduates.

Indeed the typical expression of the latter—rowdyism—represents an attack upon norms, or a testing of their elasticity, within an established framework of common values. However, normative organizations depend upon a high degree both of selectivity and of socialization. The expansion of higher education, particularly for countries maintaining open-door entry procedures, such as France, West Germany and the United States, has led to a diversification in the initial kinds of value commitments held by students. Since an increased entry has not been accompanied by a proportional increase in staffing, socializing pressures have weakened. The British tutorial method has declined as a teaching relationship and the reliance of continental universities on the lecture theatre has been reinforced. The rapid need to recruit staff has led to a further reduction in value homogeneity and the intensity of subject specialization in their commitment to respective national associations rather than to the local campus.[67] It is for this reason that so many of the interpretations of student unrest in these countries centre upon the loss of community and are basically pessimistic of its rediscovery,[68] as selectivity and socialization are progressively weakening.

Remunerative. The universities of northern Europe have shown slighter and rather more recent difficulties in obtaining *calculative* commitment from students. Typically remunerative organizations depend upon initial selectivity rather than subsequent socialization to bring about congruence. In particular, market mechanisms are relied upon to produce the appropriate calculative involvement in students; tuition is not treated as a 'free good', as the existence of the Swedish system of loans indicates, and consequently students contracting debts for higher education are assumed to place more value on the tuition they receive than on alternative uses of these resources. However, greater availability of places in conjunction with increased parental affluence reduces the efficacy of market mechanisms in this respect, as direct student investment decreases and indirect parental consumption grows. Furthermore, 'the interposition of the government between the universities and their student-consumers has created a situation in which universities cannot meet demand and tap directly resources for satisfying student-consumer preferences'.[69] Consequently calculative commitment is lowered, and in the absence of strong socialization remains at its initial level. As yet this process has not gone very far, but the example of the United States shows that its accentuation can result in a change from remunerative to normative power.

Coercive. While the previous two types of universities have experienced fairly recent difficulties in bringing about a congruent compliance structure, this is germane to systems of higher education based on coercive power. For it is only in the early days of a new totalitarian régime that alienative commitment is congruent. Most such régimes on assumption to power are prepared to treat order as their primary goal in higher education, and maintain it through purge and policing. Their objectives are primarily negative: to demobilize a potential source of opposition, to destroy existing privilege, and to discourage free discussion and publication. But once order has been consolidated in university and society, the attempt is made in both to convert coercive power into legitimate authority. In the universities this can mean endeavouring to transform commitment either to the moral, through selection of the orthodox and supplementary indoctrination, or to the calculative, through holding out occupational and financial prizes. It is in the latter direction that the Spanish Opus Dei influence has operated, largely owing to their strong endorsement of economic development. However, such situations are intrinsically unstable since the alienative commitment congruent with the establishment of the régime, when it persists, endangers its entrenchment. Yet order in the universities remains a primary objective of the régime, and its periodic use of coercion in crisis prevents the universalization of its moral or calculative appeals to legitimacy. Thus conflict is endemic in such universities, and it is interesting to note that authors stressing the long tradition of student unrest tend to draw most of their supportive examples from times and places where coercive power characterized higher education.[70]

Remunerative/Coercive. Where two types of power can be sustained in combination, the resulting control over subordinates will be greater, but there remains an enduring possibility of their mutual neutralization.[71] In the case of Russia this degree of control has been greater than elsewhere, and almost completely successful in eliminating conflict. Nevertheless the Soviet Union and to a greater extent the People's Republics have experienced constant difficulties from near or partial neutralization. A recent example is the present Russian difficulty over teacher placement, which stems from stimulating a calculative involvement in taking up this profession and simultaneously dictating that the first years of its practice should be spent in areas where the social benefit will be greatest and the individual pay-off least. In other words, neutralization and corresponding reduction in control tend to occur unless the different types of power are segregated in their application or in terms of those to whom they are applied. Both methods have been employed, the curriculum has been partitioned into vocational and ideological sections and establishments for the training of party cadres separated off from others, but these tactics have been less successful in the rest of Eastern Europe. For there the pressures towards neutralization are greater as shifts towards calculative involvement involve repudiation of the external (or as many would see it, foreign) coercive régime and lead it in turn to reinforce its control in the universities. Thus the familiar cycle of educational thaw (move to calculative involvement), accompanied by political audacity—repression (intensification of alienative involvement)—educational inefficiency *vis-à-vis* economy due to neutralization—thaw, though of course other factors are involved here.

Such differences in the predominant types of power that characterize systems of higher education have the effect of rendering equally diverse the orientations of student activism. This is because students seeking to undermine and change university norms and values must orientate their opposition against the specific kind of legitimation used to justify them. While norm-directed student movements seeking reform accept the legitimacy of authority, value-directed groups not only reject it, but try to weaken the commitment of other students. Hence the latter must engage in attempts to deprive the authorities of their *particular* claim to legitimacy rather than indulging in a *generalized* attack upon authority. In other words, as a value-directed movement seeks to extend its influence to others, its orientation becomes increasingly constrained by the framework of institutional values shared by authorities and committed students alike.

While a frequent tactic used by value-directed groups to increase their support involves the exploitation of common grievances about means rather than ends, these are subsequently assimilated into an overall attack upon the basic source of legitimation. Consequently oppositional ideologies, for all they may borrow from a restricted common stock of ideas, terminology and symbolism, show a variation in emphasis in the four types of higher education. In the *normative* it is the lack of moral integrity in the self-professed disinterested scholars that is stressed, and their corrupt and venal relations with polity and economy that are unmasked, however remote these may be. Such iconoclasm spreads feelings of moral outrage, which when extensive lead the claim to disinterestedness to be transferred from the fallen idols to the last of the just—the students themselves. In the *remunerative* more emphasis is placed on underlining the consequences (not the fact) of the universities' integration with the economy. It is information and analysis, albeit ideologically interpreted, which is diffused rather than outrage. As Allardt and Tomasson have pointed out, in Scandinavia the 'homogeneous social composition of the countries and the absence of any large deprived social groups'[72] have created difficulties for the expansion of value-directed movements. The absence of equality of educational opportunity within the Welfare State has, however, been a rallying-point in the sixties. In the *coercive*, it is those freedoms which power limits most stringently, visibly and proximately that constitute the focus of opposition. Indeed, reactions to overt repression can be sufficient in themselves to weld a mass movement which succeeds in overriding important ideological differences among students. However, if the totalitarian régime begins to reveal pluralistic tendencies, faction and schism can divide the value-directed movement, as may be beginning to occur in Spain. In the *coercive/remunerative*, emphasis is jointly placed on both the repressiveness and inefficiency of authority. The 'Open Letter' of Kuroń and Modzelewski[73] written to the Party in Poland provides an excellent example of this dual denunciation.

Increased repression in higher education due to political crisis has periodically drawn the outlook of Polish and Czech students closer to those of their counterparts in coercive university systems.

Furthermore, each value-directed movement will search not only to recruit additional allies within higher education, but will also seek support from social groups outside the universities. As Feuer has argued, 'every student movement tries to attach itself to the "carrier" movements of more major proportions—such as a peasant, labor, nationalist, racial or anti-colonial movement'.[74] Success in finding a ready 'carrier' movement largely determines whether unrest remains restricted to the universities or spreads to the wider society. Feuer detects a historical trend towards a lesser availability of 'carriers' as countries develop towards the advanced post-industrial economy stage. 'Student movements will arise frequently in advanced industrial countries, but more than ever they will experience the frustration of not finding in their own societies a carrier movement or supporting class to which they can join themselves. As a consequence, the élitism in student movements will lack the countervailing populism of the past. And the idealism of student movements will partake even more of the character of a fantasy.'[75] However, it is argued that Feuer's analysis requires both modification and specification, since it is not equally applicable to the four types of higher education discussed.

Normative. It is this type of university that corresponds most closely to Feuer's analysis; student activists have experienced difficulties in finding carrier groups, and their activism conforms to the predicted consequence of this failure. Student radicals have increasingly rejected (and been rejected by) the Communist party, established Labour Parties, the Trade Unions and the old liberal intellectuals. The rejection of such carriers is largely founded on ideological grounds, but the resistance of these groups to student infiltration and influence stems not only from divergent aims, but also from the fact—more pronounced in this type of university than others—that while higher education itself is highly regarded, the general public holds students in low esteem.[76] The result is that any alliances are extremely temporary (as in France during May 1968) and that activists are thrown back, by necessity and desire, onto the extra-parliamentary opposition groups as carriers. Such groups are frequently too weak to substantially reinforce the student activism and, as they are generally single-issue movements, too single-minded to accept goal diversification—they may make more use of students than students make of them.

Consequently, activism turns inwards against the university instead of outwards against society. As Daniel Bell remarks for the U.S.A., 'disruption in the society at large is at present impossible; here the New Left has been forced to retreat more and more into the University and to resort to more grandiose dreams and megalomaniacal visions'.[77] (Exactly the same can be said of French activists during the last two years.) Their impact upon other social institutions being repulsed, the university is treated as a surrogate for society, it stands in for the world and its problems[78]—'What the SDS could not do to the larger society it could attempt against the university: to wreck it'.[79] Their influence upon other social groups being rejected, students themselves are seen as the agents of social change. Such 'historical élitism' arises through a process similar to the thinking of C. W. Mills—a process of elimination of other potential revolutionary forces.

Remunerative. In this type of university, as has already been discussed, value-directed movements will be small in relation to norm-directed ones. The latter are actively engaged in negotiation with the authorities for increased participation and representation. The difficulties experienced by activists in recruiting internal support are mirrored in their search externally. Since it is the norm-directed groups that have established links with adult agencies of collective bargaining, student radicals are more quickly precipitated towards the extra-parliamentary opposition groups. While the same cycle follows, as in the case of the normative universities, the entrenchment of majority norm-directed movements dampens the backlash in the Scandinavian universities. Thus while in both normative and remunerative systems student radicals have difficulties in finding carriers, the reaction back upon the university is much more intense in the former than the latter.

Coercive. As Feuer admits, where there is an oppressive military élite or an absence of democratic policies, the chances of intergenerational co-operation are increased. Under such circumstances it is easier for the value-directed group to ally itself with external political carrier groups. While the régime will seek to prevent the interpenetration of opposition movements and to control students as a political force, it will only be partially successful in times of crisis. For the existence of such a régime in itself provides and defines a range of grievances representing a common denominator between students and other groups. The control of freedom of association in Spain is a case in point. However, while the presence of carrier groups can, depending upon the degree of governmental surveillance, increase the intensity and social import of student activism, the latter is itself constrained in the process. The need to sustain a working basis with the carrier groups and to develop joint action in the most feasible directions restrains the irrationalist tendency of the student movement. The reverse trend, of students deflecting their carriers 'in irrational directions',[80] will be less marked the more overtly oppressive the régime. It is significant in this connection to note the coincidence between an increased proclivity of Spanish students to factionalism and the attempt of the Opus Dei to introduce a technocratic legitimation for the régime.

Coercive/Remunerative. The outcome of the search for carriers by activists in such universities represents a mixture of that obtaining in the remunerative and coercive. There is a general difficulty in Eastern

Europe of finding major carrier groups beyond that of writers and artists because the calculative involvement of many in the régime predisposes towards the development of norm-directed movements, the chances of which would be prejudiced by close connection with militant students. On the other hand, the coercive nature of the régime at least provides the basis for a potential alliance. Thus in Czechoslovakia it took the presence of the Russian tanks to bring about a co-ordinated action between students and workers. Nevertheless the possibility of such co-operation and the memory of past occurrences in Hungary, Poland and Czechoslovakia appears to act as a restraint upon irrationalist tendencies.

The perspective adopted throughout this introduction has been comparative. The discussion has sought to emphasize the importance of national differences in the structural relations linking the university to other social institutions in influencing cross-cultural variations in student organization and forms of action. It has been argued that the degree of integration of the university with the polity influences the form of student political organization, while that with the economy affects the dominant orientation of student action. In conjunction, relations with these two social institutions condition the major type of authority exercised by the universities, and the intensity of student conflict has been seen as a function of success in gaining student commitment to the dominant authority-structure and its values. Such an attempt to account for comparative differences in no way involves an exhaustive treatment of the phenomenon, neglecting as it does any consideration of changing value-systems, particularly those affecting potential or actual students, among other factors. However, the major point this analysis has underlined is the diversity of manifestations of a phenomenon, which, because of its international character during the sixties, has too often been treated as uniform. Furthermore, a discussion situated at the macro-sociological level by definition minimizes complexities and variations, especially of national data, since it accentuates predominant institutional patterns and neglects subordinate ones. Thus the contributions that follow demonstrate more clearly the diversity of national manifestations of student unrest and their relationship with variations in university and society.

Notes

1. P. Altbach, *Student politics and higher education in the United States—A select bibliography* (Harvard University Press 1968).
   Centre for Educational Research and Innovation (O.E.C.D.), *Bibliography on 'Student Unrest'* (Paris 1969).
2. For a discussion of Internalist and Externalist Explanations see W. P. Metzger, 'The Crisis of Academic Authority', *Daedalus*, summer 1970.
3. L. S. Feuer, *The Conflict of Generations* (Heinemann, London 1969).
4. J. Nagel, *Student Power* (Merlin Press, London 1969).

5. W. P. Metzger, 'The Crisis of Academic Authority', op. cit. (note 2) p. 574.
6. For a detailed discussion of the factors underlying the slow development of a macro-sociology of education see, Margaret Scotford Archer, 'Egalitarianism and the Sociology of Education in England and France', *Archives Européennes de Sociologie*, Vol. XI, 1970.
7. R. J. Havighurst, *Comparative perspectives on Education*, (Little, Brown, Boston 1968).
8. Ibid. Introduction xi–xvi.
9. Margaret Scotford Archer and Michalina Vaughan, 'Education, Secularization, Desecularization and Resecularization', in D. Martin and M. Hill (eds.) *A Sociological Year Book of Religion* No. 3 (S.C.M. Press, London 1970).
10. Cf. F. Harbison and C. A. Myers, *Education, Manpower and Economic Growth* (1964). See also R. Castel and J. C. Passeron, *Education, développement et démocratie* (Mouton, Paris 1967).
11. For comparative Western European data see, R. Knight, *Trends in University entry: An Intercountry Comparison*, Unit for economic and statistical studies on Higher Education, No. 20 (London 1967), p. 187.
12. E.g. Alexander King, 'Educational Management and Policy-Making' in G. Z. F. Bereday (ed.) *Essays on World Education: The Crisis of Supply and Demand* (O.U.P. 1969).
13. For a discussion of these themes in developing nations see J. S. Coleman (ed.) *Education and Political Development* (Princeton U.P. 1965), Introduction.
14. C. Kerr, *The Uses of the University* (Harvard U.P., Cambridge, Mass. 1963), particularly pp. 41 f.
15. T. Parsons, 'The Academic System: a Sociologist's View', in Daniel Bell and Irving Kristol (eds.), *Confrontation—The Student Rebellion and the Universities* (Basic Books, New York 1969), p. 173.
16. It has been suggested that the multiversity as described by Kerr has not succeeded in resolving the conflict between 'service' and 'scholarship' by internal differentiation. This has not been resolved, but according to Roszak, 'the impasse has been given a name and has become a substitute for a solution. The name is "multiversity".' T. Roszak, *The Dissenting Academy* (Chatto and Windus, London 1969), p. 10.
17. E.g. Alexander King, op. cit. (note 12) discussed four types of demand which may prove incompatible in the long and short term or be perceived as such. These are:
   1. The demand of the individual for the development of his potential and preparation for a career.
   2. The manpower requirements of the economy.
   3. Consumer demand for education as desirable in itself.
   4. The demand inherent in social change and in accordance with politically determined goals.
   See also P. H. Coombes, *The World Educational Crisis: A Systems Analysis* (O.U.P. 1968).
18. T. Parsons, op. cit. (note 15), p. 180.
19. Criteria suggested by E. Ashby and cited by J. Blondel, 'The State and the Universities', *Sociological Review: Monograph 7*, October 1963.
20. J. Blondel, 'The State and the Universities', *Sociological Review, Monograph 7*, 'Sociological Studies in British University Education', October 1963, p. 36.
21. G. Z. F. Bereday, B. Holmes, J. A. Lauwerys, 'The Higher Learning', *The Yearbook of Education (Higher Education)*, 1959.
22. I. Weinberg and K. N. Walker, 'Student Politics and Political Systems: Toward a Typology', *American Journal of Sociology*.
23. Ibid, p. 82.
24. Cf. M. Shimbori, 'The Sociology of a student movement—A Japanese case study; *Daedalus*, Winter 1968.
25. For discussion of these organizations see the appropriate chapters.
26. A. Mineo, 'The Italian Student Movement' in J. Nagel (ed.) *Student Power* (Merlin Press, London 1969).
27. I. Weinberg and K. N. Walker, 'Student Politics and Political Systems', op. cit. (note 22), p. 90.
28. R. Cornell, 'Students and Politics in Communist Countries of Eastern Europe', *Daedalus*, Winter 1968, p. 170.
29. Ibid., p. 176.
30. Ibid., p. 167.
31. A. Mineo, 'The Italian Student Movement', in J. Nagel (ed.), *Student Power*, op. cit., p. 113.

32. I. Weinberg and K. N. Walker, 'Student Politics and Political Systems', op. cit. (note 22), p. 86.
33. Ibid., p. 88.
34. A. H. Halsey and S. Marks, 'British Student Politics', *Daedalus*, Winter 1968, p. 124.
35. I. Weinberg and K. N. Walker, op. cit., p. 85.
36. R. E. Peterson, 'The Student Left in American Higher Education', *Daedalus*, Winter 1968, p. 312.
37. S. M. Lipset, 'The Activists: a Profile', in D. Bell and I. Kristol (eds.) *Confrontation—The Student Rebellion and the Universities* (Basic Books, New York 1969).
38. R. Hofstadter and W. P. Metzger, *The Development of Academic Freedom in the United States* (Columbia University Press 1955), p. 6.
39. R. Cornell, 'Students and Politics in Communist Countries of Eastern Europe', op. cit., pp. 168–169.
40. N. Hans, 'New Professional demands in Europe', in *The Yearbook of Education—Higher Education*, 1959.
41. While education is a rising-cost industry, largely owing to the built-in cost increase in teachers' salaries, these costs are rarely passed on to the consumer in terms of rising prices to students. Cf. J. M. Buchanan and N. E. Devletoglou, *Academia in Anarchy* (Basic Books, New York 1970), pp. 22 f.
42. Ibid.
43. P. H. Coombes, *The World Educational Crisis: A Systems Analysis* (O.U.P. 1968), p. 69.
44. Cf. A. Kerr, *Universities of Europe* (Canterbury Press 1962), Ch. on Denmark.
45. J. M. Buchanan and N. E. Devletoglou, *Academia in Anarchy*, op. cit (note 41), p. 47.
46. P. Bourdieu and J.-C. Passeron, *Les Héritiers* (Éditions de Minuit, Paris 1964).
47. J. M. Buchanan and N. E. Devletoglou, *Academia in Anarchy*, op. cit., p. 8.
48. P. Marris, *The Experience of Higher Education* (Routledge and Kegan Paul, London 1964).
49. P. Bourdieu and J.-C. Passeron, *Les Héritiers*, op. cit.
50. P. Marris, *The Experience of Higher Education*, op. cit., p. 71.
51. Ibid., pp. 126 and 129.
52. P. Bourdieu and J.-C. Passeron, *Les Héritiers*, op. cit., p. 96.
53. Irving Kristol, 'A different way to restructure the University', in D. Bell and I. Kristol (eds.) *Confrontation—The Student Rebellion and the Universities* (Basic Books, New York 1969), p. 152.
54. J. Newman, 'Education and Politics in Britain' in J. Nagel, *Student Power* (Merlin Press, London 1969), p. 6.
55. A. Touraine, *Le Mouvement de Mai ou le Communisme Utopique* (Seuil, Paris 1968).
56. See respective contributions.
57. P. H. Coombes, *The World Educational Crisis*, op. cit., p. 87.
58. R. Dahrendorf, 'Recent Changes in the Class Structure of European Societies', *Daedalus*, Winter 1964.
59. A. Touraine, *Le Mouvement de mai*, op. cit. (note 55), pp. 177 f.
60. A. Etzioni, *The Semi Professionals* (Free Press, New York 1969).
61. P. Bourdieu and J.-C. Passeron, *Les Héritiers*, op. cit., pp. 88 f.
62. Cf. S. M. Lipset, 'The Activists: a profile', in D. Bell and I. Kristol (eds.) *Confrontation* (Basic Books, New York 1969); R. E. Peterson, 'The Student Left in American Higher Education', *Daedalus*, Winter 1968.
63. A. Etzioni, *Complex Organizations* (Glencoe, New York 1961).
64. Ibid., pp. 13–14.
65. This extension involves applying Etzioni's analysis to different types of higher education, whereas Etzioni himself when comparing universities with other complex organizations largely considered them as failing in the normative power category.
66. Ibid., chapter on 'Selection, Socialization and Organizational Quality'.
67. T. Roszak, 'On Academic Delinquency', in *The Dissenting Academy* (Chatto and Windus, London 1969), p. 23.
68. E.g. Colin Crouch, *The Student Revolt* (Bodley Head, London 1970).
69. J. M. Buchanan and N. E. Devletoglou, *Academia in Anarchy*, op. cit., p. 32.
70. See for example, L. S. Feuer, *The Conflict of Generations*, op. cit.
71. A. Etzioni, *Complex Organizations*, op. cit., ch. 1.
72. E. Allardt and R. F. Tomasson, 'Stability and Strains in Scandinavian Student Politics', *Daedalus*, Winter 1968, p. 158.

73. S. Kuroń and K. Modzelewski, *An Open Letter to Communist Party Members* (*Revolutionary Marxist Students Speak Out*), ed. G. L. Weissman (Merit Publishers, New York 1968).
74. L. S. Feuer, *The Conflict of Generations*, op. cit., p. 8.
75. Ibid., p. 280.
76. For a possible explanation of this paradox see J. M. Buchanan and N. E. Devletoglou, *Academia in Anarchy*, p. 70 f.
77. Daniel Bell, 'Columbia and the New Left' in D. Bell and I. Kristol (eds.), *Confrontation*, op. cit., p. 106.
78. N. Glazer, 'Student Power in Berkeley', ibid., p. 6.
79. Daniel Bell, 'Columbia and the New Left', op. cit., p. 96.
80. L. S. Feuer, *The Conflict of Generations*, op. cit., p. 8.

2. CZECHOSLOVAKIA

Milan Hauner

Historical introduction (until 1945)

Czechoslovakia—as she is known today—appeared as an independent state no less than twice in this century, following each world war. Her present educational system, therefore, strongly reflects this unusual symbiosis of tradition and change, benefiting and suffering from both simultaneously. Historical events repeatedly caused a radical break with the preceding era, for the Czechs and Slovaks, the two major nationalities constituting the Republic in 1918, had experienced a separate cultural and administrative development for almost nine hundred years. The Czechs were in many aspects privileged because their cultural and political development had been closely connected with the kingdom of Bohemia, which was linked with the most culturally advanced parts of Europe. Hence the first Latin university beyond the Alps and east of the Rhine was founded in Prague by the Emperor Charles IV in 1348. Later on, particularly during the fifteenth and sixteenth centuries, the Bohemian Reformation promoted education and culture. Czech humanism reached its zenith in the person of J. A. Comenius who, forced into exile, never saw his ideas put into practice in Bohemia. Owing to the loss of political and religious independence at the outbreak of the Thirty Years' War, Czech culture succumbed to the concentrated efforts both of the Counter-Reformation, carried out by the powerful order of Jesuits, and Germanization, introduced step by step by Habsburg centralism. It is to this age of religious and national persecution that the roots of the future myth of resisting physical supremacy by intellectual superiority should be traced. Consolation and strength had been found in the heroic past of the Bohemian kingdom; in the Hussite movement with its leading martyr Jan Hus; in the study of Czech literature, for which the translation of the Bible by Bohemian Brethren at the end of the sixteenth century had constituted the basis for future linguistic revival. Village teachers and parish priests, together with a few representatives of the Czech aristocracy and urban middle class, inspired by a common cultural sympathy, became engaged in rebuilding a modern Czech nation. Thanks to enlightened reforms, religious toleration was introduced and serfdom abolished in 1781. Moreover, the Czech provinces of the Austrian Empire received their first system of compulsory education lasting six years in 1776. A comprehensive educational scheme was set up, including the first model vocational schools, state engineering and technical colleges, already organized on the basis of modern educational theories.

Throughout the nineteenth century, the main issue of Czech cultural emancipation was resistance against all efforts at Germanization, directed from Vienna rather than from the German-speaking population in Bohemia, with whom the Czechs had coexisted for centuries. Gradually the Czechs scored some success, at least in the field of education. By 1886 the two languages, Czech and German, were recognized as equal in the elementary schools.[1] At the secondary level, German was the only language of instruction up to 1859, when the first separate Czech gymnasia appeared.[2] The training of teachers for elementary schools was organized on the basis of their national languages in State teachers' colleges. However, in higher education, the only Czech university in Prague (divided since 1882) had to compete with four or five German-speaking universities in Austria by 1900. Still, Prague preserved its position of being the unique capital in the monarchy, with two separate universities and higher technical colleges similarly divided for Czech and German students.

Distribution of students and professors in Prague by 1900[3]

	students	professors
Czech University	2,805	189
German University	1,162	168
Czech Technical College	1,023	80
German Technical College	419	57

In contradistinction to the cultural and educational emancipation in the Austrian part of the monarchy, where the historical provinces of the Bohemian kingdom were located (Bohemia, Moravia, Silesia), the Hungarian part, with its Slovak minority, showed a depressing picture. Here the whole education was subjected to thorough-going Magyarization by all the means which both State and Church had at its disposal. The Slovak literary language appeared as late as the middle of the nineteenth century. In 1875 the leading Slovak cultural institution for preserving the language, 'Matica Slovenská', and the only three Slovak denominational gymnasia were dissolved.[4] In 1899, Hungarian was introduced as a compulsory subject in all schools, beginning with the elementary level, for eighteen to twenty-one hours per week. By 1907 only 50.56 per cent. of men and as few as 36.56 per cent. of women among the Slovak population were literate.[5] There was no university on Slovak territory until 1912, when a Hungarian one was founded in Pressburg (now Bratislava).

When the Republic was created in 1918, education underwent a genuine change. The central and century-long theme in Czech literature, the idea of self-defence against German expansion, at last ceased to represent the national *raison d'être*. However, the dilemma presented by a multinational society continued to underline the need for democratic co-operation and mutual respect, which was championed by Thomas G. Masaryk (1850–1937), the first President of the Republic. The first pressing task to accomplish in the field of education was the restoration of education in Slovakia: from the elementary school up to the university. In 1930 there were for each 1,000 inhabitants, 81.9 illiterates in Slovakia against only 12.6 in Bohemia.[6] With regard to higher education, in addition to the Czech and German[7] universities in Prague, two other universities were founded in Brno and Bratislava by 1919. Some German and all Magyar establishments of higher education were taken over by the Czechoslovak state, and a few new foundations were made later. While the coexistence of several nationalities within one State was still a source of frictions, that of several religions ceased to be a problem. Several new theological faculties were created for the different denominations.

Distributions of students in Prague by 1913/14 and 1928/29[8]

Czech University	4,740	9,213
German University	2,295	4,463
Czech Technical College (ČVUT)	2,779	5,080
German Technical College	1,903	2,034

The tragic events of 1938/39 led to the decomposition of Czechoslovakia's special multicultural symbiosis. Under the Nazi occupation, the Czechs were to be deprived of all opportunities to be adequately educated, and among the population it was the intelligentsia that became the primary target of Nazi persecution. As the result of a student demonstration against the Germans during which a student of medicine, Jan Opletal, was killed, the Nazi authorities ordered all Czech institutions of higher education to close down on 17 November 1939.[9]

Changing patterns of development in the structure of higher education after 1945

After the liberation in 1945, the restored Czechoslovak Republic expelled the majority of her German population guilty of collaboration with Nazism. Therefore all German institutions, including educational establishments, ceased to operate. Thus ended the centuries-long bilingual tradition in Bohemia and Moravia.

University teachers and professors, many of whom had recently returned from concentration camps, resumed their lectures. Yet inner tensions and political disputes soon transformed universities into platforms for political rivalries between the supporters of the Communists and their opponents. The conflict reached its peak at the end of February 1948, when the dramatic coup was staged in Prague and the Communist Party won the day. Still, at this time the Communists succeeded in gaining and preserving the support of the majority not only among the workers but even the intellectuals, who believed that Czechoslovakia's parliamentary tradition would continue.

While education developed and expanded in conformity with world trends, the most radical transformations occurred as a direct result of the profound political changes in Czechoslovakia since 1948. Two more universities were founded after 1945: one in Olomouc (1946) and the other in Košice (1959), the centre of Eastern Slovakia. Higher technical schools (similar to colleges of advanced technology in the United Kingdom) expanded and differentiated with much greater speed. Besides those at Prague, Brno, and Bratislava, a new higher technical college was founded in Košice (1952), and higher colleges of chemical technology were set up in Prague (1952) and Pardubice (1950). A number of independent technical faculties, such as mechanical and electrical engineering, building and construction, transport, chemistry, nuclear physics, mining and metallurgy, were established. The study of agriculture and economics is provided for in autonomous institutions outside the universities. Two Institutes of Physical Education and Sport were founded in Prague and Bratislava in 1953. The Institute of Culture and Journalism was established in 1959 to train journalists and librarians. The School of Arts and Crafts in Prague (1885) was raised in 1946 to the 'higher' educational level, and the Academy of Music (1811) was similarly transformed in 1945. A parallel academy was opened in Brno in 1947, and Slovakia received her School of Fine Arts, Music and Dramatic Arts in 1949. Seven independent faculties of education for the training of future teachers in regional towns replaced the old Teachers' Colleges.[10]

One of the precautions of the new régime was the exclusion of all faculties of theology from the university complex in 1950. Although the number of students was limited, they varied as to denomination: there were two catholic seminaries, in Litoměřice (344 students) and in Bratislava (184); the Comenius evangelical college in Prague for the Protestant Church of Czech Brethren (73); the Hus theological faculty for the Czechoslovak State Church, created in 1918 as a compromise between Catholicism and Protestantism (70); the Slovak evangelical college in Bratislava (56), and one college for the Russian Orthodox Church in Prešov (41), founded in 1950.[11]

There exists a separate category, the Higher School of Politics, which until 1969 was not open to ordinary students. It was known as the Higher Party School (or in mocking jargon as the 'Sorbonne of Vokovice', after the Prague suburb where it is located), and controlled exclusively by the Party apparatus, for which it provided cadres.

The structure of education

The landmark for reform in Czechoslovak education after 1948 was the 'United School' Act, whose author and protagonist was Zdeněk Nejedlý,[12] the despotic ruler and high priest of Czech culture in those years. As a result of this Act a uniform network of comprehensive schools was set up. All remaining private or religious schools were abolished. The scheme was largely inspired by the Soviet system, which had no relevance to the Czech tradition, but has, nevertheless, often been slavishly imitated.

At the elementary level, compulsory education was extended over nine years to the age of fifteen. Leaving the nine-year school, pupils could usually enter a network of secondary schools preparing for a school-leaving certificate, which is required for entrance to institutions of higher education. In the first place there are the three-year *General Secondary Schools* (S.V.V.Š.), which are poor replacements for the excellent traditional gymnasia. The second source of applicants are the four-year *Secondary Vocational Schools*, covering a wide range of subjects and aiming at training specialists with intermediate qualifications for the national economy. The third source for entry to higher education are the four-year *Secondary Schools for Workers*, which steadily grow in proportion. They are a result of the social revolution accomplished since 1948. Although the objective of raising the number of school-leaving certificate holders is undoubtedly democratic in its inspiration, the results were not entirely satisfactory.[13]

To show how the nationalities were variously reflected in the educational process, the population of Czechoslovakia totalled in 1968 14,333,000, from which 9·285m. were Czechs (8·38m. in 1950), 4·197m. Slovaks (3·24m. in 1950), 0·563m. Hungarians (0·368m.), 0·113m. Germans (0·165m.), 0,058 Ukrainians and Russians (0·067m.), 0·046 of other nationalities, mainly Poles.[14] There are elementary schools for the Ukrainian, Polish and Hungarian minorities, in which Czech or Slovak are compulsory subjects, and for the Hungarians there are even secondary and special vocational schools.

All institutions of higher education in Czechoslovakia are established by Government decrees—the Law of 18 May 1950 amended in 1956 and 1966. The State also exercises its function as proprietor and supreme director. The courses are gratuitous, and all Czechoslovak citizens have the right to attend them, but textbooks have to be bought by the students themselves. Universities and other higher-level institutions are under the control of the Ministry of Education exercised by the State Council of Higher Schools.[15] This links upwards to the corresponding department in the Central Committee of the Communist Party.

The head of each autonomous institution of higher education has traditionally been a rector (Vice-Chancellor), assisted by pro-rectors for research and educational questions, and a quaestor (deputy for financial and administrative matters, appointed by the Minister). Each faculty is headed by a dean (decanus) who is assisted by deputies for various matters (pro-decani). Furthermore, there is for each faculty a scientific council, replacing the traditional senate, and dealing with all major problems under the chairmanship of the dean. Representatives of students and non-academic employees could attend meetings of the council, but had no votes. Since January 1968 and in particular during 1969, the students demanded an adequate share in university or faculty self-government,[16] though they were not unanimous about how strong their participation should be: whether parity, two-fifths or only one-third. Their hopes vanished with the new Law of 17 December 1969,[17] when any guarantee for academic freedom ceased to exist even in theory. Universities have now been submitted to the almost arbitrary power of the Minister of Education. He has now not only the right of dismissing and appointing rectors, deans and other dignitaries, but also—regardless of election by the faculty or university scientific council —the power to replace any lecturer or professor by people who in his opinion fulfil the 'moral, political, educational, scientific or other preconditions'[18] even if they have no academic qualification.

Number of students in Czechoslovakia[19]

	Total No. of Students	Part-time incl.	Female incl.	Professors and Readers	Other Teaching Staff
1959–60	79,332	20,773	19,240	1,473	7,456
1961–62	113,394	35,341	29,390	2,049	10,767
1963–64	141,943	47,228	37,720	2,301	11,433
1964–65	144,777	52,095	35,891	2,672	12,216
1965–66	144,990	49,967	37,355	2,925	12,463
1966–67	142,373	46,225	37,284	3,188	12,319
1967–68	137,497	38,161	39,036	3,361	12,258
1968–69	137,654	40,698	40,698	3,631	12,772

The number of foreign students totalled 3,402 in 1968–69, and many of them (941) studied at the 'University of 17 November'.[20] The largest institution is the Charles University, with 19,516 students in twelve faculties, followed by the Higher Technical College in Prague (Č.V.U.T.), with 13,718 students. The cultural and educational centre of Slovakia is Bratislava, with its Comenius University comprising

12,939 students in eight faculties, and its Higher Technical College with 10,631 students.[21]

The socialist system has helped to raise the number of students and graduates significantly. The average number of students per 100,000 inhabitants was 201 in 1930–34, and has risen to 563 in 1955–59. The trend is of course towards increasing the annual output of graduates. It was forecast that by 1966–70 some 125,000 students would graduate, which represents an increase of 62 per cent. on the 1961–65 figures.[22]

The number of students is determined by reference to the 'Higher Schools' Production Plan', which is a part of the global State Development Plan for the national economy, carried out since 1948 usually in five-year stages. These requirements gave a definite priority to the scientific and technical subjects. Positive results were, unfortunately, almost inseparably accompanied by negative side-effects. Although social barriers restricting access to higher education were eliminated and school and examination fees abolished, the early adoption of 'class struggle' criteria resulted in a notable loss of standards and formalization of some studies.

Admission of students is carried out through special commissions. Apart from the general and intellectual criteria of suitability for higher education, the applicant's moral and political profile was also considered. In the sixties the requirement that the majority of students should originate from the working class and the peasantry weakened. Nevertheless, preference was often given to applicants with at least one year's working experience.[23]

Students have to pass, during their (average) five years of study (i.e. ten semesters) a number of oral exams and certificates, which are held at the end of each semester. Final examinations are held before a State examination board and usually consist of two parts, the preparation and defence of a thesis and the final oral examination. Postgraduate studies, usually lasting three years, are divided into two periods: during the first, the graduate 'aspirant' has to pass all examinations prescribed by the regulations (special subject plus two foreign languages), and then present a thesis. Research projects, because of the rigid system of central planning, must be prepared a long time beforehand in order to be approved, which involves a lengthy procedure, and finally be included in the State Economic Development Plan.[24] The research is mainly carried out by the Academy of Sciences (founded in 1952 from the remains of the old 'Emperor Franz Joseph Czech Academy for Sciences, Belles Lettres, and Arts', created in 1882). Its foundation benefited scientific research, but this development created some disadvantages, which soon became apparent in the growing rivalry between Academy and University. The role of university teachers was now merely seen as teaching and writing textbooks, a redefinition which was not entirely accepted by the university staff. As far as extramural education is concerned, in addition to the well-attended part-time courses at universities,[25] a wide range of lectures, some of them of the highest standard, is organized by the Evening People's Universities and Socialist Academies.

Student life and welfare

One of the most remarkable achievements under the socialist régime, despite its arbitrary penalization of children of 'class enemy' origin, was undoubtedly the equalization of opportunities. Although it is gradually developing in most advanced countries of Western Europe as a consequence of the scientific revolution, in Czechoslovakia, as in the other socialist countries, this radical change instead resulted from ideological pressures. As a result of this the present student generation in Czechoslovakia is considerably more homogeneous than its predecessors. On the other hand, the growing feminization of some institutions of higher education surpassed recognized needs and reversed the balance between the two sexes.[26]

As was already mentioned, there are neither tuition nor examination fees for Czechoslovak students. Most scholarships for undergraduates in need of financial assistance are provided from State grants, but the amount is not always satisfactory and it is necessary to earn supplementary money. Regional communal committees also provide grants for students who undertake to work for that particular region during a certain minimal period. Higher grants are made by some industrial enterprises to students who are taking combined courses. Those who, while in employment, are enrolled for part-time courses, enjoy certain special privileges and benefits in terms of financial assistance and free time. All students are also entitled to reductions on city transport and trains while visiting their homes and families. In addition to State grants, an extra premium can be paid for good academic results. The number of students receiving Government grants was 41,726 in 1968–69, of whom 22,873 were Czechs and 15,428 Slovaks.[27]

Accommodation for students living away from home is provided by a network of residential hostels and halls of residence. The charges are very modest, but the older hostels resemble dormitories, with three and even up to ten people sharing one single room. Private lodgings are very scarce because of the appalling housing shortage. Although new modern hostels are being built, the present number and capacity could hardly be called satisfactory.

Student residential hostels in Czechoslovakia[28]

	1964–65	1968–69
No. of beds	57,322	60,150
No. of accommodated students	57,110	63,299

Until recently it was generally required that each student should be a member of the single organization, the Czechoslovak Union of Youth (Č.S.M.), which directed student activities at the universities through its subordinate bodies, the Student Council (Vysokoškolská rada), and in Prague, the University Student Regional Committee (Vysokoškolský obvodní výbor). Limited student participation was granted on admissions commissions and on councils dealing with student scholarships. The International Union of Students (I.U.S.) was responsible for contacts with students abroad. At the time of its creation in 1946 in Prague, it comprised about fifty national student organizations all over the world. During the cold war a number of non-communist organizations left the Prague Union. Already prior to 1968 several vocational student offices were set up, providing, for example, part-time jobs for students in the Prague area and a bureau for international holiday work-camps.

There was practically no independent student newspaper until 1966, when the weekly *Student* began to appear.[29] Student problems were also discussed within the limited space devoted to them in the central organ of the Č.S.M.: *Mladá Fronta*. But all editors were under strict control or exercised auto-censorship until the very beginning of the Prague Spring 1968. Charles University edited its own paper *Karlova Universita*, but it was not a student weekly properly speaking. In addition, there were some faculty papers of poor quality and very limited circulation.[30] The students in Bratislava edited their own paper *Echo*.

The emergence of the student movement as a political force

Motto: 'I consider the rule of law, not only in the narrow legal
sense, as the most urgent need that our society has to
resolve.'

Ladislav Mňačko, in *Kulturný Život* (22.6.1963)

The historical and structural framework outlined in previous sections makes it easier to understand most of the differences and particularities that characterize the student movement in Czechoslovakia in general, and in Bohemia, Slovakia, or in Prague in particular. It developed very slowly and discontinuously, but underwent rapid acceleration prior to its suppression in April 1969.

After the take-over in February 1948, all non-communist student organizations were abruptly silenced and some of their leaders arrested. It is said that about 10,000 non-communist students were dismissed from Charles University by 1949.[31] Children of parents labelled as 'exploiters' were often prevented even from attending secondary schools. Soon, under the enforced central youth organization, the Č.S.M., the pro-government policy was adopted at universities and no deviation permitted even in theory. Distinguished professors and scientists were forced, under fierce attacks by fanatical students, to resign from their posts, or to recant and adopt conformist attitudes. University life became collectivized, faithfully following the Soviet example. Through means of 'study groups', supplementary weekend activities called 'brigades', organized for the sake of helping the national economy in plants and farms, the students were transformed into a docile and submissive social stratum.

When the first major crisis struck the socialist camp in 1956, it found the students in Czechoslovakia unprepared and unconscious of having a specific role to play. The Twentieth Congress of the Soviet Communist Party announced an era of de-Stalinization and liberalization. It gave a strong impetus to Czechoslovak intellectuals, who for the first time since 1948 transformed their Second Writers' Congress in April 1956 into a platform from which guarantees of essential civil and artistic freedoms were demanded. Both events inspired the spontaneous manifestation of student discontent during the traditional May Day procession, called *Majáles*, a sort of merry kermesse with allegoric figures, humorous placards, improvised 'happenings', and so on, which were to be repeated in later years. One of the common features of Czech culture and education, the solidarity between writers and students, reappeared in the new socio-political context. Still no loud echo among the workers was heard, though some minor strikes occurred. The explanation of this relative calm lay partly in the economic situation, which did not yet show signs of the forthcoming stagnation. Also the reputation of the Communist Party, already under the firm leadership of its dogmatic First Secretary Antonín Novotný, remained unshaken by the Twentieth Congress. The insurrections in Poland and especially in Hungary were presented to the Czechoslovak public as counter-revolutions, and the atrocities during the purges in the early fifties had not yet been officially disclosed. However, it was precisely in the cultural field where liberalism began to emerge. Censorship was loosing its grip, and thus a number of remarkable works escaped its control. It was as early as 1957–58 that the Czechoslovak cinema, theatre and literature began to show non-conformist tendencies. The Party began to fear that it might eventually lose its control over those who up to now were regarded as obedient and loyal servants of culture and education. Inquiries in some Prague faculties produced disquieting results. The overwhelming majority of students turned out to be politically uninterested, lacking true ideological fervour, and sharing many religious and other 'bourgeois prejudices'.[32] The membership of the Č.S.M. steadily decreased and the organization lost half of its members within five years.[33] Almost all top functionaries of the Č.S.M. were already in their thirties, a type of career Party servant from the apparatus with a boorish attitude to any problem exceeding their monotonous routine. This discrepancy between the rulers and the ruled, between a handful of intransigent and uneducated bureaucrats on the one hand, and dissatisfied youth on the other, was particularly acute and somehow more articulate in universities.

It is difficult to indicate any particular date to mark the emergence of the student movement as a specific and independent force. It seems that the juncture should be sought in the year 1963 (i.e. at the time of economic difficulties; the presentation of the new economic reform by Professor Ota Šik's team; permission for individual trips to Western countries, etc.). The Third Writers' Congress, also held in 1963, and the partial rehabilitation of thousands of victims of the political trials, contributed greatly to the growth of social criticism.

In the meantime the students acquired further experience in their search for self-expression. The *Majáles* in 1962 and also the kermesse in 1965 and 1966 ended in turmoil, with police intervention to prevent alleged 'anti-socialist provocation', as it was officially termed. Some students were expelled and there was no student body which could defend them at this time. The great majority of students accepted their prescribed roles, as diligent citizens to whom the State and the Party granted the privilege of study, and were in return prepared to serve the national economy wherever they would be appointed.

The only hope of achieving some gradual and limited improvements through a policy of restrained reformism was within the legal framework of existing Č.S.M. organization. The University Student Committee, the V.O.V., assigned to the Central Committee of the Č.S.M. in Prague, became infiltrated throughout 1965 by a number of radical students who represented mainly the 'group of five', which was soon accused in the Party's jargon as a 'faction'.[34] Some of its leaders were to become popular in the following years: Lubomír Holeček, Jiří Holub, Jan Kavan, Jana Kohnová, Karel Kovanda, Jiří Müller, Zdeněk Pinc, Miroslav Tyl, Zdeněk Zbořil. The original aim of this group had merely been a transformation of the rigid structure of the Č.S.M. organization into a more contemporary body, and to give the university a more adequate share in it. The programme called 'federalization of the Č.S.M.', still very much within this old framework, was proposed by Jiří Müller at the student conference in December 1965. This can be considered as a starting point in the formation of a specific political consciousness among Czechoslovak students. Müller's proposition that 'The Union (i.e. Č.S.M.) has even to play the role of the Party's opponent when it is necessary'[35] provoked an alarmed reaction and unleashed the watch-dogs of the Č.S.M. and Party apparatus.

The following year brought about more radicalization, and the conflict overlapped with the usual and well-established dispute between the V.O.V. and the Central Committee of Č.S.M. Thanks to the co-operation among the apparatchiks and absolute control over the mass media, through which the facts were either disclosed or distorted, the radicals were forced into silence. But this was not enough. Jiří Müller learned at the end of December 1966, to his astonishment, that he was expelled from his faculty and enrolled for compulsory military service. The same fate met his ardent defender and friend Lubomír Holeček. The students then realized that no understanding between the V.O.V. and the Central Committee of the Č.S.M. was possible any longer, and that there was no hope for even limited reforms within the established framework.

The Prague Spring[36]

Simultaneous with the attempts of ultra-conservatives to maintain the establishment, parallel undercurrents in the politico-economical and cultural sphere helped to promote anti-dogmatic socialism. Although there is no evidence of any preconceived co-operation between the courageous speakers at the Fourth Writers' Congress[37] held at the end of June 1967, and the activities of radical students at the Fifth Congress of Č.S.M. held about the same time, the echo was very strong. The writers and editors from the banned weekly *Literární Noviny* were invited by students who expressed their solidarity and in a way continued their activities under the harmless cover of a new society, 'Academic Circle of Arts Friends'.

Unexpectedly, the demonstration of students from the largest Prague hall of residence at Strahov on 31 October 1967 changed the situation and helped to intensify the mood of disillusionment and scepticism and transform it into a more articulate protest.[38] The demonstration was brutally suppressed by the 'forces of order', though the students only asked for 'more light', owing to the permanent failure in electricity supply. At this moment the V.O.V., supported by a number of faculty and hostel councils, began to act on its own responsibility: they demanded an objective and impartial investigation, including the punishment of some policemen who had inflicted incurable injuries upon several students during the riot. Still, the position of V.O.V. remained relatively correct towards the Č.S.M., whose top functionaries did everything in order to silence this unpleasant affair. The attitude of the Č.S.M. was subject to heavy criticism, in particular from the student rank and file. New patterns of self-governed faculty councils based on representative elections were quickly set up. Their model had been first developed (in December 1967) by the faculty of philosophy, which traditionally functioned as vanguard in student movements. The Č.S.M., with its numerous branches, was slowly but inevitably declining from the moment it lost its bureaucratic supremacy and ceased to be faced by a silent majority. The student unrest—if we may call it so—together with the writers' opposition was the immediate catalyst bringing about the decisive crisis within the Party leadership, and reaching its height in the dismissal of its First Secretary, Antonín Novotný. In April 1968 the Student Parliament was established in

Prague and the V.O.V. ceased to exist. In May the Union of university Students (S.V.S.) with its two federal parts for Bohemia (plus Moravia) and Slovakia was created, putting an end to student participation in the Č.S.M.[39]

Students became more directly involved in politics and demonstrated on numerous occasions in the Prague streets. Thus they accelerated the abdication of Novotný as President. Their spontaneity at this time was determined both by a desire to avoid allegations of provocation and by the lack of any far-reaching political programme, properly speaking, as too much energy had been concentrated upon structural change in their own organizations.

Although the domestic scene was so rich in events, contacts with students abroad were developed and discussions organized. Czech students staged a protest demonstration in April against the suppression of their Polish colleagues and the growth of anti-semitism there. The manifesto of two arrested Polish intellectuals, J. Kuroń and K. Modzelewski, attacking the bureaucratic degeneration of the present régime, was translated and distributed in Prague. Numerous rather improvised discussions took place with students coming from Western Europe, especially from Germany (Rudi Dutschke was in Prague on 4 April 1968) and from France after the May rebellion. At a number of international conferences the Czechoslovak students defended their attitude of support for the new liberal course.[40] Though there were many common points, it would nevertheless be entirely wrong to say that the student movement in Czechoslovakia came under the direct influence of the different ideologies which the New Left has been constantly diffusing.[41] The main inspiration came from the abundant domestic resources, which provided the students with such appalling experience of manipulation in a far more primitive form than their Western counterparts could even imagine.[42] Yet the student criticism of the present Czechoslovak society and its institutions never degenerated into purposeless destruction.

The discrediting deeds and affairs of the old régime (for example, rumours of a military coup that Novotný wanted to launch, and General Šejna's escape to the West) and above all the irredeemable burden of crimes inflicted by it during political trials in the fifties,[43] contributed to the withdrawal of its conservative members. After the abolition of censorship and with its re-animated editorship, the *Student* was indisputably the most radical newspaper. However, it would be incorrect to assert that its articles were decisive in stimulating student activities. For example, the tract 'Head Against the Wall' by the dissident philosopher Ivan Sviták found a comparatively small audience. Yet the heritage of twenty years of dictatorship could not disappear within a few months, nor could the acquired stereotypes of acquiescence. Its traces were still visible in the lack of genuine democratic training and behaviour among the students. Ideals of democratic freedom among the youth were naturally more inspiring than most of the attractive utopianism expressed in Marcuse's books. Demands for legal justice and direct participation in the new pattern of youth organizations seemed to them more imminent. One of the Czechoslovak student leaders, Jan Kavan, summarized it as follows: 'For us, the classic civil liberties assume the utmost importance. In a socialist society, freedom of speech, freedom of the press, freedom of assembly and freedom of association are essential if the people are to exercise any control at all. . . .'[44] On the other hand, the so-called progressive communists, who for various reasons sacked Novotný, still thought in terms of monopolistic rule and were therefore distrusted by the students. Isolated attempts were made by some intellectuals[45] and students in factories, because most of the workers were still confused and often misused by the conservative elements of the Party apparatus by this time. When in April the liberal Communists issued the 'Action Programme', it produced in fact less effect than the later 'Manifesto of 2,000 Words', which could be considered as the first serious appeal for an alliance based on a community of interest between workers and intellectuals against the apparatchiks. The onslaught of Soviet tanks on 21 August accelerated this process.

After the invasion: 'normalization' or 'all power to the Soviets'?

Despite the terrible shock which the August invasion inflicted, especially upon the younger generation, the student movement was still capable of preserving its coherence. The first reaction of young people when they learned about the sequels to the Moscow communiqué of 27 August was a wrathful refusal ('Betrayal!') and as a result of this, the editors of the *Student* decided to discontinue their weekly at once.[46] In the difficult search for an adequate policy, given the presence of foreign troops, the students tried to preserve their influence in the sphere of domestic policies. Yet without any gross exaggeration it could be said that they developed into the major political driving force until Dubček's replacement by Dr Husák in April 1969.

There were two practical alternatives offered to the Czechoslovak people with a view to continuing the post-January course. The first trend seemed to be undisputed at the beginning. It involved nation-wide enthusiasm for the unity which had been reached during the spontaneous one-week non-violent resistance against the invaders. This sentimental and popular nationalism soon became almost a legend, and despite the submissive attitude of the political leadership, students followed this path together with all sections of the population. They swallowed with some verbal protests the first hard measures of censorship such as the temporary ban imposed on a number of newspapers, and suppression of minor political groups like 'K.A.N.' (Club of

Committed Non-Party Members) and 'K-231' (Society of Former Political Prisoners). Although the students did not feel convinced by promises that the stationing of Soviet troops had only been temporary, they accepted the line of slow 'normalization', provided that the essential achievements from the post-January 'Action Programme' would be guaranteed. There was a danger that loss of dynamism in student politics would help this strong current gain a majority,[47] especially among those students for whom the main priority was structural and organizational change in education, improvement of student conditions and welfare and so on.

The second trend stressed the chance of associating the workers with the intelligentsia in order to exercise more pressure against right-wing elements who wanted to switch back to the pre-January situation. It was left to a relatively tiny minority of radical students to grasp this unique chance and use it at once before it would be too late. Their first extraordinary test, because so non-conformist and defiant in a country where socialism was an official doctrine, happened during the November student strike. The students wanted to show that they dissociated themselves from guilt over what was going on in occupied Czechoslovakia, and in particular from the tactics of 'lesser evil' advocated by the present political leaders.[48] Thus they decided to occupy the premises of their faculties on the anniversary of the International Student Day on 17 November. The strike lasted four days, and it was estimated that about 60,000 students joined the strike in Bohemia and Moravia, but with a considerably smaller proportion in Slovakia, where radical students found only a few supporters. Although the authorities tried to conceal facts about the student strike, the public was kept informed through posters and bulletins of the Student Press Agency named T.A.I.S.S. The sit-in was soon transformed into a popular festivity in which young workers together with writers and actors took part and discussions, panel sessions and seminars were organized. Workers and even farmers from co-operatives sent their greetings and material as well as financial support. In some factories token strikes as signs of solidarity with students were announced.[49] The moderate programme of the student sit-in was set out by the S.V.S. in the famous 'Ten Points':[50]

1. The basis of our policy is and shall be the Action Programme of the Communist Party as accepted at the April Central Committee session.

2. There shall be no policy behind closed doors; in particular the flow of information between citizens and their leadership shall be restored.

3. Introducing censorship in the mass media of communication is temporary, and shall not last longer than six months.

4. Freedom of assembly and association shall not be violated.

5. The freedom of scientific research, literary and cultural expression shall be guaranteed.

6. Personal and legal security of citizens shall be guaranteed.

7. Those people who have lost the confidence of the nation and who have never clarified their positions shall no longer stay in their posts.

8. The forming of Councils of Employees as bodies of enterprise self-government shall continue.

9. Freedom to travel abroad shall be guaranteed.

10. In the sphere of foreign policy, Czechoslovakia shall not participate in actions which would contradict the feelings of the Czechoslovak people, the United Nations' Charter and the General Declaration of Human Rights.

The acceptance of those ten points, especially by workers' Trade Unions, prevented the authorities from launching a witch-hunt for student agitators. There was a legitimate fear that the infection of student unrest could easily spread to secondary schools and, above all, to factories.[51]

The student strike gave a new incentive to public action in Czechoslovakia. In particular the radical section of the S.V.S. concentrated on forming a genuine union with the workers through drafting a common programme. Practically all workers' Trade Unions concluded bilateral agreements with the S.V.S. and a number of associations of the intelligentsia. One of the most remarkable ever signed by both students and workers together was the treaty of 19 December 1968 between the S.V.S. and the most powerful Trade Union organization of metalworkers.[52] Specific student claims exceeding the minimum ten points were compiled, together with particular trade unionist requests, and completed by essential demands for political freedom and direct socialist democracy appealing to citizens of all categories. Workers' representatives were invited to attend sessions of the student parliament, and vice versa. Although this policy of a united front may have achieved some limited success, it soon proved inadequate to cope with the real power situation. Very few people seemed to realize that time had already been working in favour of the conservatives, that verbal declarations of disagreement covered with plenty of signatures, though impressive, could not stop those who possessed the full panoply of physical force from disintegrating the people's opposition. Instead of cautiously elaborating all possible alternatives, how such and such illegal abuse of power, which the authorities were potentially ready to use, should be opposed, illusions of success slowed down the process and resulted in a sort of premature euphoria.

Jan Palach's self-immolation of January 1969, followed by other student martyrs like Jan Zajíc on 25 February,[53] shattered this obvious fallacy, and their behaviour had a traumatic influence on the Czechoslovak population. The students took the leadership in organizing public processions and hunger strikes during the funeral. The first direct accusation of treason was levelled at the political leadership (the declaration of students of the faculty of philosophy on 17 January). However, the outcry of grief could not be translated into rational politics. There was never an ultimatum clause formulated, capable of transforming the latent force into being. The policy of defiance was still concerned very much with affects rather than effects. None the less, the search for an authentic union between students and workers was an outstanding achievement, far more successful than, for instance, similar attempts in France or Poland during the spring of 1968.[54]

The basic theses of the radical student group were summarized by one of its leaders:[55]

> What are the plans of my generation in 1969? (1) To pursue a current of political thought opposed to all forms of Stalinism and yet not indulging in dreams. For us it is a necessity to reject some of the dreams of the New Left in the West. With such dreams we will be buried. (2) To maintain our links with the working class and trade union organizations. We speak daily in factories to gatherings of up to a thousand workers. Last week there were 200,000 people at our public demonstration. We do not tell workers what they should do: we simply try to share our experience with them. The trade union movement is now ready for a political struggle and can only, conceivably, be stopped if subjected to extreme illegal repression.

In spite of many similar good intentions expressed by setting up workers' councils,[56] the counter-offensive of the conservative elements began to undermine the numerically superior forces of resistance. There was no feasible programme for joint action against the persistent 'normalization', which was backed by the intransigent majority of the Party's apparatus and the presence of Russian troops. The student movement itself could not escape certain repercussions of the slow but conspicuous disintegration.[57] On top of this, the trade unions were not able to accept the crucial thesis which the radical students defended: non-adherence to the National Front, which assembled all mass organizations for electoral purposes and was under practically complete control of the Communist Party.

The final test came before long. After the spontaneous anti-Soviet demonstration on 31 March and 1 April resulting from the Czechoslovak ice-hockey victory over the Soviet team, the U.S.S.R. resorted to a policy of ruthless pressure which brought about Dubček's resignation. At this moment the lack of resistance was crucial. A handful of faculties in Prague, without any support from other organizations, launched an isolated strike. No suppression from outside was necessary, for it ceased through student disillusionment with their own powerlessness and the lack of interest displayed by many.[58] Above all, no support came from the trade unions. The united front of resistance was doomed to failure from the very beginning, for it was characterized by a mixture of spontaneous verbosity and national sentimentalism on the one hand, but on the other by the absence of essential attributes required for a genuine political struggle, such as firm leadership and a complex programme. As far as the radical students were concerned, their aims stemmed from primarily moral incentives, but never infringed the recognized legal framework. This proved to be their political dilemma because the ruling authorities could easily manipulate the very meaning of legality and direct it against them. Though forced by events to evolve tactics of nation-wide union based on the alliance between students and workers, it could not be translated into an effective political strategy. The apparent success which the radicals had scored at the last Congress of the S.V.S. in Olomouc at the end of April 1969, by not accepting the adherence to the National Front, was understood as an open challenge to the régime.[59] The opposition of the radicals by constitutional means forced the new Party leadership to dissolve the S.V.S. Censorship was reintroduced and a dozen nonconformist newspapers ceased to circulate. Frontal attacks against radical students appeared in the 'normalized' press.[60] However, the Czech radicals did not give up and refused to recognize the ban of the S.V.S.[61] It was a desperate struggle of an isolated minority against superior forces of oppression. The reliability of workers' unions proved to be temporary and the Slovak Union of University Students (Z.V.S.) gradually dissociated itself from the Czech movement from January 1969 onwards, becoming more conformist once Czechoslovakia was transformed into the federation of two administrative units.[62] No organized defiance was possible any longer and the spread of frustration among large masses of the population now became inevitable. Final verbal protests reflected this tragic impotence.[63] The only alternative consisted in reasserting the traditional Czech reliance upon spiritual superiority against brutal physical force.

And yet student radicals continued to address people at home and abroad, appealing in the name of their political ideals and recent experiences in Czechoslovakia:[64]

> . . . the original slogan 'Society is not free because the intellectuals are oppressed' has changed into the completely new and perhaps more accurate 'Only when the immediate producer enjoys full and true democratic rights as citizen in society—only then may the intellectuals have the right to talk about their own freedom.'

This message may be regarded as an attempt at seeking co-operation with the western New Left by presenting the experience of the Czechoslovak 'teaching model'.[65] So far the appeal has passed unnoticed.

Notes

1. *Ottův Slovník Naučný* (O.S.N.), Vol. XXI. By 1900 there were in the Austrian part of the monarchy some 19,251 elementary schools of which 7,725 were German and

5,046 Czech; the rest distributed among other nationalities. From the total population of 26,150,000 in the Austrian half, 9,170,000 were Germans and 5,955,000 Czechs.

2. *O.S.N.*, Vol. VI, item 'Čechy'.
3. *O.S.N.*, Vol. XXI, item 'Rakousko'.
4. *O.S.N.*. Vol. XXIII, items 'Slovensko', 'Slováci'.
5. *O.S.N.*, Vol. XXIII, XXV.
6. Cf. weekly *Květy*, No. 12, 1969.
7. Needed for the powerful German minority of more than two and a half million by 1918.
8. *O.S.N.*, Supplement, 1–2, item 'Československo'.
9. Celebrated now as the International Student Day by the I.U.S.
10. World Survey of Education, UNESCO, 1966, p. 381 n.
11. The number of students for 1968 is given in brackets. (In: *Statistical Yearbook of Č.S.S.R.*, 1969, p. 494.)
12. Zdeněk Nejedlý (1878–1962), professor of music at Charles University, with a wide range of interests in literature, aesthetics and history, became after the First World War one of the leading Communist intellectuals. He spent the war years in Moscow, where he dedicated himself to a policy of neo-Slavophilism. In his position as the powerful President of Academy of Sciences (since 1952) and Minister of 'Education, Sciences and Arts' (1948–1953), he developed a policy with strong monopolistic features. No intervention into his domain was imaginable, and the ruling Stalinists had full confidence in his autocratic management.
13. It was planned that by 1979 the majority of young people would be provided with full secondary education and certificates roughly corresponding to the British G.C.E. The facts are not confirmed yet. In *World Survey of Education*, p. 381.
14. Figures in brackets indicated for 1950. The explanation for the drop in the figures for the German and Ukrainian population lies less in emigration than in their progressive assimilation. This is particularly relevant for the German minority, which has not even the right to be educated in its own language, apart from optional courses.
15. After the introduction of the new Federal Act of January 1st, 1969, there are now two separate ministries for education: one in Prague for Bohemia and the other in Bratislava for Slovakia.
16. Cf. *Universita Karlova* No. 3 (1968); Nos. 4, 8, 13 (1969).
17. Text in Czechoslovak Government Paper No. 163, 1969.
18. Ibid.
19. *Statistical Yearbook of Č.S.S.R.*, 1969, p. 483.
20. The 'University of 17th November' was founded in Prague in 1961 and has a similar purpose to the 'People's University' in Moscow. It is largely devoted to languages and social sciences for overseas students from Asia and Africa.
21. *Statistical Yearbook of Č.S.S.R.*, 1969, pp. 484–6.
22. *World Survey of Education*, p. 388 n. The number of graduates leaving schools totalled 13,852 in 1968. Cf. *Statistical Yearbook of Č.S.S.R.*, 1969, p. 488.
23. Already in 1957 the percentage of students from working-class families at the faculty of philosophy was 23.71, from peasant families 5.71. (See *Tvorba*, No. 15/57, quoted in: P. Tigrid, *Marx na Hradčanech*, p. 109; New York 1960.)
24. Out of the total state expenditures of 151,394 million crowns in 1968, 3,021 m. were invested in education, culture, and sport, 1,192 m. in science and research. (The total G.N.P. was 153,906 m. crowns in 1968; see *Statistical Yearbook of Č.S.S.R.*, 1969, pp. 26, 164–6.) Some statistics give the total budget for education in 1968 as 12,226 m. crowns (*International Yearbook of Education*, UNESCO, 1968, p. 135).
25. Nearly half of the students enlisted at faculties of Law and Philosophy were part-time students (*Statistical Yearbook of Č.S.S.R.*, 1969, pp. 484–6).
26. A very high proportion of female students is found in arts, medicine and particularly in teachers' institutes (more than 90 per cent.), which results in a steady decline of this important profession at primary and secondary levels (cf. weekly *Květy*, No. 12 (1969)).
27. *Statistical Yearbook of Č.S.S.R.*, 1969, p. 490. The amount paid in total was 165 million crowns.
28. Ibid., p. 491.
29. The *Student* ceased to circulate after the Moscow Diktat in August 1968 and was replaced by *Studentské Listy*, whose first copy appeared on 25.2.1969 and the last on 29.4.1969.
30. Their number varied. In February 1969 there were about nine faculty papers circulating in Prague (cf. *Universita Karlova* No. 11, 1969).

31. Cf. G. Mond in *East Europe*, January 1970. About 1,000 students and 50 lecturers from the faculty of philosophy in Prague alone. (*Literární Listy*, No. 13, 1968.)
32. *Učitelské Noviny* No. 14, 1959; quoted in P. Tigrid, *Marx na Hradčanech* (New York 1960), p. 39.
33. Cf. H. Klímová, J. Kavan: 'Jak to bylo s těmi vysokoškoláky', in *Literární Listy*, No. 2, 1968.
34. The term 'radical students' is widely accepted in the Czechoslovak student movement, though it may differ from the interpretation usually given to this notion by the West European New Left.
The five Prague faculties were: engineering, natural sciences, nuclear physics, law, and philosophy. Cf. H. Klímová, J. Kavan, op. cit. (*Literární Listy* No. 2, 1968); J. Kavan, 'David a Goliáš', in *Student* No. 11, 1968.
35. Ibid.
36. Owing to limited space, the author has to confine himself to a very sketchy outline, following basically the role played by the students. The account is based mainly on author's personal experience and interviews with a number of direct participants.
37. Cf. publications: IV. *sjezd čsl. spisovatelů*, Prague 1968; D. Hamšík, *Spisovatelé a moc* (Writers and Power), Prague 1969.
38. *Universita Karlova* No. 5, 1968.
39. *Reportér* No. 38, 1968.
40. Cf. also G. Mond, op. cit. (note 31).
41. The ideas of the New Left were expressed in Czechoslovakia in a rather inconsistent way by a few individuals. Members of the 'Movement of Revolutionary Youth', a small nucleus of students and young workers in favour of Maoist and Trotskyist ideas, were reported to have been arrested in January 1970 (cf. *Der Spiegel* No. 5, 1970; *The Times*, 17.1.1970; *Le Monde*, 16 and 20.1.1970).
42. J. Šiklová, 'Existuje u nás "New Left" ', in *Listy* No. 3, 1968.
43. Cf. 'The Piller Report', published in *The Sunday Times*, 1.3.1970.
44. J. Kavan, 'The Testament of a Prague Radical', in *Ramparts*, vol. 7, 1968, p. 58; also in *International Herald Tribune*, 20.10.1969, Milovan Djilas on the New Left.
45. Ivan Sviták in *Literární Listy* No. 8, 1968.
46. Open letter of the editors of the *Student* on 27 August 1968 (published in *Black Book*, ed. by R. Littell, London 1969).
47. *Studentské Listy* No. 5, 25.3.1969, stated that the majority of students prefer social and educational matters to exclusively political ones. In contrast with this, the radical student leader Holeček was saying '. . . to be preoccupied to-day with social and educational problems is a luxury'. (Ibid.)
48. P. Tomàlek's Report from Prague in *New Left Review* No. 53. ('Never before had we realized how great an influence we could have . . .', p. 16, ibid.)
49. Full report in *Universita Karlova* Nos. 6–7, 1968; *Reportér* No. 45, 1968, p. 11.
50. Cf. *Studentské Listy* No. 1, 1969; P. Tomàlek in the *New Left Review*, op. cit.; A. Dasbach, 'Czechoslovakia's Youth' in *Problems of Communism*, March–April 1969.
51. Cf. the joint Proclamation of the Central Committee of the Communist Party, the Government and the National Assembly to the students, published in *Universita Karlova* Nos. 6–7, 1968, p. 7.
52. The Union of Metalworkers represented nearly one million employees (cf. *Svědectví* No. 37, p. 136, 1969).
53. Their last messages and poems written with the highest moral integrity reveal their bitter despair and disappointment at growing tendencies of compromise, reconciliation with the invaders, and the unavoidable indifference of the silent majority. (Cf. *Studentské Listy* No. 1; *Listy* No. 12, 1969; *Universita Karlova*, 13, 1969.)
54. Cf. Interview with J. P. Sartre in *Universita Karlova* No. 8, 1969; *Listy*, 6, 1968.
55. Lubomír Holeček's speech at the Bertrand Russell Foundation Conference in Stockholm, in *New Society*, 13.2.1969, p. 233.
56. The leader article of the *Listy* on 20 February, No. 7, 1969, significantly carried the heading 'All Power to the Workers' Councils'.
57. Cf. *Universita Karlova* No. 13, 1969; *Studentské Listy* Nos. 3 and 5.
58. *Universita Karlova* No. 20, 1969.
59. Cf. Karel Kovanda explaining the programme of the radical section for an independent student organization which would not be a docile instrument in the Party's hands, in *Universita Karlova* No. 20, 1969, 17, 1969.

60. E.g. series of articles in *Rudé Právo*, the main Party daily, written by Josef Ondrouch in May 1969.
61. Statement passed by the Extraordinary Congress of the Czech Student Parliament on July 2, 1969.
62. *Studentské Listy* No. 2, p. 7.
63. E.g. *Listy* No. 13, 1969, the leader article *Capitulation and Courage*.
64. Manifesto signed by student leaders Jiří Müller, Karel Kovanda, Lubomír Holeček, published in *The Observer*, 18.5.1969; 'Czech Students Alongside the Workers'.
65. Ibid.

3. POLAND

Michalina Vaughan

Post-war expansion and reorganization

The expansion of higher education after the advent of the People's Republic corresponded not only to an economic need for trained cadres—since war-time losses had been particularly heavy among the intelligentsia, as a result of repressive policies against this group[1]—but also to a political need. The new régime was not unexpectedly determined to broaden access to higher education and to recruit future graduates from among the social classes considered as revolutionary, i.e. the manual classes. Regardless of opinions and activity during the twenty years between the wars, almost every intellectual had the stigma of being 'alien' because of his connections—no matter how indirect—with the pre-war ruling class.[2] The remaining intelligentsia was not only depleted, but distrusted: hence the high priority attached to the rapid production of trained personnel.

To this end, the number of higher educational establishments was increased, as was student intake, and the latter form of growth has remained a constant characteristic in the fifties and the sixties. In 1938 the total student population had been approximately 50,000 in 32 establishments, six of which were universities. Under the People's Republic the network of 76 degree-granting establishments includes 8 universities (only one of which is private—the Catholic University of Lublin), 7 Schools of Higher Economic Studies, 5 Teacher Training Colleges, 10 Medical Schools, 16 Art Schools, 7 Agricultural Schools, 17 Polytechnic and Higher Technical Schools, 4 Higher Schools of Physical Training and 2 Theological Academies.[3] Therefore they differ widely from the pre-war institutions, which were less vocational in character and offered courses in the traditional academic subjects. Furthermore, the student population (whose increase is shown in Table 3.I) includes those who take correspondence courses or attend evening classes; such part-time students endeavouring to acquire professional qualifications represented one-third of the total in 1968–69.[4]

Table 3.I—*Number of students and of students graduating: 1946–69*

Year	Students	Graduating
1937–38	49,534	6,114
1945–46	55,998	3,860
1950–51	125,096	21,722
1955–56	157,465	21,650
1960–61	165,687	22,391
1965–66	251,864	26,728
1966–67	274,471	31,933
1967–68	288,788	

Source: *Rocznik Statystyczny*, (G.U.S., Warsaw 1968), p. 443

The target figures for the next decades are 380,000 students in 1975 and half a million in 1985, in order to fulfil the estimated requirements of the planned economy.

This link between educational and economic planning corresponds to a prerequisite of socialist policy, and is in striking contrast with the pattern of pre-war academic laissez-faire. Higher education has thus undergone a planned expansion with a view to performing specific tasks, related to official economic and social policy, and defined by State legislation as including 'the pursuit of creative scientific research, the provision of scientific workers capable of undertaking both teaching and research, the instruction and education of cadres and of an intelligentsia qualified to perform functions requiring a high level of scientific competence, and the preservation and development of national culture and technical progress'.[5] This is indicative of the emphasis on specialist training and on applied science—which is of course much more pronounced in the Higher Schools and is the *raison d'être* of the polytechnic/technical sector, where one-third of the whole student population is registered. Consequently the rate of expansion has been considerably higher in the technical and scientific subjects than in the humanities. According to Szczepański, the pre-war number of students in the former disciplines had been multiplied by ten in 1963–64, whereas in the latter it had only quadrupled.

A corollary of State control over expansion has been State intervention in the organization of higher education. Thus the precise tasks to be performed by these establishments have been periodically redefined in connection with shifts of emphasis in economic and employment policy, as well as in the ideological assessment of subjects or courses. Furthermore, the structure and organization of the educational system have also been frequently revised to take account of the variations in degree of autonomy granted to the teaching staff. While the integration of education with the economy is a stable feature of educational policy, the complementary integration with politics has been a source of constant organizational change. According to Szczepański, 211 legislative provisions on higher education were enacted in the period between 1945 and 1968 and introduced 1,350 different organizational or structural reforms.[6] Thus every successive intake of students experienced change in curricula and/or examination procedure before graduating. To sum up the general trends of these reforms, it could be stated that during the first phase, until 1947, more latitude was left to the teaching staff—both in scientific and administrative matters—than between 1948 and 1955, when ideological training was emphasized and centralism prevailed. After October 1956, a liberalized educational policy was gradually introduced and the corresponding legislation (November 1958) emphasized the economic rather than the political integration of higher education and its scientific rather than its ideological goals. However, a fourth phase has followed the student protests of March 1968: it is characterized by a tightening up of central (ministerial) and party control over appointments and discipline, as well as by a priority given to ideological and political education. This policy—which can be termed reactionary, since it is both a reprisal induced by the March movement and a regression to the past—is formally summarized by the law of December 1968,[7] which contains the first legal recognition of the Polish United Workers' Party as a participant in the administrative bodies of each University. The competence of party representatives is not limited to political and ideological education, but extends to all matters of scholarships, students' housing, access to students' canteens, etc. Apart from this party control over the practical aspects of student life, the right to expel any student 'guilty of collective offenses or offenses particularly damaging to society or against law and order or the interests of the State'[8] is given to the Minister for Higher Education and to the Rectors (heads of educational institutions) appointed by him. Administrative centralization is evidenced not only by the replacement of elections by appointments (the Rectors appointing Deans and the Minister or the Rectors being empowered to appoint associate professors from among pedagogically and ideologically suitable, though not fully qualified, staff 'in accordance with the interests of the socialist State, without having to consult collective or advisory bodies'), but also by the replacement of relatively autonomous professorial chairs by institutes in which teaching and research are carried out by teams.[9] Thus a major aspect of this reorganization is the limitation it introduces on the prerogatives of the teaching staff. This is a logical outcome of the distrust in which academics have been held by the government throughout the period of educational expansion.

The academics and the intelligentsia tradition

In 1944 the surviving academics had such scarcity value that there was no alternative to co-operating with them in organizing higher education anew. However, from the outset there was a clash between the professoriate, attempting to maintain traditional standards of quality, and the Communist Youth Organization (A.Z.W.M.-Życie), which was determined to hasten a quantitative increase in working-class and peasant intake. To this end, pre-university entry courses were organized by A.Z.W.M.-Życie in 1946 for youngsters of manual origin with incomplete secondary education. They met with vigorous criticism from university teachers. Nor were protests emanating from this group limited to academic matters: in 1948–49[10] the Workers' Party repeatedly denounced the universities as centres of reactionary thought.

Although the composition of the teaching body was necessarily modified as a result of expansion involving new appointments[11] and of retirement affecting pre-war professors,[12] the attitudes denounced at the beginning of the Stalinist period were again diagnosed ten years later. 'The influence of bourgeois trends, attitudes of social passivity and of ideological distrust have a large following among the professoriate and particularly among the young',[13] stated the minister for Higher Education at the party Congress in 1959. The 'privatization' of ideals among an important section of the professors and assistants was denounced at the same Congress.[14] In fact, the series of statements demanding a restoration of free speech in 1961–62 and the 'Manifesto of the 34', signed by many eminent academics in 1964, do not seem to be indicative of 'privatization' in the usual sense of this term, but of an independence traditionally associated with the teaching profession. The fact that the young academics, trained and appointed under the People's Republic, met with the same accusation as their elders undermined the view that it sufficed to train a scientific cadre under socialism in order to ensure its political reliability.

Since the attitudes of academics bridged the 'generational gap', an explanation for their persistence was sought in the ideological bias pervading the teaching of those disciplines that are most closely connected with philosophical and political issues. '. . . The social sciences . . . in spite of existing achievements—represent the most backward sector of the scientific front. . . . (yet) shaping the socialist consciousness of society, and particularly of the young generation, have no less importance for the development of socialism than the construction of its material, economic bases'.[15] In this statement at the Second Party Congress in 1959 Gomułka emphasized the need for designing a 'cultural policy in the ideological disciplines, such as philosophy, sociology, economics, and to a great extent education, the legal sciences, the historical sciences etc.'[16] Thus attention was clearly drawn to the 'danger spots' represented by certain fields of study singled out from among other disciplines because a greater degree of commitment to Marxist–Leninist orthodoxy should be required from academics engaging in teaching or research in them. This difference was spelt out by Gomułka at a meeting between the Central Committee of the Party and a group of scientists in 1968:

> The social sciences are such that I would call them fundamentally different from the exact sciences. Indeed in the field of exact sciences the political standpoint of the scientist does not have a decisive influence on the results of his research, and even a person with backward, reactionary views, but with a deep store of knowledge in his speciality may achieve creative, useful and progressive results by his work. In the field of the social sciences it would be difficult to find a scientist holding backward, reactionary, anti-socialist views whose work was progressive and valuable . . . the standpoint of the researcher in these disciplines cannot be dissociated from his ideological and political standpoint. The results of his research, and particularly their interpretation fill specific ideological and educative and propaganda-political functions. Therefore the party must and will interfere in this scientific field, since this derives from its role of leadership.[17]

This postulate contrasts with the recognition that problems arising in the exact sciences can only be solved by the scientists themselves. Thus the assumption that a generation of academics were untrustworthy and that the influence of their teaching should be checked is supplemented by the broader hypothesis that the very study of certain subject-matters is a potential source of ideological unreliability. Consequently, in the social sciences, party control is equally imperative over students as over teachers, over post- as over pre-war graduates (in 1962 the former represented 80 per cent. of the population educated at the higher level).[18] The new intelligentsia is not assumed to be more reliable than the old.

The students and the creation of a new intelligentsia

While educational expansion at other levels was intended to raise the literacy, numeracy, and the occupational skills of the mass, higher education was specifically aimed at producing a new élite, access to which is necessarily restricted. The number of places available (annually fixed by the Minister of Education) remains insufficient to meet the demand: thus in 1969 there were about 100,000 applications for 41,120 places.[19] Chances of entry vary with the specialism and with the institution selected, since both the supply of places (created in the light of national needs assessed by planning authorities) and the demand (number of applicants) differ widely. Thus in the early sixties the percentage of rejections oscillated from 24 to 60 per cent. of applicants, depending on the subjects and the establishments considered.[20]

To manipulate the supply of university places so as to produce the specialists required by the economy is an essential aspect of educational policy. However, it is equally important for ideological reasons to ensure that selection procedures facilitate the access of working-class and peasant youth to higher education. Otherwise future graduates would be predominantly recruited from among the children of intellectuals, whose home background gives them an initial advantage (evidenced by their performance at secondary level and in university entry tests). This would result in the perpetuation of the old, rather than the recruitment of a new intelligentsia, and would be in direct contradiction with both the egalitarian tenets of Marxism–Leninism and its emphasis on the dictatorship of the proletariat. Therefore the selection committees of academic institutions cannot apply criteria of intellectual merit alone, but have to operate a system of quotas based on social background and fixed by the Minister for Higher Education. Thus in 1950 the quota for entrants of working-class and peasant origin was 60 per cent. of the total intake.[21] The increase in the representation of the manual classes among the student population was initially considerable, providing a sharp contrast with pre-war recruitment patterns.[22] However, 'the percentage of entrants of working-class and peasant background has never ceased to decrease as one moves away from the initial impulse, as if the university system through its very inertia acted as a brake'.[23] This trend is illustrated by Table 3.II.

Table 3.II—*Entrants of manual background as a percentage of yearly intake of higher educational establishments*

Year	Working-class origin	Peasant origin	Both together
1951–52	39.1	24.9	64.0
1952–53	35.9	25.1	61.0
1953–54	33.9	25.9	59.8
1954–55	34.6	24.4	59.0
1955–56	32.2	24.0	56.2
1956–57	30.7	22.0	52.7
1957–58	25.0	21.1	46.1
1958–59	27.8	21.3	49.1
1959–60	28.2	20.1	48.3
1960–61	27.0	13.3	40.3

Source: J. Szczepański, *Pedagogiczne Problemy Wyższego Wykształcenia*, (P.W.N., Warsaw 1963), p. 123.

This gradual decrease became more accentuated after the thaw of October 1956 and the ensuing reduction in external pressures on uni-

versity authorities. Consequently a system of bonus points was introduced in 1964 by the Ministry to 'equalize the chances' of candidates
originating from the manual classes. In addition to the points given to
reward the best results at secondary leaving stage and those gained at
the university entry test,[24] a bonus equal to at least one-tenth of the
highest possible score is attributed on the basis of social origin. The
fewer the candidates with the appropriate social background applying
for entry to a given faculty, the higher the bonus granted to them.
Although this system has been defended on egalitarian grounds,[25] it
has also been criticized because of the arbitrariness inherent in the
manual/non-manual distinction, which penalizes not only the children
of clerical workers, but also those of the post-war graduates of proletarian origin. Academics have accused bonus points of lowering the
quality of the university intake, and also of being awarded too late to
help the truly underprivileged. Indeed it is when pupils are channelled
from primary schools into general rather than technical secondary
instruction that their educational future is determined; this selection
made at the age of fourteen is undoubtedly influenced by social factors,
rural pupils being at a particular disadvantage. 'The process of selection
for higher education occurs between primary and secondary, so that
most provisions made at the stage of university entry are merely "a
condiment after a meal".'[26] Thus in 1968 only 28.2 per cent. of lyceum
pupils came from working-class or peasant families,[27] and a plea was
made in the press for extending quotas of social origin to all these
general secondary establishments, or at least to some of the most
renowned. Unless such a reform is introduced, attempts to broaden the
social basis of university intake will be frustrated—by the dearth of
applications from the 'underprivileged' categories.

'We expected a crowd of working-class and peasant children to rush
to the universities; but this has not been the case.'[28] The disappointing
results of the bonus points system show clearly that it is not the entry
tests that represent the main obstacle to a greater representation of the
manual classes in the student population. It is in fact the preference
demonstrated by secondary leavers of this background for the more
vocational courses offered by polytechnic schools and teacher training
colleges that accounts for their concentration in these establishments,
outside the universities.

The choice of a branch of study and that of a type of educational
establishment appears to be made by reference to economic and other
criteria (such as the religious—characteristically the Theological
Academy is the only institution with an overwhelming majority of
applicants from the manual classes), which are not given the same
weight in different milieux. Thus intellectuals tend to consider the lack
of a university education for their children as tantamount to social
demotion, whereas there is no unanimity among the manual classes in
regarding education as the best avenue to promotion.[29] Inclined to

Table 3.III—*Breakdown of candidates for entry into higher education in 1965 (by social background and type of establishment)*

	Social origin of applicant			
Establishment	*Working-class*	*Peasantry*	*Intelligentsia*	*Artisans and others*
Universities	25.7	14.9	52.3	8.1
Higher technical schools	38.1	17.4	40.9	3.6
Higher schools of agriculture	19.9	34.8	39.7	5.6
Higher economic schools	36.7	19.4	39.6	4.3
Teacher training	39.1	23.6	31.8	5.5
Medical schools	23.1	14.2	57.1	5.6
Art schools	21.2	9.6	62.4	6.8
Theology	25.2	50.2	19.2	5.4

Source: *Rocznik Statystyczny* (Warsaw 1965), p. 421.

assess it as an investment rather than to value it for its own sake, manual workers are somewhat less able and distinctly less willing than intellectuals to help their children during a period of full-time study. Hence the predominance of students with an intelligentsia background in 'day-time' higher education, and that of manual workers in evening and correspondence courses. The latter represent a short-term investment in occupational mobility rather than a long-term investment in social mobility, and moreover are mostly undertaken by adults emancipated from their family.

Social background is an important variable not only at the stage of applications for entry, but also during the completion of a degree course. In his research on 'the role of social origin in the formation of cultural patterns in two student milieux', Nowak found that 'young people whose parents belong to the intelligentsia and have been educated at higher level are best adapted to, and have the highest social status at the Faculty'.[30] The conflict between value systems which students of manual origin must face at university is a contributory factor to their high failure rate,[31] especially at the end of the first year. While in all fields of study the overall failure rate is considerable, it is distinctly lower in the establishments which provide vocational training rather than dispensing academic culture. For instance, approximately 40 per cent. of students complete their course in the time prescribed in such institutions as the Higher Agricultural School and the Higher School for Statistics and Planning, whereas in Warsaw University only 25 to 29 per cent. of the students do so.[32] 'The Achilles heel of our higher education is the efficiency of the courses. Although there are in Poland 86 students per 10,000 inhabitants, this yields only 8.4 graduates.'[33] Consequently the choice of vocational education at higher level does not necessarily reflect differences in aspirations held, but considerations of expediency; it is still entrants from manual backgrounds who can least afford to 'take a chance' in the more academic courses.

Apart from the difficulties epitomized by a high failure rate, students have to face economic hardships and/or to rely on parental aid. State scholarships are only granted in cases of proven need, and the criterion fixed in 1959 has been increasingly difficult to meet, since real wages have increased less than nominal. Thus in 1962, 52.8 per cent. of the student population were in receipt of a grant, in 1963 49.8 per cent., in 1965 50.5 per cent.;[34] in 1968–69, there were 95,000 scholarships—including 1,936 graduate grants—for 300,000 students.[35] In addition, halls of residence only provide for the housing of 41.6 per cent. of students;[36] this scarcity of places accounts for the predominance of 'local recruitment' among university entrants, particularly in Warsaw, where accommodation remains a major problem. Thus the material conditions under which students have to work are difficult and could provide a legitimate source of discontent. On the other hand, while employment upon graduating is virtually guaranteed,[37] the structure of remunerations is such that economic prospects are bleak and the opportunities for rapid promotion are virtually non-existent. The 'wastage' of graduates, stagnating in posts for which they are over-qualified, is frequently mentioned as a major source of disenchantment among young intellectuals, both at the university and in later life.[38] However, these anxieties and grievances have not been the substance of student protest under the People's Republic. It is always on general issues of nation-wide politics, rather than on specific educational or economic problems affecting the students as a group or as members of the intelligentsia, that this protest has focused.

Student organization and student protest

1944–56—The Stalinist period
The politicization of student life in Poland pre-dates the Second World War, since in the late thirties there were frequent and often violent confrontations between the extreme right-wing, anti-semitic Phalange, and the left, divided between four student groups. Each of these four reappeared in 1944–45 and was linked to one of the major legal political parties: 1. *A.Z.W.M.-Życie*, connected with the Polish Workers' Party (P.P.R.), and its youth organization Z.W.M. (total membership: 100,000 in 1945, trebled by 1948), continued the pre-war tradition of the communist student organization *Życie* ('The Life'); 2. Under its pre-war name, *Z.N.M.S.*, the Organization of Young Independent Socialists, was linked with the Polish Socialist Party (P.P.S.) and its youth organization T.U.R. (total membership in 1948: 150,000); 3. *A.Z.W.M. Wici*, the University Organization of Young

Peasants, not only possessed a long pre-war tradition, but—like the Polish Peasant Party (P.S.L.) led by Mikołajczyk—had a broad support from urban as well as rural opponents to the sovietization of the régime; it was loosely linked with the Youth Organization *Wici* (total membership: 400,000 in 1945; 255,857 including 3,240 students in 1948); 4. The student section of the Organization of Young Democrats (Z.M.D.), known as Z.P.M.D. before 1939, was an emanation of the Democratic Party (S.D.), whose membership was mainly among intellectuals and the urban petty-bourgeoisie, and was linked with the small Association of Democratic Youth (Z.M.D.) with a total membership of 20,000 in 1946.[39]

During this period, formal ties between student political groups and other bodies, such as the unions and the non-academic youth organizations, were not well articulated, and political activities in academic circles were separately organized. This relative autonomy was gradually reduced until it disappeared almost completely in the fifties. Yet, even in the early days of the People's Republic, there were strong personal links between the leadership of student organizations and the corresponding political parties.[40] The competition—particularly between A.Z.W.M.-Życie, on the one hand, and the Socialist and Peasant Organizations, on the other—remained intense, while anti-communist opposition parties were legal, and centred on the interpretation of Poland's relationship to the Soviet Union. The extreme left propagated the view that the wartime resistance had been led by the communist People's Army (A.L.) while the Home Army (A.K.), which acknowledged the London émigré government, had played a pernicious role and staged the Warsaw uprising as an anti-Soviet diversion. Thus a major feature of the late forties was the concentration of political debate, in academic life and in the country as a whole, on national problems such as the territorial losses on the Eastern border and the dependability of the new alliance (in the light of the earlier German-Soviet pact and of the Russian non-intervention in Warsaw). A large number of students, predominantly of intelligentsia background, held views that had been shaped during their service in the A.K., the majority resistance movement, and were to the right of all four student groups. Their interpretation of patriotism was very similar to that upheld by the Catholic Church, whose organizations—although formally designed as purely religious—provided an alternative centre of attraction for academic youth and a constant target for attack for the extreme left.[41]

It was outside the framework of the four official organizations that student protests took the form of overt demonstrations—as on the 3rd of May (date of the pre-war national holiday) 1946 in Cracow, when Soviet tanks threatened several thousands of student demonstrators—or of creating clandestine groups in opposition to the régime—such as that discovered in Cracow in 1954. The elimination of official opposition in 1948—marked by the fusion of the major parties, communist, socialist and peasant, into one United Workers' Party (P.Z.P.R.)— was accompanied by the amalgamation of all youth organizations into the Association of Polish Youth (Z.M.), and all academic youth organizations into the Z.A.M.P. From then on the concept of political pluralism vanished from student politics. Consequently only 15,000 out of the 25,000 members of the four former student organizations joined the Z.A.M.P. Yet its subsequent growth was rapid, turning it into an ante-room to the Party for the student rank and file (in 1949 it counted 25,857 students and in 1950, 42,017).[42] When the Z.A.M.P. was dissolved in 1951, students made to join the sole remaining youth organization, the Z.M.P., were deprived of any political grouping of their own. As a result, the ideological control of the party over student politics was tightened up, and mass student affiliation to this official body became a feature of the early fifties. In 1951, 70 per cent. of all students were Z.M.P. members,[43] and a post in the hierarchy of this organization was frequently a start to a political career. 'The typical politician who was a candidate for promotion to a high post in 1968 was born between 1925 and 1931; he was active in the Z.M.P. machine or occupied a responsible post in the student movement.'[44] Yet the failure of the Z.M.P. leadership was made obvious in October 1956.

1956—The Thaw

The end of the Stalin era, marked by the Twentieth Party Congress of the Soviet Union, stimulated demands for political and intellectual liberalization in Poland, as in other eastern European countries. In the short run at least, the Polish opposition to Stalinist centralism seemed particularly successful. The thaw consisted of a double phenomenon: the prevalence of Gomułka's faction within the Workers' Party and the emergence of an articulate, critical left among the intelligentsia. On the one hand, the new party leadership after October 1956 no longer rigidly enforced ideological conformism. On the other, Catholicism no longer represented the only philosophical alternative to Marxist orthodoxy.

The Z.M.P. leadership had not only failed to anticipate the defeat of the Stalinist faction within the Central Committee of the Party, and the subsequent relaxation of governmental controls over academic life, the press and the mass media. They had also assumed, on the basis of post-war experience, that student political protest would necessarily rally round the Church, against whose influence Z.M.P. campaigns had been directed throughout the early fifties. Yet, although clerical organizations survive in most higher educational establishments (of which only the University of Lublin is under the direct control of the Catholic hierarchy[45]) and are ritualistically attacked at Party Congresses from time to time—they were no longer instrumental in mobilizing student opinion after the first years of the People's Republic.

The generation of students who entered higher education in the mid-sixties had been brought up under the new régime. They no longer considered the traditional right as politically 'credible'—they rejected its obsession with the pre-war past and its anti-collectivism. Yet they themselves perpetuated an old tradition by attributing to the intelligentsia a special responsibility for formulating national ideals and for assuming leadership in times of crisis. Their heroes were writers and artists breaking away from socialist realism, young academics, such as Kołakowski in Warsaw, and journalists, particularly the team who issued the periodical *Po Prostu*,[46] the organ of the new debating clubs where the errors of Stalinism were critically appraised and attempts were made to devise new patterns of socialist humanism. For the Marxist revisionists, Yugoslavia provided an exemplary solution, whereas those who held more moderate views considered Finland as an alternative model.[47] This increased involvement in the contemporary international scene was matched by a renewed interest in recent Polish history, particularly in the wartime relationship with the Soviet Union.

It is this atmosphere of intense political debate among the intelligentsia, this rethinking of the country's political future, which has become known as 'the Polish October' or, more romantically, 'Spring in October'. The name is misleading, since it refers to an outburst of anti-régime (and, some have argued, anti-Russian) protest in Poznań in October 1956. The participants in this demonstration were mainly manual workers, with some unorganized local student support. The Poznań incident stimulated fears of counter-revolutionary agitation and thus served to strengthen Gomułka's hand against Stalinists in the party. Thus it contributed to bringing in the political new deal which —especially in its first year—resulted in greater intellectual freedom. The workers' street-fighting in October permitted the continuation of the nation-wide debate among the intelligentsia to which the label of 'Polish October' remains affixed.

Attempts made by Z.M.P. leaders to contribute to this debate and to remain in control of student life failed. Their organization was liquidated soon after the Poznań events and was gradually replaced by several co-existing youth associations:

1. The Association of Socialist Youth (Z.M.S.)
2. The Association of Rural Youth (Z.M.W.)
3. The Association of Polish Students (Z.S.P.)
4. The Association of Polish Scouts (Z.H.P.).[48]

While the first two were explicitly political and formally connected with the Party, the Z.S.P. claimed to defend the occupational interests of students rather than to disseminate an ideology. Its origins could be traced back to 1951, when it had been organized as a centre for student self-help and mutual assistance, while the political sphere was left to the Z.M.P. Not being officially linked with the Party, it had considerable appeal after October 1956 as a comparatively apolitical body; its membership reached approximately 50 per cent. of the student population.[49] Subsequent events showed that the Z.S.P. was neither as representative of student opinion nor as free from Party influence as had been initially surmised.

From 1957—The Hardening Up

The accusation of revisionism levelled at the *Po Prostu* team and the order to discontinue its publication resulted in demonstrations by Warsaw students, violent intervention by the police, street fighting in the capital between the 3rd and the 7th of October 1957, and finally a series of arrests and expulsions from the Party. This was a turning point in the history of the régime, marking the disavowal by Gomułka of the 'mirage' of 'a socialism which does not resemble that socialism erected by the Party and by millions of men'. The ensuing reshuffle in Party leadership was accompanied by the replacement of those youth leaders who had been most involved in the October reappraisal. Some emigrated, others withdrew from politics, and a new generation controlled the three official associations. This take-over was described in the Polish press as a triumph of realism over idealism, of expediency over enthusiasm, of opportunism over revisionism.[50] The legislation on higher education was more liberal than during the Stalinist period; the Z.S.P. made contact with foreign student organizations; revisionist opposition seemed to have been replaced by an 'ideology of withdrawal', which left to the cadres of the official associations a monopoly of militancy. Yet warnings against 'anti-socialist forces among students'[51] and attacks against 'a consumer's outlook on life . . . in a large part of student youth'[52] continued within the Party.

Widespread disenchantment among the students after the failure of the October movement remained a latent threat in the early sixties. It became manifest from 1964 onwards when new leaders emerged and formulated a programme which is both more explicit, more original and more extreme than the proposals launched for social and political reform in 1956. Yet there is a similarity between the two episodes: in 1956, it was Leszek Kołakowski, then assistant at Warsaw University, who became the main exponent of student protest in the weekly *Po Prostu*; in 1965, it was Karol Modzelewski[53] and Jacek Kuroń[54], both assistants at Warsaw University, who were on trial as the authors of an 'Open Letter to the Party' and as the leaders of student opposition. In both cases, young teachers were recognized as more representative of student opinion than official organizations. In both cases they were Marxists, and their criticism of the régime was based on its departures from socialist ethics. In both cases the existence of the People's Republic was recognized as an unalterable fact, as was its participation in the socialist camp. Hence there is a major doctrinal difference between criticism emanating from such radical academics and the previous type of student protest—of the late forties and early fifties—in which the basic premises of Marxism were rejected. In 1956, it was no longer Western liberalism but Yugoslav workers' councils that constituted a source of inspiration for the followers of Kołakowski. In 1964 Kuroń and Modzelewski described workers' self-management in Yugoslavia as a mere technocratic device to maximize production, and appealed for an antibureaucratic revolution to liberate the working class. Thus a slide to the left appears to have occurred with the advent of a new generation of young teachers and students entirely brought up under the People's Republic, deeply impregnated with Marxist ideology, but highly critical of the concentration of all political initiative within the party leadership,[55] of the bureaucratic control over the economy[56] and of the preventive censorship[57] stifling freedom of expression and research. The revisionism of the Italian Communist Party, the Cuban socialist experiment and the Chinese cultural revolution—as well as back-reference to the thaw, referred to as the 'Polish Spring in October', usually recalled by teachers and assistants rather than actually remembered by students—formed the background to this ideological crisis.

In the 'Open Letter', Kuroń and Modzelewski emphasize that it is mainly the young who are robbed of prospects by growing unemployment, rural overcrowding, the housing shortage and savings on higher education, 'which deprive peasants and workers, as well as the small-town youth of their opportunities for advancement. In the face of the growing difficulty of finding a place in the life of society, the young people in every social stratum are most affected by the economic, social, ideological and moral crisis, and are potentially at every level of society the most revolutionary element.'[58] Yet those among whom the manuscript of the Open Letter was circulated and discussed belonged in fact to a privileged minority—attending either the top forms of the most fashionable gymnasia in Warsaw or studying one of the social sciences in the most renowned Universities (Warsaw, Cracow and Wrocław). Many of them were the children of well-known party members, occupying posts of responsibility in the government and/or the party machine. Most of them belonged either to the party or to the Z.M.S. They were not among the economically deprived and they enjoyed special opportunities, for example passports for travel abroad, in addition to their educational advantages. Given this socio-political background, it is hardly surprising that many of them should have been either Jewish or of Jewish descent. This was neither a coincidence, nor the result of the 'Zionist plot', 'unmasked' during the first wave of student trials in 1956 and relentlessly denounced by the press ever since. In fact, it was merely a reflection of 'the relationship which established itself between the revolutionary party in Poland and the Jewish population and of the role played by Jews at various times in the (pre-war) Polish Communist Party (K.P.P.) and the communist movement. It is the final outcome of a process which has lasted for a whole half century.'[59] Since the disproportionately high representation of the depleted Jewish minority in the leadership of the student movement is directly related to a similar imbalance in the composition of the party leadership, it is not irrelevant to mention the historical causes of this phenomenon.

The alleged Zionist plot
Throughout the pre-war period, the K.P.P. membership was 'nationally unrepresentative'[60] since approximately a quarter of the rank-and-file and a higher proportion of the leadership were recruited from among the Jewish minority. This concentration was due to the emphasis placed by the party programme on the abolition of any form of national or racial discrimination. The 'internationalism' of the K.P.P., which attracted the Jews, was a deterrent for the Polish intelligentsia in particular, and for other social classes as well—both because of deep-rooted antagonism to Russia and of a heightened sensitivity (ever since Partition) to issues of national sovereignty. Moreover, Jewish party members were less suspected of Polish nationalism, and this played an important part in the personnel policy of the Komintern. A similar attitude prevailed after the war. Jewish survivors—most of whom had spent the war years in the Soviet Union and a number of whom were 'ideologically reliable' members of the former K.P.P.—played a considerable part in the foundation of the People's Republic by staffing the new Workers' Party (P.P.R.) and the emerging State administration. This early influence was further reinforced after 1948, when the right-wing nationalist deviation had been denounced and when the reliance on Jews occupying high posts in the party executive, the foreign service, the army and the security machine represented a continuation of the pre-war view that they were less prone to this deviationism. However, in the late fifties the revisionist crisis deeply affected Jewish members of the party—whose proneness to leftist deviationism became obvious through their participation in the 'October Left'. Attacks on party dogmatism emanated mainly from the creative intelligentsia (especially writers), from university teachers (particularly in the social sciences) and from the so-called 'ideological apparatus' (press, radio and television); in all these fields, there was a comparatively high proportion of Jews—precisely because they had been considered as trustworthy during the previous period. Thus the anti-revisionist campaign launched in the sixties soon acquired anti-semitic overtones, intensified by the earlier prominence of the Jewish minority during the Stalinist period.

> The official statement [is] that it is not Jews, not 'Sionists', but 'revisionists' who are the main danger. . . . But the attack against the Jews was exceptionally convenient as a screen, and was calculated moreover to win the support of at least a section of society, whereas it is difficult to conjure

up emotion against the abstract and not very comprehensible concept of 'revisionism'. [61]

It was thus argued before the Central Committee of the party that 'between these two trends (revisionism and Zionism) there largely existed a personal union'.[62]

The official explanation of student unrest is centred on the concept of a Zionist-revisionist plot, extending beyond the academic milieu, but finding a particularly fertile ground among the young, whose idealism and political inexperience were exploited for subversive ends.

> The supporters of revisionism were not idle . . . they took advantage of academic freedom to infiltrate their views into the minds of the young, they selected assistants and students in their own image, they persecuted those who did not share their views. Thus the revisionists retained strong and dominant positions in the faculties of philosophy and economics of Warsaw University, and to a certain extent in law, education and history as well as in some institutes of the Polish Academy of Science. . . . A group of scientific workers, graduate students and undergraduates of the faculties of history, economics, philosophy-sociology and mathematics-physics of Warsaw University conspired to produce an anti-party political program calling for the overthrow of the socio-political order existing in our country. The main part in the activity of this group was played by K. Modzelewski . . . and J. Kuroń.[63]

This interpretation of student revolt as being localized and engineered rather than widespread and spontaneous is the only version compatible with the allocation of responsibility for it to individuals presented as subverting rather than leading students. It was expressed by the prosecution during the first trial of Kuroń and Modzelewski in 1965[64] and provided the official justification for the subsequent series of repressive measures against academics and students,[65] most of whom were Jewish and all of whom were Marxists. During this period, the growing restlessness in higher educational establishments was expressed in informal and small group meetings; it was in halls of residence rather than in the official student organizations that criticisms of governmental policy (particularly with regard to censorship and to the limitations on political freedom within the University) could be voiced. It was in these halls that the programmes of reforms demanded by students during the demonstrations of March 1968 were discussed and crystallized. Kuroń and Modzelewski's Open Letter had been intended as a background document for such discussions—both authors emphasized its provisional and experimental character during their trials. While the views on the inevitability of a future revolution may not have been generally shared or even widespread, their attacks against the party bureaucracy and its monopoly of decision-making certainly coincided with the opinions of most writers, university teachers and students. The growing discontent of the intelligentsia with the policy of the party—in which the tough-minded group of 'partisans' who control the political police was acquiring a predominant influence at the time —became manifest in January 1968.

1968—The March Events

The episode which triggered off the series of protests from the 'creative' intelligentsia and of students' demonstrations leading up to the 'March events' was an unlikely beginning for a Zionist-instigated movement. It concerned a drama written in the nineteenth century by the national poet Mickiewicz, entitled 'The Forefathers', whose denunciation of tyrannical government could still be construed as topical by a receptive audience. However, it was the allusions to Tsarist occupation of Poland which were alleged by the authorities to be detrimental to friendship with the Soviet Union (rather than plain anachronistic), when the National Theatre in Warsaw was ordered to discontinue the performances of this play.[66] Writers, artists and students protested against this administrative decision and against its motivation (challenged by the publication of a favourable review in the Moscow *Pravda*). Official retaliation consisted in the expulsion of several students from Warsaw University. A manifestation of solidarity was held in the courtyard of that university on the 8th of March and was sternly repressed. The confrontation between students and the militia—reinforced by 'party activists representing the working class', a majority of whom were identified as members of the secret police—continued for several days, culminating in street fighting on the 11th. The protest movement spread to provincial institutions, particularly to the Universities of Cracow, Wrocław and Toruń, while clashes with the police were occurring in Cracow, Poznań and Katowice. This outburst—denounced by Gomułka on 19 March as a Zionist-revisionist plot—became known, to parallel the former 'Spring in October', as 'the Polish early Spring'. It was to prove short-lived: heavy reprisals against the student leaders[67] (who were mainly Z.M.S. members, but not involved in Z.M.S. leadership), the dismissal of sympathetic university teachers[68] and the refusal to re-enrol those students who had actively participated in the sit-ins and demonstrations, ushered in a new period of 'social discipline' in higher education.

Even the briefest account of the March events shows that they involved the whole of higher education—and not isolated faculties in which the alleged plot was supposed to have been perpetrated. It shows also that the students who actively participated in them were not a minority—in fact whole sections of the official organizations such as the Z.S.P. at Warsaw University explicitly adhered to the movement. Furthermore, the teaching staff expressed solidarity with the students both in resolutions passed by the Councils of Faculties and through the Teachers' Union.[69] Hence it is possible to characterize the protest movement as being 'academic' rather than limited to students. A major difference from the October movement was that in 1968 the working class—leaving aside isolated expressions of solidarity from a few industrial establishments—remained passive. Whereas in 1956 the intelligentsia was not isolated from the rest of society, the March events were initiated within the sphere of higher education and did not really spread beyond it. While it has been shown that the police surrounded working-class districts and prevented students from entering factories to make appeals for workers' support, anti-intelligentsia propaganda was also used to cut off the students from the manual classes. In the press and in leaflets circulated during the March events the emphasis on the Jewish origins of students' leaders and of their teachers, as well as on the positions of those leaders' parents in the political hierarchy, was a direct appeal to anti-semitism and to bitterness against the privileged. The inadequate representation of the manual classes in the student body was stressed, though no reference was made to its fluctuations or to the major centre of protest—the Warsaw Polytechnic School—having a particularly high intake of workers' children. The purpose of official propaganda was thus to depict the new intelligentsia as genetically alien and politically hostile to the working class—although this was tantamount to proclaiming the failure of educational policy both with regard to student selection and to ideological formation.

It is consequently to be expected that great emphasis will be laid on the criterion of social origin (and presumably also of ethnic origin?) in admitting students to higher education in future years. Since the Jewish minority represented only 0.1 per cent. of the population in 1969 and is still being reduced by emigration, racial homogeneity in the student population may well be achieved. It is indicative in this respect that in the most recent series of student trials—in February 1970—none of the accused were Jewish, and that they were sentenced for maintaining contacts with a review published in France by Polish émigrés (Kultura)[70]. Social homogeneity appears more difficult to achieve, and the problems encountered in filling the manual-class quotas are unlikely to be lessened in the future. Even the wider provisions of educational facilities at secondary level—which the economy can ill afford—would not suffice to solve this problem in the absence of a complete change in the value-system of the manual classes. Thus in the seventies the student population will presumably still be largely recruited from among the intelligentsia. Therefore, when it becomes impossible to blame student protest on the lack of national integration of a dwindling ethnic minority, it will be a logical development to attribute student unrest to the lack of social integration of the intelligentsia as an occupational minority. The March events have already confirmed the accuracy of the diagnosis that 'alienation in our country is an elitarian disease'.[71] The repressive measures taken since 1968 show the official determination to contain the symptoms, rather than to investigate the causes of this phenomenon.

The new policy has consisted in striving to secure ideological uniformity and—to this end—increasing the part played by official students' organizations in higher education. Membership of these organizations is essential for obtaining scholarships and/or gaining access to halls of residence, while entry to the Party is—since 1968—only from the Z.M.S. or the Z.M.W. for students and graduates. Thus short-term practical and long-term political considerations alike prompt students to join these bodies[72] whose common programme—co-ordinated by the National Committee for the Co-operation of Youth Organizations (O.K.W.O.M.)—emphasizes ideological formation, physical work and subordination to party leadership. University sections of military training, to which virtually all able-bodied male students belong, also contribute to spreading a new atmosphere of discipline, nationalism and—somewhat paradoxically—anti-intellectualism in higher education. Under the law of December 1968, student organizations appoint delegates who participate in a purely advisory capacity in the councils assisting Rectors and Deans. Thus a return to the regimentation of the pre-October period has been achieved since 1968—but without restoring the monopoly of one organization (although the Z.M.S. plays a leading part in formulating ideologically orthodox views). In spite of the plurality of allegedly representative bodies, no channel for the expression of student dissent exists—predictably, since such dissent is a punishable offence.

The outbreak of student protest in Poland in March 1968 ought not to be considered in a purely national context, since it stems from an ideological crisis which has spread throughout Eastern Europe and affected Marxist parties in the West. Not only were expressions of solidarity with Czechoslovakia indicative of a common concern for national independence and the humanization of socialism: the political programmes elaborated by Polish students[73] embody the same proposals for reform that were launched in Prague during the brief period of liberalization. Yet a major difference between the two countries—and between the March events and the earlier Polish October—is the limitation of protest to the creative intelligentsia and the academic community. The failure of the Polish student movement can be accounted for both by this isolation and by the lack of support from any faction in the party—contrary again to the precedent of October 1956. However, the history of student organizations under the People's Republic shows clearly that the enforcement of ideological orthodoxy in higher education has repeatedly failed, and that the youth leaders chosen to encourage conformity have either repudiated it themselves or lost control over their 'constituencies'. Thus the present tightening-up of political control over academic life is unlikely—in the light of precedent—to prove successful in the long run, for all its short-term repressive efficacy. The cycle of protest, scapegoating, and ideological hardening, followed by protest again, appears to be a permanent feature of the twenty-five-year-old relationship between university and Party, and to epitomize it. Yet this relationship is only one aspect of the more lasting, less predictable and ultimately decisive relationship between university and society.

Notes

1. Out of 2,460 university teachers in 1939, 700 were killed in the war. Cf. J. Szczepański (ed.), *Wykształcenie a Pozycja Społeczna Inteligencji* (PAN 1959), p. 481. Cf. also K. Estreicher, *Cultural Losses of Poland: Index of Polish Cultural Losses During the German Occupation 1939–44* (London 1944).
2. A. Borucki, *Kariery Zawodowe i Postawy Społeczne Inteligencji w P.R.L.* (1945–59) Wrocław–Warszawa 1967.
3. Cf. B. Simon, *Education in the New Poland* (1954), and S. Żółkiewski, 'Nowoczesna organizacja nauki i szkoły wyższe', in *Nowe Drogi*, 5/192, May 1965, p. 110.
4. Data compiled from *Trybuna Ludu* by G. Mond, unpublished research.
5. Cf. W. Wesołowski and J. Koralewicz-Zębik, in J. Szczepański (ed.), *Przemysł i Społeczeństwo w Polsce Ludowej* (PAN 1969), p. 459 and Statistical Yearbooks for the years 1964–69.
6. *Dziennik Ustaw PRL* No. 68, 1958, p. 338.
7. Cf. *Dziennik Ustaw* No. 46, 1968, p. 517 f.
8. Idem.
9. Cf. R. Mistewicz, 'O nową strukturę wewnętrzną szkół wyższych' in *Nowe Drogi*, 10/233, October 1968, and M. Karaś, 'Uniwersytet—postęp i tradycja' in *Nowe Drogi*, 2/237, February 1969, p. 50 f.
10. Cf. C. Majdarzyk and W. Markiewicz, 'Nauki społeczne w ostatnim ćwierć wieczu' in *Nowe Drogi*, 7/242, July 1969, pp. 118 f.
11. There were 6,237 teachers in higher education in 1946–47 and approximately 19,000 ten years later (cf. J. Szczepański, 'Wykształcenie a Pozycja Społeczna Inteligencji', op. cit. (note 1), p. 475).
12. According to S. Żółkiewski, then Minister for Higher Education in 1959, a quarter of the university staff were due to retire within the next five years (cf. *Nowe Drogi*, 4/118, April 1959, p. 362). Cf. also H. Golański, 'Dziś i Jutro kadr naukowych' in *Nowe Drogi*, 2/141, February 1961, p. 108 f.
13. Idem, p. 365.
14. J. Wieczorek, Report to the Second P.Z.R. Congress, 4/118, op. cit., p. 410.
15. W. Gomułka in *Nowe Drogi*, April 1959, 4/118, pp. 73–4.
16. Ibid.
17. W. Gomułka in *Trybuna Ludu*, 22.10.1968. Cf. also A. Żabiński, 'Problemy pracy ideologicznej Z.M.S.' in *Nowe Drogi*, 11/234, November 1968.
18. Cf. W. Wesołowski in J. Wiatr, ed. *Studies in Polish Political Structure*, PAN 1967, p. 5. Cf. also M. Charkiewicz, 'Zmiany w strukturze wykształcenia ludnossci' in *Nowe Drogi*, 7/182, July 1964, p. 326.
19. Cf. *Trybuna Ludu*, 27.2.1969.
20. Cf. J. Lagneau, *Stratification et Egalitarisme; Théorie et Pratique de la différentiation sociale en pays socialistes*, mimeographed doctorate thesis, University of Paris, n.d., p. 149 (data for 1962).
21. Idem, p. 159.
22. Cf. H. Wittlinowa, *Atlas szkolnictwa wyższego*, Warsaw 1937, p. 25: in 1934–35 the social origin of students was as follows: bourgeoisie and landed aristocracy: 9.1 per cent.; professions and intelligentsia: 57.8 per cent.; petty bourgeoisie and 'kulak' peasantry: 19.4 per cent.; smallholders and manual workers: 13.7 per cent.
23. J. Lagneau, op. cit. (note 20), p. 160.
24. The tests are in three subjects, that which is most closely connected with the future studies having the highest coefficient.
25. Cf. E. Polański, 'W sprawie doboru kandydatów na wyższe studia' in *Życie szkoły wyższej*, No. 5, 1966: 'It is of course impossible to make fully objective choices; but the postulate that chances should be equalised at the start remains justified.'

26. Cf. *Trybuna Ludu*, 19.4.1968.
27. J. Szczepański in *Życie Warszawy*, 2–3.6.1968.
28. Z. Kitlińska, 'Pierwsza próba analizy nowego systemu rekrutacji' in *Życie szkoły wyższej* No. 6, 1968.
29. Cf. A. Sarapata, *Studia nad uwarstwieniem i ruchliwościoi społeczna w Polsce*, Warsaw 1965, pp. 366 f.
30. I. Nowak, in *Przegląd Socjologiczny*, tome 20, 1966, p. 147.
31. Cf. J. Szczepański, op. cit. (note 1), pp. 483 f.
32. Cf. W. Kata in *Życie Szkoły Wyższej* No. 9, 1968, pp. 5 f.
33. J. Wójcik in *Współczesność* No. 12, 1968.
34. Cf. T. Kołodziejczyk, 'Wynik w Portfelu' in *Polityka* No 33, 19.8.1967. In pre-war Poland only 5.5 per cent. of students received subsidies of any kind—cf. H. Wittlinowa, op. cit. (note 22), p. 31.
35. *Rocznik Statystyczny* 1968, p. 460. Cf. also A. Rajkiewicz, 'O zatrudnieniu absolwentoów szkół wyższych' in *Nowe Drogi*, 8/207, August 1966, p. 88.
36. *Rocznik Statystyczny*, 1968, p. 459.
37. Although the right of graduates to employment is not binding on the authorities and there has been some unemployment of arts graduates in the fifties.
38. Cf. K. Lutyńska in J. Szczepański (ed.), op. cit. (note 1), p. 7 f. Cf. T. Izydorkiewicz, idem., p. 354 f., cf. also Z. Bauman in *Kultura* No. 12 (Paris 1968), p. 6 f.
39. Data on the membership of student and youth organizations compiled by G. Mond from *Robotnik*, 15.7.1948, p. 1 and *Pokolenia* No. 3, July–September 1968, p. 133 f.
40. Former A.Z.W.M. Życie leaders include not only many members of the Political Bureau and of the Central Committee of the Party in the late fifties, but also Leszek Kołakowski, the main exponent of the ideology of the Polish October. Former Z.N.M.S. leaders gravitated towards university teaching and the arts.
41. Cf. M. Rybicki, 'O Postęp na Wyższych Uczelniach' in *Nowe Drogi* No. 4, July–August 1949, p. 35.
42. Out of these 42,017, 6,549 belonged also to the United Workers' Party and 1,279 to the United Peasant Party; 30.9 per cent. were of working-class origin, 27.7 per cent. of peasant origin, 33 per cent. of intelligentsia origin and 6.6. per cent. belonged to other social categories. Cf. *Pokolenia*, op. cit., p. 153.
43. Cf. Z. Zemankowa, 'Wyższe uczelnie w walce o nowe kadry' in *Nowe Drogi*, September–October 1951, p. 74 f.
44. *Polityka*, 11.1.1969.
45. The Catholic University of Lublin is the only religious, non-State higher educational institution in Eastern Europe. It is financed by Polish Catholics and run on systematically apolitical lines. It has remained open, although several of its faculties have been temporarily closed by the government. It has been a target for constant criticism in the press and for severe fiscal levies.
46. The circulation of the weekly *Po Prostu* went from 30,000 in November 1955 to 150,000 in November 1956, and its editor, E. Lasota, got almost as many votes as Gomułka in the Parliamentary election in January 1957. The failure of the Polish October was marked by the order to discontinue its publication given by the Party leadership in late September 1957.
47. Cf. W. Jedlicki, 'Quelques remarques sur le révisionnisme polonais' in *Esprit* No. 2, 1968, p. 269 f.
48. Mainly active in secondary establishments, but whose leadership is composed of university students and assistants (e.g., Kuroń).
49. Cf. C. Wiśniewski, 'Z.S.P. przed nowym rokiem akademickim' in *Nowe Drogi*, 10(137), 1960, p. 153 f.
50. Cf. *Tygodnik Powszechny*, 7.7.1962, p. 2.
51. Z. Zemankowa, 'Problemy wychowawcze wyzszych uczelni', in *Nowe Drogi*, October 1958, p. 40.
52. J. Wieczorek, op. cit. (note 14), p. 410.
53. Karol Modzelewski is the adopted son of a communist leader who was the first Minister of Foreign Affairs of the People's Republic. He is a graduate of the Law Faculty of Warsaw University and in 1964 was a fellowship holder and a teaching assistant in economic history in that Faculty. He belonged both to the K.Z.P.R. and to the Z.M.S. and was expelled from both immediately after his arrest by the secret police as the co-author of 'An Open Letter to Communist Party Members' (published in English,

edited by G. L. Weissman, under the title *Revolutionary Marxist Students in Poland Speak Out*, Merit Publishers, New York 1968).

54. Jacek Kuroń, a history graduate and teaching assistant at the faculty of education of Warsaw University, was arrested and banned from the K.Z.P.R. at the same time as Modzelewski, in November 1964.

55. Cf. J. Kuroń and K. Modzelewski, 'Open Letter', op. cit., p. 19: 'The decisions of the élite are sovereign and made without consulting the workers or the rest of society. Neither the workers nor the mass of the party members can influence these decisions.'

56. Ibid., p. 51: 'Every new advance of industry under the conditions of production for production's sake can only increase the contradiction between the developed productive capacity and the low level of consumption, thereby contributing to the development of the crisis. . . .'

57. Ibid., p. 67: 'Any displays of independence connected with the development of social thought and the enrichment of culture and ideological life in certain circles—discussion clubs, cultural societies, and others—are particularly subjected to strict surveillance and treated as potential dangers by the government. The same holds true for any sign of independent political and ideological activity and discussion in the most active units of the youth organization and the party.'

58. Ibid., p. 66.

59. W. Bieńkowski, *Motory i Hamulce Socjalizmu* (Paris 1969), p. 43.

60. A. Werblan, 'Kontrybucja do genezy konfliktu', in *Miesiecznik Literacki*, June 1968.

61. W. Bieńkowski, op. cit., p. 51.

62. A. Werblan, op. cit., loc. cit.

63. Ibid. Cf. also B. Pleśniarski, 'Praca Ideowo Wychowawcza w Szkołach Wyższych' in *Nowe Drogi*, 3/328, March 1969.

64. Kuroń and Modzelewski were arrested in March 1965 and sentenced in July to three and three-and-a-half years' imprisonment respectively for circulating the 'Open Letter'. They were released in Summer 1967 and rearrested in March 1968 during the student demonstrations. They were tried again in January 1969 and sentenced to three-and-a-half years for 'belonging to a secret organization and making contact with a Trotzkyist organization in Western Europe'. They were let out in 1971.

65. These include the trial of three lecturers at Warsaw University (Hass, Smiech and Badowski) in January 1966, the expulsion of Kołakowski from the Workers' Party, the suspension of Michnik and five other students from Warsaw University, and the prosecution of Nina Karsov.

66. Cf. W. Bieńkowski, op. cit. (note 59), p. 38 f. and *Polskie Przedwiośnie* (*Dokumentów Marcowych tom II*) (Paris 1969), p. 13, emphasizing that no anti-Russian demonstrations took place, contrary to the official version (for which see W. Gomułka's report to the Party on March events, *Nowe Drogi*, 4/227, April 1968, p. 5).

67. Apart from Kuroń and Modzelewski, student leaders condemned for participating in the so-called commandos of Warsaw University include S. Blumsztajn, S. Kretkowski, J. Lityński, J. Dajczegwend, W. Górecki, A. Michnik, H. Szlajfer and Barbara Toruńczyk.

68. Kołakowski, Bauman, Brus, Baczko and Maria Hirszowicz—all of them social scientists of Warsaw University.

69. Cf. *Wydarzenia Marcowe* (Paris 1968), pp. 136–7 (written statements of support from the Councils of several faculties of the Universities of Warsaw, Cracow and Wrocław, and of the Polytechnic Schools of Warsaw and Wrocław).

70. The review *Kultura* and the Polish Literary Institute attached to it (which has published Kuroń and Modzelewski's 'Open Letter' and documents on student protest (see notes 65 and 69) was denounced by Gomułka in April 1968 as a reactionary organization financed by the C.I.A. and by Zionists, and accused of fomenting the March events (see note 66 above). The accused in the 'Kultura trial' (M. Kozłowski, K. Szymborski, J. Karpiński, Maria Tworkowska and Maria Szpakowska) were all graduate students and/or teaching assistants at Warsaw University. Further trials are expected soon, particularly in Cracow, in connection with this case, and arrests have also been made in Prague, Czech intellectuals being also implicated.

71. J. Chałasiński, 'Problem narodowości' in *Przegląd Socjologiczny*, vol. XX, 1966, p. 38.

72. In late 1968 the Z.M.S. had 64,000 student members, (plus over 400,000 secondary school pupils); the Z.S.P. 180,000; the Z.M.W. 150,000 students and secondary pupils. (Cf. G. Mond, op. cit. (note 39)). 152,000 Party workers were active in the Z.M.S. and Z.M.W. (Cf. T. Rudolf, 'O młodzieży w tezach' in *Nowe Drogi*, 9/232, September 1968.)

73. The thirteen points drawn up at the Warsaw Polytechnical School and the statement of March 28th drawn up by representatives of Warsaw and Cracow Universities stressed the need for greater independence and impartiality of the judiciary, for an extension of parliamentary powers, and for the protection of individual rights granted by the Constitution.

4. U.S.S.R.

Nigel Grant

The structure of higher education

Soviet universities do not dominate the higher educational scene like their British counterparts; indeed, so different is their relationship with other higher institutions that it is of doubtful value to attempt to give them separate consideration at all. British universities are primarily—current academic mythology to the contrary notwithstanding—concerned with training for the higher professions. In the U.S.S.R., on the other hand, these functions are spread more widely over a variety of institutions at comparable level. Doctors, dentists, engineers and technologists, lawyers and economists, and most specialist teachers for secondary schools, are trained in medical, technical, legal and other specialist institutes. The universities thus have a more limited role in providing courses in the humanities and the pure sciences, a role filled in the U.K. only by the arts and science faculties. Some of the graduates become research workers or specialists of some kind; the majority, however, join their counterparts from the pedagogic institutes teaching in the secondary schools.

The universities therefore make up a much smaller part of the higher educational system than is the case in Britain. The figures make this clear enough. There are 794 higher educational institutions (*Vysshie uchebnye zavedeniya*, hence the useful abbreviation *VUZ*); of these, only 45 are universities.[1] Actually, since they tend to be large institutions, their share is greater than this figure might suggest. Still, with 7.3 per cent. of the total student body and 7.9 per cent. of the graduates, they form one of the smaller categories of VUZ. By way of contrast, the various types of technical and polytechnical institutes account for no less than 44.1 per cent. of the students and 38.1 per cent. of the graduates. (1968 figures; for details, see Table 4.I.)[2]

In standard and esteem, too, the gulf that is usually assumed in Britain between the universities and the rest is not apparent in the Soviet higher institutions. Since they are all subject to the same kind of ministerial control, one of the props of the British binary system is missing; they are also organized internally in much the same way. In

Table 4.I—Students and Graduates by Type of Higher Institution, 1968

Type of Institution	Students		Graduates	
	No.	%	No.	%
Universities	325,700	7.3	40,300	7.9
Pedagogic Institutes	894,200	20.0	139,200	25.5
Art Institutes	37,800	0.8	5,600	1.1
Medical Institutes	302,500	6.8	37,300	7.3
Legal and Economic Institutes	562,800	12.5	64,000	12.5
Agricultural Institutes	375,300	8.4	38,500	7.5
Technical Institutes	1,971,400	44.1	194,700	38.1
Total	4,469,700	100.0	510,600	

Table 4.II—Entrants and Graduates in day, evening and external courses, 1950–1968

		1950	1960	1965	1966	1967	1968
Entrants:							
	Total	349,100	593,300	853,700	897,500	888,100	887,900
%	Day	65.4	43.5	44.3	47.6	49.2	51.0
	Evening	2.6	13.0	14.7	15.0	15.2	14.8
	External	32.0	43.5	41.0	37.4	35.6	34.1
Graduates:							
	Total	176,900	343,300	403,900	431,800	479,500	501,600
%	Day	82.5	66.6	55.7	53.1	52.1	52.3
	Evening	1.1	4.9	10.8	13.0	13.7	14.6
	External	16.4	28.9	33.6	33.9	34.2	34.9

many minor but possibly psychologically important respects there is little to choose between them. All have such titles as 'professor' and 'reader' for their senior academic staff. The system of diplomas and higher degrees is the same. Professions such as teaching that draw their members from different types of VUZ do not distinguish for salary purposes between university diplomas and those taken elsewhere. Nor do the universities dominate the field of academic research to anything like the extent taken for granted in the U.K. It is true that their contribution is out of proportion to their share of the higher educational sector, but research is carried on in all types of VUZ, notably in the technical institutes, where there is often close collaboration with industry. Nor are the universities the apex of the pyramid; this is to be found not in the higher educational sector at all, but in the special research institutes. Legally, then, and to a large extent functionally, all classes of VUZ are equal.

But in practice some are more equal than others, and some less. It is probably true that the universities as a group enjoy greater prestige than most other institutions. Conversely, many of the smaller pedagogic institutes, which train most secondary school teachers, are widely . regarded as 'second-class institutions',[3] and often find it difficult to compete with other VUZy in attracting staff and students of high calibre.[4] But one should not make too much of this, for the differences in prestige are generally greater between individual institutions than between categories. The Universities of Moscow and Leningrad have an extremely high reputation, and places in them are greatly sought after; but so have many of the technical institutes. Engineering is probably the most highly regarded profession in the U.S.S.R., and such VUZy as the Kalinin Polytechnic in Leningrad or the Moscow Power Institute enjoy a reputation greater than that of many universities. Nor are the pedagogic institutes uniformly low in esteem; those of Moscow or Leningrad, or the foreign language institutes there and in Gorky or Minsk, are quite different from the more remote 'mini-institutes',[5] and are more highly regarded than the Universities of, say, Alma-Ata or Dushanbe. Though the differences are real both in reputation and standards, there is no clear-cut distinction between the various categories of higher educational institution.

To keep the record straight, however, it is necessary to make some mention of another sector of the educational system which, though having no direct parallel in the U.K., does fill some of the roles assigned in Britain to the non-university side of the so-called binary system. Although not formally part of the higher educational system, the secondary specialized schools (*srednie spetsial'nye uchebnye zavediya*) are nevertheless relevant to it, as they provide most of the training of what might be loosely termed lower professional level. These schools, sometimes called *tekhnikumy* or technical schools, provide professional training in music, art, librarianship, economics, clerical work, nursing, communications, transport and construction, agriculture, and often a wide range of qualifications in engineering, technology and applied science.[6]

These schools share some of the characteristics of both secondary and higher education. At present, compulsory education in the U.S.S.R. ends with the completion of the eight-year school at the age of about fifteen. Very few, however, leave at this point. The majority stay on to complete the full ten-year course leading to the school-leaving certificate (*Attestat zrelosti*, literally 'attestation of maturity'). Of the rest, some enter *vocational technical schools*, trade courses of two or three years roughly equivalent to apprentice training, and some enter secondary specialized schools. For those who go in at this stage the course usually lasts for four years, and includes general education up to ten-year school standard; graduates are thus equipped to take up their professions or go on to higher education. Alternatively, students may enter secondary specialized schools after finishing the ten-year school; in this case, the course is usually of two years' duration and concentrates on professional subjects, the general element having been taken already.

There seems to be a growing tendency to take this second road, though official figures do not make this clear. There are signs that the authorities are trying to keep their options open. On the one hand, present policy is to make ten-year schooling compulsory in some form by 1971, and statements by the Minister of Education have indicated that the preferred course is for students to complete ten-year schooling before going on to work or further study. On the other hand, not all are expected to do this—about 75 per cent., according to the Minister; the rest will go either into vocational-technical schools (continuing with their general education part-time) or into secondary specialized schools. It is plain, then, that they will continue to exist at a secondary level for at least some students for some time.[7]

Numerically, the secondary specialized schools are comparable with the higher institutions. They have now slightly fewer students (4,262,000 as against 4,470,000), but thanks to the shorter courses they release a much larger number of specialists into the economy—902,800 in 1968 compared with 510,600 graduates from the VUZy.[8] They come under the same administrative machinery as the VUZy—some run by specialized ministries—the system as a whole coming under the U.S.S.R. Ministry of Higher and Secondary Specialized Education, not the Ministry of Education, which is responsible for the general schools. The secondary specialized schools cannot be dealt with here, but they have to be borne in mind lest the general parity of the higher institutions should give too one-sided a picture.

One example of the way these two sectors overlap is in teacher-training. At one time the division of function was clear-cut, but reforms of the past few years have begun to blur the distinctions. Three main types of institution produce teachers for the schools, namely:

(i) *Universities* train subject specialists for the secondary classes, forms V–X (approximately age 11–17). Courses last for five years and concentrate on one special subject, which accounts for between 60 and 70 per cent. of the total time. Professional subjects such as pedagogy, psychology, teaching method and teaching practice are an integral part of the curriculum (about 10–15 per cent. of most courses).[9] Although not all university students intend to teach, the majority are qualified to do so. In the event, between 60 and 70 per cent. find themselves in the secondary schools.[10]

(ii) *Pedagogic Institutes* also train teachers for the same level. The approach is somewhat different, however, rather more time being given to teacher-training subjects. The course for single-subject specialisms lasts for four years, double-subject specialisms for five; most students take the latter. Although officially at the same level, university graduates are widely held to be at least a year ahead of their colleagues from the pedagogic institutes in mastery of their special subjects; on the other hand, they are said to be about a year behind in educational theory and professional expertise.[11]

Pedagogic institutes also train some primary-school teachers, though with the exception of some of the smaller republics their contribution is not large. These four-year courses were established when the 1958 'Khrushchev reforms' envisaged, among other things, higher educational qualifications for *all* teachers. As yet, however, this has not been carried through; even now, only 11.5 per cent. of primary teachers hold higher qualifications. According to Ministry officials, it will be at least ten years before the pedagogic institutes can entirely take over the training of primary teachers.[12] Meanwhile, their main function remains the training of secondary specialists; they are, in fact, the chief source, with 119,800 graduates compared with 38,000 of all kinds from the universities.[13]

(iii) *Pedagogic schools* (*pedagogicheskie uchilishcha*, or *peduchilishcha* for short) are secondary specialized schools which train all kindergarten teachers and the great majority of teachers for primary schools (over 70 per cent. of whom have qualifications from this source),[14] and over a quarter of the teachers of music, art, physical education and labour training. There has been considerable dissatisfaction for some years with the standard of training in the *peduchilishcha*, hence the attempts to replace them with VUZ courses. This has so far been unsuccessful for a number of reasons, including faulty prediction of the number of teachers required, and the present expansion of secondary schooling, which is putting enough strain on the pedagogic institutes already without the additional burden of taking over all primary training as well. In the meantime there has been much heart-searching about the quality of the *peduchilishcha*, and widely reported attempts to improve them.[15] Even if the higher institutes do eventually take over the training of primary teachers, the pedagogic schools will still, of course, have a part to play in the system, since it is not suggested that the training of kindergarten teachers should move into the higher sector.

Internally, higher institutions are run on much the same lines. The basic unit is the department (*kafedra*, literally chair), consisting of all the academic staff and headed by the departmental chairman. The departments in one major area make up a faculty (*fakul'tet*), which is generally more narrowly defined than in this country: one finds faculties of geology or chemistry rather than science; philosophy or history rather than arts. Each faculty has a council of leading staff, headed by a dean. The chief controlling body of the whole institution is the academic council (*uchonyi sovet*), consisting of members elected by the faculties and headed by a rector. This body is responsible for the academic work of the institution, and is in some respects not unlike the Senate of a British university.

The resemblance soon ends, however, as the institutions are subject to a much greater degree of control than the U.G.C. ever dreams (one assumes) of exerting. At first glance, the external administrative machinery is simple enough. Major policy decisions are taken by the Central Committee of the Communist Party and the Council of Ministers of the U.S.S.R. At national level, these are worked out by the Ministry of Higher and Secondary Specialized Education of the U.S.S.R., and at the level of the fifteen Union Republics are further elaborated by the Republic Ministries of Higher Education,[16] with due regard to the special conditions of the area. Finally, they are passed down to the VUZy themselves for translation into action. It appears to be a neat chain of command, with the competence of each level clearly determined, from the central authorities in Moscow right down the line to individual institutions from Riga to Vladivostok.

Actually it is far from being as simple as that. The pattern of ministerial responsibility is much more complex. Although the Ministry of Higher Education is responsible for the system as a whole, it does not run all the VUZy directly; many of the specialized institutes come under other ministries, such as Culture or Public Health, and most pedagogic institutes come under the Ministry of Education. Between various ministries there is a network of information and consultation, often informal.

Another complication is the role of the Communist Party which, as in all fields of Soviet life, operates parallel to the machinery of government. This ensures a further degree of vertical control, from the Central Committee's Department of Education, Higher Schools and Science right down to the powerful party and Komsomol (youth league) branches in the institutions themselves. Horizontally, the party maintains links with branches in the locality outside the institution. Needless to say, party decisions carry at least as much weight as those originating in the formal chain of command.

A substantial degree of uniformity is thus ensured. Even the curricula (*uchebnye plany*, literally 'instructional plans') are prescribed in great detail, laying down not only the subjects to be taught in any particular course, but the years in which they appear, the number of hours per week to be devoted to each, the distribution of time to lectures, seminars and practical work, the number of examinations, tests and essays, and so on.

There are some breaks in the pattern. Most of the plans leave aside a proportion of curricular time, upwards of 10 per cent., for optional or elective courses, and simply suggest the kind of thing that might be offered. Most of them make provision for 'special courses', 'courses determined by the peculiarities of the Republic or VUZ', and the like. This is not a wide choice either for the student or the institute, but it is there and has been increasing. Some institutions manage to avoid the prescribed curricula altogether and use their own individual curricula. This is quite commonly done by many of the major universities and some of the more prestigious and well-staffed colleges of other kinds, such as the more prominent technical institutes and larger pedagogic institutes in Moscow, Leningrad and Minsk. This is not a matter for unilateral action, however; ministerial approval is still required at every stage.

These are official ways of departing from the norm, but there are plenty of unofficial ones as well. One hears, for instance, of required courses not being offered owing to lack of suitably qualified staff. There have been complaints about undue leniency in examinations in some of the smaller colleges. There have been cases where periods of 'productive work practice' have been turned into protracted potato-picking on collective farms to help out a local labour shortage, to the detriment of the students' academic work.[17] Sometimes the elaborate schemes of work are simply ignored; in some of the smaller pedagogic institutes, for instance, students' teaching practice is used mainly as a device to solve teacher shortages in the schools, the syllabus being 'liquidated in practice'.[18] How much of this goes on is hard to judge, but it seems to be quite common the further one gets from the major cities. In some cases the authorities know well enough what the situation is, but are unable to do much about it—they can hardly, for instance, conjure staff into being. In others, the channels of information seem to have become clogged. Either way, even in a highly centralized system it seems that the size and complexity of the country, plus a fair amount of bureaucratic muddle, impose practical limitations on the exercise of power.

The functioning of the system—admissions, courses and degrees

Any holder of the attestation of maturity from the general school can apply for admission to a higher institution. This is not enough in itself; candidates have to take an entrance examination as well. At one time holders of gold medals from the secondary schools were exempted from the examination, but Khrushchev put a stop to this in 1958 in his attempt to hinder the obvious growth of a professional élite.[19] His policy was not particularly successful, and one of his other innovations —giving preference to applicants who had been working for two years— has largely fallen into disuse. The requirement that all take the entrance examination, however, remains. The examination is not the only criterion; school records and testimonials from Komsomol organizations or trade unions also play their part. In effect, entry is competitive, and the competition is becoming keener all the time. Certainly the number of places has grown considerably—it has nearly doubled in the last decade—but secondary education has been expanding even faster. The chances of getting into a higher institution vary greatly from place to place and category to category, but, according to the Minister of Education, work out at about one in three on average.[20] Applicants can try for only one institution at a time—there is nothing like U.C.C.A.— which gives rise to a good deal of frustration and shopping around for places where chances of getting in are known to be better, with a view to transferring to something more congenial later on. (Students are not supposed to do this, but it happens none the less.) There is some disquiet about the vagaries of the selection system, but while the gap between supply and demand exists, no one seems to have much idea what to do about it. Meanwhile, an educational system which is substantially comprehensive at primary and secondary level remains highly selective at the tertiary stage.

One way of alleviating this pressure is the extensive use of part-time courses. There are other reasons for emphasizing these as well as pressure of numbers. They are somewhat cheaper, since part-time students do not receive maintenance grants or require hostel accommodation. In the technical disciplines at least, they may be a useful way of maintaining contact between theoretical and practical work. They make higher education available by correspondence to students in remote areas. They make it possible for large numbers to pursue higher education while remaining in their jobs, thus minimizing the drain on the manpower force that the expansion of higher education might otherwise cause. It has also been argued that part-time study keeps the student in touch with the realities of working life, thus discouraging the growth of a professional élite cut off from the masses and seeing education as a means of social self-promotion. Less is heard of this than during Khrushchev's time; though some may still expect a socio-political bonus of this kind, the reasons for the emphasis on part-time study have been overwhelmingly practical.[21]

About half of the students in the U.S.S.R. are now studying part-time, some of them attending evening classes but most of them 'externally'—that is, they do most of the work by correspondence, and attend their institutions for consultations with tutors, etc., for ten weeks in the year, being released on full pay for the purpose. The part-time contingent has fluctuated in the past couple of decades. Between 1950 and 1960 it rose from 43.6 per cent. of the total number of entrants to 56.5 per cent. In the last ten years, however, the proportion has been going down again; in 1968, full-time entrants once again made up the majority (51.0 per cent.). (For details, see Table 4.II.)[22] The reasons for the increase during the 1950s have already been noted; the more recent decrease can be attributed to practical difficulties. Part-time courses are no doubt cheaper to provide, but they are less efficient. Naturally, the students take longer than in full-time courses—one year more in theory, rather more than that in practice. They also tend to attain lower standards, and are more liable to fall by the wayside. This point will come up again later; meanwhile, it can be noted that part-timers have consistently been a minority of the graduates, even when they were a majority of the entrants. (See Table 4.II again.)

Full-time students are paid grants ('stipends') according to the year of study; they increase as the course progresses, though the reasons for this are not altogether clear. They vary to some extent from one type of institution to another, in an attempt to entice students to less popular but important fields of study. They also vary according to the students' performance. Those whose work is unsatisfactory may lose all or part of their stipends for the following year, though this seems to be uncommon; on the other hand, those who do particularly well are awarded extra 'personal stipends' which in some cases can nearly double their income. There is no space here to attempt to evaluate the real worth of the stipends, but generally they are low, not much more than half an unskilled worker's wage. This is to some extent offset by the absence of fees of any kind and by the cheapness of hostel accommodation, but most students still have to rely on help from their families or on spare-time jobs to make ends meet.

On graduation, students are liable to be assigned to jobs wherever they are most needed for a period of up to three years. There are many exceptions, however. Many students are seconded for their courses by their employing enterprises and are therefore committed already. Others may have ties in a particular area, possibly dependent relatives, and if one has a spouse already working in, say, Moscow, one will not be sent off to work in the Arctic.[23] The remainder are given a choice of available jobs in order of merit in the final examinations. The universities afford a good example of this system, and at the same time illustrate its drawbacks. Since most university courses include teacher training, graduates are qualified to teach whether they intended to or not. Apart from a few with a real vocation for teaching, the ablest graduates tend to choose research work; for the rest, the attitude seems to be, 'If I can't get a job in science, then I'll be a teacher'.[24] Of those, the ablest snap up the teaching posts in the cities, thus leaving the rural schools to those at the bottom of the list.

This is not a popular system, nor is it particularly effective. Some graduates simply fail to turn up. This is usually got round by sending the diploma to the employing body so that the graduate has to turn up to collect it; many, however, do not stay the full term, but come back to more congenial posts in the city, which seem quite easy to arrange. There are many ways of doing this unofficially, and though unauthorized leaving of jobs before the time has expired is well enough known to the authorities, there is not a great deal they can do about it. As one Ministry official put it, 'Well, what can we do? Put them in jail? How would that help the rural schools?' Finally, even those who do turn up for unpopular jobs and stay for the full period can then leave quite legally and take up work somewhere else. The main victims of this system are the rural schools themselves. While it is true that university graduates tend to drift from teaching, they are in any case only a small proportion of the teaching force; but pedagogic institute graduates do drift from country to town whenever they can, since remote-area payments and free accommodation are an inadequate compensation for being deprived of the amenities of city life.[25] Thus the rural schools (where half the country's children are taught) receive the less able graduates and fewer of them, and have an unhealthily high rate of staff turnover. It is not surprising that one of the major headaches in the U.S.S.R. is the gap between town and country in the level of attainment and aspiration in the general schools.[26] It will doubtless remain so until something can be done to improve communications and the standard of living in the villages, a Herculean task that goes far beyond the competence of the educational system.

Most courses in higher institutions last for five years, though some (such as single-subject specialisms in pedagogic institutes) last for only four and others (such as medicine) for six.[27] They are all specialist courses in the sense that they concentrate on one subject area (for example, Russian literature and language, mathematics, electronics, soil science), and the relevant ancilliary subjects (such as Old Slavonic, dialectology or folklore in the first example, organic and inorganic chemistry and hydrology in the last). This makes them more specialized than the courses in many European and certainly American universities—there is no equivalent of the general or ordinary degree. As has been noted, over 10 per cent. of the time is devoted to optional or elective courses, not necessarily within the special field; otherwise, the courses are run according to the prescribed uniform pattern. Students are required to decide their special field right from the start. Changing courses is not unknown, but it is neither common nor encouraged.

In one sense, however, the courses are less specialized than they appear, since they quite deliberately include non-specialist subjects. In the first two years physical education and a foreign language have to be taken by all students. The object of this is to mitigate the specialization of the rest of the course.

Finally, there are the political courses that appear in all curricula, regardless of subject. These are variously named, but usually contain three main areas: the history of the Communist Party of the U.S.S.R.; political economy (Marxist, of course, though Western economists are occasionally brought in to be proved wrong); and Marxist–Leninist philosophy. Classes in 'scientific atheism' are included, and sometimes listed separately. The amount of time given to political courses varies (they are less prominent in technological curricula than in the humanities, for instance), but it is rarely less than 10 per cent. of the total. Indeed, in most pedagogic institute curricula their share of total teaching time is greater than that of pedagogy, psychology and teaching method put together.

It is obvious that the authorities regard these courses as of the highest importance in 'shaping the materialist world outlook of the students';[28] whether the students take them seriously is another matter. They are notoriously the dullest taught elements in any curriculum; there are frequent complaints about this and calls for more imaginative presentation, but in such a sensitive area it seems that the teachers prefer the security of dullness to the risks of lively treatment. The students have to attend, but are said in many cases to sleep through the lectures, or work for other subjects in the back rows if, as one student put it, 'the lecturer is one we respect. If he isn't, then we work in the front rows as well.' The students have to pass examinations in the political subjects, and do so by the time-honoured process of regurgitation. All this may make them more knowledgeable about Marxism, though the general rule that required subjects are the first to be forgotten may well apply. There is little evidence that it does much to 'shape their world outlook'; the extent to which they are favourable or hostile, or simply apathetic, has little to do with political teaching, for which even the most fervent Marxist–Leninists find it hard to summon much enthusiasm. There are believers and unbelievers, but the preaching itself, according to one observer, 'is about as effective as compulsory chapel'.[29]

Students seem much less interested in politics than in their career prospects, social lives, and their specialist subjects. The last certainly keep them busy enough; for most of the course, they are liable to be kept at it for as much as six hours a day, six days a week, with regular tutorials, essays and tests as prescribed by the ministerial plans. Lectures are compulsory, though skipping of classes is not unknown. Reading lists are long, but students are as adept as any at spotting likely questions in advance. It is widely felt that students are over-taught and over-examined, but the final examinations do not count for everything. The last year is devoted largely to the preparation of a diploma thesis or project, and the final assessment is based on this as well as the examinations. If all is well, the student qualifies for the award of the first degree, known simply as the diploma. There are no classes of honours, but the diploma may be awarded with distinction—useful for those wishing to apply for higher studies.

Higher degrees are of two kinds, the Candidates of Sciences and the Doctor of Sciences. Both require advanced study and original research, and carry considerable prestige and financial advantage. The Candidate degree requires at least three years of further study, and involves both course-work and research for publication. It may be taken part-time or, more commonly, full-time, but with rather more generous grant-support than for undergraduate courses;[30] in 1968, 55,000 post-graduates (*aspiranty*) were studying full-time, just over 41,000 part-time.[31] As a rule, graduates are expected to work for two years or more before applying for post-graduate study. Comparison of standards is fraught with difficulties, but it would be reasonable to regard the Candidate degree as roughly the equivalent of the British Ph.D. The Doctorate is a more demanding and much more rarely awarded distinction, involving several years' work after the Candidate degree, with the publication of major research. It is roughly at the level of such higher doctorates as the D.Litt. or the D.Sc. At present, there are only 20,000 Doctors of Sciences, as compared with 186,400 Candidates.[31]

Strictly speaking, higher degrees are not awarded by the institution but by the Ministry. The VUZ makes the recommendation, but confirmation of the award lies with the Ministry's Higher Qualification Commission or VAK (*Vysshaya attestatsionnaya kommissiya*). One result of this arrangement is that work for higher degrees need not take place in higher educational institutions at all, let alone the universities. In fact, of the 25,000 *aspiranty* graduating in 1968, over 10,000 were studying in the scientific research institutes, which are as well qualified for this as the universities or colleges. There are over 98,000 post-graduate students, 56,500 of whom are studying in VUZy, which still leaves the research institutes with a substantial role to play in the higher degree system.[31] There is no suggestion, incidentally, that such degrees taken outside the VUZy are in any way inferior to those taken inside; the VAK, after all, has to approve them in either case.

The scientific research establishments look after not only a large proportion of the *aspiranty*, but the bulk of the ongoing research as well. That, after all, is what they are for. The main task of the VUZy remains teaching; nevertheless, they are concerned with research, partly because this is a useful way of spreading the load, partly because the staff are to hand, and not least because this is felt to be good for the teaching in keeping the lecturers from sinking into a rut. At one time it was required that all teachers in higher institutions spend an average of three hours a day on research. This proved, not surprisingly, unrealistically precise and was dropped, but staff are still expected to treat research as one of their main priorities.

Current problems

Although Soviet higher education is spared the turmoil so obvious in other countries, there are still problems in plenty, as current press discussion makes clear enough. There are signs, for instance, that the authorities are worried about the widespread political apathy among students. Not that there is much overt disaffection, but the present indifference is felt to be nearly as bad as political interest of the wrong kind. Courses in Marxist–Leninist theory seem ineffective in galvanizing young people into more active support for the régime or, more to the point, its present policies. Nevertheless, the importance of this work is still insisted on: 'Higher educational institutions must develop the younger generation as bearers of the great work of Lenin, bring up students in the spirit of high Leninist principles, communist consciousness, and opposition to bourgeois ideology.'[32] The need for improvement, however, is widely recognized, and the suggestions pour in.[33] In a few cases, they have been acted upon; one VUZ[34] attempts to break down the barrier between the ideological courses and what students regard as 'the real course' by constructing the syllabus so as to bring in the work of other departments such as languages, physics, biology and literature. There have been attempts to give the political courses a new look by bringing in the findings of sociology,[35] until recently a discipline highly suspect in the U.S.S.R. The Komsomol organization is supposed to play a central role in political education, but there are signs that it is not pulling its weight, paying more attention to its social activities or even becoming dormant altogether. For a body supposedly 'the active helper of the party in the building of higher education'[36] this will not do, and much ink has been spilt in discussing ways of improving the work of the Komsomol in 'the formation of the students' communist ideology'.[37] In one college (the Chuvash pedagogic institute) an optional course on 'fundamentals of propagandist work' has been set up.[38] This theme has become more and more insistent, and was commonly linked with the build-up to the recent celebrations of the centenary of Lenin's birth, to which the higher educational journals (like others) gave a great deal of space.[39]

How effective all this has been is difficult to say. Most of the reports on attempts to improve political teaching claim some degree of success, but these are hard to evaluate since it is not clear how failure would be recognized; it is perfectly possible, indeed frequent, to go through all the motions of conviction while basic indifference remains unruffled. There is no real student unrest, political or other. Not, at least, overtly; but this does not mean that a state of happy unanimity prevails either. It is common knowledge that many dissident student groups exist. Some of them take up a religious position (the 'God-seekers'); for them, church-going itself is a criticism of the official ideology. This is of course not illegal, but it does sometimes bring them under some pressure, particularly if the Komsomol branch is active. There do not seem to be any Maoists, but there are the strict Leninists, who take the view that the Soviet Union has been on the wrong path since Lenin's death, and Socialist Humanists, who think it was going wrong even before that. These are embarrassing, of course, since they need point no further than the Soviet Constitution and the stated principles of the régime for justification of their own positions. For this reason they are more dangerous than the clandestine groups to the Right which reject the Revolution altogether. None of these groups is large or active. There is a certain amount of *samizdat* (self-publication), the circulation of type-script books or articles from a critical standpoint, usually on the Left. Occasionally this is jumped on by the authorities, but very often is winked at; typed copies of Dr *Zhivago* have been going round the universities for years. There are unofficial neo-Marxist discussion groups, run largely by committed Marxists who find the compulsory courses and the official activity of the Komsomol little to their taste. But this is usually as far as it goes. A few students joined the dissident teachers in protesting about the imprisonment of Daniel and Sinyavskii, the invasion of Czechoslovakia, the treatment of the Tatars and similar actions. They were promptly expelled. Expulsion of dissidents is nothing new, though it does seem to have increased in the last few years. No figures are available; the numbers appear to be small, but enough to discourage imitation. There is little future, as most see it, in active protest if it simply means being thrown out. Even the politically discontented, then, with very few exceptions, follow the usual course of compliance followed by evasion. The 'silent majority' of students are largely indifferent, however, take the political situation as a fact of life and get on with their own concerns. They are well aware of how much they have to gain from acquiring a higher education, how much to lose from falling foul of the authorities. Since few of them seem to feel fundamentally hostile to the régime itself (as distinct from some of the things that it does) the risks involved in protest do not seem worth while.

Mere acquiescence, however, is not enough. The present indifference, though surely a logical outcome of the tight control of political discussion and activity, worries the authorities. The call has been raised, therefore, for greater participation by students in the running of their institutions. As we shall see presently, however, it is both initiated and controlled by the authorities themselves; what is envisaged is not a real change in existing relationships, but participation within the existing framework.[40]

Another important problem is student drop-out. The rate varies from place to place, as do the reasons for it, but there have been a number of detailed studies, among them one on the higher institutions in Sverdlovsk.[41] There, the drop-out rate rose from 4.6 per cent. per year in 1958–59 to 7.4 per cent. in 1962–63, levelling out slightly thereafter. It was at its highest in some of the technical institutes (notably the Forestry Institute with 10.2 per cent.) and in the natural science departments (7.5 per cent. in the Agricultural and Pedagogic Institutes and in the University). In other fields, notably in the humanities, things were somewhat better. Still, the average rate for all the institutions over a six-year period worked out at 5.3 per cent. per year—which meant that a quarter of all students admitted to a five-year course failed to graduate. Some of the casualties were attributed to 'living conditions', but most were academic, such as failure to attend classes or 'lack of proficiency'. The last was by far the largest category, accounting for 36.6 per cent. of drop-outs.

Two categories of student seemed to do particularly badly. The *stazhniki*—those who had worked for two years or more after leaving school—lost 45.6 per cent. of their number during the university course, compared with 25 per cent. of those who had come straight from school. Their difficulties were attributed to being out of touch with their subjects and being out of practice in studying. The other group, not surprisingly, was that of the part-time students. Those taking correspondence courses were falling out at the rate of 12.7 per cent. per year, while those taking evening classes were even more vulnerable (14.3 per cent. per year), higher in the university but lower in the technical courses. Again, the reasons given were usually academic.

The Sverdlovsk study is useful because it gives more detail than is usually available. It is not, of course, typical of the country as a whole in every particular; but it is generally conceded that on a national scale between a fifth and a quarter of those entering the first year do not gain the final diploma. The special difficulties of the *stazhniki* are general, as are those of the part-time students.

Among the reasons for these difficulties, one suggested is that students embark too light-heartedly on part-time courses:

> The difficulties of combining study with work are well known. Not all the students who undertake to study without giving up their productive work clearly visualise the difficulties facing them.[42]

But the institutions are blamed also:

> It is well known that the workers in the system of part-time education are striving to bring it as close as possible to full-time education. It is undeniable that the part-time form . . . has the greater achievements . . . but it must not be forgotten that the external and evening form . . . . . . requires a different system of organization of the teaching process. . . . [It] should be individualized as far as possible. The evening and external departments are trying in every way possible to copy the curricula and working programmes of the full-time departments. In our view, this is not correct.[43]

There follow demands for more flexibility, experiment, 'modernization of the teaching process', improvement of methods, better use of audio-visual aids and more attention to the particular problems of part-time students and their working conditions.

But the concern is more general than this. There have been constant complaints about the inadequacy of equipment and textbooks, over-crowding, the inefficiency of some of the teaching, and the instability of curricula. Even the two great pillars of traditional higher education, the lecture and the examination, are being looked at with a more critical eye. There are many accounts of better results being obtained through seminars and work-projects than formal lectures.[44] As for examinations, it is true that many still place a rather naïve trust in them (the author of the Sverdlovsk report, for example), but others are aware that even the most refined examinations are pretty blunt instruments; and though no one has yet managed to suggest a viable alternative (particularly for determining admissions), many are urging that for the final assessment the diploma thesis is a much better indicator of knowledge and ability than the examination, and should be given more weight.[45]

While the discussion on means of improvement goes on, there is a growing feeling that some margin of error in admissions is inevitable. The author of the Sverdlovsk report seems to accept this, though phrasing it rather oddly:

> Naturally, a small percentage of drop-out for personal reasons is un-avoidable, but no one should or will keep lazy, blockheaded or morally unscrupulous people in the higher educational institutions just for the sake of keeping up the number of students.[46]

Stripped of the rhetoric, this seems to suggest that some wastage is to be expected and accepted. In fact, the same author does say that the VUZy should admit more students to allow for drop-out, thus main-taining the required number of graduates.

Nor is all well in the research field. Ideally, there should be close co-operation between the higher institutions, the research establish-ments, the ministries and other interested bodies such as industrial enterprises, hospitals, schools and the like, and certainly there have been many successful joint ventures. Research is planned according to the national need and co-ordinated on a nation-wide scale, with the VUZy and other agencies all playing their part. It often breaks down in practice, of course; research has an awkward habit of not going according to plan, and the complex machinery often creaks and some-times fails to function. The Academy of Pedagogic Sciences, for instance, was taken to task in 1965 for failing to co-ordinate educational research, with the result that there was much 'dissipation of resources', and it had to be totally reorganized.[47] The drawbacks of this kind of arrangement, especially in view of the Soviet tendency to bureaucratic confusion, are apparent enough. On the other hand, there are obvious advantages to both sides in a link between the institutions and the national economy, and at least the existence of the research establishments makes it possible for the VUZy to play their part in research without having their teaching function smothered by it.

The teacher-training system has problems of its own. Although officially at the same level, there are clear disparities between the universities and the pedagogic institutes. In the institutes it is felt that the level of work in the specialist disciplines compares unfavourably with that of the universities, hence the 'brain-drain' of more highly qualified staff.[48] But the universities have their failings too; they devote less time to the pedagogic disciplines and take them less seriously, which is thought to have an adverse effect not only on the students' competence but on their motivation as well: 'Secondary teachers trained in the universities do not love their profession, but regard themselves as temporary guests in the schools, and as soon as possible get out of the educational field.'[49] Perhaps for this reason, suggestions that the institutes might be turned into university faculties have met with rather a frosty reception on both sides.[50] There have been the usual calls for improvement, but major structural change seems unlikely for the time being.

Obviously enough, these problems call for action, and we shall turn now to some of the steps that are being taken. One great difficulty, however, is that the present state of instability gets in the way of effective change. Curricula, for instance, are often changed or modified abruptly before the institutions have settled down to the previous ones; there have been many complaints about this, one to the effect that 'this sort of thing happens nearly every year'.[51] Changes there have to be, but if they are to improve matters much they will require to be thought out with care; a further series of tinkering is likely to cause more confusion, or to evoke the common response of minimal conformity to new policies which, even if it makes for a quiet life, does not hold out much hope of real improvement.

Developments

Following a crescendo of complaint about the shortcomings of higher education, in 1966 the Central Committee of the Communist Party and the Council of Ministers issued a resolution 'On measures to improve the training of specialists and perfect the guidance of higher and secondary specialised education in the country'.[52] Having noted with satisfaction the positive achievements, and spelled out the tasks of higher education in political training, research, teaching, and their application to national needs, the resolution complains that 'the higher and secondary specialised institutions do not always cope with these tasks, and there are substantial shortcomings in their work'.

The Ministry of Higher and Secondary Specialised Education of the U.S.S.R., as well as other ministries and departments . . . are making inadequate use of the rights granted to them to guide the methodological, research and ideological work of these institutions, and they are exercising inadequate control over the training of specialists. The Ministry does not carry out systematic work to raise the qualifications of teachers . . . it does not ensure the preparation of enough worthwhile standard textbooks. . . . There are serious shortcomings in specialist training. . . . Educational and material facilities . . . do not fully measure up to present-day requirements. . . . Not enough is done to involve the higher educational institutions in problems of national importance.

There is a good deal more of this, criticizing the VUZy for insufficient ideological work, ineffective liaison with the schools, and a host of other defects. Not surprisingly, the special difficulties involved in part-time study are noted:

It has therefore been proposed . . . that provision be made for the further priority development of full-time instruction. . . . At the same time, it is necessary to draw up a list of specialisms in which specialists will receive training through the system of evening and external instruction.

While part-time higher education still has a part to play—'one of the most important achievements in the cultural revolution in our country', as one commentator has it[53]—that part is clearly to be a smaller one than formerly. The enrolment figures tell the same story.

In view of the tendency of teaching staff to make insufficient allowance for the peculiar conditions of part-time study, more attention has been given to training specialist teachers for this kind of work, and to the design of courses and methods. This is partly the responsibility of the Ministry, but it is made clear that the institutions themselves are expected to play their part on their own initiative.[54] There are some instances where this is being done quite successfully, though how general this is there is no way of knowing. But we have seen that the shortcomings of current methods are not confined to part-time courses. The 1966 resolution authorized the Ministry to set up four special institutes for raising the qualifications of teachers of the social sciences. There are also provisions for the Ministry to assume direct control of a number of VUZy which 'will serve as a base for generalising and developing educational and methodological materials, compiling textbooks and study aids, and providing training and further training for the research and teaching personnel for all higher educational institutions'.

But exhortation and example was not enough; control was felt to be necessary, and so was information about the actual state of affairs in the institutions. It might be thought that there should be plenty of both already, but centralized systems can be extremely clumsy. Hence, presumably, the direct take-over of the intended model institutions; hence, too, the mounting of a full-scale governmental inspection of *all* higher institutions in the country 'with a view to strengthening control over the quality of the training given to specialists'.

This is obviously an enormous task, and it will be some time before the finding can be properly collated, let alone acted upon. So far, the year 1968–69 has been taken up with inspecting science courses in technical and pedagogic institutes and some of the professional courses in technical, agricultural and medical colleges. There has also been some wider study of part-time courses in general, entry to higher education, the teaching load of professors, and one or two other broader issues. Altogether, over 200 departments have been looked at. In 1969–70 it is the turn of art, economic, sport and legal institutes, and there is to be a general examination of teaching methods, research, and the internal organization of the institutions.[55] Clearly it is going to take years if the original intention of a full-scale inspection is adhered to. It may be, however, that there are expected to be benefits from the *possibility* of a visitation, in much the same way that a conspicuous police-car has marked effects on the observance of speed-limits.

There has also been greater emphasis on the need for more flexibility, devolution of decision-making to the VUZy themselves, and greater participation in the running of the institutions and planning of their work by staff and students. The resolution puts it thus:

> The Ministry . . . has been entrusted with the task of formulating draft regulations . . . that will provide for a further democratization of the activities of the institutions, increased rights for their directors, and greater independence in deciding educational, scientific and economic questions, as well as greater initiative and increased participation on the part of the students' civic organizations.[56]

Some aspects of the centralization of the system have certainly been proving irksome for some time. Even before the resolution, it was being pointed out with some force that 90 per cent. of the decisions referred to the Ministry could well be taken locally, and that the curricula and syllabuses were 'too standardized as a rule'. Not that there was any suggestion of complete devolution, but rather more flexibility within the existing system was called for: 'Naturally, it would be wrong to deny the need for model curricula and syllabuses, but we must not permit them to prevent VUZy from showing individuality in the training of specialists.'[57]

Reform of this kind, logically, has to affect not only the relationship of ministry and institution, but the internal organization of the institution itself:

> In order to create conditions under which scholars can participate more

actively in determining the direction of development . . . it would seem necessary to limit somewhat the undivided authority of the rector. The academic council should be given the right to elect a rector for a fixed term.[58]

In 1969, the 'Decree on the higher educational institutions of the U.S.S.R.' made most of the same points, with particular reference to 'further democratization' and greater involvement of staff and students.[59] As elsewhere, participation has come into vogue:

> The student is an active member of the VUZ collective. He has the right, through the social organizations, to participate in the discussion of the problems of improving the educational process and ideological up-bringing work, and also . . . the award of stipends, the allocation of places in hostels and other questions connected with the students' academic and social life. He takes part in the social life of the collective, in the work of the sports sections, artistic and scientific-technical circles, student clubs and amateur groups. The decree guarantees the graduate work in his specialism.

This is not exactly an upsurge of student power. The 'social organizations' are, of course, the Komsomol and the Communist Party, and there is nothing new in the involvement of the Komsomol (to which most students belong, at least nominally) in the activities mentioned. What the authorities do have in mind is the closer and more effective involvement of the students, and there are many discussions going on at the moment on ways to enliven the sometimes moribund Komsomol organizations.[60] It is made clear enough that further participation is expected to run along the approved lines, and that the students have obligations as well—to study Marxism–Leninism as well as their special subjects, to take part in socially useful work and in mass political and educational activity, and of course to work harder. It may well involve more participation, but not power.

It is clear, too, that the devolution of authority to the institutions and their staffs is not only to be limited, but cautious. As one pronouncement put it in 1966:

> Naturally, the granting of broad rights to the higher educational institutions in the training of specialists is not a simple matter; it must be effected gradually, starting with the most highly qualified higher school collectives. At first this should take the form of an experiment, and this will clear up all the things that cannot be foreseen. The sooner we proceed to the solution of this problem, the less painful will be the shift towards more rational methods of administering the higher school.[61]

The experiments have been proceeding since then, and are still being widely discussed. How far the easing-up will go cannot yet be judged; so far it has been modest enough, but at least there has been a step in the direction of greater flexibility.

Throughout the discussions, it has been realized well enough that one of the most obvious needs is for more money. From the 1966 resolution to the latest decree, there have been provisions to improve the 'material base' of the system, including the appointment of additional teaching staff, rather more favourable budgetary allocations for capital expenditure, and so forth. Needless to say, it is not enough, but at least it helps. Since many of the defects noted can be traced to inadequacies of equipment, laboratories, lecture-rooms, hostels and the like, even a modest injection of money is welcome. It comes, of course, with constant exhortation to work harder to make better use of facilities, think up more effective methods, plan teaching and research better, and so on. Money may be short but exhortation has never been lacking. Whether it will work is another matter.

It would be a mistake to adopt too gloomy a view. For all the undoubted shortcomings that have been raked over in the past few years, the fact remains that the U.S.S.R. has managed to establish higher education on a massive and still growing scale while maintaining standards, in technology and the sciences at least, that can perfectly well stand comparison with those of any other system. The biggest problem, perhaps, is not so much what is happening inside the institutions as the pressures building up outside. At present, about 60 per cent. of the age-group now goes on from the eighth form to the ninth and tenth; by 1971, ten-year schooling is to become generally compulsory.[62] To go by past experience,[63] it will doubtless take longer than that to make it effective, and of course not all will succeed in taking the attestation of maturity. Nevertheless, the number of potential entrants to higher education is bound to rise considerably. As we have seen, the competition for places is already acute, and in spite of the growth of the higher educational system it is likely to get worse, which has ominous implications for social peace; the younger generation in the U.S.S.R. have come to expect increasing educational opportunities, and if these are blocked for too great a number, and no viable alternative found, they may well become much more restive than they are at present. Part-time study has been extensively used to alleviate the problem in the past, but as we have seen, this brings severe problems of its own. The pressure on places also highlights the problem of admission procedures, which is at present rather crude; but it is doubtful if sophistication of testing will help much—the experience of some other countries, including Britain, suggests that much more refined examination gradings are still rather a poor predictor of performance in higher education.[64]

Whatever success the Soviet Union may have in sorting out some of the practical problems and bringing more flexibility into the system —and this will require changing some habits of mind as well as administrative practices—it is likely that they will be left with the problem of growing pressure from the expansion of the general school system. There is no clear solution to this one that is not shatteringly expensive in cash and manpower alike, and a sufficiency of these is not on the horizon at the moment. Although it is doubtless small comfort to the Soviet authorities, this is a problem shared by other advanced countries of the modern world.

Notes

1. N. S. Egorov, 'Sovietskii universitet'. *Vestnik vysshei shkoly*, 3, 1968, pp. 3–7.
2. Raw figures from *Narodnoe khozyaistvo SSSR v 1968 godu: Statisticheskii yezhegodnik.* (Statistika, Moscow 1969.)
3. G. M. Mikhalev, 'Sovershenstvovat' podgotovku uchitel'skikh kadrov'. *Sovietskaya pedagogika*, 6, 1965, pp. 104–109.
4. 'Slovo pedagogicheskomu vuzu.' *Uchitel'skaya gazeta*, 9 February 1967.
5. Mikhalev, op. cit.
6. Ministerstvo vysshego i srednego spetsial'nogo obrazovaniya SSSR: *Spravochnik dlya postupayushchikh v srednie spetsial'nye uchebnye zavedeniya SSSR v 1966 godu* (Vysshaya shkola 1966).
7. M. A. Prokofiev, 'Segodnya i zavtra nashei shkoly' (*Pravda*, 12 December 1966).
8. *Narodnoe khozyaistvo S.S.S.R. 1968.*
9. N. Grant, 'Problems and developments in teacher education in the U.S.S.R.', *School and Society*, 25 November 1967, 95, 2297, pp. 451–55.
10. I. S. Dubinina, I. M. 'Slepenkov: Universitet—uchitel'—shkola'. *Vestnik vysshei shkoly*, 3, 1965, pp. 15–18.
11. Oral communications.
12. Oral communications.
13. *Narodnoe khozyaistvo 1968.*
14. Ibid.
15. E.g., 'Pedagogicheskoe uchilishche', *Uchitel'skaya gazeta*, 6 January 1966; 'Srednee pedagogicheskoe', *Uch. gaz.*, 2 February 1967.
16. Some of the Union Republics have their own Ministries of Higher Education, while in others a single Ministry of Education is responsible for the entire system. At this level too, of course, other ministries are involved.
17. Mikhalev, op. cit.
18. 'Kakoi dolzhna byt' pedagogicheskaya praktika', *Uch. gaz.*, 1 April 1965.
19. For an account of the 1958 changes, see Bereday, Brickman and Read (eds.), *The Changing Soviet School* (Boston 1960), N. Grant, *Soviet Education* (Penguin 1968).
20. M. A. Prokofiev, 'Vuzy—shkole'. *Vestnik vysshei shkoly*, 9, 1966, pp. 7–11.
21. Nicholas De Witt, *Education and Professional Employment in the U.S.S.R.* (Washington 1961).
22. Raw figures from *Narodnoe khozyastvo 1968.*
23. That this gives rise to a sudden increase in marriages among final-year students shortly before the examinations is widely stated, but difficult to verify.
24. Mikhalev, op. cit.
25. There were salary differentials in favour of urban teachers, but they were abolished in 1964.
26. Ya. Pilipovskii, 'Selskii uchitel'—problemy, suzhdeniya', *Uch. gaz.*, 25 May 1967.
    Prokofiev (*Pravda*, 12 December 1966) notes that in many rural areas the targets for numbers of pupils going on from the eighth to the ninth class had not been reached. *Narodnoe khozyaistvo* gives separate figures for secondary school enrolment in rural and urban areas, which tell the same story.
27. Ministerstvo vysshego i srednego spetsial'nogo obrazovaniya SSSR: *Spravochnik dlya postupayushchikh v vysshie uchebnye zavedeniya SSSR v 1966 g.* (Vysshaya shkola, Moscow 1966).
28. 'Novoe polozhenie o vuzakh.' *Vestnik vysshei shkoly*, 3, 1969, pp. 3—7.
29. Oral communication.
30. This may be as high as the normal salary of the *aspirant*.
31. *Nar. Khoz. 1968.*
32. E.g., G. A. Chigrinov, Sovershenstvovat' metodiku istoriko-partiinogo kursa.' *Vestnik vysshei shkoly* 10, 1969, pp. 70–74.

33. N. I. Mokhov, 'Sovetskii student i obshchestvennye nauki.' *Vestnik vysshei shkoly* 2, 1969, pp. 3–7.

34. G. P. Smirnova, 'Edinii perspektivnyi plan v deistvii.' *Vestnik vysshei shkoly* 2, 1969, pp. 64–67.

35. L. S. Fridburg, 'Trudy sotsiologov v prepodavanii nauchnogo kommunizma.' *Vestnik vysshei shkoly* 10, 1968, pp. 82–85.

36. V. N. Shostakovskii, V. P. Groshev: 'Aktivnyi pomoshchnik partii v stroitel'stve vysshei shkoly.' *Vestnik vysshei shkoly* 10, 1968, pp. 3–9.

37. E.g. A. M. Kalnberzina, 'Plan perspektivnyi, edinii, kompleksnyi.' *Vestnik vysshei shkoly* 7, 1969, pp. 60–66. P. S. Nikitin, 'Kafedra i vuzovskii komsomol.' Ibid., pp. 66–67. A. N. Belov, 'Komsomol i formirovanie kommunisticheskogo mirovozzreniya studentov'. Ibid., 10, 1968, pp. 10–11. Etc.

38. A. M. Tokarev, 'Kurs "Osnovy propagandicheskoi raboty".' *Vestnik vysshei shkoly* 7, 1969, pp. 67–70.

39. See almost any issue of *Vestnik vysshei shkoly* during 1968 and 1969; the main article usually had to do with preparations for the 'Lenin jubilee' either in the form of celebrations or signal efforts in honour of the occasion.

40. 'Novoe polozhenie o vuzakh.' *Vestnik vysshei shkoly* 3, 1969, pp. 3–7.

41. M. N. Rutkevich, *Vestnik vysshei shkoly* 7, 1965.

42. Ibid.

43. A. I. Bogomolov, 'Povyshat' kachestvo podgotovki zaochnikov i vechernikov.' *Vestnik vysshei shkoly* 8, 1969, pp. 3–8.

44. E.g. T. N. Fedotova, 'Studenti i lektsiya.' *Sovietskaya pedagogika* 6, 1969, pp. 97–107.

45. E.g. A. Z. Nazyrov, 'Nuzhny li gosudarstvennye ekzameny?' *Sovietskaya pedagogika* 5, 1969, pp. 100–104. G. N. Balanok, 'Vysshaya forma samostoyatel'noi raboty studenta.' Ibid., 12, 1968, pp. 72–83.

46. Rutkevich, op. cit.

47. 'Deistvovat' edinym frontom.' *Uch. gaz.*, 3 July 1965.

48. 'Slovo pedagogicheskomu vuzu' *Uch. gaz.*, 9 February 1967.

49. D. O. Lordkipanidze, 'Sozdat' pedagogicheskuyu atmosferu v universitetakh.' *Sov. ped.* 5, 1965, pp. 100–104.

50. Mikhalev, op. cit.

51. Ibid.

52. V TsK KPSS i Sovete Ministrov SSSR: 'O merakh uluchsheniya podgotovki spetsialistov i sovershenstvovanii rukovodstva vysshim i srednim spetsial'nym obrazovaniem v strane.' *Izvestiya*, 10 September 1966.

53. Bogomolov, op. cit.

54. Ibid.

55. A. V. Krupin, 'Gosudarstvennoe inspektirovanie vuzov.' *Vestnik vysshei shkoly* 11, 1969, pp. 3–7.

56. See note 52.

57. M. Anuchin, *Izvestiya*, 14 August 1966.

58. Ibid.

59. Novoe polozhenie o vuzakh.

60. See Notes 36 and 37.

61. Anuchin, op. cit.

62. V TsK KPSS i Sovete Ministrov SSSR: 'O merakh dal'neishego uluchsheniya raboty srednei obshcheobrazovatel'noi shkoly.' *Pravda*, 19 November 1966.

63. In some areas, the 1958 reforms had still not been fully implemented by the mid-1960s or even later.

64. Recent work of the National Foundation for Educational Research is as yet incomplete, but findings so far do much to cast doubt on the value of G.C.E. as a predictor of performance in degree examinations.

5. SPAIN

Salvador Giner

After a long period of forced stagnation, Spanish culture, education and science are now entering a phase of intense change. Under the present circumstances, however, this does not necessarily mean progress —or not yet. For one thing, the change taking place is discontinuous: while in some areas it is easy to detect improvements, in others deep rifts are developing and conflicts breaking out whose solution is certainly not in sight and seems dependent upon the occurrence of political change. These factors contribute to the difficulties experienced by researchers in obtaining a clear overall picture and, *a fortiori*, in giving a satisfactory analysis of the situation.

Such difficulties are also encountered in analysing a sphere of culture where change is particularly intense at present: in studying the present generation of students in higher education, one finds new sets of values and cultural attitudes, new patterns of recruitment, a renewed political awareness, a heightening of political activity and activism, an emergence of ideologies and, last but not least, a numerical growth of such proportions that it is already having serious consequences upon the occupational structure of the country as a whole. Even the most elementary outline and discussion of these changes must be undertaken from a political angle. Although public power and policies always play a decisive role in the realm of higher education in any modern society, for some—like Spain—the observer is forced to approach the entire theme from this standpoint.[1]

Economic and cultural trends which are essentially non-political have of course affected higher education over the last decades, and they help explain much of what is happening now. Yet the type of state which emerged in Spain in 1939 was such that the whole world of higher learning became integrated with it; clearly this happened to a greater extent, and in a very different sense, than in other European countries north of the Pyrenees.

For clarity's sake this paper will attempt to distinguish between three main political periods in the recent history of higher education in Spain. It will stress major features of each epoch—rather than minor fluctuations, localized exceptions and trivial events.

Towards the Fascist model (1939–54)

Discussions on 'how fascist' the Spanish state is—or rather, has been—are not infrequent, and arguments on this relatively unprofitable question have not yet flagged.[2] For the purposes of the present topic only one fact about Spanish Fascism need be stressed—namely, that the degree of influence of 'strictly' fascist institutions and behaviour patterns had a differential impact on various aspects of society in the years following the final defeat of the Republic. While some areas—such as the Church and banking, and social groups like the upper classes—remained immune, others were significantly affected by it: for example, primary education and state economic planning. Still others underwent a serious attempt at 'fascistization': this was the case with the trade unions, the youth organizations and the university student body. It must be stressed that in this latter category it was an attempt which, in the end, was to meet with failure, as other supportive sectors of society lacked the degree of either 'fascistization' or fascist control which they had reached in, say, Italy during the same period.

As far as the universities and other institutions of higher learning and education were concerned, the drive went far enough to mark out a distinct period of their history. As elsewhere in Europe, this was characterized by the common pattern of terror, paralysis of creativity and a very grave regression (rather than mere stagnation) in the cultural life of the country. Two factors made this possible: the first contributory element was the presence, dating from before the outbreak of the Civil War, of militant fascist groups within the University. The S.E.U. (*Sindicato Español Universitario*) was a fascist-syndicalist group created in 1933, soon after the foundation of its mother-organization, the Falange.[3] It appeared as the fascist alternative to the chief students' union, the F.U.E. (*Federación Universitaria Española*) which was staunchly republican, and soon began a policy of violence against it. As the Falangists themselves now recognize, 'at the zenith (of the pre-Civil War anti-Republican) struggle, the Falange lived almost exclusively upon the structure of its University cadres'.[4] This was so, amongst other reasons, because the limited number of Falange militants at that time, coupled with the national ambitions of the party, put the greatest pressure on its (relatively) numerous student members not to struggle in the restricted area of university politics alone. With their para-military training and organization, S.E.U. militants were able to join in the uprising in a most efficient manner. They soon began to man and, to a large extent, control the propaganda, radio and press apparatus of the right-wing forces. They never, however, forgot their university connection.[5] A very high mortality rate in combat, the aura of being, supposedly, the rising youthful force of the 'New State', their claim to be the intellectual élite of the régime, as well as certain external events, such as the spectacular expansion of the Axis from 1939 to 1941, apparently gave this Falangist group a unique claim and opportunity to 'conquer' the university—to use an expression dear to its members.[6]

The opportunity for creating a fascist university was also enhanced by the large-scale emigration of the republican intelligentsia, which deprived it of its most creative and valuable members. Furthermore, the new régime had launched a witch-hunt or purge—officially known under the euphemism of *depuración*—against those supposedly sinister free-thinkers, members of an international masonic conspiracy whose sole aim had allegedly been and still remained the destruction of 'eternal Spain'. The seriousness of this policy was demonstrated by the ensuing terror during the post-war years and by the provisions of such legal decrees as the notorious 'law for the Repression of Communism and Free-Masonry'. Under these circumstances it appeared that the Falange would easily have a free rein in the University, from which so many of its early members originated. Veterans crammed the reopened classrooms and received privileged treatment at the examinations. Student delegates of the S.E.U.—since 1940 the sole student political organization—appeared in the Falange uniform, as did other members of the party. Later, the 1943 University Law[7] established that even the Rector of each University must be a member of the Falange and that every teacher must swear allegiance to the régime. An atmosphere of triumphant fascism seemed to impregnate universities, and it appeared as if a thorough 'fascistization' of higher education was at hand.

Yet the new régime was the result of a mixture of co-operating but distinct right-wing forces. As in most of the other complex institutions of the post-Civil War, universities largely reflected the general power structure, without any need for further purges. Politically they were subject to two forms of control: the Falange controlled the student body, while Catholics of extreme traditionalist orientation predominated amongst the staff. This group shared out amongst themselves the academic spoils of a war whose devastating effects upon Spanish culture cannot be overemphasized: chairs were taken over by the incompetent in an unprecedented manner. It should be noted that the republican intelligentsia had managed to achieve, over approximately forty years preceding the outbreak of the war, a notable competence in science, philosophy and some of the social sciences. The memory of 'republican' achievements, as will be shown, has never ceased to play an active role in contemporary Spanish university life. With a few exceptions, Falangists were not in a position to compete for posts of responsibility on the staff: they had too short a history to possess a senior generation of militants who could be defined as scholars, scientists, or intellectuals to fill the staffing gap. University Falangists almost immediately realized the extreme danger that this represented for their future, especially as they sensed that their national party chiefs were already compromising with conservative forces of the winning side—the military, the landowners, the Church. In the National Council of the S.E.U.[8] in 1940 they still felt strong enough to publicly denounce 'anachronistic military dictatorship', in the words of the comrade who opened the congress,[9] and to threaten those who 'wanted to destroy and undermine their pending revolution'. At the same meeting, Joaquin Ruiz Gimenez—who was to become minister of education years later—defended several postulates, some of which, using his own terms, can be summarized as follows:

1. The Spanish University will be thoroughly committed to Catholicism and to Falangism. 'The purest dogmatic orthodoxy' and Falangist beliefs must be enforced.

2. Each university must completely control any 'cultural movement' that takes place within its orbit. Its authoritarian tutelage must extend from the humblest primary school to the highest cultural organizations in the territorial area allocated to it.

3. Chairs will be filled by the traditional system of *concours* (*oposición*) but the 'moral and political purity of professors and teachers will be strictly controlled by the Falange'.[10]

The years that followed, however, saw an erosion of some of these principles. The military dictatorship, of course, was not immune from the Falangist threat. It was for this reason that, in an early attempt at neutralization, some of the most vocal and militant S.E.U. members of 1939 and 1940 were conveniently 'bureaucratized' and given posts and privileges—in the process a number of them were even to become ministers in later years.[11] It is worth noting that this erosion of 'revolutionary' Falangism took place without liberalization. One of the most important agents of the process of decline was the militarization of the student body. This occurred in two different ways. Firstly, the creation of the *Milicia Universitaria* flattered the students by giving them the opportunity to carry out their military service in an 'élite corps', while it isolated them from the *classes dangereuses*.[12] Secondly, a campaign of anti-Soviet propaganda was aimed at recruiting the most active, militant students for the Division which was to leave for the Russian front, on the Nazi side. About two thousand students joined it,[13] and among them were many of the most revolutionary and idealist Falangists, already disillusioned with the 'pending Falangist revolution' in their country. As one Falangist writer has implied, by fighting on the Eastern Front, their revolutionary *élan* was conveniently spent,[14] especially as many never came back. Yet some of those who returned became the first protagonists—and victims—of an act of student violence against the régime, a bomb attack on one prominent general.[15] As a reprisal an S.E.U. member was executed, and acts of this type against the militaristic, non-Falangist power élite were never repeated.

Throughout this first period of student life, and especially after 1942, the S.E.U. leadership began to accept the régime with all its consequences. Consequently, they were prepared both to act as a 'campus police' and to organize whatever demonstrations of solidarity with the régime or of hostility to certain foreign powers the government deemed opportune. Nothing else seemed to remain of the brief moment of elation after victory, except perhaps for the Falangist control over some cultural activities—whose quality always left much to be desired. In 1945 the defeat of the Axis meant the complete domestication of the S.E.U.: subservient officers were nominated and, following the new government line, much emphasis began to be placed upon the religious element in life. 'Too much science'—the then Minister of Education, Ibáñez Martín, explained—'does not bring you near the Supreme Being.'[16] There were some reactions against these policies throughout the period although they originated solely from the S.E.U. rank and file. (Although the republican F.U.E. was clandestinely reorganized in Madrid in 1946, and lasted until 1950,[17] it was ineffective and succumbed to repression.) Thus in 1956, the year that marks the first watershed between the phases demarcated here, Falangist S.E.U. militants were still clamouring for 'agrarian reform', 'Falangist revolution', etc. By that time, though, politically minded non-Falangist students were already working under cover of the S.E.U., or taking part in its 'actions' and demonstrations in order to redirect them to other targets. The 1951 general strike in Barcelona had already been joined by such students, and the 1954 mass demonstrations in Madrid, officially staged against England and demanding the reversion of Gibraltar also turned—after violent charges of police—into a demonstration against the government. The purges that the government inflicted upon the S.E.U. further debilitated its cadres. Henceforth it only attracted some opportunists, and soon even these began to discard it as futile.

This period had seen the collapse of a Falangist University, the maintenance of a backward-looking structure of higher learning, and a university which had reached its lowest point in modern history: over-bureaucratized, corrupt, legalistic, unexpanding, rigid and, worst of all, dogmatic and poor. Furthermore, the government had set up in 1939 the *Consejo Superior de Investigaciones Científicas* (C.S.I.C.), or Higher Council for Scientific Research, a continuation of a body founded by the Republic which absorbed the small funds earmarked for research in the national research budget, leaving nothing to the universities. It may be of interest to mention that one of the *Consejo's* chief aims was to 're-establish the Christian and basic unity of the sciences, destroyed in the Seventeenth Century',[18] and that its first president (from 1939 to 1966) José María Albareda, was a rising personality of what then appeared as a little-known Catholic 'sect', the *Opus Dei*.

The struggle against the ancien régime (*1955–65*)

After 1951 Spanish universities began to admit students who, born during the brief Republican period, could hardly remember the war. Their parents had no doubt countless times given them the stern advice not 'to meddle in politics'—a pattern of socialization not unknown in pre-Civil War Spain, but now emphasized by a majority of families. These students had undergone schooling during the years of doctrinaire militancy and utter poverty, the forties and early fifties. It was only in 1952 that the *per capita* income of the average Spaniard slightly exceeded that of the last year of peace—1935—after remaining well below that mark from 1940 to 1950.[19] For this reason, they saw themselves, like their counterparts in the other Mediterranean societies, as a very fortunate stratum. More than ever the university system seemed unchangeable: the twelve state universities, with their rigid systems of faculties and chairs, their incredibly underpaid non-professorial staff, their networks of influences for passing exams or, indeed, obtaining a chair, seemed immutable. The higher technical schools also seemed invulnerable and impervious to change: *numerus clausus* made entry very difficult; but a degree from, say, the *Escuela de caminos*, opened the way to considerable social prominence. Indeed, after the decline in Falangist activism, the parasitical bureaucratization of the S.E.U., and the growth in Church influence from 1945 onwards, the University was viewed by the livelier and more aware students as a stale, *ancien régime* affair, under the veneer of a nineteenth-century Napoleonic reform and of the fascist rhetoric still used by the régime. (It is in this strictly allegorical sense that the concept of an *ancien régime* university is used here; it will also help to convey the feeling of disgust and shame that overcame the student political and cultural élites of that generation when they realized the increasing gap between their country and the new world emerging elsewhere in Europe at the time.)

The student population remained static through this period. There were 64,281 university students by 1957 (as against 33,623 registered during the first full academic year under republican auspices—1932–33), but then numbers remained stationary until 1963–64. On the other hand, students entering higher education in the early fifties followed the same vocational patterns as their predecessors: greater numbers went into Law and Medicine; girls and nuns flocked to Philosophy and Letters; Pure Science faculties were half deserted; Pharmacy was sought after by those whose parents already owned a pharmacy, thus aspiring to the secure life of the monopolistic shop-keeper: the examples could be multiplied. Basically, the majority of students came from the traditional strata that could afford to give their children an education, almost invariably sending them to the nearest university. In spite of some growth of *colegios mayores* (students' residences), family ties and dependence continued to be kept throughout the period—as they are still today, though to a slightly lesser extent.

Yet, these were the students who first 'politicized' Spanish universities after the 1939 débâcle; they challenged the S.E.U. authority, gained some freedom for themselves, publicly manifested their democratic and republican beliefs, and utterly rejected the 'eternal and imperial Spain' whose scions they were supposed to be. Their success was, in practical terms, far from complete: the régime was too strong and their own numbers too small. Above all, the predominant political attitudes in society were not in their favour. (This point often tends to be overlooked by left-wing critics of the régime, who overemphasize repression and police action: these were all too efficient but, in addition, the necessary consensus was always lacking at least in the middle and upper classes whence the students came.)

Towards 1955, members of this generation were entering their second or third year in the university. Their first years as students had coincided with a period which—in the circumstances—may be described as particularly favourable for a *prise de conscience* of their situation. Apart from the decisive generational fact mentioned above—their lack of 'vested interests' in, or direct experience of, the Civil War—a number of humane catholic (or lukewarm Falangist) intellectuals had managed to occupy posts of responsibility in the Ministry of Education and in the Universities. (This may have been allowed to happen by the Government in order to acquire greater international respectability. This policy, incidentally, was partly successful: in 1952 Spain was admitted by UNESCO as a member.) In 1951 Ruiz Giménez, an 'open'—not yet considered as left-wing—Catholic, was appointed Minister of Education. Simultaneously, the Nazi-sounding ministerial Department of Propaganda was taken out of the Ministry of Education and transferred to the apparently less virulent Ministry of Information and Tourism (*sic*). Antonio Tovar, a repentant Falangist (although not yet publicly so), a man of 'liberal' leanings, was nominated to the Rectorship of Salamanca, and Pedro Laín, a man of similar persuasion, Rector of Madrid University. The effects were soon felt. The University became the only relatively free arena of political discussion in the entire country. A slight—but qualitatively important—degree of liberalization was felt in the more sophisticated journals.[20] French Catholics, disciples of Maritain, began to meet regularly in San Sebastián with Spanish liberal Catholics. Even the theoretical organ of the régime, the *Revista de Estudios Políticos*, notorious in the past for its defence of the *caudillaje* (*Führerprinzip*) doctrine, began to open its pages to a less fascist political science and, soon, even to sociology.[21] Simultaneously, certain books and publications from abroad began to be occasionally available on request. Informal seminars were organized to study and discuss them and did not always meet on university premises. Some—such as the *Seminario Boscán*, held over a period of almost three years in Barcelona and inspired by the literary critic Josep María Castellet—can in retrospect be considered as very significant for the attitudes and orientation of the younger members of today's intellectual community.

The politicization of these student élites occurred very rapidly, as could be expected of a country whose polity presented the characteristics then prevalent in Spain. Thus, to give two examples, the commemoration of the death of the philosopher José Ortega, in 1955, in a joint public lecture organized by members of the Boscán literary seminar, led to its forcible dissolution; in November of the same year the preparation for a first National Conference of Young Writers in Madrid was stopped by the government. The students involved in events such as these—even when they were not arrested or directly bothered by the police—began to give up all hope of being able to go along with the 'policy of the outstretched hand' advocated by the 'liberal' Ministry. Frustration made them see that radicalization and political action were the only way out. By the winter of 1956 incidents against the S.E.U. broke out in Barcelona; later outbursts in Madrid became more serious as some bloodshed combined with Falangist over-reaction led to a government crisis. The 'hawks' claimed that the active student opposition to the régime was the consequence of the 'soft' Ministers' policies. As a consequence, Ruiz Giménez and Raimundo Fernández Cuesta (Minister of the régime's political organization, the *Movimiento Nacional*) were deposed. Finally, in May 1956, political trials against rebellious students began.[22]

All this, of course, further radicalized the students. By now, clandestine political parties and the first free organizations had appeared, such as the U.D.E. (*Unión Democrática de Estudiantes*) in Madrid, gathering Christians and Socialists; the *Nueva Izquierda Universitaria*, a forerunner of the left-wing F.L.P. (*Frente de Liberación Popular*) both in Madrid and Barcelona; M.S.C. (*Moviment Socialista de Catalunya*) in Catalonia; and the Communist Party. Needless to say, the latter was systematically accused of plotting and inspiring everything that was happening in the universities. For this reason, it paid a heavy toll in casualties, but it also soon began to lose members in periodical internal crises due, above all, to the extreme conservatism of its central leadership, combined with their disregard of internal democracy. In this connection it is significant that in 1956, just after the first outbreak of the crisis between the government and the students, when temperatures were running highest against the régime, the exiled C.P. Central Committee ordered all its members to subscribe to an improbable policy of 'national reconciliation' between the victors of 1939 and the vanquished—the most active of whom were too busy avoiding prison and torture to seek reconciliation with anybody in power. The reasons for this incongruous policy of appeasement lie beyond the scope of this paper and must be sought in the general policies of Soviet Communism within three years of Stalin's death, but its consequences for the fate of communism in Spanish universities or, indeed, amongst contemporary Spanish intellectuals, are most relevant.[23] Both students and intellectuals have been leaving the C.P. ever since, either in intermittent waves or by a constant trickle of individual desertions, because of the inconsistency—as they saw it—between their own revolutionary interpretation of Spanish social reality and the party's ultra-conservatist policy.[24] Easy parallels, of course, may be drawn with the situation in Italy and France: the fact that these two countries were not undergoing a similar dictatorship during the same years only underlines the well-known generality of the phenomenon.

It was against this general background that the first steps towards the institutionalization of a democratic and independent organization were taken by the students. Until then we encounter only unofficial demonstrations or small clandestine parties and more or less ephemeral illegal 'students' unions'. But in 1957, in defiance of the S.E.U., the Barcelona students openly managed to hold the First Free Students' Assembly (surrounded and locked in by the police). Of course, the recently reshuffled government responded swiftly by repression and academic sanctions; but in the end it had to give in in other matters. As a result of the 1956 and 1957 events the S.E.U. was reorganized (October 1958). For the first time it included representation, though only at its lowest levels, the *consejos de curso* and *cámaras sindicales*; such democratic representation as was granted soon began to be used as an increasingly more threatening instrument for the struggle against the authorities. The 1957 victory set a pattern to be replicated in the years immediately following until, between 1962 and 1965, the S.E.U., fully eroded, became extinct as far as the majority of students was concerned.

Until 1965, however, the government clung tenaciously to the S.E.U. as *the* (and its) only existing organization in higher education. Of course, after 1957—and in spite of the good will of Falangist squads—it could not rely on it as a satisfactorily repressive weapon; thus police in often clumsy disguise made their appearance in classrooms to the bemused surprise of their 'fellow students'. In order to achieve a measure of success with the students, several experiments were tried, which all failed in political terms. While the T.E.U. (*Teatro Español Universitario*) managed to create some fairly good theatre groups—who did their utmost to put on revolutionary plays—it is also true that the S.U.T. (*Servicio Universitario del Trabajo*)—an organization through which students got jobs as miners, fishermen, peasants and industrial workers during the long vacation—was a dangerous experiment, which made many students politically sensitive, whilst others used it to 'spread the word' amongst the workers. After a crisis and a reorganization, the S.U.T. experiment was hurriedly called off.[25] By 1960 and 1961, students' strikes aimed to prove that the S.E.U. was useless and impotent, unless it became thoroughly representative. This the government could not grant, for the whole political structure of the state apparatus was based on 'vertical' unions, with officers nominated from above. If one union were to break away from this pattern, the others would try to follow suit. Faced with such dilemmas the government hesitated and bid for time. Meanwhile, an atmosphere of freedom—albeit limited to internal matters—was growing within the student bodies in the different universities: they were perhaps more busily engaged in political debates, cultural activities and seeking links and co-ordinating their actions with the outside world—especially during the vast 1962 strike waves in mining and industry—than they were in their struggle with the authorities and the government. This intense 'internal' activity mainly consisted in the formation and development of political parties as well as clandestine students' unions, some of which—like the Barcelona-based *Inter*—achieved a remarkable degree of efficiency, seriousness and harmony among the various parties competing for their control.[26]

As the power of the clandestine unions rose, the idea of controlling the S.E.U. began to wane. Yet in 1962 and 1963 free unions in many universities still thought it expedient to occupy as many posts as possible in the ailing S.E.U. in order to complete its disintegration. By the autumn of 1964, in the course of an eventful 'Week of University Reform', originally planned as a series of cultural events in several universities, the crisis between the S.E.U. and the students reached deadlock, and the period under consideration came to a close: the students and their free unions completely ignored the existence of the S.E.U. This opened the way to the serious disturbances which took place early in 1965, after the Madrid students had held another Free Assembly of Students—the fourth in Spain since 1957.[27]

The huge and peaceful assembly of six thousand Madrid students on the University campus had found widespread and very active support amongst teachers and a number of professors. It was perhaps this unprecedented fact that prompted the police into rash and brutal action against the students and staff who marched through the campus in quiet and orderly manner to deliver a petition at the Chancellor's house. Police repression and academic sanctions included the expulsion or suspension of five professors.[28] Simultaneously, the Government was bent on reaching some agreement with the students: during the months preceding this latest clash frantic attempts had been made to negotiate with the students' freely elected representatives—who by now ignored S.E.U. officers as if they did not exist or belonged to the secret police. This contradictory policy triggered off further demonstrations, and a few more assemblies took place in the most provincial and isolated universities. Once thirteen out of Spain's fourteen university districts had officially and openly rejected the S.E.U., international recognition of the illegal unions was forthcoming. The French U.N.E.F., for instance, not content with recognizing them as the only existing students' organizations in Spain, sent its president to take the chair at a free assembly in Barcelona. By the end of February, in cloak-and-dagger conditions, delegates from all over Spain managed to meet in the same town, helped by the whole union apparatus, which had been mobilized to mislead the police as to their meeting place and whereabouts. The Government gave in—that is, conceded as much as its nature could allow: the Decree of 5 April 1965 interred the S.E.U. and created the Professional Students' Association, a vague name for a nebulous institution one of whose aims was to avoid conflict with the official 'vertical' union structure.

The students had already gained some victories in their struggle against the *ancien régime* University: moral reprobation of favouritism, academic incompetence and authoritarianism were widespread; the acceptance of representative, free unions was universal; strong demands for a democratization of student recruitment were constantly heard; a significant number of teachers—especially young ones who had been students and led the revolt in 1956 and 1957—were also unambiguous in opposing the government. The students—as the socialist professor Enrique Tierno said in a celebrated article—had 'discovered complexity': in the post-war, semi-fascist years everything was black or white; one was either a fervent defender of 'eternal Spain' or her deadly enemy, deserving only moral—if not physical—extermination.[29] Now the young generation of students accepted political complexity—pluralism as well as the religious, cultural and national diversity of their country. This, in a sense, expressed a wish—though by no means a nostalgia—for a return to Republican conditions. In this, as in many other ways, the Spanish student disturbances and movements were different (some would say 'behind') similar forms of generational conflict which were then beginning to develop in other universities. Thus the Berkeley campus atmosphere in and after 1964 was totally alien to the Spaniards who, between 1955 and 1965, had been struggling for associational and academic freedoms and cultural progress of a kind unrelated to the millenarian and violent student *gauchisme* which was then appearing elsewhere. In contrast to these emerging movements—typical of more affluent societies—Spanish students had been struggling for 'classical' liberal goals: free unions, a modern educational system, the development of science and research, and free circulation of ideas. Concomitantly, they had often integrated themselves with political parties with a long republican tradition, thus claiming a political legitimation for their actions which was linked with the kind of legitimation they desired for the general polity: this again contrasted with the isolated political units of young people which were already forming in other western countries—such as the University of California rebels or the Dutch provos—and which took their stand precisely against such liberal traditions and conceptions of legitimacy.

The following years were still marked by opposition to what has been called, in the present context, the *'ancien régime* university', i.e., obscurantism and professorial feudalism (*caciquismo de cátedra*). But these were not going to be the only, nor perhaps the chief characteristics of the new period.

Modernization without democracy (1965–71)

1. Quantitative Transformations and Attitudinal Change

1965 represented more than one divide. The government, which by that time had already adopted the style of technocratic and 'apolitical' efficiency characteristic of the latter stages of the régime, the so-called *desarrollista* ('development') ideology, had still failed to give a thought to a serious reform of higher education. However, secondary education statistics had been indicating for a long time that the intake of higher education was bound to rocket in the coming years. The following table clearly shows the speed of this growth:

Table 5.I—*Number of students registered in Spanish State Universities from the Academic Year 1957–58 to the Academic Year 1969*

1957–58	64,281
1958–59	62,985
1959–60	63,787
1960–61	62,105
1961–62	64,010
1962–63	69,377
1963–64	80,074
1964–65	85,148
1965–66	92,983
1966–67	105,370
1967–68	123,896
1968–69	139,266
1975–76	383,000 (estimated)

Source: *Anuario Estadístico de España, 1969*. Figures do not include students in Higher Schools of Technology. 1975 estimate. FOESSA'S *Informe 1970*, Madrid 1970, p. 963

This quantitative transformation can be explained by certain changes in the economy and in the mentality of the middle classes, not only in the size of the latter. (Yet it is precisely the increase in numbers of university graduates which is already helping to transform the middle classes themselves from a traditional set of strata with low mobility rates and 'secure' jobs to a more dynamic, individualistic, professionalized and technically minded new middle class.) The changes in the economy consist basically in the process of sustained expansion, which puts Spain's rate of industrial growth during the sixties immediately behind that of Japan, thus placing her second in the world in this respect. This expansion soon had its effects upon the purchasing power of the lower middle classes, who often now could afford to send their children to university. Thus the lower classes have continued to be excluded from higher education, and this to a greater extent than elsewhere. (By all accounts class-discrimination, or *clasismo*, is universally recognized in Spain as the worst of the present evils.)[30] But economic modernization, intense urbanization and increased intranational and international mobility of the population were also having effects upon the outlook of youth. There is evidence that the numbers of students who, in spite of the nature of the primary and secondary education, gave up Catholicism in this period is considerable. Secular and hedonistic values also made important inroads in the students' mentality. More significant perhaps, the students who now prefer a good university education to merely being rich has increased. As could be expected, regional differences remain strong, but the general trend is towards greater modernity of approach to every aspect of life, be it the attitude towards the other sex, religion, the merits of individual achievement or universalistic values.[31] By and large, then, the ideological victory of the régime in this field had been ephemeral: the trends of modernization of which the Republic had been one expression and which it intensely fostered during its short life have come to the fore again, further promoting the wave of economic expansion whose early effects had given them a new impetus.

The changes in mentality and the new possibilities of the social division of labour in contemporary Spain can best be illustrated by the following data:

Table 5.II

(A) *Number of students registered in several faculties*

	Faculty			
Academic Year	*Economics, Politics and Commerce*	*Law*	*Medicine*	*Science*
1957–58	4,082	17,847	16,592	10,397
1966–67	16,850	14,781	22,991	21,523

(B) *Number of students registered in Higher Schools of Technology* (*Architecture, Engineering, etc.*)

Academic Year	No. registered	No. of degrees obtained in that year
1959–60	17,439	709
1966–67	36,038	1,312

(C) *Number of students registered in Higher Schools of Fine Art*

Academic Year	No. registered	No. of degrees obtained in that year
1957–58	9,138	421
1966–67	3,901	481

Source: *Annuario Estadístico de España, 1969*

Given the growth in numbers over this period it is clear that one can hardly speak of modernization in some fields of study such as pure science, where the influx of students just keeps ahead of their overall growth in numbers. But other data more than warrant such assumption. One of the most important and—for a Mediterranean society such as Spain— one of the most revealing is the drastic reduction in absolute and relative numbers of Law students, to the advantage of Economics and Commerce. (Not surprisingly there is only one Faculty of Politics in the country.) Another datum of equal weight is the steady growth in the intake of women in the universities. During the first full academic year under the Republic only 6 per cent. of the students were women; by 1966–67 the women had risen to 30 per cent. of intake.

2. The Government's Response to Change and the Educational Policies of the Opus Dei

Until 1969—the year that marked the complete political triumph of the Opus Dei organization—the Spanish Government had not tried to tackle the problems of higher education except by piecemeal and erratic reforms. However, the assumptions of some sociologists of education that there appears to be a high positive correlation between levels of secondary and higher education and intense economic growth or considerable economic development[32] seemed to obtain in Spain before that date. In 1960—in spite of a decline in the *per capita* income from $362 in 1958 to $292, owing to financial austerity measures, the economy began to enter the phase of intense growth and development which has characterized it until the present time.[33] It was from the same year onwards that the percentage of the budget devoted to educational purposes began to rise, marking a definite change of attitude in the ruling élite towards these matters.

Table 5.III—*Percentages of Spanish Governmental Budget devoted to education compared, in some years, with* per capita *income*

Year	Percentage	Year	Percentage	Per Capita Income $
1925	6.04	1960	8.57	292
1930	5.36	1961	9.72	
1935	6.60	1962	9.65	382
1940	5.51	1963	8.92	
1945	4.79	1964	11.41	500
1950	7.86	1965	10.60	583
1955	8.22	1966	12.75	656
		1967	11.74	606
		1968	11.37	676
		1969	13.81	738
		1970	14.47	800

Source: for percentages—R. Tamames, *Estructura Económica de España*, Madrid, Guadiana, 1969, p. 721: for incomes—in 1969 U.S. $ corresponding to Spanish 1958 pesetas, *Informe social, 1968*, Asociación Católica de Dirigentes, Barcelona, 1969, p. 57. For 1969 and 1970—*España Hoy*, Ministry of Information, Madrid, April 1970, No. 2, p. 78 and *Extebank* Sept. 1970, p. 2 (1$ = 70 pts.).

Moreover, in 1969, the ministries of Education and Finance announced a joint plan of educational development, to be financed by special taxation and loans from the private sector. This plan was connected with a White Book on Education published earlier in the year by the new Minister of Education, José Luis Villar Palasí. (Professor Villar had been appointed to the Ministry after the deterioration of student and university relations during the year 1967–68, and remained in it after the November 1969 reshuffle which had marked the 'total' victory of his faction, the Opus Dei.) The White Book openly recognized some of the anachronisms of Spain's system of education, the rigidity of the university structure, its neglect of scientific specialization, and even its evident painfully inegalitarian flaws.[34] Critics soon expressed doubts as to whether the White Book's ambitious plans would ever be realized: on economic grounds alone the sums to be raised were fantastic for the Spanish economy, they said, implying also that they would be assigned to education only if greater political changes came about. Supposing that at least two-thirds of the educational expenses were to be financed by the State, they would represent, in the years to come, no less than 40 per cent. of the budget, on the optimistic assumption that the budget would represent at least 15 per cent. of the G.N.P.[35] The scope of such provisions can be appreciated if one considers that, in 1966, Spain was spending only 2.46 per cent. of its national income on education—the smallest percentage in Europe.[36] As if to confirm these strictures, the joint plan of the Ministries of Education and Finance—which appeared months later—did not meet such requirements. At the moment of writing it is at the earliest stages of implementation and all that can be said is that it certainly will allow for some much-needed additional expansion in buildings, educational materials, increase in teachers' salaries and student scholarships, and further development of second universities to alleviate great overcrowding in the universities of the two great metropolises. This statement is, of course, extremely vague; but Spanish Government plans being what they are,[37] it is impossible to be more explicit at this stage.

By and large, increased educational budgets, large fund-raising plans and their immediate effects in the improvement of higher education have accompanied the rise in power and influence of the Opus Dei more closely than the rise and fluctuations of the standard of living of the Spaniards. And, as already mentioned, real expansion has taken place since control over the government has been assumed by the Opus. By 1968 other ruling groups and personalities had realized that higher education reform was inevitable. Paradoxically, the first reaction to this, aggravated by the fear that the Paris May events of 1968 would be repeated in Spain, was to launch a new wave of repression in the first months of 1969, when a national state of emergency was called. (The earlier Law of Banditry and Terrorism had conveniently been disinterred the year before to deal with Basque separatism and workers' unrest.) It soon became clear, though, that the mere recrudescence of police-state tactics could not solve the problem. It was at this juncture that the Opus acquired a decisive majority in the Government. Amongst the factors that made this possible one at least is relevant in the present context: the Opus had been claiming for a long time that it alone held the key to the solution of Spain's problems in every field, and especially in higher education, the 'key', of course, being modernization without democracy. (Not even the most dogmatic materialist could have put it more clearly than Sr. López Rodó, a member of the Opus and Minister and Commissioner for the Economic Development Plan at the end of 1969: 'The government's number one objective is to reach a per capita income of $1,000; the rest, be it social or political, will in consequence be solved by itself, as a matter of course'.)[38]

It is not possible to give here an account of the internal characteristics of this interesting religious association,[39] nor to attempt a sociological explanation of why and how it arose in the framework of modern Spanish society. Suffice it to say that one of the decisive factors for its rise to power lies precisely in its attitudes to higher education. From its very beginnings, in pre-Republican Spain days, the Opus emphasized the importance of 'improving and Christianizing the world' through the occupation of 'posts of responsibility' in society by selected individuals. The obvious channel at the time seemed to be the university. As early as 1939 an Opus Dei man was chosen for the 'highest post of responsibility' in *Consejo*, the National Council for Scientific Research. Later on, studious members of the lay order obtained university chairs in spite of growing, though unpublicized, protests.[40] This was the Opus' chief activity in the area of education until 1947. After that date it began to spread in other directions, first in publishing by controlling the learned journal of the *Consejo* and founding a publishing house.[41] By 1949 the Opus had managed to establish the 'Studium Generale of Navarre' in Pamplona, a private institution of higher learning. It escaped no one that *studium generale* stood for University and, although private universities were not allowed by law in Spain, the Jesuits and the Augustines already had higher education centres in the country.[42] After some difficulties the Studium Generale became the fully-fledged University of Navarre in 1962.

In view of later developments, it is doubtful that—as the otherwise acute critic of contemporary Spanish issues, Professor Aranguren, claimed—the Opus was 'withdrawing from the conquest of the state university', as it had already been defeated there.[43] Far from being defeated, the Opus' policy has consisted in a double strategy: the control of the official educational levers *and* the establishment of a flourishing private university, assuming that this type of diversification would ensure future survival. Thus by the end of 1969 at least sixty full professors or *catedráticos* in the state universities could be identified as members or ex-members of the Opus. Also many of their chairs were amongst the most strategically important. The numbers of Opus lecturers was presumably much greater.[44] Meanwhile, the Opus' influence in state universities has grown uninterruptedly, often indirectly helped by political repression. Thus, when staff are expelled or suspended *en masse* (as in the Barcelona disturbances of 1966[45] or during the 1969 state of emergency) it is always the 'liberal' non-Opus intelligentsia that suffers. Their own chances of occupying 'posts of responsibility' are thus further curtailed, their degree of alienation from their own institutions greatly heightened.

The reasons for the academic and political success of the Opus Dei are to be sought in the combined influence of economic development and conservative dictatorship. The Opus' system of religious beliefs provides adequate legitimation, whilst its avowed 'apoliticism' and 'end-of-ideology' ideology make it very reliable to the military and the oligarchy in power; on the other hand, its achievement-oriented criteria of social promotion, its constant emphasis on 'modernity', efficiency and technical competence have given the régime just the kind of organization that could make it survive at least through the sixties and early seventies. Simultaneously, these possibilities increased its attractiveness for young university people, who saw in it an easy channel of upward mobility in a society where this phenomenon was in many ways restricted. Finally, upward mobility through the Opus did not operate independently of the patterns of patronage that still pervaded much of Spanish society and gave this organization deep cultural roots. Selective recruitment among the students, rather than mass attraction—imposed, amongst other things, by the secretive elements of the institution—precluded the formation of an Opus Dei student movement, or even of a free union controlled by it. Opus Dei students have tried to keep out of trouble, and have been on the defensive ever since an early clash with Falangists. As if to prove their 'independence' *vis-à-vis* the Opus Dei ruling élites, however, there have been in the past a few disturbances at the University of Navarre which rather belong to the folk-lore of the situation.

3. The rise of public criticism

Many pages of the White Book seem to echo time and again the traditional 'opposition' attacks upon the structure of Spanish education. In fact, the White Book appeared after a renewed wave of criticism, which was made possible in the sixties by a precarious, but insufficiently noticeable, period of 'liberalization' in some areas of public opinion. Professor Angel Latorre's thoughtfully critical *Universidad y Sociedad* (1964) was followed by other books and studies in the same vein (some of them incorporating belated recantations of Falangism).[46] The influential Christian left-wing review *Cuadernos para el diálogo* published special issues devoted to educational problems in 1966 and 1969,[47] where a considerable number of intellectuals of various persuasions expressed their critical views in no uncertain terms. Some writers even managed to express their unorthodox opinions in the dailies.[48] Later a series of pamphlets specializing in educational matters began to appear, and some symposia were published.[49] More revealing, perhaps, of the tenor of criticism is the fact that in all these publications economic and budgetary studies of higher education and scientific research as well as sociological enquiries into the social origin of the students loom as large as purely ideological attacks on the prevailing system.

Some of the arguments expressed in this wave of criticism are old, such as the perennial complaint about the lack of research funds, or the demands for more academic freedom and freedom of opinion. Others are also familiar, but cast in a new form, such as pleas for the democratization of the university. Statistics are produced which show the overwhelmingly inegalitarian traits of Spanish higher education, accompanied by undisguised attacks on recent policies which have aggravated class discrimination; for instance, the opening of the so-called Labour Universities. Grave deficiencies in the staff-students ratio are pointed out: one report in 1970 stated that 26,000 teachers were needed instead of the actual 8,000.[50]

There is, in addition, a new body of literature on the specific problems of university life, for instance the low pay—often much less than a pittance—received by assistant lecturers and lecturers, or the absurd system of *oposiciones*, and the corruption of the method whereby a chair is obtained. (Not surprisingly, criticism of this last aspect is still weak—while in theory it ought to be central. Perhaps this has something to do with the fact that many of the critics themselves are *catedráticos*.)[51] Another specific problem which now attracts attention is the staggering number of drop-outs in higher education (more than 50 per cent. in 1967): reports link this situation with the lack of scholarships and to the general weaknesses of primary and secondary education.[52] On the other hand, the government is directly blamed for the brain drain which, in some fields, has reached nearly *total* proportions.[53]

At least some members of the new governing élite—evidently made up of more competent and intelligent men than in the past—are now trying to answer and assimilate these strictures from the 'opposition'. Yet it remains doubtful to what extent they will be able to introduce some of the new unavoidable structural changes without endangering the permanence of the present political arrangements. The nature of recent moves and crises at governmental level shows that this problem is very central to the oligarchy. The project for a General Law of Education passed by the Cortes in 1970 tried to find precisely such an answer to the problem.

4. The diversification of the student world

The process of modernization of certain structural aspects of Spanish society was accelerated during the sixties. Likewise during that period, and very markedly after 1965, the students began to acquire new sets of attitudes. Throughout the history of the régime their political stand of course varied geographically as well as by party, faction or ideology; yet, when it came to the crunch, it was nearly always a question of 'them'—the authorities—and 'us'. This dichotomy simplified matters, and as long as the régime lasts will be a source of student unity. Yet, definitely, a diversification of strategies, and interests and a growth in complexity of the student movement has now set in, bringing the Spanish student life much closer to—though not making it identical with—student life elsewhere in the West.

To begin with, internal student solidarity has been broken in some areas by the professionalization of some graduates. Thus, hostility against private schools such as the Opus Dei University of Navarre or the Jesuit Faculty of Chemistry in Barcelona—whose graduates readily found jobs even without official titles—had already been strong. But it was the suppression of *numerus clausus* in the technological schools that triggered off professional strikes and protests—quickly labelled as 'reactionary' by other left-wing students. These protests by students who had managed to get admitted, often after great financial sacrifice by their families, into the *écoles d'élite* marked the beginning of a pattern —the strictly occupational protest—which is now almost as familiar in Spain as in several other industrialized countries. According to some left-wing critics of the situation, this 'professionalization' of protest is now stronger than the tendency 'that subordinates the problems of the University to the great political options'.[54] However, it would be wrong to infer—even if such an assumption were correct— that the future of student unrest will be increasingly restricted to the expression of occupational grievances. A politicization of occupationally based conflict amongst students is a typical phenomenon of certain modern societies; in some countries, students with an insecure professional future have related their distress to the issues of the wider society as they saw them. For the time being, though, it is clear that the first phase in the diversification of the student movement has consisted in its split into two trends, the 'political' or revolutionary one, and the 'professional interests' one, not always exempt from conservatism. In this new context, between 1965 and 1967, the 'professional associations' with which the government had tried to replace the S.E.U. fell under the attack of the perennially rebellious student body. Simultaneously, a new, well-organized, free union was formed, the S.D.E.U. (*Sindicato Democrático de Estudiantes Universitarios*) with the explicit intention of creating a stable organization: the time of the improvised free assemblies had gone, the students proclaimed.[55]

During 1968 and 1969 the S.D.E.U. grew in prestige, efficiency and size, under conditions that would have broken its predecessors: special campus plain-clothes police, shock police patrols on the university premises, repeated suspensions of courses, expulsions of students, and arrests and trials before a special court, the *Tribunal de Orden Público*. Two facts are worth mentioning in this period: the intensity of S.D.E.U. activity and student unrest in the provincial universities which had been quiet until then, such as Santiago; and the heightened degree of solidarity of the staff with the students. This solidarity itself began to acquire new forms, often linked to events which were by then taking place beyond the Pyrenees. Thus, many 'liberal' professors and teachers accepted open 'critical judgment' sessions (*juicios críticos*) from their students and engaged in professional self-criticism. It must be stressed that these developments—soon forbidden by the rector in Madrid— went on in an atmosphere of civility which contrasted with similar exercises elsewhere; but then the situation was also different in Spain. The proclamation of the state of emergency in January 1969 ended all this.

It did not, however, end the further process of political diversification of the student body, that is, the multiplication of its active minorities. The first new element, predictably enough, was the emergence of the *gauchiste* groups which soon and inevitably collided with the S.D.E.U.— destroying it as a national union—and with parties supporting traditional 'republican legitimacy'. The *gauchistes*—of either Maoist, Trotskyist, or anarchist extraction—began to pose problems not altogether dissimilar to those created in less dictatorial contexts. However, left-wing F.L.P. members or F.L.P. sympathizers continued to carry weight, in spite of the F.L.P.'s endemic crises, and so did, of course, the C.P. Yet the C.P. has remained under attack from the left to this day because of its above-mentioned conservatism, and as a result has suffered the same loss of prestige amongst students as in other European countries.[56] Simultaneously, the common cause with the workers—which had been an ideal since 1955, and had become a reality in 1962—finally materialized. Yet, be it because of fairly effective police action or because of serious workers' distrust of the students as children of the privileged, durable contact and common action have tended to be limited to small groups of intensely active students. This, once again, may look like a situation not unfamiliar in, say, London or Berlin; however, it can be asserted that because of both the dictatorship and the still 'backward' socio-economic structure of the country, the alliance between the students' and the workers' own clandestine organizations is anything but utopian in Spain as, for instance, the Madrid May Day demonstrations of 1968 clearly showed. Acts and declarations of mutual solidarity are still common enough.

The years to come will witness further effervescence if not outright rebellion in the universities. Generational change, political immobilism, an erratic pattern of economic growth, and very deep changes in the mentality of the younger people, all combine to create a situation of permanent active dissent. Finally, the introduction of a campus police, the hated *policía universitaria*, since 1968 and the constant threats of further toughness by the government is bringing about a state of permanent chaos, at least up until the winter of 1971.[57] And yet, all these factors put together would not warrant such a statement if the society in which they arose were as a whole hostile to the students' rebelliousness. The students of 1956 and 1957 were practically alone in an atmosphere of silent antagonism in the street, and vocal disapproval by their fearful middle-class parents. Those of the 1970s live in a country again full of social tensions, where intense 'repoliticization'[58] is now taking place at *all* levels of society. Ethnic minorities are again restless— if not openly rebellious, as in the Basque country; workers are more militant than ever; the Church openly defies the régime; members of the political establishment clamour for some form of political pluralism, and there are signs of restlessness even in the ever-subservient army.[59] It is this revival of the political awareness and activity of the many, compared with the narrower range of choices left to the ruling few, that will make the final collapse of the régime possible.

The government has tried at last to face some of these problems with the new Education Bill, which attempts to introduce a more enlightened programme. Yet it is clear that the basic principles for which a democratic and progressive university always stands, the preservation of cultural freedom and the advancement of science and learning amongst a broad collectivity, will not fully materialize until a new régime is inaugurated.

Notes

1. For a substantiation of this assertion, cf. S. Giner, 'Spain', in M. S. Archer and S. Giner, *Contemporary Europe: Class, Status and Power* (Weidenfeld & Nicolson, London 1971), pp. 125–161.
2. Cf. H. Thomas, 'Spain', in S. J. Woolf (ed.) *European Fascism* (Weidenfeld & Nicolson, London 1968), pp. 280–301; J. Solé-Tura, 'The Political "Instrumentality" of Fascism', ibid., pp. 42–50.
3. D. Jato, *La Rebelión de los Estudiantes* (Madrid, 1967), pp. 130–132.
4. M. Valdés, Introduction to D. Jato, op. cit., pp. 12–13.
5. Ibid., loc. cit.
6. D. Jato, op. cit., p. 422.
7. *Ley de Ordenación de la Universidad Española*, article 40.
8. Took place at the Escorial, from 4th to 8th January 1940.
9. Comrade José María Guitarte. D. Jato, op. cit., pp. 427–428.
10. D. Jato, op. cit., pp. 428–429.
11. I.e. Srs. Fernández Cuesta, Ruiz Giménez, Romeo Gorría.
12. The 'fascist' *Milicia universitaria* was disbanded after 1945; instead, students entered special army units for N.C.O. training.
13. A. Peña, 'Veinticino años de luchas estudiantiles', in *Horizonte Español* 1966 (Ruedo Ibérico, Paris 1966), Vol. II, pp. 169–212.
14. D. Jato, op. cit., pp. 448–449.
15. On 14th August, 1942. The intended victim was General Varela.
16. A. Peña, op. cit., p. 171.
17. Until 1952, in exile. In 1947 it had been severely damaged by repression and political trials.
18. Quoted by D. Artigues, *El Opus Dei en España* (Ruedo Ibérico, Paris 1968), Vol. I, p. 37.
19. R. Tamames, *Estructura economica de España* (Guadiana, Madrid 1969), 4th ed., p. 592.
20. Such as *Alcalá*, the Madrid S.E.U. review; or *Revista*, a magazine published in Barcelona by the ex-Falangist poet Dionisio Ridruejo.
21. For the theory of Hispanic *caudillaje* see the work of Professor Javier Conde and that of the other totalitarian disciples of Professor Carl Schmitt.
22. A. Fontán, *Los Católicos en la Universidad Española Actual* (Punta Europa, Madrid 1961), p. 114.
23. For a description of the 1956–57 situation see A. Peña, op. cit. (note 13), pp. 169–212.
24. Cf. F. Claudín, *Las Divergencias en el Partido* (privately published, no place given, 1964, *passim*).
25. The S.U.T. has survived to this day in a subdued form.
26. Others were the F.U.D.E. (*Federación Universitaria Democrática Española*) founded in 1961 and centred in Madrid. The C.U.D.E. (*Confederación . . .*) later embraced both organizations.
27. For a good account of these events see 'Chronicle' in *Minerva*, Vol. III, No. 3 (Spring 1965), pp. 420–428. Also E. Tierno, 'Students' opposition in Spain; in *Government and Opposition*, Vol. I, No. 4, 1966, pp. 467–486.
28. Professors Aranguren, Tierno, García Calvo, Aguilar Navarro, Montero Diaz. Professors Valverde and Tovar resigned.
29. Quoted by M. Jiménez de Parga, 'Nuestra Universidad y nuestra sociedad', in *Cuadernos para el diálogo*, 5th special issue, May 1967, p. 13.
30. For class percentages cf. J. Rubio *La enseñanza superior en España* (Gredos, Madrid 1969). The author notes that children of the poorest strata achieve 8 or 9 per cent. of the student body of the higher technical schools, certainly a 'European' average. In the universities percentages have been abysmally low—less than 2 per cent.—although important changes have been reported for 1968 and 1969. One critical author puts the percentage of students of working-class origin at 4.69 per cent.: R. Conte, 'Universidad' in J. M.

Spain

Areilza *et al.*, *España perspectiva 1969* (Guadiana, Madrid 1969), p. 128. For *clasismo* in general cf. O. Bohigas *Les escoles técniques superiors i l'estructura professional* (Nova Terra, Barcelona 1968).

31. Cf. J. L. Pinillos, 'Actitudes sociales primarias: su estructura y medida en una muestra universitaria española', in *Revista de la Universidad de Madrid* No. 7, 1953; J. F. Tezanos, M. A. Dominguez, 'Los universitarios y la religión, in *El Ciervo* No. 142, December 1965; J. L. Pinillos, *Actitudes sociales de los universitarios madrileños*, unpublished research, although cf. *Time* magazine, Vol. 67, No. 3, 16th January, 1956. Cf. also *Revista española de la opinión publica, passim*, since 1965, amongst other sources.

32. N. J. Smelser and S. M. Lipset, 'Social Structure, Mobility and Development', in N. J. Smelser and S. M. Lipset (eds.), *Social Structure and Mobility in Economic Development* (Routledge & Kegan Paul, London 1966), p. 32.

33. Such growth and development have been erratic and still present many dangerous features (cf. J. M. Muntaner, 'Los altibajos del desarrollo económico español', in *Destino* No. 1696, 4 April 1970, pp. 16–17), but this is quite another matter.

34. Ministerio de Educación y Ciencia, La Educación en España: *Bases para una política educativa* (Official publication, Madrid 1969), *passim*.

35. Article in *España Económica*, quoted by R. Tamames, op. cit. (note 19), p. 723. Yet a report from a commission in the Cortes claims that the expenses incurred by the Educational Reform Act now discussed by that body will be yearly only 15 per cent. of the state budgetary credits (see *Noticiero Universal*, 12 March 1970, p. 10).

36. Turkey excluded.

37. The incompetence and inexactitudes of government planners can be measured by the several criticisms which have appeared on the two development plans. Cf. Tamames, op. cit. (note 19), pp. 779–800 and A. López Muñoz and J. L. G. Delgado, *Crecimiento y Crisis del Capitalismo Español* (Edicusa, Madrid 1968), *passim*.

38. M. Niedergang, in *Le Monde*, 31 October 1969, p. 2.

39. Cf. D. Artigues, op. cit. (note 18), *passim*, for this purpose; also his 'Qu'est-ce que l'Opus Dei?' in *Esprit*, November 1967, No. 11, pp. 707–744, and especially J. Ynfante, *La prodigiosa aventura del Opus Dei* (Ruedo Ibérico, Paris 1970).

40. Probably the earliest open clash between Opus Dei students and others (in this case Falangists) occurred during the academic year 1949–50, at the Colegio Mayor César Carlos.

41. It first took over the Consejo's learned journal *Arbor*: its first publishing house, Rialp, was founded soon after.

42. Although their students had to sit final examinations in State Universities in order to be granted degrees.

43. D. Artigues, op. cit. (note 18), p. 155.

44. J. Ynfante op. cit. (note 39), pp. 60–62.

45. When the participants in a free assembly of students, teachers and intellectuals, held in the Franciscan Sarrià Monastery, were locked in by the police. Mass arrests followed.

46. A. Latorre, *Universidad y Sociedad* (Ariel, Barcelona 1964); P. Lain, *El Problema de la Universidad* (Edicusa, Madrid 1969); A. Tovar, *La Universidad en la Sociedad de Masas* (Ariel, Barcelona 1968); all *passim*.

47. *Cuadernos para el Diálogo*, June–July 1966, Nos. 33–34; May 1967, Special issue No. 5; October 1969, Special issue No. XVI.

48. Cf. S. Giner, 'La Ciencia y la Sociedad Española', in *Diario de Barcelona*, 7 February 1965, p. 13; 'Situación de la docencia universitaria de base', in *Diario de Barcelona*, 7 March 1965, p. 15; 'La Universidad y el diálogo', *Diario de Barcelona*, 4 April 1965, p. 14.

49. Cf. Editorial Nova Terra, Barcelona: *Dossier Universitario* series; and *La Universidad* (Ciencia Nueva, Madrid 1969), *passim*.

50. F.O.E.S.S.A. *Supplemento*, March 1970, p. 20.

51. Obviously this statement is not aimed at those competent and distinguished scholars or scientists who have obtained chairs during this period. Scandals during *oposiciones* have often accompanied nominations to chairs when it became clear that the appointment was rigged. This may be a hopeful sign that the system will be challenged in the future. On patronage in The Madrid Faculty of Medicine, see *Sábado Gráfico* 31.7.1971, p. 9.

52. J. A. Aguirre, *et al.*, *Así está la Enseñanza Primaria* (Gaur, San Sebastian 1969), *passim*; F.O.E.S.S.A. 'Informe sobre Educación Superior', cf. *Vanguardia*, 25 March 1970, p. 7.

53. Out of the 2,372 who graduated (M.A.) in pure physics over nineteen academic years, by 1969 only forty-two worked in their field in Spain; 1,730 worked abroad (75 per cent.);

700 had other jobs; and *twenty only* were in higher research. Cf. *Ibérica*, Vol. 17, No. 6, 15 June 1969.

54. I Fernández de Castro, *De las Cortes de Cádiz al Plan de Desarrollo* (Ruedo Ibérico, Paris 1968), p. 356. On the professional strikes of engineering students, cf. *A.B.C.*, Weekly Supplement, 18 January 1970, pp. 28–33; and constant reports in the Spanish press, Spring 1970. Cf. especially discontent in the new Autonomous University of Barcelona, Faculty of Medicine.

55. M. Tuñón de Lara, 'Le Problème universitaire espagnol', in *Esprit*, Mai 69, No. 381, p. 848.

56. G. Hermet, 'Les Espagnols devant leur régime', in *Revue française de science politique*, Vol. XX, No. 1, February 1970, p. 27.

57. R. Conte, op. cit., p. 116.

58. Ibid., p. 34.

59. Cf. proceedings of XI Plenary Assembly of the Spanish Episcopate, Madrid, December 1969, as reported in *Le Monde* over first fortnight of the month. It was the first time that the ultras of the hierarchy spoke against the government. For the military, cf. speech and subsequent dismissal of General Ariza, Director of the General Staff College (*Le Monde*, 12 May 1970), p. 4.

Both trends have been gathering momentum during the early months of 1971.

See attack on Opus Dei by Captain General of Granada (*La Vanguardia*, 19 January 1971), p. 7.

For Church, *The Times*, February, 5th.

For 1969 unrest and halting policies, R. Conte, op. cit., is an excellent detailed account.

6. FRANCE

Margaret Scotford Archer

The history of educational change and the development of the sociology of education have shown a remarkable degree of parallelism in France from the late eighteenth century onwards. Four major stages can be detected in which educational studies have consistently appraised and evaluated the institutional changes taking place. The continuity of the Napoleonic model in higher education, administratively centralized and concerned with the professional training of state servants in Faculties and Grandes Ecoles, was mirrored, until the Third Republic, by a series of historically oriented studies, written from a variety of politico-philosophical points of view. Secondly, the movement culminating in the 1877 reform of higher education, which initially hoped to reduce the rigid hierarchical organization of the Imperial University and to replace the narrow and insular faculties by real universities, teaching a wide range of subjects, stimulated the more analytical work of Durkheim and Lapie. However, the failure of such reformism, clear by 1896, when the title of university was simply conferred upon existing groups of faculties, destroyed hopes for the foundation of real universities in France and halted this tradition in the sociology of higher education.[1]

The first decades of the twentieth century represented a considerable lull in educational studies, but gradually the preoccupations of the 'école unique' movement, which sought to reform and democratize the relationships between primary and secondary schooling, began to be reflected in a growing body of research examining the social background to educational achievement. Thus the third stage, particularly as represented in the work of Pierre Naville and Alain Girard, was marked by an almost exclusive concern for the pre-university phase and a complementary neglect of higher education. Although the problems of the universities, particularly those relating to numerical expansion, were mushrooming throughout this period and were accentuated after World War II, they received little systematic attention from sociologists. It was only in the sixties, and in effect when higher education began to constitute an urgent political problem— after student involvement with the Algerian crisis and with the need for expanding technical expertise—that the fourth stage began to take shape. The early work of sociologists like Bourdieu, Passeron and Castel was still marked by an extension of the preceding type of research to higher education, but it began to break away from the narrow concerns of student social composition to present a thorough analysis of the functioning and values of universities themselves.[2]

However, it was the events of May 1968 which were to consolidate this stage, since they gave rise to an unprecedented output of research, analysis and documentation in the field of higher education. In many of these studies, recent developments in sociological theory were first brought to bear on questions of student origins, condition and destination, and the relationship of the university to the wider social structure. While the recent outbreaks of student unrest appear to have had the universal effect of stimulating the sociology of education, this impact, in both its quantitative and qualitative aspects, appears to be particularly marked in France. It is for this reason that the present discussion will concentrate upon the period beginning in 1968 and upon the body of theory developed in connection with the events of the last two years, since much of this appears to have a relevance wider than the national context. However, it is first necessary to briefly fill in the developments in higher education that constituted the background to the present crisis.

The retention of the open-door policy of university entry for all possessing the *Baccalauréat* led to a massive numerical increase of students, particularly in the period after World War II. By 1967 its intake had trebled over fifteen years to equal that of secondary education eleven years earlier (440,000). A combination of demographic growth and increased educational aspirations were creating a quantitative growth which existing institutions could not absorb and whose implications for quality were increasingly feared. Numerical increase did not, however, mean democratization—in 1964 only 6 per cent. came from manual or peasant families; children with parents in the liberal professions, top management or higher civil service had more than one chance in two of a university education, while the son of an industrial worker had less than two chances in a hundred.[3]

The *de facto* 'solution' to this problem has been a 40 per cent. failure rate on average at the end of the first year, which an ex-Minister of Education likened to 'organizing a shipwreck to find who could swim'. Despite student and staff dissatisfaction with this situation, the government has firmly rejected the notion of pre-entry selection, and sought to solve the problem by founding new universities and faculties, thus meeting demand by increasing supply. In the sixties, six new universities were opened in provincial towns and the University of Paris tried to cope with its overflow by founding new faculties in the suburbs at Orsay and Nanterre. Yet four years after its opening the latter had already exceeded its planned capacity.

It is in this context of unplanned and largely unregulated growth of higher education that the post-war development of student politics and syndicalism must be seen. The changes occurring over this period in the national students' union (U.N.E.F.)[4] are symptomatic of a general trend; beginning after the war to style itself as a trade union and declaring in its Charter of Grenoble that 'the student is a young intellectual worker', its subsequent development was one of increasing politicization, reaching its peak during the Algerian crisis. In the early sixties the growing political involvement of students frequently implied their affiliation to extremist groups, particularly of the left, operating outside the framework of the main political parties (including the Communist party), none of which had supported students over Algeria. The following table indicates the distribution of political preferences, and their bias to the left, in a sample from the national student body investigated in 1961–62.

Father's Occupation	Extreme Left per cent.	Centre per cent.	Extreme Right per cent.
Agricultural, industrial, clerical workers	71	26	3
Craftsmen, shopkeepers, medium-level managers	60	23	17
Top-level managers, higher civil servants, professionals	54	28	18

Source: P. Bourdieu and J.-C. Passeron, *Les Etudiants et leurs Etudes*, 1964. In Paris, however, there are not only more students from the high bourgeoisie (63 per cent. as against 49 per cent. in the provinces), but they are also more left-wing. Parisian student politics are thus not a simple function of class origins.

In the immediately post-Algeria period the development and differentiation of left-wing factions continued and their representation on the U.N.E.F. grew, but in the absence of specific political or syndicalist targets, their overall influence waned. A new phase began in 1966—the intensification of the Vietnam War provided a political rallying point and the Fouchet plan for higher education a stimulus to syndicalism. Vietnam was doubly important in leading the Communist Party again to purge from its student group (U.E.C.) the main critics of party policy, who then joined or created other factions, and secondly in providing an issue over which such groups could sink their differences.[5] It is thus not without significance that while the first strike taking place at Nanterre in November 1967 concerned the application of the Fouchet reforms, the invasion of the Administration building on 22 March 1968 was in protest over student arrests during a Vietnam demonstration.

The events taking place in France between May and June 1968 are frequently subdivided into three major phases; the period up to 14 May, generally termed the University phase, saw the development of the student movement from Nanterre to the Sorbonne and to other universities, culminating in large-scale fighting and the famous 'night of the barricades'; the period between the 15th and the 27th May, frequently called the economic phase, witnessed the outbreak of strikes among technical and professional employees as well as industrial workers, reaching the unprecedented total of eight million strikers, many of whom occupied their factories and work places; after this date followed the political phase of the crisis, in which the political parties and unions struggled to regain control of the situation and the defence of the Vth Republic appeared less than certain.[6] The May events stimulated the publication of a mass of descriptive accounts, interpretative commentaries, philosophical, educational and sociological analyses. Over two hundred books and major articles on the subject have already been published. Basically they are addressed to two problems, whose discussion will occupy the rest of this chapter. Firstly, what accounted for the outbreak of these events, and what form did they take? Secondly, how did the events in France reach an intensity, degree of violence and political importance rarely paralleled in the rest of Europe?

The interpretation most frequently advanced, particularly in official circles, to account for the May events depends heavily upon the chain-reaction analogy. The events are viewed as a series of episodes, tenuously linked by both accident and opportunism and amplified by a multiplicity of contributory factors; 'everything began to form a chain of events which were totally unnecessary and basically futile'.[7] In the standardized imagery employed, Nanterre constituted the 'detonator' or 'spark'; a 'trail of powder' led from it to the Sorbonne,[8] its 'resonance' triggered off strikes, particularly among young workers, and its 'amplification' by the mass media provided popular support and helped precipitate political crisis. There are, however, two distinct groups endorsing this interpretation and endowing it with very different implications—the first, made up of spokesmen for the major political parties, holds conspiracy responsible for the unfolding of the May events, the second merely points to various mechanisms leading to the greater intensification of conflict in France than elsewhere in Europe, without making any assumption of subversive activities.

The events of May represented a similar crisis for parties of the Left and Right alike, escaping their control, denouncing their concerns and condemning their mutual collaboration in 'consumer society'. If it were not until late April that the notion of toppling the Gaullist régime was voiced by the movement, the idea of replacing it with a government headed by Mitterand or Mendès-France, or particularly by the Communist Party, was never seriously considered. Since the most striking aspect of the movement was that it constituted 'more than a crisis for Gaullism and a crisis for the left',[9] the similarity between their interpretations is relatively unsurprising. To the government, while certain 'legitimate' education grievances led to dissatisfaction in the student body, its mobilization and militarization was blamed (in the words of the Minister of Education) on the 'action of small extremist groups, often anarchists, determined to use all possible means to throw the universities into disorder'.[10] Thus the Minister divided students into a large majority, wishing to modernize a basically nineteenth-century university, and a very small minority belonging to Anarchist, Trotskyite and Maoist 'groupuscules', with ulterior political motives. The demonstration of 6,000 students on 6 May, chanting 'nous sommes un groupuscule', did little to correct the official view. In fact, it was intensified from the extreme Right by publications from *Occident*, with its scares about money distributed from Peking to pro-Chinese groups (as a protest over the Vietnam talks), films from the West German S.D.S. on street-fighting techniques, and supplies of ammunition from East Germany.[11] Despite the proportions reached by the movement and the obvious unlikelihood that a crisis involving over ten million could be stage-managed by factions whose membership was numbered in dozens only two months earlier, the government stuck to its viewpoint. One of the first actions of de Gaulle upon declaring the election was to ban extremist organizations, including the J.C.R. and F.E.R. (Trotskyite), U.J.C. (M.-L.) (pro-Chinese) and the 22 March Movement (which started at Nanterre); one of his first actions upon winning it was to constitute a working party on the reform of Higher Education. For Gaullists the conspiracy theory had a double function—it freed them of responsibility for an artificially stimulated revolt, while simultaneously heightening fidelity to the régime in the face of subversion. Moreover it had similar functions for the Communist Party.

As early as 1963, as the P.C.F. was having difficulties with its dissident youth section, Waldeck Rochet criticized those 'bourgeois ideologists who flatter youth so as to prevent them seeking what is really new. Towards this end they fabricate an artificial conflict between the generations'.[12] After this date the party virtually lost control over its student group, the U.E.C., many of whose members left to join other factions. In May the groupuscules were held responsible for misleading the working class, for trying to 'artificially graft a revolution on this organism, which it was bound to reject as a foreign body it could not and did not wish to assimilate'.[13] Not only were the groupuscules denounced as detrimental to the interests of the students and the working class,[14] they were also claimed to be infiltrated and manipulated by the government.[15] 'Gaullism believed that it could inflict a durable defeat on the Communist Party in May by pushing it towards a confrontation and the use of force.'[16] Indeed the belated participation of the Communist C.G.T. in the strike after 13 May was explained by Séguy (its leader) as a blow against those *provocateurs* who had sought to engage the working class in revolution, and as a redirection of the conflict towards traditional union claims. Thus both Gaullists and the Party sought not only to dissociate themselves from the events, but also to minimize their importance. This, as Touraine argues, seems to spring from the inability of the Right to conceive of large-scale conflict in advanced industrial societies after the 'end of ideology' and of the Party to acknowledge that such conflict need not be directed against capitalistic property and could occur without Communist leadership. The response in both cases was identical—if the vast majority of students and workers had participated because of 'legitimate' grievances, then educational and wage reform would suffice to rob the groupuscules of their following.

Rejecting explanations based upon conspiracy, the second group, advocating a chain-reaction theory, substitutes a plurality of alternative mechanisms which amplified student protest into social conflict. Thus to Raymond Aron, while it seemed likely that less than 10 per cent. of students had revolutionary aims, it was the operation of 'the classical mechanism, provocation–repression, repression–riot, riot–repression, triggered off by governmental clumsiness or provoked by ringleaders (that) mobilized public opinion and teaching staff in favour of students'.[17] In a similar vein is Edgar Morin's statement that 'the "Leninist" daring of the 22 March movement was confronted on the other side of the barricade by "Kerenskyism" which facilitated its growth'.[18] Somewhat differently, Chombart de Lauwe advances the thesis that revolt was favoured by the convergence of several crises which became linked to that in the University. Protest originating in Higher Education 'suddenly let loose latent aspirations which had long been contained'.[19] Thus for example, the working class benefited from the occasion to define its fundamental claims more clearly.

Such interpretations have a strong tendency to minimize the importance of the origin of the May events—student unrest having been reduced to the role of detonator, attention immediately moves elsewhere. This is evidenced by Chombart de Lauwe's statement that 'if the revolt had not begun from Nanterre, it would have broken out elsewhere';[20] it is even clearer in Morin's analysis, 'If at the start the French revolt had no basic originality, its impact must be traced to phenomena of progressive amplification and intensification'.[21] Thus the early 'University' phase of the events gets only cursory attention from this standpoint, which after a brief acknowledgement of the archaic form and content of higher education, passes on to accentuate a variety of factors spreading and intensifying conflict on the national level. In other words such theories are really more concerned with explaining why events in France assumed proportions unmatched in the rest of Europe, than with the reason why such events broke out in the first place. This essentially comparative analysis is addressed to two basic problems. How did the movement spread from one faculty to engage the national student body; how did a national student movement escape isolation to result in economic and political crisis?

Five major factors are frequently cited to account for the national-expansionist rather than local-isolationist tendencies in French student activities. Firstly, the high degree of administrative, legislative and budgetary centralization of the educational system represents a structural 'orientation' towards the national and away from the local. The standardized application of educational legislation throughout the country, together with the low degree of freedom at the university or faculty level for its adaptation to prevailing demands, serve to prevent problems from being considered as local issues or from being dealt with autonomously. It was the introduction of the Fouchet reform which stimulated conflict in the Faculty of Nanterre; it was the impossibility of working out a solution or even of administering discipline *in situ* which transferred the crisis to the Sorbonne, when Nanterre students were ordered before the Disciplinary Committee of the University of Paris. Secondly, the very centralization of the system has been influential for the development of a parallel structure in student associations. The more explicitly these have defined themselves as agencies for collective bargaining the more they have stressed the importance of critique and action at national level.[22] Thirdly, the fact that political activities were officially forbidden within the universities had the unintended consequence of engaging committed students in national politics. This resulted in a stimulation of political groups for students outside the university and concerned with major issues rather than the development (as in England) of university political groups (whose concern with abstract theory has often precluded their active participation, even at constituency level). Furthermore, student involvement in the political groupuscules[23] reacted upon the strictly student associations such as the U.N.E.F.,[24] and led to greater politicization than that of comparable organizations elsewhere in Europe. 'If U.N.E.F. is compared with similar foreign associations, a great difference can be seen between them. In Italy there is a very apolitical union, in Germany there are very apolitical student associations and by contrast in France there is on the one hand a union which was comparatively politicized and on the other hand a number of political groups with equally strong commitments'.[25] Fourthly, the politicization of student groups was stimulated, as those purged from or disenchanted with the Party, particularly over Vietnam, increasingly attached themselves to the universities instead. From 1966 onwards the Party had been systematically and vigorously expelling the pro-Chinese element from its youth groups, and had been seeking to destroy the Trotskyite J.C.R., whose aim was to separate the C.G.T. from the P.C.F.[26] Thus after the Stalinist period there was a growing interpenetration of student groups and political factions, with their wider frame of revolutionary reference, and their desire for action outside the established parties and unions. Finally, the part played by student groups, and particularly the U.N.E.F., during the Algerian war helped to crystallize their role in national politics (as supporters of the Third World—hence the significance of Vietnam) and also produced an experienced leadership unparalleled in north and western Europe. Thus to Morin the May movement was, characteristically, 'far better organized and directed by its factions, by revolutionary leaders who form a political staff of an exceptionally high quality in terms of action and thought'.[27] Taken in conjunction, such factors help explain the speed and degree to which student protest developed at the national level in France, as opposed to other countries where local autonomy of action and organization acted as brakes.

However, from the chain-reaction standpoint, the extension of the movement outside the universities, until an unprecedented figure of ten million workers went on strike, requires evidence of mediatory factors transmitting the 'resonance' beyond higher education. Many have stressed the role of the mass media and specifically of radio and television (once they escaped Government control) in giving national significance to events concentrated in the Latin Quarter. Others have accentuated the popular support deriving from outrage at police brutality—'a large discrepancy existed between the repression applied and the reprehensible act, and it is from this gap that the events of May grew'.[28] Such factors may account for the passive support of popular opinion (on 8 May, Polls registered four-fifths of Parisians in favour of the students), but are inadequate to explain the strike action undertaken. More important are considered to be, firstly, the relative absence in France of student grants (available to less than 10 per cent.) as a factor reducing worker hostility to a privileged group, and secondly the degree of contact that certain groupuscules had previously established, particularly between young apprentices and students. The two Trotskyite groups, J.C.R. and C.L.E.R., as well as the pro-Chinese U.J.C. (M.-L.), had published student–worker papers, been active in the apprentice centres, where the C.G.T. was particularly weak, and generally established channels of communication with industry, which, without endorsing the conspiracy theory, can be said to have facilitated the spread of student ideas and policies. Finally the willingness of the C.F.D.T. (the second largest French union) to declare strikes, more in opposition to the C.G.T. than in direct support of the students, contributed to the political crisis. To many this degree of worker support was apparent rather than real; it merely reflected a bandwaggoning effect through which different elements sought different ends. 'The student revolt acted as a detonator for the strike of workers, but despite appearances the latter was the *inverse of the former*; while students sought to transcend the consumer society, the workers attempted to gain a greater share in it.'[29]

Frequently (and especially in its official version) the chain-reaction interpretation is linked to the pessimistic mass-society thesis. Thus to the 'Giscardian' Griotteray 'the abusive degree of centralization, the absence of intermediary bodies, facilitated this paralysis of nervous centres and this disintegration of civic forces capable of resistance'.[30] The antidote proposed was regionalism, to create secondary groups in a necessarily centralized technological society. This perhaps provides the theoretical context in which de Gaulle's unsuccessful 1969 referendum on regionalization can be understood. However, this thesis is far from being a Gaullist prerogative, and plays a significant part in Raymond Aron's interpretation of the events.[31]

As has already been argued, the chain-reaction analysis is essentially comparative; it correctly underlines those factors accounting for the greater scope of events in France. However, in concentrating upon causes of intensification or continuation this outlook tends to minimize, if not ignore, problems about its origin.

> The example of other countries in which student agitation, however active, remained circumscribed within the University, is invoked in order to demonstrate that a chain of small events gave rise to a great one. It would be better to ask what was new in the action taken at Nanterre and why the University is a place from which contestation can spread to the rest of society.[32]

In extreme cases, causes of origin are dismissed, being incorporated into the causes of continuation, as for example in the statement that 'the closure of Nanterre was basically of no consequence. But when the closure of Nanterre brought its students to camp in the courtyard of the Sorbonne . . . Paris was convulsed.'[33] Thus such an interpretation fails to answer the fundamental problem: *Why the students?*

Attempts to answer this question must, in any country, be centred upon the student condition itself—a condition which can be analysed at two different levels, on the one hand in the university, on the other in society. Of the two major analyses of students as a social group made by French sociologists in the sixties, that of Bourdieu and Passeron seeks to understand student attitudes and actions from their condition in the university, while that of Touraine, from their condition in the social stratification system. They can be compared to the extent that both concentrate upon and hold as central the relationship between the student condition and the student destination. In doing so, both provide national, not trans-national, interpretations of this condition, in the context of a specific social institution in a particular social structure at a given time.

To Bourdieu and Passeron the modern student condition is characterized by *anomie*, a discontinuity between the means and ends of study. This precludes the possibility of students having a rational relationship with either their present activities or future destinations. Rational student conduct—which would involve only those means which are adequate to attain certain unambiguous goals—is specified by reference to an Ideal Type, derived by a logical development of the concept 'student'. Firstly, since 'to study is not to produce, but to produce oneself as a potential producer', the student is therefore an intellectual apprentice and 'has not and cannot have any other task than working towards his own disappearance as a student'.[34] Secondly, the concept also implies that by studying a student prepares for a professional future. Therefore the most rational manner in which to be a student 'would consist in organizing all present actions by reference to the requirements of professional life'.[35] Actual student conduct is then analysed as a deviation from this type.

The oversimplification involved in this type is admitted, in view of the multiple and incommensurate functions with which education is endowed, but it is claimed that any educational system at a given time concentrates more on one end than on others. Thus 'the contemporary French system seems to serve traditional rather than rational ends and directly works at forming cultured men rather than professional men'.[36] Hence the whole of higher education is conducted as though *all* students were future members of the cultural intelligentsia. Yet this goal is not a rational project for the vast majority of students, for whom it is unattainable. This entails a collective bad faith, as many are brought to dissimulate the nature of their present work through pretending about the future to which it leads. Thus, far from University studies leading to an unambiguous and attainable end, the opposite occurs, as everything works together 'to mask the truth of their work, by separating their present from their future, the means from the ends they are supposed to serve'.[37] As the future is indeterminate, present studies can have no *raison d'être* for the majority of students—their actions must be irrational.

Thus the temporary state of being a student is made autonomous in the traditionalistic university, which provides two different but equally acceptable models of behaviour as substitutes for the rational apprenticeship role. The 'exam-hound' narrows his horizons, treating the examinations as an end in themselves, unrelated to what lies beyond them; the 'dilettante' looks to distant and indistinct horizons of intellectual adventure. Both are forms of an illusion in which the apprenticeship is considered an end in itself, which involves a negation of the true ends of apprenticeship—entry into a profession, even if this be an intellectual one. A by-product of the unreality characterizing the student condition is that few attempts are made to rationalize their activities or to acquire those techniques appropriate to the attainment of specific goals. In so far as the goal remains indefinite, the student who wishes to give sense to his activities must engage in self-mystification by confusing his studies with some aspect of intellectual adventurism. Indeed this mystification may be necessary, since attempts to make rational the means of study risks making them incompatible with the nature of the ends, which are more traditional than rational. In this they are aided and abetted by the teaching staff, who employ all kinds of charismatic ingenuity to prevent their reduction to a strictly instrumental role in the professional training of students. In preferring to remain as 'masters' communicating personal gifts of culture, they reinforce the irrationality of students—'Any rational relationship with the foreseeable future being broken, the present becomes a time of fantasy in which even the idea of useful techniques or the usefulness of techniques is excluded.'[38]

However, all students cannot and do not play the game of irrationality to the same degree, since the future does not have the same ambiguity and indeterminacy for all. The inclination to unreality is determined jointly by the situation in which the student finds himself, and by his social origins. Those enrolled on more vocationally oriented courses, particularly in the Grandes Ecoles, will be less prone to it, as will be students from less privileged backgrounds, for whom the pursuit of a career is more vital, and women, for whom the future is (culturally) less ambiguous. It is thus when the future can be forgotten without risk and where the situation itself provides the lowest future-orientation that dilettantism is greatest.

These characteristics are found in their most concentrated form in Paris. It is no accident that Paris students, condemned to spatial co-existence, passive learning and individual competition, together with the easiest access to culture and politics, have the greatest tendency to substitute for rational criticism conceptual and verbal terrorism (for example in non-directed education), thus projecting the need for integration onto the ideal level of integration for integration's sake.[39] However, these tendencies towards dilettantism, intellectual adventurism and millenarian philosophies will be most pronounced among the privileged students in the Letters Faculties. Certain disciplines in particular, such as Sociology, not only attract students who are vocationally uncertain, but at the same time favour vocational uncertainty,[40] thus cumulating the conditions predisposing to such tendencies.

If the myth of auto-education, an aristocratic utopia specific to small élitarian groups, wishing themselves to determine the ends of their own activities, has met with such a success lately, it is perhaps because this ideology filled the deepest and least avowed aspirations of Parisian and bourgeois Arts students, by instituting a permanent fête: in the fête a group may assert its integration by appearing to intensify symbolic exchanges; it can maximize the gratifications afforded by integration by giving itself a show of group solidarity without this game having any other end than the reinforcement of integration.[41]

The unreality of the student condition also leads to the (unrealistic) search for meaning and community in the political factions.[42] Such conformity to anti-conformity is a method of surmounting *anomie*. Hence the student condition, particularly in certain disciplines, leads to mystification, which par excellence 'consists in magically negating oneself as a student, by denying the Professor as Professor, through the fiction of participation in creating culture; in other words by believing that one has finished with being a student when in fact one has only refused to be a student without imposing on oneself the patience and the work necessary to cease being one'.[43]

Alain Touraine, on the other hand, attempts to explain contemporary student attitudes and actions by examining the student condition in the new class structure of an advanced industrial society. The changing mode of production in such societies, now more dependent upon planning than capital accumulation, collective rather than private investment, and manipulation of needs and information rather than direct exploitation,[44] gives rise to a new dominant class—the Techno-Bureaucrats;[45] 'If the principle governing membership of the old dominant classes was property, the new dominant class would define itself primarily by reference to knowledge, that is by a certain level of education'.[46] The high prestige and generalist instruction given in the different Grandes Ecoles, outside the university framework, frequently by civil servants rather than professors and leading to a final *concours*, not an examination,[47] constitutes the means of entry to the new ruling class. In this, Touraine brings together two recent preoccupations of French political commentators—the recognition that the scientific revolution has a growing impact on the class structure (clear in the recent work of Garaudy[48]) and the fear that the growing influence of the Grandes Ecoles combats any attempts to democratize education (seen in the coining of the term *Enarchie*[49]). In this context 'the May movement is one of the first class conflicts which have broken out in advanced capitalist societies'.[50] In it the Techno-Bureaucracy was opposed not by the working class, but by professionals, communications workers, journalists, research officers in the public and private sectors, and including apprentice professionals—students: a class which occupies subordinate positions under the technocratic mode of production, and is deprived of decision-making power. To Touraine this must not be taken 'for a new stage of the proletarian movement, but for a new form of class conflict, as different from the old as are the *Commissariat au Plan* and I.B.M. from the ironmasters and family mill owners'.[51]

Control over education becomes a central aspect of social conflict, since for the first time it becomes a productive force in advanced economiés and ceases to be solely concerned with cultural transmission.[52] It is because of this changed role of education (a change which is as yet far from complete) and its growing importance as a source of man-power trained in the skills of social engineering and mass-manipulation, that student protest itself becomes a central aspect of class conflict.

> In May as never before, it was not the working class which entered into social combat but a set of seemingly diverse elements, students, lecturers, research workers, technicians and those engaged in cultural production, who occupy the same position in technological society as did skilled workers in the early phases of industrialization.[53]

In the past it was a minority of skilled workers rather than the whole proletariat who defined conflict with the entrepreneurial class. Con-temporary students perform the same role—they are not a class but they engage in class conflict.[54] Thus student action is rational, since it springs from concern over future occupational roles and over the increasing integration of the student condition with technocratic production. Those supporting the students have similar relations to production: the old working class cannot unite with them since it sees students as future members of the ruling class, but the new technicians and experts do, realizing that the vast majority of students will only execute policy, not determine it.[55]

Far from acting as 'outcasts' in Marcuse's terms, students engaging in conflict in May were neither marginal men nor an intellectual *avant-garde*, but those directly concerned with their professional situa-tion.[56] However, Touraine, in pursuing his parallel between workers and students in the two industrial revolutions, distinguishes within the student body between those playing innovatory and supportive roles.

> In fact it is in the modernising sectors of the French University—and the recent progress made by economics courses is undeniable—that student action has most chance of developing and imposing itself in the future. It is in the most archaic sectors, the faculties of letters, that the revolt originated, but in the same way that the movement of workers never derived lasting strength from declining sectors of industry, which were also capable of revolt or of defensive measures but not of innovating future action, so too the future of student action lies in the modern faculties and will not develop unless the university modernizes.[57]

Thus in complete opposition to the analysis of Bourdieu and Passeron, Touraine concludes that it is precisely where the educational and economic systems are most highly integrated that student protest will be greatest.

Because of the high level of disagreement between the two inter-pretations and their future predictions, their major points have been schematized in the following table for ease of reference.

Touraine	Bourdieu/Passeron
1. Analyses student attitudes/actions from student condition in the contemporary class structure.	Analyses student attitudes/actions from student condition in the contemporary university.
2. Major task of university education is increasingly related to production—its goals are rejected by many.	Major task of university education is culture transmission—studies have no clearly defined goals.
3. Student action due to integration between the means/ends of studies.	Student action due to lack of integration between means/ends of studies.
4. Results in rational action among students—occupational rejection/political action.	Results in irrational action among students—dilettantism/millenarianism.
5. Greatest among students following the most vocational disciplines—Paris Economics students leading/Letters students supportive action.	Greatest among students following the least vocational disciplines—Paris, privileged Letters students.
6. Unity characterizes the student movement.	Diversity characterizes the student movement.

As advanced, the two analyses are striking in their degree of mutual exclusiveness, and when applied to the May events it becomes evident that the strengths of each interpretation neatly pinpoint the weaknesses of the other. Thus Touraine's thesis can account for the condemnation of future jobs and the wish to change the goals of higher education by students, their engagement in rational political action, and the support given in this undertaking by those studying vocational disciplines, research workers and certain categories of professional workers. While such aspects are more difficult to account for on the Bourdieu-Passeron thesis, this in turn is better able to explain other facets of student protest—anxiety over job shortage, the desire for educational reform, the predominance of Letters students and the irrational subjectivist side of the movement symbolized by the occupation of the Odéon theatre.

Touraine admits that 'the most obvious weakness of our interpretation is that the French university is still far from being a technocratic institution . . . the experience undergone by students, above all in the faculties of letters corresponds more closely to the crisis of the traditional university than to the rigors of the new'.[58] This, it is claimed, accounts for the movement beginning as a cultural outbreak, closer in nature to populism than to the class struggle, since the technocratic adversaries were not well defined; but when it spread beyond the universities this gave way to social conflict. However, to Touraine it is false to separate these two elements since 'students speak of culture as workers speak of work'.[59] Thus he seeks to defend the essential unity of the student movement by claiming that the cultural-educational reformism and the political activism merely parallel the reformist and revolutionary themes of workers under early capitalism. It is only through constant appeal to this worker-student analogy for the two industrial revolutions that the claim for unity is sustained (as has been seen for the Letters students likened to workers in declining industries). Thus having detected the central tendency of the movement, other trends towards different goals are merely said to have 'overflowed' from it.[60]

The non-political, irrational, 'anti-society' element of the movement, which negated problems, turned in upon itself and instituted the fête at the Sorbonne and Odéon, does not deny the unity of the movement, since 'the anti-society is not the movement itself, but the response to the impossibility of action'.[61] Similarly the strictly modernizing impulse of certain professionals during May, (of architects, doctors and barristers) is seen as a rejection of the same source of power as that governing the universities. Again the strike of O.R.T.F. workers for objectivity, *not* politicization of the media, is construed as an attack on technocracy, which depends upon manipulation of information.[62] Yet leaving aside the analogy, which itself is non-explanatory, the diversity of these various trends is equally compatible with an acceptance of their different causation and objectives. The class framework has been imposed too rigidly, even if the assumptions made about the change in nature of the stratification system could be accepted uncritically.

In stating that those students from less privileged backgrounds together with those studying vocationally oriented disciplines will be more concerned with improving the methods of higher education, while the privileged Letters students will be more inclined to irrational action, Bourdieu and Passeron clearly anticipate diversity in the student movement. However, when dealing with the latter category there tends to be an implicit assumption of a common reaction to the situation of *anomie*. This irrationality may take different forms—dilettantism, idealism, millenarianism or membership of political factions—but in all cases this is basically viewed as retreatism. There are a few hints (the mention of auto-education for example), and perhaps there would have been more had the book been written only slightly later, that retreat into irrationality can also lead to a politically oriented reaction to *anomie*. Already the authors had noted membership of the political groupuscules as one of the responses to the *anomic* condition of some students. Where they did not go far enough was in showing how anti-rationalist philosophies interacted with political ideologies and in turn reacted back upon the university.

Thus both theories appear to provide partial rather than exhaustive accounts of student attitudes and action; the origin of the May events seems to lie in the interaction between groups committed to rational political action (in Touraine's sense), and ultimately seeking social conflict, and others seeking integration in the university community through idealism (in the sense of Bourdieu and Passeron). The typical product of this amalgam was a 'transgressive' association aiming at educational and political change—the 22 March movement of Nanterre. Pinner's description of the composition of such organizations is in exact accordance with the foregoing analysis—'Thus, for the typical members of transgressive organizations, role images are either unavailable because of the uncertainty of their professional future or unacceptable because of their opposition to the traditional system of social roles'.[63] It is precisely this dual aspect of the movement which accounts for the frequency with which commentators have stressed its originality and their inability to identify historical precedents or analogies. This duality also does much to explain the frequency with which two types of interpretation are advanced (and the contradiction between them): on the one hand, the range of theories which, like Touraine's, assimilate student action to some category of political conflict undertaken in defence of group interests; on the other, the school of thought extending beyond Bourdieu and Passeron and viewing the movement as even more idealist in nature, 'an "existential demand", a "spiritual revolution", a kind of ethical transformation, the expression of an irresistible need for individual liberation'.[64] The former has difficulty in accounting for the strong utopian aspect of the movement, the latter for its obvious elements of political engagement;[65] both try to overcome these difficulties by assuming their trend to be dominant and the other subsidiary and usually in decline. Instead it is suggested that the movement was fundamentally dualistic, and only acquired the magnitude it did within the student body because of it. In other words, the anti-rationalism of students without academic goals fused with the political ideologies held by students rejecting academic goals, to produce the philosophy of this transgressive association. There are two kinds of supportive evidence which can be cited in relation to this hypothesis; the first involves an analysis of the component groupings active during the events, the second an examination of the major ideas advanced by students during this period.

The initial development of the 22 March movement at Nanterre occurred outside the political groupuscules and grew from opposition to the application of the Fouchet reforms. At the start 'it did not possess any kind of political knowledge enabling it to state in advance its aims or the events which were to follow'.[66] In its early negation of any difference between teachers and taught, the 22 March group was much closer to the ideas of the International Situationists (influential at Nanterre) and their stated antirationalist aim of 'leaving no specialist master of a single specialism'.[67] While the movement remained at Nanterre, its activities bore more resemblance to the Situationist desire to 'make art'[68] than to political goals advocated by the various groupuscules. It was when unrest developed within the Sorbonne that fusion with the groupuscules occurred, in terms of common action and the emergence of shared values, as the vocabulary of revolution permeated the student body, partly engineered by the factions, but aided by the isomorphism of industrial and educational conflict—occupations of workplace, strikes, erection of barricades etc. Gradually, with their knowledge of tactics, organization and facilities, the political groups came to 'regularize and channel the movement without ever controlling it'.[69] However, towards the latter stages of the Sorbonne occupation, as political leaders felt they headed a movement capable of overthrowing the bourgeois state, fissures reappeared, the idealists seeking integration separating out from the neo-Marxists seeking revolution. 'It is here that the rich and triumphant unity of the student commune began to crumble and the political commune to detach itself and sometimes to oppose itself to the university commune.'[70] For the political leaders educational questions were not only secondary, but risked being a source of diversion. The intensification of this trend has been aptly characterized by Touraine in stating 'It was Cohn-Bendit who turned the rebellion into a movement, Geismar who lived it as an uprising and Sauvegeot who sought to transform it into a political force'.[71] But while the factions wished to turn the universities into 'red bases', the idealists retreated, and the student commune turned in upon itself, instituting the fête in the Sorbonne and Odéon. Far from being a simple response to blocked action, this was the real expression of the idealists' irrational search for integration—the sit-in for its own sake. Touraine is right in saying that it was because the movement was not fully politicized that in June it could not retreat and reformulate its strategy, but this—it is maintained—was because a major part of the student body was never politically motivated, and the moment of fusion passed precisely when political and educational concerns ceased to be complementary.

There is sufficient evidence from student pamphlets, speeches and slogans[72] to indicate the extent to which the preoccupations of idealist (and privileged) students fused for a time with the political concerns of the factions, both being modified in the process to constitute a shared ideology. The idealists could accept the revolutionary vocabulary, firstly because for them too the technological society was a barrier to their aspirations and, secondly, because to them the appeal to the working class involved not solidarity with contemporary workers, but obeisance before the historical myth.[73] The resultant ideology was not merely, as some have defined it, a mixture of the red and black flags, but the joint product of bourgeois idealism and neo-Marxism.[74] Of the examples available perhaps the most significant is the use of the key concept *global contestation*, or *perpetual contestation*. During May, the verb 'to contest' was constantly used intransitively; its object was left vague, or at best was defined as 'the system as a whole'.[75] Unlike its use by the unions, in the sense of to contest or to claim *something*, for many students it designated an end in itself. Similarly the movement did not delineate a specific group to replace the technocratic élite, but instead used the slogan 'l'imagination au pouvoir'—'which announces a transformation of mental processes . . . a clear expression of the will to rediscover, underneath the layers of acquired culture, profound sources of creativity and thus real culture'.[76] The concern is more with changing man, releasing his repressed creative potential, than with changing governing élites. The method employed, 'creative violence', is less a means to a political end than a method for attaining self-fulfilment. Again the worship of spontaneity, the highest accolade the movement conferred on itself, was less of a political tactic than a metaphysical tenet. As Morin remarked in this context, 'clearly one is very far from Lenin but very close to Bergson'.[77] Finally, student opposition to the 'consumer society', stressing not the relation with production but the manipulation of consumption, involves a distinction being made between 'real' and 'artificial' needs in terms of a cultural value-system. Thus the revolution sought by the movement concerned change 'not only in the system of property ownership or of the régime . . . but also of civilization'.[78] It was this dualistic nature of the movement which accounted for the popularity of Marcuse's thought, his works providing links between Freud and Marx, subjectivism and activism, unreason and revolution, and thus uniting the two groups.

However, the movement was also dualistic in the sense that at no time did all members of either group accept this lowest-common-denominator of bourgeois idealism and neo-Marxism, and their differences became progressively accentuated. On the one hand the idealists moved deeper into subjectivism; on the other, the factions became more concerned with political strategy. Some students were well aware of the false equation implicit in the common platform of the worker and student struggles: 'for the former it is above all a struggle for life which is involved; for the latter a struggle to obtain a superior form of life; for the former this requires a social revolution, for the latter an existential revolution'.[79] It was an acceptance of this difference that underlay such slogans as 'Marxism is the opium of the People'; 'To make a Revolution is to break our internal chains'.[80] Thus total irrationality and complete subjectivism characterize this sector of the movement, which

> denounces a priori every absolute
> of normality
> of objectivity
> of rationality
> The unfounded principle, of the existence of absolutes, masks the only characteristics of man which are essential.[81]

Thus the 'moral' imperative of this group was to 'take our desires for reality'.[82]

However, as events progressed its political leaders became increasingly concerned with defining the actual role of students in stimulating confrontation with the ruling class. It is for this sector that the work of Althusser was even more relevant than that of Marcuse. The book subsequently produced by the Cohn-Bendits is devoted not only to negating the Party view that the sole role of students is to reinforce the pickets, but also to affirming that 'the proletariat alone is capable of changing society'.[83] By pursuing a real conflict (in a variety of ways) between oppressed groups and the ruling class, this section of the movement retained the Marxist tenet that alienation can only be solved through struggle, and not independently of it.

La Loi d'orientation de l'enseignement supérieur[84]

After the Gaullist success at the polls, it was clear that the government held to its chain-reaction theory, and since the only major reform it was willing to make concerned higher education, that its policy consisted only in dismantling the detonator. The working party established in August under the new Minister of Education, Edgar Faure, followed this through to its logical conclusion of a massive overhaul of the universities. Agreement was reached on the defects of the system which the events had highlighted—the inertia of its structure, rigidity of its centralization, its obsolete teaching methods and the detrimental role played by the traditional examination procedure. The three major principles of the new law were those of autonomy, participation and orientation. The first sought to destroy the structure of the Napoleonic university by abolishing faculties in favour of real universities of a pluridisciplinary character, with greater administrative, financial and pedagogical autonomy, leading to increased flexibility, adaptability and experimentation. The second referred to a greater representation of students on all the new and more localized administrative councils of the universities. The third rejected pressures in favour of selection for entry to university,[85] preferring to maintain the open-door policy and to concentrate upon a greater degree of student orientation during the first year of studies. Thus through 'autonomy' the government sought to prevent the escalation of conflict, through 'participation' to provide for its arbitration at the local level, and through 'orientation' to remove its source. Vocational orientation was thus the key principle, and accordingly the First Article of the law states that universities 'must provide students with means for their orientation and for the best choice of future professional activities, and to this end provide them not only with the necessary knowledge but also with preliminary training'.

It is clear, however, that the two interpretations presented, that of Bourdieu and Passeron, and of Touraine, lead to very different expectations about the success of the Law. On the one hand, through increasing vocationalism and thus defining the end of instruction more clearly, students should now enjoy a more rational relationship with their studies, and discontent due to the anomic student condition should decline proportionally.[86] On the other, to Touraine the reform is analogous to policies of industrial recuperation in centring upon specific changes while ignoring the wider political issues.[87] Far from destroying the movement, the increased vocationalism of higher education will intensify protest over the uses to which knowledge is put.[88] If—as it has been argued—these two theories refer to distinct groups of students (the bourgeois idealists and the neo-Marxists) who interacted during May, the Law may be expected to have a differential impact upon them, reducing the potential for unrest among the former, while stimulating it among the latter. The distance should have widened between these two groups and their chance for co-ordinated action have been reduced. While to a certain extent this has taken place, delays in the implementation of the law and modifications in its terms preclude anything other than a tentative and interim assessment of its impact.

The Law foresaw a lengthy and complex process of institutional change—the formation of units of teaching and research which would later be regrouped into new pluridisciplinary universities and provide student and staff members for their councils, a process far from complete at the beginning of 1970.[89] As Maurice Duverger commented at the time, the future of French universities was more dependent upon the application of the Law than on its passing.[90] Unsurprisingly the faculties, and particularly those of Paris, often resisted their breakdown into pluridisciplinary units, seeking instead to constitute exclusively medical, legal or scientific universities.[91] After the deadlock reached in Paris and Bordeaux, the Minister of Education, Olivier Guichard, was forced to deliver his ultimatum, that in default of acceptable proposals for the reorganization of these universities reaching him before 10 March 1970, the subdivision would be established by the Ministry, and under any circumstances the transformation of a traditional faculty into a university would be excluded.[92] Nevertheless such resistance had already delayed the application of the Law one year longer than planned—this phase having been scheduled for completion by 15 March 1969.

Yet the rationalizing impulse of the Law, whose insistence upon pluridisciplinarity represented an attempt to group subjects logically according to their interconnected career outlets rather than to traditional criteria, largely petered out in application. It may be doubted whether the foundation of such small and highly differentiated units of teaching and research (143 for Paris alone), while democratic in intention, was the optimum method for arriving at an integrated and coherent restructuring of the universities. In the provinces the plans advanced for subdivision and regrouping 'were often swayed by memories of May 1968 or by political affinities rather than scientific ones'; the lawyers, for example uniting with the medics in 'calm' and conformist universities, while letters and sciences became linked in radical and 'progressive' universities.[93] Despite ministerial assurances the same was feared for Paris, and the project submitted by the rectors and subsequently approved in March did little to allay it. The thirteen universities in all and seven in Paris-Centre, (replacing the five faculties), showed the extent to which the government had followed the preferences of the strong faculty pressure-groups.

Of the seven universities in Paris-Centre,[94] only I, V and VII show greater pluridisciplinarity than the faculties they replace. The remaining four tend to be more restricted than previously since some contain only part of the older faculty. Thus Paris II is essentially devoted to law but, unlike the faculty, will not prepare for degrees in economics. In the same way Paris VI resisted the application of the Law even more successfully, to become an exclusively scientific university. Similarly Paris III, already nicknamed 'Berlitz University', shows a considerable degree of specialization, and Paris IV a return to the traditional Humanities. Vagueness in the terms of the Law, with its references to linking disciplines 'as far as possible', while allowing new universities to concentrate upon a 'dominant vocation', certainly facilitated this wide range of interpretations of pluridisciplinarity. There is doubtless much justification for stressing the rationalizing intent of the Law and accentuating it in preference to mixture for mixture's sake, as in the case of the Modern Language (Paris III) and Science (Paris VI) universities. What is more serious, as Duverger has argued, is the resurgence of traditionalism, which conforms to neither the letter nor the spirit of the Law—'It is most regrettable that the Sorbonne pre-dating Lavisse and Durkheim has been reconstituted, based on Latin, Greek and so-called "belles" lettres, together with the Law School of the Nineteenth century'.[95] Thus overall the process of restructuring has tended, despite appearances, to favour the maintenance of the *status quo* and to capitulate to its partisans.

Obviously these changes and the delay they have occasioned have considerable implications for the other two principles of the Law— orientation and participation. In the case of the former it is yet unclear how far restructuration will increase the students' scope and flexibility of choice within a given university. It seems likely that there will be a considerable variability between establishments in this respect, at least in the short run. However, in March, Guichard promised students a free choice of university, unconstrained by geographical region[96] and if (as now seems very unlikely) this became practice it would have an important effect on increasing choice and facilitating self-selection. As far as participation is concerned, the implementation of management councils with student representation has been prevented by the delay. It is now impossible in Paris to hold the necessary elections during the present academic year, which postpones the application of this aspect of the Law until 1971–72. Meanwhile the prospects of most students are as uncertain as ever.

In the present situation, two factors appear of major importance:

that the extreme slowness of structural change may ultimately lead to the disenchantment of student reformists, and that the immediacy with which 'political information' was allowed into the faculties may strengthen the political factions. The main danger arises from the slow application of the Law and the incoherent position in which it places students in the interim. Most in the 1969–70 session entered a faculty that they knew would disappear in several months without having much idea of what would replace it. In the short term the student condition in the university had been made even more illogical; if this were prolonged, many might again make common cause with the groupuscules. For the moment, it appears that the analysis presented is correct, the 'bourgeois idealists', basically satisfied with the intentions of the reform bill, have awaited its implementation fairly quietly. So far the majority of students and their (strengthened) reformist associations have not only refused to participate, but have fiercely condemned the current activities of activists as hostile to student interests.[97]

The student political factions, prominent during the May events and banned in June 1968, have since renamed and reformulated themselves.[98] Perhaps the strongest influence the events have had upon them has been to re-enthuse their populist idealism and to strengthen optimism as to a proletarian alliance. In addition, they have served to increase insistence upon the need of violence to advance the cause of the people.[99] Paradoxically, however, this resurgence of faith in the revolutionary character of the working class has been accompanied by few signs of their ability to provide carrier organizations, perhaps among other things because of stricter Union surveillance during the last three years. This has resulted in the common pattern of violence being turned inward against the university itself. The outbreaks taking place during the early months of 1970 provide classic examples of the use of the university as a surrogate for society. For, unlike the pattern two years earlier, there was very little attempt to find an educational nail upon which to hang political confrontation.

Yet in the most important respect the clashes of February and March 1970 differed from those of 1968—they attracted the condemnation, not the support, of the vast majority of students. The insults and attacks upon the Dean of Letters at Nanterre[100] only served to isolate the extremists further and contributed towards the 'marginalization' of violence. This was particularly clear with the outbreak of armed battles at the Assas centre of the Law Faculty in Paris during March (which led to its closure for forty-eight hours), for this was a confrontation restricted to right- and left-wing extremists.[101] The apparent isolation of the extreme Left has stimulated the counter-offensive of the neo-fascist Right, which has never been numerically strong in the last few years. Only at one point during March did there appear any chance of a new revolutionary coalescence among the student body, and this once more centred upon Nanterre. The authorization of police intervention to restore order on the campus, which involved revoking the former legal exemption of the university from common policing, immediately led to battles with left-wing extremists. The major slogan used by the latter—'Les flics hors du campus'—united the various groupuscules and rallied some considerable support. Moderate and right-wing groups condemned the Dean for actions which could lead to the closure of the faculty, and it was undoubtedly memories of what had resulted from this in 1968 which led the authorities to avoid escalation by a speedy withdrawal of the police.

Thus the end of the academic year 1969–70 in no way represented a conclusive point in the attempt to restructure and hence restabilize higher education in France. On the contrary, it is the forthcoming years, the first of the full application of the *loi d'orientation*, which will test the viability of the new formula. Yet the variety of modifications in its provisions and the multiplicity of interpretations given to its terms appear to have gradually robbed it of any chance to provide a coherent university structure. Its strong rationalizing impulse of providing students with a logical relationship to their courses and hence increasing the calculability of the student condition has been progressively diluted by the entrenchment of traditionalism.

Notes

1. Cf. A. Prost, *L'enseignement en France 1800–1967* (A. Colin, Paris 1967).
2. Cf. Margaret Scotford Archer, 'Egalitarianism and the sociology of education in England and France', *Archives Européennes de Sociologie*, 1970.
3. P. Bourdieu and J.-C. Passeron, *Les Héritiers* (Ed. de Minuit, Paris 1964), Ch. 1.
4. U.N.E.F. (Union national des étudiants de France). The main student union, which at the beginning of the sixties contained two main groups, the 'minos', who despite the label were in the majority and belonged to various parts of the extreme Left, and the 'majos', made up either of apolitical students or those with right-wing affinities. In 1968 Jacques Sauvageot estimated its membership at 70,000, but claimed that its followers included more than half the student body. In H. Bourges, *La Révolte étudiante: les animateurs parlent* (Seuil, Paris 1968), p. 76.
5. The pro-Vietnam committees (C.V.N.), initially established by the P.S.U. party, recruited their members not only from among students and the general public but also from lycée pupils. The left-wing political factions all tended to be actively involved on such committees, including the two Trotsky groups, J.C.R. and F.E.R., and the pro-Chinese U.J.C.(M.-L.).
6. The most complete account of the May events is L. Rioux and R. Backmann, *L'explosion de mai* (Robert Laffont, Paris 1968).
7. Jacques Perret, *Inquiète Sorbonne* (Hachette, Paris 1968), p. 16.
8. Epistémon, *Ces idées qui ont ébranlé la France* (Fayard, Paris 1968), p. 21.
9. Edgar Morin, et al., *Mai 1968: la Brèche* (Fayard, Paris 1968), p. 66.
10. Alain Peyrefitte, quoted by L. Rioux and R. Backmann, *L'explosion de mai* (Robert Laffont, Paris 1968), p. 59.
11. For a summary of the extreme right view see F. Duprat, *Les Journées de Mai '68* (Nouvelles Editions Latines, Paris 1968). The general conclusion is that 'Rien ne fut assurément moins spontané, rien ne fut moins improvisé que les émeutes du Quartier Latin' (p. 182).
12. Waldeck Rochet, *La place des étudiants dans la bataille pour le progrès, la paix, la liberté, le socialisme* (C.P.F., Paris 1963), p. 11.
13. F. Fonvieille-Alquier, *Les Illusionnaires* (Laffont, Paris 1968), p. 163.

14. Article by Georges Marchais, *L'Humanité*, 3.5.68.
15. Fonvieille-Alquier, op. cit. (note 13), p. 75.
16. L. Salini, *Mai des Prolétaires* (Ed. Sociales, Paris 1968), p. 69.
17. R. Aron, 'Le sort de l'Université dépend des étudiants', *Figaro*, 15.6.68.
18. E. Morin, *Mai 1968: la Brèche*, op. cit. (note 9), pp. 68–69.
19. P. H. Chombart de Lauwe, *Pour l'Université* (Payot, Paris 1968), p. 22.
20. Chombart de Lauwe, op. cit., p. 21.
21. E. Morin, op. cit. (note 9), p. 68.
22. 'The fact that the movement developed in the provinces was due to the action of the U.N.E.F.'—Jacques Sauvageot, quoted in H. Bourges, *La Révolte Étudiante: les animateurs parlent*, op. cit., note 4.
23. A list of these organizations can be found in L. Rioux and R. Backmann, *L'explosion de mai*, op. cit. (note 10), pp. 9–12: P. Seale and M. McConville, *French Revolution 1968* (Heinemann, London 1968), also provides an adequate summary of their development (in English). Those of major importance include U.E.C. (Union des étudiants communistes), the official Communist student group, which gradually freed itself from Party control in the mid-sixties; U.J.C. (M.-L.) (Union des Jeunesses communistes (marxistes-léninistes), pro-Chinese; J.C.R. (Jeunesse communiste révolutionnaire), the Trotskyite youth group of the French section of the Fourth Internationale, i.e. followers of Pierre Franck; F.E.R. (Fédération des étudiants révolutionnaires), previously named C.L.E.R., a Trotskyite student group of those breaking away from the Fourth Internationale, following Pierre Lambert; J.A.C. (Jeunesse anarchiste communiste), anarchist youth group; I.S. (Internationale situationniste).
24. Both the U.E.C. and J.C.R. were active in the U.N.E.F., the former after 1962, the latter after 1966, when it provided a Vice-president and two committee members for U.N.E.F. An index of the growing influence of the groupuscules is the support given by U.N.E.F. in 1966 to the I.S. publication, 'De la misère en milieu étudiant', which specifically condemns the U.N.E.F.'s attempts at university reform. This document is reprinted in R. Viénet, *Enragés et Situationnistes dans le mouvement des occupations* (Gallimard, Paris 1968).
25. Jacques Sauvageot, quoted by P. Labro, *Ce n'est qu'un début* (Ed. Premières, Paris 1968), p. 213.
26. For a brief summary of the relationship between the Communist Party and its youth section see P. Seale and M. McConville, *French Revolution 1968* (Heinemann, London 1968), Ch. 2.
27. E. Morin, op. cit. (note 9), p. 70.
28. Christian Charrière, *Le Printemps des Enragés* (Fayard, Paris 1968), p. 37.
29. André Philip, *Mai 1968 et la foi démocratique* (Aubier-Montaigne, Paris 1968), p. 15.
30. Alain Griotteray (Preface V. Giscard d'Estaing) *Des barricades ou des réformes* (Fayard, Paris 1968), p. 52.
31. R. Aron, *The Elusive Revolution* (Pall Mall, London 1969).
32. C. Lefort, 'Le désordre nouveau', in E. Morin, *Mai 1968: La Brèche*, op. cit. (note 9), p. 44.
33. J. Perret, *Inquiète Sorbonne*, op. cit. (note 7), p. 26.
34. P. Bourdieu and J.-C. Passeron, *Les Héritiers* (Minuit, Paris 1964), pp. 83–84.
35. Ibid., p. 86.
36. Ibid., p. 88.
37. Ibid., p. 87.
38. Ibid., p. 96.
39. Ibid., p. 57 f. 'It is understandable that, culminating all privileges the bourgeois students of Paris are better able than all others to manifest a lack of deference and detachment from their studies . . . and are more ready than others for political audacities which give them the satisfaction of sharing in an intellectual concensus.' (p. 72.)
40. Ibid., p. 18, 'the Faculty of Letters, and within this disciplines like sociology, psychology or languages, can serve as a *refuge* for students from the most educated classes who, being socially "obliged" to undertake higher education, orientate themselves, since they have no clear vocation, to those studies which at least appear to supply them with a social label.' For the students from less privileged backgrounds entry to such disciplines may be a forced choice.
41. Ibid., p. 75.
42. While the University of Paris has the greatest proportion of students of bourgeois origins,

it also has the highest percentage of students with left-wing affiliations. In the provinces left-wing opinions, on the contrary, are closely related to less privileged origins. It is also in Paris that more students with left-wing opinions refuse to support one of the left-wing parties (p. 69).

43. Ibid., p. 85.
44. A. Touraine, 'Anciennes et Nouvelles Classes sociales', in G. Balandier (ed.), *Perspectives de la Sociologie contemporaine*, (P.U.F., Paris 1968), p. 130.
45. Ibid., pp. 133–135.
46. Ibid., p. 135.
47. For a discussion of the historical development and present relevance of the Grandes Ecoles see M. Vaughan, 'The Grandes Ecoles of France', in R. Wilkinson (ed.), *Governing Elites* (Macmillan, New York 1968).
48. R. Garaudy. The author was expelled from the French Communist party in 1970 partly for claiming that Russia was incapable of adapting to the scientific revolution, and for calling for a new definition of the working class to include the new technological and scientific workers.
49. J. Mandrin *Enarchie; Les mandarins de la société bourgeoise* (La Table Ronde de Combat, Paris 1967). The term refers to the latest Grande Ecole to be founded, the Ecole Nationale d'Administration for the training of higher civil servants (non-technical), and the power and prestige enjoyed by its recruits.
50. A. Touraine, *Le Mouvement de Mai ou le Communisme Utopique* (Seuil, Paris 1968), p. 62.
51. Ibid., p. 191.
52. Ibid., p. 283.
53. Ibid., loc. cit.
54. Ibid., p. 26.
55. Ibid., p. 177.
56. Ibid., p. 277.
57. Ibid., p. 244.
58. Ibid., p. 27.
59. Ibid., p. 266.
60. 'The social crisis provoked two seemingly opposed responses, which both overflowed the developing social movement; on the one hand the tendency towards modernisation, perfectly acceptable to the technocrats, on the other the proclamation of the anti-society, engrossed in its own verbiage', ibid., p. 218.
61. Ibid., loc. cit.
62. Ibid., p. 210.
63. F. A. Pinner, 'Tradition and Transgression: Western European Students in the Post-War World', *Daedalus*, Winter 1968, p. 144.
64. M. Niel, *Le mouvement étudiant ou la révolution en marche* (Le Courrier du Livre, Paris 1968), p. 13.
65. The difficulties stemming from the first position have already been illustrated from the work of Touraine. Those deriving from the second can be shown from the following statement of Niel's where student political engagement is viewed as a transitory stage of the movement: 'It is a real psycho-social transformation which is developing. . . . Many students and young workers remain dependent upon marxist-leninist ideology. They only envisage revolution according to trotskyist, maoist or castrist schemas. Not having understood the necessity of changing their "mental structures", they cannot reject absolutes, nor Bibles, idols or flags.' Op. cit., p. 115.
66. Epistémon, *Ces idées qui ont ébranlé la France*, op. cit. (note 8), p. 19.
67. E. Brau, *Le Situationnisme ou la Nouvelle Internationale* (Collection Révolte No. 3, Paris 1968), p. 11.
68. Ibid., p. 15. See also R. Viénet, *Enragés et Situationnistes dans le mouvement des occupations*, op. cit.
69. E. Morin, *Mai 1968: la Brèche*, op. cit. (note 9), p. 19.
70. Ibid., p. 24.
71. A. Touraine, *Le Mouvement de Mai*, op. cit. (note 50), p. 47.
72. Cf. U.N.E.F. and S.N.E.-Sup., *Le Livre noir des Journées de Mai* (Seuil, Paris 1968).
73. C. Prévost, *Les Etudiants et le gauchisme* (Ed. Sociales, Paris 1969), p. 55. For a similar interpretation, see also J. Chateau, *L'étudiant périmé* (Vrin, Paris 1968).
74. It is not suggested here that neo-Marxism was not idealist, merely that its content and preoccupations differed from those of the bourgeois idealists.

75. C. Prévost, op. cit., p. 43.
76. G. Michaud, *Révolution dans l'Université* (Hachette, Paris 1968), p. 64.
77. E. Morin, *Mai 1968: la Brèche*, op. cit. (note 9), p. 34.
78. J.-M. Domenach, in *Esprit*, May 1968.
79. M. Niel, *Le mouvement étudiant ou la révolution en marche*, op. cit., p. 25.
80. Slogans quoted by M. Niel, op. cit. (note 64), pp. 44 and 46.
81. From 'Nous sommes en marche', *Censier*, Mai 1968.
82. Slogan quoted by Epistémon, *Ces idées qui ont ébranlé la France*, op. cit. (note 8), p. 85.
83. G. and D. Cohn-Bendit, *Obsolete Communism* (Penguin, London 1968), p. 27.
84. For the text of this law, see *Le Monde*, 17–18 November 1968, and for its discussion in the National Assembly, *Le Monde*, 5–12 October 1968. Despite fears from the Gaullist extreme Right ('all universities will be communist two years from now') and condemnation from the extreme Left (that co-management did not go far enough and that the old Faculty structure would reassert itself), the major parties restricted themselves to textual criticism and to proposing amendments. The law was adopted by the National Assembly in October 1968 by 441 votes to 0, the Communists and 6 Gaullists abstaining.
85. Many agreed with the statement by Jacques Perret that 'Selection, full-time study, grants and a virtual assurance of entry to a career afterwards are inextricably related'— *Inquiète Sorbonne*, op. cit. (note 7), p. 109.
86. Many of the provisions of the *Loi d'orientation* are very close to those advocated by G. Antoine and J.-C. Passeron, *La Réforme de l'université* (Calman-Levy, Paris 1966).
87. A. Touraine, *Le Mouvement de Mai*, op. cit. (note 50), p. 245.
88. Touraine argues that the only real solution lies in the formation of a strongly anti-technocratic university. 'When power was in the hands of a Monarch or of Oligarchies, the writer, the journalist, the artist could defend public liberties against domination of a personal nature. Faced with the powerful machinery of the techno-bureaucracy, only an organization, itself powerful and anti-technocratic in its aims and methods, can take over this role.' Ibid., p. 288.
89. For a list of universities created and their decrees published by the end of 1969 see *Le Monde*, 14.11.69.
90. M. Duverger, 'Les contradictions de l'Université nouvelle', *Le Monde*, 12.9.69.
91. For example, the attempt by the Dean of the Paris Science Faculty, M. Zamansky, in the name of the staff of this faculty, to transform it into a single 'Science University of Paris' (*Le Monde*, 29 January 1970).
92. *Le Monde*, 3 February 1970.
93. Maurice Duverger in *Le Monde*, 26 February 1970.
94. The texts creating these Universities are published in *Journal Officiel*, 22 March 1970. A resumé appeared in *Le Monde*, 22–23 March 1970. Apart from the seven universities of Paris-Centre, the remaining six are: Paris VIII, the experimental University of Vincennes, concentrating on contemporary studies, languages and human sciences; Paris IX, the experimental University of Dauphine, orientated towards management studies and applied economics; Paris X, the University of Paris-West at Nanterre, including law, letters and some technology; Paris XI at Orsay, predominantly scientific with a bias towards medical applications; Paris XII (Créteil) and Paris XIII (St.-Denis) existed mainly on paper at the time of writing.
95. Maurice Duverger in *Le Monde*, 26 March 1970.
96. *Le Monde*, 22–23 March 1970.
97. The incidents at Nanterre during the 19–25 January were condemned by the reformist Comité de liaison étudiant pour la rénovation universitaire (C.L.E.R.U.) as well as by the history and geography section of S.N.E.-Sup. (*Le Monde*, 29 January 1970).
98. Of the major factions dissolved by law on 12 June 1968 the following have been renamed. *Trotskyite groups:* Federation des étudiants révolutionnaire (F.E.R.) gave rise to the Alliance des jeunes pour le socialisme (A.J.S.) and Alliance des étudiants pour le socialisme (A.E.S.), while the Jeunesse communiste révolutionnaire (J.C.R.), reassembled as La Lique Communiste. *Maoist:* Union des jeunesses communistes marxistes—léninistes (U.J.C.M.-L.) has largely been reconstituted as La Gauche Prolétarienne. The situation is, however, considerably more complicated than this indicates.
99. Cf. Jean-Paul Sartre, 'Les Casseurs', *Le Nouvel Observateur*, No. 288, 18–24 May 1970.
100. Commenting upon his being attacked by students the previous week the Dean of Letters, M. Ricoeur, a strong supporter of student claims during the May events, made the following points: firstly, that some of those present were not enrolled at Nanterre, and

secondly that a process of 'groupusculization' was occurring, 'each extreme left-wing group, submitting to the pressure and blackmail of a more extreme group against which it cannot defend itself. . . . In my view this is the tragedy, that the extremists basically seek nothing further from the University. For them the University is simply the place where they apply a revolutionary strategy.' (*Le Monde*, 1–2 February 1970.)

101. Right-wing groups such as Union-Droit, Mouvement Restauration Nationale (ex-Action-Française), and Mouvement Jeune Révolution Université, had arranged a common meeting with Italian neo-Fascists and German neo-Nazis (N.P.D.). (Maurice Duverger, 'Un contre Mai', *Le Monde*, 13 February 1970.) A three-point contract was proposed at Assas to be signed by all student groups, agreeing to forbid the stocking of arms in the faculty, to respect the posters affixed by other groups, and to cease attacks against persons. (*Le Monde*, 11 February 1970.)

7. *WEST GERMANY*[1]

Dietrich Goldschmidt

The present university situation in West Germany (Federal Republic of Germany—F.R.G.—plus West Berlin) is determined by the following features.

The number of university students, German and foreign taken together, has grown significantly since the end of the second world war. In 1950 there were 114,000 students registered at the various universities: in 1969 there were 252,000.[2] In West Germany's first five years of existence the number of students stagnated, but after 1954 it increased by almost 7 per cent., or 10,000 per annum.[3] To cope with this influx the existing universities expanded considerably. New universities were founded and their staff of professors, lecturers and assistants was enlarged. However, the number of students grew more quickly than the university system expanded, so that overcrowding is faced in many disciplines. Admission—officially unrestricted—is limited in subjects like medicine or pharmacy at almost every German university. The growing number of applicants turned down is, of course, an indicator of the poor functioning of the educational system in West Germany. Since continued increases in the number of students must be expected, there is an urgent need to further enlarge the capacity of the universities by a quantitative reform. That their growth cannot go on without a fundamental qualitative reform is realized by all agencies concerned, but there is considerable debate about the direction this necessary change should take.

In the past the German tradition of university learning—particularly in the disciplines of the arts and of the social sciences—was to let the student choose his courses almost at will and to let him determine the number of years he wanted to stay at the university before taking his final examination. A minimum time-span—four years at least—was prescribed for the student's studies before he could apply for his diploma; however, there was never a maximum limitation set on his stay at the university as long as he could find ways of financing it. Thus the German university gave the student an education remarkably free from the time limits and organizational pressures that characterize universities elsewhere in the world. This 'academic freedom', in the past, had influenced scientific imagination and academic outlook within Germany's higher educated class, but with the growing demand for university training this freedom contributed to a chaotic situation characterized by overcrowding and disorientation. Studies became less effective year by year and this, in turn, made students remain longer at the university, so making for still more overcrowding—a vicious circle which gave rise to high drop-out rates and even further extensions of study time. In the end, this prolongation of regular studies made university teachers believe that they could add even more demands to the regular syllabus of examination requirements, as the students were expected to have learned more in the surplus time they spent at the university. So, of course, the teachers also contributed to the prolongation of the students' course of study.

At present, the actual time needed for the completion of studies is on average six years in most subjects, instead of the prescribed minimum of four years, and a period of even eight years or more is not exceptional.[4] A study by Kath *et al.* not only indicated this but also revealed differences between disciplines. The sample for this study consisted of 2,000 students of all faculties who entered the Free University of Berlin, the Universities of Bonn and Frankfurt/Main, and the College of Commerce and Economics at Mannheim in the summer term of 1957. Eight years later, i.e. by the winter term of 1964/65, the percentage of those who had completed their courses and graduated was as follows: Pharmacy 82; Law 77; Medicine 74. These three disciplines are characterized by one or more of the following features: a compulsory attendance requirement; a rigid course structure; intermediate examinations; a compulsory period of practical work preceding the course of study. In the faculty of Economics and Social Sciences only 65 per cent. of the sample had completed their course of study. In the faculty of Arts, where there is the strongest insistence on the principle of 'academic freedom' combined with comparatively little orientation toward a future career, only 37 per cent. of the sample (41 per cent. men and 32 per cent. women) had graduated after eight years. The number of those who had not yet taken their final examinations was 25 per cent. In the faculty of Science, 56 per cent. of the sample had graduated, but here was also found the largest number of students still studying (27 per cent.). In all the disciplines considered it was the female students who most frequently gave up before completing their courses.

DROP-OUTS			
Subject	*Female*	*Male*	*Total*
Medicine	29%	10%	16%
Law	24%	16%	17%
Economics and Social Sciences	37%	21%	24%
Science	35%	12%	17%
Arts	53%	25%	38%
Amongst the arts: transfers who obtained an alternative qualification (e.g. at a Teachers' College)	25%	11%	17%

If one considers that the *Abitur* is usually taken at the age of 20, and adds $1\frac{1}{2}$ years of national service for men before entering the university, then the normal age of graduates on entering a profession is about 26 to 29 years, or when further training on the job is necessary (e.g. for teachers at secondary schools) even 30 years. This situation means excessive stress for most of the students, as they have not only been restricted and dependent during their best early years, but also take their first step in professional life after having experienced frustrations and breakdowns within the organizational setting of the university.[5]

In German universities the teaching of many subjects has become unsatisfactory. University professors often confine themselves to very specialized fields and, as a result, teach their students as though they intended to make university professors out of them. Of course such a scholastic 'ivory tower' community may well meet the need for scientific research and progress, but it cannot satisfy the majority of the students' demands for higher education and professional training. Only very recently have experiments with more structured courses begun at some universities and in some disciplines. There are other institutions like Teachers' Training Colleges and Technical Colleges that educate students for performing very clearly prescribed future jobs. However, recent attempts to 'qualify' these institutions as 'academic' lead to somewhat similar problems of one-sided and disorganized curricula as in traditional university teaching. Pure professional training is always regarded as of 'lower' order. The so-called 'academies' designed to train engineers, social workers and economists, having hitherto performed the role of specialized colleges, are now involved in a process of 'academization' which aims at integrating all institutions of this level into a comprehensive system of university education.

The 'third level' of education, all education beyond secondary schools, is by tradition fragmented—mainly because three parallel streams constitute the system of secondary education:

(a) The secondary general school (*Hauptschule*), comprising the 5th to the 9th grade and leading to practical work in trade, industry and farming, i.e. skilled labour of many kinds, via apprenticeships which are combined with part-time vocational schooling, known as the 'dual system'.

(b) The secondary technical school (*Realschule*), comprising the 5th to the 10th grade and leading to white-collar middle-rank positions in trade, industry, hospitals, etc., via special full-time technical schools and colleges.

(c) The academic high school (*Gymnasium*), comprising the 5th to the 13th grade and ending with graduation for university entrance (*Abitur*). This type of education opens the way to all qualified spheres of professional life via further training at universities and special colleges.

The traditional system of rather rigid streaming in secondary education produces selection at the age of 10 years of (mainly middle-class) pupils for the academic high school, with its bourgeois tradition. Of course, the same over-representation of these classes can be found in the student body of the universities too. Only 7 per cent. of university students are sons and daughters of industrial or farm workers, while almost 30 per cent. of the students are children of civil servants, and about the same percentage come from those whose parents are white-collar workers.[6] Though there are, in principle, opportunities for those who did not get their *Abitur* to obtain it along a 'second path towards education', i.e. through evening schools and special colleges, they usually need so much extra effort that the percentage of those who succeed by this means and go on to university or college is almost negligible.[7]

A factor that reinforces this sort of selection even further is the system of scholarships. Though university fees are low and in some cases not charged at all, scholarships are restricted to a very small number of highly qualified students, and to a limited group, which represents 30 per cent. of those students whose parents, according to a strict means test, cannot give them the support necessary for minimum subsistence.[8] So the majority of students are financed by their parents, something obviously only the well-to-do can afford. About one quarter of the students therefore have to spend a considerable amount of time working at unskilled jobs to cover all or at least a large part of their living expenses.

University students have constantly pointed to the shortcomings of the present university system, first by internal reform discussions, then by demonstrations and political campaigns. In 1960 the German National Union of Students (V.D.S.), the official student representative body, published a memorandum under the title 'Farewell to the Ivory Tower',[9] declaring their intent to awaken student responsibility for social and political problems outside the institutional framework of the university. They formulated explicit demands for the integration of the different streams of education, increased stress on developing highly qualified manpower, promotion of international student exchanges, and for political commitment. The German Socialist Student Federation (S.D.S.) followed in 1961 with 'The University in the Democratic State',[10] a highly detailed and comprehensive analysis of the function of the university in West Germany, coupled with a strong demand for a thorough democratization of society.

However, despite these and other sophisticated declarations, next to nothing happened in the way of effective reform until the student protest movement grew active, arranging sit-ins, teach-ins and lecture-strikes. The Free University of Berlin became the core of the protest movement, perhaps because students there enjoyed the institutionally guaranteed right to participate in university administration—what is known as the 'Berlin Model'—and perhaps also because of a particularly strong discrepancy between the claims made for democracy in this city and the real patterns of political behaviour. The general process of active confrontation with the representatives of the traditional university began exactly twenty years after the capitulation of Nazi Germany, on 7 May 1965, when a well-known journalist was denied the right to speak to the students on the grounds that he had once been said to have made disparaging remarks about how free the 'Free University' was. This, of course, was an incident which aroused much indignation because it smacked of one-sided political tutelage. Distrust of positive co-operation between the students, the university administration and the city council grew so strong that, in the end, the police force dealt fiercely with student demonstrations everywhere and on every occasion.[11] The fact that a Berlin student was shot dead by a policeman in June 1967 made students' solidarity spread through Germany; their struggle for better conditions of study, better curricula, less individualistic examinations was—for a certain time—overshadowed by purely political demands, such as for peace in Vietnam, atomic disarmament, or against the enactment of emergency laws in West Germany, and the power of newspaper monopolies.

Most influential within the German student protest movement was the Socialist Student Federation (S.D.S.), an intellectual, rather small but highly aggressive group, which had been founded as a student organization of the German Social Democratic Party (S.P.D.), but separated from it in 1959. Because of the radical political views of this organization, the severance of all ties with the parliamentary system became the explicit objective of the S.D.S. programme for action. When, in 1966, the grand coalition between Christian Democrats and Social Democrats was set up in Bonn, the Socialist Student Federation became the leading force of the so-called 'extra-parliamentary opposition' (A.P.O.), a popular youth protest movement with its stronghold in Berlin. Its idea was that there could be no effective opposition in Parliament when the two largest parties combined; real opposition would only be possible from outside. However, the A.P.O. overestimated its influence on political decisions, and as a result, the general movement lost its impetus. The remainder split into various factions. What was originally an extra-parliamentary programme, increasingly developed into an anti-parliamentarian one, the more these groups identified themselves with the 'underdogs' in Latin-America, Africa, and Asia, in the belief that effective struggle against bad conditions could only be led by guerilla groups. As far as one can see, the student leftist movement as a whole did not follow this particular course: one part of it received protection from the newly founded 'German Communist Party' (D.K.P., not to be confused with the old Communist Party: K.P.D.), which is recognized as an official political organization under the West German Constitution; another part has split up into so-called 'red-cells' or 'basis groups', which seek to completely re-organize the teaching, and in particular the curricula of all university subjects along Marxist lines.

The official successor of the S.D.S. in the association with the German Social Democratic Party was the Social Democratic University Federa-tion (S.H.B.), a heterogeneous and rather moderate group of students who believed in chances for reform at a time when their radical predecessors had already given up all hope. Indeed, the two were complementary. The S.D.S., as *'avant-garde'*, revealed the weaknesses of the university system by staging drastic actions, which attracted much publicity; when the socialist students had thus indicated the urgent need for measures to alter prevailing conditions, the S.H.B. figured as mediator between the established authorities and the radical students, interpreting their demands in a co-operative fashion, while sticking firmly to the initial aims. Now that the S.D.S. has split up into different factions and has abandoned its central organization, the S.H.B. has gained in influence in co-ordinating socialist ideas and political actions at universities.

During the past five years all student political groups have undergone a 'radicalization', that is, they have incorporated into their own pro-grammes the demands their more radical opponents had left behind. The most evident features of this process can be seen in the Federation of Christian Democratic Students (R.C.D.S.), a kind of progressive spearhead of the Christian Democratic Party of Germany. Actually they are as 'radical' in their ideas on reform as the Socialist students were in the year 1965. The Liberal Student Federation (L.S.D.), has also adopted many of the demands formerly proclaimed by the S.D.S. Like its parent party, the Free Democrats, it has become transformed into a smaller but more active body than before. Its numbers are not as large as one might imagine, because many students of liberal inclinations are not organized at all, or rather adhere to groups like the Student Humanist Society (H.S.U.) or one of the Christian Student Associations (E.S.G., K.S.G.).

The German student protest movement has, for a long time, found little response from the general public, although the protests during the years 1965–68 indicated interest in establishing a broader basis for political action. The workers—more than members of the well-to-do middle class—were very hostile to the demonstrations and to the students' anti-authoritarian behaviour, especially in Berlin. They did not quite understand why persons who were being educated at univer-sities did not enjoy their privileges—why they were not looking forward to stepping into important and well-paid jobs in the existing society instead of seeking to transform it altogether. The reports printed in newspapers that workers preferred to read—the so-called rainbow press—were often biased and extremely intolerant towards the students' demands and actions. Incidents of aggressive public hostility were reported from every large German city; their most prominent victim was Rudi Dutschke, one of the leaders of the S.D.S., who narrowly escaped death when he was shot at by a young nationalist.

This crime came as a considerable shock to the politically responsible, as it raised the question of possible analogies with the beginnings of the Nazi movement in the twenties. Though nationalist tendencies are still alive within Germany, they now have become concentrated on such non-university problems as the East European policy of the Federal Government. In most of the federal states discussion about university reform has reverted to the academic arena with the passage of new legislation on higher education. By creating new organizational structures, this legislation has led to a consolidation of the various interest groups in universities and has brought their antagonism into the open.[12] In Berlin, for example, enactment of the new law led to the dissolution of the official student organization, the General Student Association (A.S.T.A.), which corresponded to the Students' Union in Great Britain. Instead of formulating their interests through a central, all-university body, students now have the right to participate in decision-making on legislative bodies and committees that also include professors, assistant professors and university employees,[13] although only at the department level, and by delegation from these to the senate. The idea behind this arrangement was to give the students more rights and opportunities for intramural self-determination, but to take away their claim of having a 'political mandate', i.e. the possibility to speak for all of the students on political issues.[14]

The University Laws, in so far as they have been enacted, are not meant to reorganize the structure alone, or stop the ongoing reform discussion and experimentation by means of legislation, but rather to institutionalize these efforts. The law in force in Berlin since August 1969 explicitly states that it is the duty of the Government as well as of the universities to bring about reforms, 'reform' being defined as 'the development and test of new structures, forms of organization and curricula within the universities as framed by law'.[15] However, students are not content with the direction the official development has taken. Some of their demands have certainly been met: for instance, the democratization of the universities, i.e. effective participation of students in university administration at all levels. This enables them to press for revision of the curricula in order to eliminate one-sided 'bourgeois' indoctrination. To introduce the Marxist point of view into the curricula involves restructuring studies according to a plan of minimum representation of the Marxist approach to 'problems of Capitalism', and a special university personnel policy for finding teachers able to handle such subjects. This task is strongly backed by the 'red cells', whose members often do not refrain from attempts at extortion. Because of such methods, a group of university teachers and politicians has now founded a federation called 'Pro Academic Freedom',[16] aimed at conserving some of the traditional rights of scholars. For the students, of course, 'academic freedom' means something else: a politically conscious university in the sense that its members should cease collaborating with government, industry and other interest-bound institutions, and drop their pretence of carrying on research and teaching for their own sake, free of value judgements and in political neutrality. The students' ideal aim is a university with so much autonomy that it can act as a revolutionary force within existing society. Therefore all measures not designed to alter the traditional 'content' of the university system seem to them to be purely 'technocratic'.

However, the following facts should be kept in mind during any discussion of 'academic freedom' in the German universities. The universities are not and have never been 'autonomous' in the full sense of the word. There still is and always has been a delicate division of functions and a balance of power between state administration and academic self-government. In principle, the universities are state institutions—'Körperschaften öffentlichen Rechts'; in Germany private universities have never existed. University budgets are provided and controlled by state government. All professors, though nominated by the appropriate academic body, are appointed by the state's minister of education as civil servants for life. The academic institutions, however, are solely responsible for the scientific work of the university, in particular for teaching at all levels, examinations and research projects.

Traditionally, this organizational independence of intellectual training and creative thinking in the universities did not pose a threat to the established structures of society. As university education was a privilege either of rich families or of social climbers from the middle classes, it always formed the base of recruitment for the political and economic élite, whose aim could only be to profit individually from the special conditions of social selection which were at work. Thus, the opinion that universities are a genuinely democratic institution is purely ideological. When the society is a democratic one only in a formal, procedural sense, but not in content, it cannot create 'equality of opportunity' even if it is guaranteed under the constitution.[17] Equal opportunity for young people who want to study could only be ensured by generous scholarships for the majority of them, i.e. some kind of central stipend system independent of parents' income. It would take away from many of the students the additional burden of having to work to earn their living, and would give them a better chance to choose the subject that suited their inclinations. The family's influence on the decision to train for a certain profession is too strong as long as the parents see in their children's education an investment which has to 'yield interest' in a prescribed time. Therefore the pressures deriving from the private financing of the studies influence the subject and the study-time of the youngster as well as the direction of his professional career. Here, of course, it is the duty of the government to help students in their emancipation from direct dependency on relatives, so that 'academic freedom' shall not be reduced to a shallow phrase.

Responsibility for legislation on education has hitherto rested with the eleven federal states in West Germany, as can be seen by the fact that West Berlin enacted a special law for its universities. Each state individually planned and administered the institutions, from 'kindergarten' to the universities. That the policies of the different states were barely co-ordinated with one another could be deduced from regulations governing school holidays, from the foreign languages prescribed for secondary-school education, from the examinations demanded for the *Abitur*, from the scale of university fees, and so forth. There was no uniformity. Of course an official co-ordination agency did exist—the 'Permanent Conference of the Ministers of Education' (K.M.K.)—but the states normally reached only a minimal degree of consensus.

Altogether, the Federal Government was able to exert very little central authority in the realm of education, although in articles 73 and 74 of the Constitution it has special reserved rights concerning the financing and furthering of scientific research. With the growing disproportion between student numbers and university capacity the Government came to realize that a central agency for educational planning would be necessary. Therefore, twenty years after the end of the second world war, in May 1965, it succeeded in passing a constitutional amendment[18] which guarantees its influence on the future educational development of Germany, and particularly on the 'third level' of education. Structural planning and financing of the country's universities is the main function of West Germany's Ministry of Education, newly organized in 1969, when the Social Democratic–Free Democratic coalition was formed. Since then it has stimulated much reflection about the need for over-all reform of the university system. Two consulting commissions, the 'Science Council' and the 'Council on Education' have backed this initiative. A third commission has been entrusted with educational planning and co-ordination between the Federal Government and the states. The necessary law regulating federal authority—the *Hochschulrahmengesetz*—is in preparation. Guidelines for this legislation were published by the Ministry at the beginning of 1970. They comprise fourteen theses which serve as a basis for public discussion.[19]

The 'Science Council', established in 1937, is an advisory body for 'academic affairs', i.e. for research and teaching within the university system. The 'Council on Education', now five years old, has found its task in the formulation of forecasts and reform models for the elementary and secondary level of education and for the training of teachers. Both of them have very recently published huge volumes laying down their ideas on the future of education in Germany.[20] The long-run aim of their proposed reforms is the integration of the different streams of education: the 'comprehensive schools' will be increasingly responsible for the education of all children from the age of 5 to 18; 'regional comprehensive universities' are envisaged as the framework for studies of various types. First steps in both directions have already been taken. At some places, especially in large cities like Berlin, Frankfurt and Hamburg, comprehensive schools are at work, starting with pre-school classes for under-privileged children. The integration of professional and academic training at the third level of education has been furthered by new laws which enhance the status of the Teacher Training Colleges and of the formerly non-academic 'academies'.[21] For some years Teacher Training Colleges (*Pädagogische Hochschulen*) have already required the *Abitur* for entrance and have extended their course of study from two to three or three-and-a-half years. Some have already been given university status, and the remainder will acquire it soon. They may become integrated into the 'comprehensive universities', providing satisfactory opportunities for transfer into other fields and for graduation with an academic degree.

Thus far, technical colleges (colleges of engineering, medical technology, commerce, etc.) have required graduation from secondary technical schools plus some vocational training for admission to their three-year courses. Very soon these colleges will establish higher, more academic entrance requirements and will be integrated into the 'comprehensive universities' as well. The hope of the legislators is, of course, that such measures will make the West German educational system more flexible than it has been until recently. It must indeed be flexible, or otherwise it will collapse under the growing influx and increasing discontent of youth.

In 1969, 460,000 students were registered at the various universities, colleges and 'academies'. In the next five years this will grow to 680,000 people seeking higher education. This figure, published by the recently established Federal Planning Commission on University Development,[22] is fairly reliable, since the youngsters in question are already attending secondary school. It is forecast that 25 to 30 per cent. of a given age-group will receive university training in 1980; whereas at the moment only 15 per cent. come this far.[23] According to the projections used by the 'Science Council', the attendance level will have reached the one million student mark by 1980. Of course these figures have shocked the German public; the era of 'mass university' seems to have begun. Warnings by élitist groups can be heard that an 'academic proletariat' will be the greatest evil of the future, and that one should completely close university entrance for two years in order to stop this run on professional and academic careers.[24] However, it must be stressed that West Germany, in making such an immense 'leap' forward in the years to come, will only catch up with the standard already reached by other countries in 1966/67. At that time, 38 per cent. of an age-group received university education in the U.S.A.; in France it was 29 per cent. and in Jugoslavia 30 per cent., as the 'Science Council' reports.[25]

Conclusion

How can all these reformist trends within West Germany's educational system be evaluated? Firstly and above all, it is clear that university reform would not have made a significant start if student protest had not brought tremendous individual and public pressure to bear on the authorities. On the other hand, student protest would not have reached the pitch of a pseudo-revolution if university and state administration had responded with greater vision and with less rigid conservatism.[26] In addition, the appearance of the student protest movement has changed the balance between those involved with reform. No longer are there merely two forces—the professors as representatives of the university, and government officials representing the federal states— working together in relative harmony; now a third force—students and young academic staff—has joined them, with loudly proclaimed demands and a zest for controversy. In order to ease the situation and establish new and better conditions of study and work at the universities, the political authorities feel compelled to act, even at the price of trespassing upon traditional university autonomy and professorial interests.

Secondly, while the actual reforms going on in West Germany can be divided into three groups (constitutional reforms concerning the rights of the Federal Government to stimulate, co-ordinate and support decisions on education reform; legislative reforms by state parliaments with the aim of changing university constitutions; and internal reforms of curricula and teaching methods in order to build up a flexible and politically conscious university), certain aims are common to all of them. These include the democratization of the universities, i.e. the effective participation of students in university administration and legislation, and the effective restructuring of university curricula, designed to allow the students to plan their studies and to complete them in a reasonable span of time.

The main discovery of recent years is that the comparatively small élite universities are developing into modern institutions for higher education in an ever-growing number of subjects. It fits into this picture that adult education schemes within the university context are being discussed, not in the sense of traditional university extension courses or evening classes, but as condensed instruction to provide participants with an opportunity for keeping up with the developments in their own fields. The intensity of the struggle to develop new structures and introduce new content in the university system has yielded some by-products which can be seen as an indispensable part of future reforms: the establishment of centres for curriculum research, for teaching methods, for problems of professional education, for problems of university capacity, and so on. As things stand now, it can be hoped that such new institutions will stimulate further innovation in higher education.

In this discussion of the current status of university reform, nothing could be said about the future of post-graduate studies and research, traditionally strongly linked with the general university education in Germany. Nevertheless, one should be aware that the tremendous expansion of undergraduate education will change the relation between the two sectors of university work. Certain recommendations by the 'Science Council'[27] show that one can expect a clearer distinction to develop between undergraduate education and postgraduate studies than has existed so far. Although those recommendations were rather controversial at the time of their publication, they nevertheless exerted considerable influence on the present changes of curricula.

Finally, this review of the current status of university reform in Western Germany leads to the following conclusion. The general picture is rather grim, the urgency of reforms indisputable, but we are not in a position to predict the outcome of the present changes— neither the short-term effects on the student protest movement, which during the current academic year seems to have lost some of its former impetus, nor the long-term effects of the reforms on the functioning of the universities in teaching as well as in research. We can see some promising beginnings so far as the expansion and reform of the whole interdependent system of secondary and higher education are concerned, but the crisis has not yet been overcome.

Notes

1. The author is indebted to Miss Sibylle Funk, who kindly prepared this manuscript for publication.
2. Cf. W. Albert and Ch. Oehler, 'Materialien zur Entwicklung der Hochschulen 1950 bis 1967', Vol. 1, 1st ed. (H.I.S., Hanover 1969), p. 99 and Statistisches Bundesamt (ed.), 'Hochschulbesuch' (Kleine Hochschulstatistik) Wintersemester 1969/70, in A. Fachserie, *Bevolkerung und Kultur*, Reihe 10 (Bildungswesen, Stuttgart 1970).
3. W. Albert and Ch. Oehler, op. cit., p. 96.
4. Cf. G. Kath, Ch. Oehler and R. Reichwein, 'Studienweg und Studienerfolg' in *Studien und Berichte*, Vol. 6 (Institut für Bildungsforschung in der Max-Planck-Gesellschaft, Berlin 1966).
5. Cf. D. Goldschmidt, 'Psychological Stress: a German Case Study' in J. Nagel (ed.) *Student Power* (Merlin Press, London 1969), pp. 59–72.
6. G. Kath, 'Das soziale Bild der Studentenschaft in der Bundesrepublik Deutschland' (Deutsches Studentenwerk, Bonn 1969), p. 39 f.
7. About 2 per cent. of the university students come from a special preparatory college for adults or have graduated from a technical college.
8. G. Kath, op. cit., p. 72 f.
9. 'Abschied vom Elfenbeinturm, Einheit der Bildungswege, Nachwuchs und Forderung, Studium im Ausland, Mut zur Politik', (Verband Deutscher Studentenschaften (ed.), Berlin 1960).
10. 'Hochschule in der Demokratie, Denkschrift des Sozialistischen Deutschen Studentenbundes', Verlag 'neue Kritik' 1st Ed. (Frankfurt/Main 1961).

11. 'Die Rebellen von Berlin, Studentenpolitik an der Freien Universität. Eine Dokumentation von Jens Hager' (Kiepenheuer & Witsch, Köln and Berlin 1967).

12. The Berlin universities were the first ones to be completely reorganized. Cf. 'Das neue Gesetz uber die Universitaten des Landes Berlin' (Senator für Wissenschaft und Kunst (ed.), Berlin 1969).

13. According to §10 of the Berlin University Law the University Senate consists of 11 professors, 6 assistant professors, 5 students and 2 non-academic university employees. Practically this means that students and assistant professors, together with the employees, can outvote the professors.

14. Cf. U. K. Preuss, *Das politische Mandat der Studentenschaft*. Mit Gutachten von R. Havemann, W. Hoffmann und J. Habermas/A. Wellmer (Suhrkamp, Frankfurt/Main 1969).

15. Cf. University Law of Berlin, §2.5.

16. The official inauguration took place at Bonn on 18 November 1970.

17. Cf. Article 12 of the Constitution of the F.R.G.

18. Article 91.b.

19. Cf. 'Thesen des Bundesministers für Bildung und Wissenschaft zur Vorbereitung von Informationsgesprachen uber den Entwurf eines Hochschulrahmengesetzes' in *Schriftenreihe Hochschule* No. 2 (Bonn 1970).

20. Cf. 'Strukturplan für das Bildungswesen' (Deutscher Bildungsrat (ed.), Bonn 1970); and 'Empfehlungen des Wissenschaftrates zur Struktur und zum Ausbau des Bildungswesens im Hochschulbereich nach 1970' (Köln 1970).

21. Cf. the 'Fachhochschulgesetze' of the Federal States.

22. Cf. *dpa-Dienst für Kulturpolitik* No. 43, 26 October 1970, p. 2.

23. Cf. 'Uberlegung zur Entwicklung der Studentenzahlen' in 'Empfehlungen des Wissenschaftsrats zur Struktur und zum Ausbau des Bildungswesens im Hochschulbereich nach 1970', p. E.17.

24. W. Schlaffke, 'Akademisches Proletariat?' in *Berichte des Deutschen Industrieinstituts zu bildungs—und gesellschafts politischen Fragen*, 2, 1970, No. 1 (Köln 1970). W. Arnold, L. Kroeber-Keneth and E. Luscher, *Alma mater moribunda. Oder: Ist die Universität noch zu retten?* (Quelle & Meyer, Heidelberg 1970).

25. Ibid, p. E.18.

26. It could be argued that student unrest has developed in those places (Berlin and Frankfurt) where universities were considered to be progressive. However, a distinction should be made between the academic 'atmosphere' of modern critical and progressive thought and the administrative actions characterized by an outlook representing rather rigid political, social and educational standpoints.

27. *Empfehlungen zur Neuordnung des Studiums an den wissenschaftlichen Hochschulen* (Wissenschaftsrat (ed.), Bonn 1966).

8.   ITALY

Guido Martinotti

Introduction

A number of aspects of the current Italian University situation are peculiar to it, or, to be more precise, while many of the same factors are also active in other countries they are found here in a particularly negative combination. In more systematic terms, one could say that the Italian university system is a rather good example of what we would *not* expect by approaching a social subsystem from a functional point of view, that is, from the assumption that social systems tend to react to external or internal stimuli by a process of successive self-adjustments, tending towards a state in which tensions are minimalized and therefore become manageable. In this case, by contrast, one witnesses a number of crucial factors coinciding to push the Italian system in the opposite direction.

The first crucial factor is the rapid growth of the student body. This constitutes the major external pressure, and while it is a common feature of most university systems in modern societies, it has been particularly pronounced in Italy during recent years. Figure 8.1 gives a general idea of the increase since the first world war.

Despite the fact that in absolute terms both new enrolments and the total number of students are still below the corresponding levels for highly industrialized countries, the relative growth rate has been very high, partly owing to a general improvement in the economic situation. It should be noted that the 'social demand' for education has been much stronger on the *input* than on the output side. In other words, the expansion of the system has been more a consequence of pressures from 'below' the university than a function of demand for graduates from the labour market. This in turn has been one of the central points of debate over the role of the Italian university in recent times.[1]

The second factor is connected with the rigidity of the Italian university system at the institutional level. This appears both in the form of imbalance between the growth of the student body and the amount of resources allocated by the government, and in the general inability of the university system to adapt its methods (examination and teaching systems) to the new situations. Even the innovations made in response to student protest have been rather random and have been gradually eroded.

The third factor is, in a way, the strategic variable since it explains the inadaptability of the system and is usually absent from functional analyses. It is the role of vested interests and of the power structure within the universities. In the Italian case the academic élite has been remarkably resilient and has been able to oppose innovation even when this was initiated from within the academic body. Such resistance has developed far beyond the level expected on the assumption that the system should move toward self-adjustment.

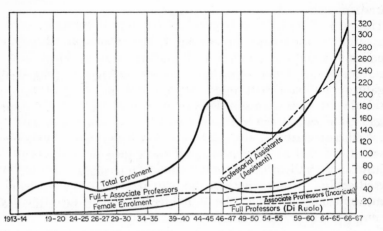

FIG. 8.1.—INCREASE IN STUDENT ENROLMENT, FEMALE ENROLMENT AND THE SIZE OF THE TEACHING BODY BETWEEN 1913–14 AND TODAY

(In thousands—figures referring to the teaching body are multiplied by 10 for each rank on the graph.)

Source: *Annuario Statistico dell'Istruzione Italiana.*

Obviously this very simple three-factor scheme does not claim to explain the Italian university situation exhaustively; it is, however, a convenient framework for a description of the situation, which will now proceed along three lines:

1. Organization of the university: faculties, disciplines and the teaching system.
2. The student body.
3. The academic profession.

Organization of higher education: faculties and institutes, disciplines, curricula and teaching systems

Some of the Italian universities are very ancient and can be counted among the first created during the early university movement at the end of the Middle Ages. Never again, however, has the Italian University gained the world-wide renown that ranked Bologna and Padua with Paris and Oxford at the beginning of the fourteenth century.

Today there are in Italy 48 universities plus a few additional institutes at university level. Practically all of them are state universities,[2] which range from very large campuses with tens of thousands of students; as in Rome (the largest), Naples and Milan, to very small ones with a few hundred students like Camerino or Macerata. Some are ancient universities like Bologna, Padova, Camerino, and Pavia, and others are of fairly recent origin, such as Milan, the Economics branch of the University of Urbino in Ancona, or the Institute of Social Sciences in Trento.

However, despite the differences in size, type of administration and age, Italian universities are rather homogeneous in their internal organization and functioning, as all must conform to precise and rigid state regulations. These regulations concern curricula, degrees, teaching and examination systems and the recruitment of professors. The rationale for such homogeneity can be traced back to the so-called 'legal value' of the academic degree. There is only one degree given by all the universities—the *dottorato*, whose legal value is nation-wide. A result of this formal homogeneity imposed through centralized control is that there is no competition among universities to have a better faculty. Admittedly there are better universities and second-rate ones,[3] but this is the effect of external factors such as the attractiveness of universities located in large urban centres, not of the tendency to form university centres of high cultural level like the Sorbonne, Oxford and Cambridge or Harvard. Because of this homogeneity it is possible to indicate traits common to the whole of the Italian system of higher education.

(a) *Length of curriculum.* Each *dottorato* has a fixed length of studies, ranging from four years for the 'Doctorate' in Law, Economics and Business, Humanities and most of the Scientific subjects, to five years for Industrial Chemistry and Geology, Architecture and all the Engineering branches, to six years for Medicine.

(b) *Curricula.* The number and type of subjects studied to obtain a degree are very rigidly fixed by law; the number of courses left optional has traditionally been very low. For instance, to obtain a Law 'Doctorate' a student has to pass twenty-one exams in four years, of which eighteen are compulsory or 'basic' (and therefore the same for all students and in all universities) and only three are 'complementary'—that is, options which the student can select from among a list of several courses. An indication of the rigidity of the system is the fact that each change in the structure of the 'basic' courses can be instituted only by a national law or presidential decree.

In 1969, however, a special law was passed allowing students to establish their own curricula from whatever courses were available in a given university, even if in other faculties. Although this law has been interpreted restrictively in many universities, where curricula still have to be submitted for approval by the Faculty, there is no doubt that this single provision—in itself an anticipation of the larger reform law now being discussed—has probably been the most momentous decision to affect Italian universities in recent years.

All in all, however, the Reform law has been a mixed blessing, since unless it can operate in the context of an entirely restructured university it will create additional tensions and confusion in an already strained situation.

(c) *Criteria of admission.* No university has entrance examinations. Admittance is based solely on possession of the appropriate lower diploma (*maturità* in the lycée system, or equivalent in other branches of secondary schools).

(d) *Teaching and attendance.* Traditionally, teaching in Italian universities has been based on very formal *ex cathedra* lectures given by professors, usually in front of a large and rather passive audience. Interaction between teacher and students is minimal, and contacts for tutorials almost non-existent, or mainly left to the professor's assistants. Most of the courses are based on some kind of institutional textbook, which is usually the so-called *dispensa*. The *dispensa* is reminiscent of the medieval *pecia*,[4] and is made up from notes of the course held by the professor, edited by himself or by one of the assistants, and published at the end of the year.[5] However, under the joint pressure of demands from younger staff, and from the students, there has been a tendency in recent years to abolish traditional *ex cathedra* lectures and to substitute seminars, or group work, involving greater interaction between students and faculty and more active participation by students.

(e) *Examination and degrees.* The system of examination is also uniform for all the Italian universities. Apart from a few exceptions in technical subjects, where practical or laboratory tests are required, or in subjects like Latin, Italian or foreign languages, where there are written tests, all other exams are *oral*.

In case of failure to pass the student can try again and again, the only restriction being that no more than two trials can be made in the same year. This provision, however, is becoming obsolete, with the shift toward easing the exams and the tendency of students to substitute voluntary withdrawal for failure.

The *dottorato* degree is obtained upon successful completion of the prescribed course plus the writing of a dissertation (apart from certain courses such as Medicine or Engineering where there are somewhat different procedures).

(f) *Recruitment of Professors.* An additional cause of the homogeneity of universities is the recruitment procedure for appointment of professors. This is effected through a national *concorso*, or contest, which will be described in detail later. In any individual university, appointments are made by the *Consiglio di Facoltà*, which is composed of all the full professors of the Faculty.

(g) *Organization and decision-making structure.* To complete this sketchy description of the structure of the Italian university, a few words should be said about the decision-making structure and the organizational structure.

For the latter it will be enough to mention that the basic organizational component is the Institute. This is usually composed of one (or more, rarely of two or more) full professors, and several *incaricati* and *assistenti*. The full professor is the head of the Institute and has responsibility for management and administration.

Institutes receive a share of the university's economic resources, but they can also have a separate budget derived from professional or research activities conducted for private or governmental agencies. Traditionally, such activities have been more characteristic of the engineering and scientific faculties, and obviously of medicine. Administration of these revenues is almost completely outside the control of the University, or any other agencies.

The level above the Institute is the Faculty, which is composed of several Institutes. The Faculty is governed by the *Consiglio di Facoltà*, composed of full professors, who alone decide on all teaching matters and also a great many administrative issues.

The Consiglio di Facoltà elects a *Preside* (Dean) every three years, who represents the Faculty in the Academic Senate, which in turn is composed of all the *Presidi* of the different Faculties in a given university.

Each university is governed by a Rector, elected by all full professors of that university once every four years. The administrative part of the organization is managed by a relatively small bureaucracy, which performs roughly the same functions as a Registrar's Office and takes care of facilities.

As it would take too long to enter here into the details of the organizational structure, it appears more useful to indicate some of the major features of its functioning. Decision-making power is not in the hands of a 'lay' body like a Board of Trustees or comparable agencies, but is almost entirely entrusted to professors. This eliminates problems of external control or internal pressures from the administration, as well as the strains that such a dual organization entails. On the other hand, however, the fact that there is no central 'managerial' authority above the individual professors renders difficult the kind of co-operation needed for long-term planning. The power structure in Italian universities essentially follows the various levels of 'zero-sum' allocation of resources. The central Ministry of Education makes the preliminary distribution of money and posts among the universities, Faculties in each University then compete for their share, and within each Faculty, Institutes compete for the final allocation. The *Consiglio di Facoltà*, then, is not so much a decision-making body, but rather an agency for resource-sharing among a group of peers. And among peers the easiest way to allocate resources is even division.

Thus each Institute has to compete with all the others, and efforts are largely directed towards avoiding excessive prominence of one or more of the other Institutes. This leads to precisely the inverse of those conditions conducive to planning, where some central mediating agency is needed to establish priorities and to concentrate resources. One of the major consequences of this (or perhaps the cause) is the prevalence of the 'amoral familism' that regulates the professional life of academics in Italy.[6]

Students

The aim of this productive system (the university) is to place a good (the graduate) on the labor market—where it will be *sold*—and on the wider system of social reproduction—where it will be *consumed*; peculiar to this product (the graduate) is the possibility of being sold on the labor market both during production (study) as a semi-manufactured good (student-worker) and at the end of the cycle as a manufactured good (graduate).[7]

So the student movement in Trento defined the university at the very beginning of the 1968 revolt.

Obviously the university is not simply a collection of teachers and students, but this relationship is the basis on which a whole set of superstructures, such as the academic profession and its power, and much of the research activity, have been successively and successfully built. We can consider the university, stripped to its barest essentials, as a system whose inputs and outputs are students and graduates, since such a flow on the one hand justifies the very existence of the institution, and, on the other, provides a standard for the amount of resources to be allocated to it by the wider society. Recent increases in student numbers, part of a trend which is obviously not limited to Italy, have had very serious consequences because of the rigidity of the system as such.

If the number of students is taken as an input indicator and the number of professors as an indicator of structural adjustment, we can identify three more or less distinct periods in the changes occurring in Italian universities since World War I. During the first period, which approximately corresponds to the inter-war years, the system was in equilibrium. It was a rather small system—77,429 students and 3,362 professors of all categories in 1938–39; student numbers grew by an average of 5 per cent. a year, and the student-teacher ratio, while increasing slightly, remained manageable (24:1 at the end of the period).

During the second phase, which includes World War II and the post-war period, the system entered into a temporary crisis. The university was swamped with students, whose number grew rapidly to a peak of almost 200,000 in 1946–47.[8] The system did not respond by increasing the number of professors, but this was reasonable as this rate of expansion proved temporary. The student-teacher ratio rose to a record 54:1 in 1946–47, but had decreased to 29:1 by 1953–54 as the war-boom intake was slowly digested.

In the final period between 1954–55 and 1966–67 the number of students increased 2.50 times, while the number of full professors increased by a factor of only 0.40.

This represents a situation radically different from the small and balanced pre-war university. In 1967–68 there were 370,076 regular students enrolled, plus 130,139 *fuori corso*, making a total of 500,215 students. Of these 127,625 (or more than one-third of the regular students) were first-year students. On the other hand, there were only 2,911 full professors, or one chair for every 171 students. It is true that together with professors one should consider the 7,199 *incaricati* and compute the ratio for only the regular students; it then falls to 37:1[9], which is still, however, considerably higher than in the first period discussed. The strains resulting within such a system can be outlined by considering the indicators of input, output and structural change contained in Table 8.I.

(a) *Input* indicators are increasing rapidly; as can be seen (a) by the percentage of school-leavers enrolling at university and, (b) by the number of first-year students. The overall size of the student body is also increasing, although less rapidly than the first-year student group. The differential between this indicator and the previous ones is an additional pointer to future expansion.

(b) *Structural change*, as indicated by the number of professors, shows on the contrary a rather low rate of growth, the lowest in fact of all the indicators.

(c) *Output*, as measured by the number of graduates, also shows a fairly low rate of increase. This will almost certainly change in the near future, but for the time being it constitutes an added strain on the system.

For all its impressive if rather chaotic growth in recent years, the Italian university is as yet not a mass university. Access to it is only granted to a small percentage of the appropriate age-group, although the exact proportion is difficult to assess because available official statistics do not provide the necessary data, and govern-

Table 8.I—*Some parameters of the Italian university system (1954–55 = 100)*

| | Input | | | Structure | | Output |
Years	(a) % Graduates from lower-level schools enrolling in University	(b) Number of first-year students	(c) Total number regular students	(d) Full Professors	(e) Total teaching personnel	(f) Graduates
Base Value		(35,893)	(136,458)	(1,852)	(16,682)	(20,203)
1954–55	56.9 100,00	100,00	100,00	100,00	100,00	100,00
1955–56	59.3 104,22	112,93	101,88	105,13	105,13	109,31
1956–57	59.2 104,04	123,01	106,53	107,18	112,53	100,86
1957–58	58.9 103,51	135,10	113,32	108,96	114,04	96,45
1958–59	57.3 100,70	139,95	120,14	112,04	125,58	103,15
1959–60	59.2 104,04	157,61	129,12	104,10	136,96	104,63
1960–61	59.6 104,74	166,35	140,44	107,61	144,95	108,31
1961–62	63.5 111,60	181,69	150,94	112,90	156,17	113,92
1962–63	71.6 125,83	209,11	165,47	118,84	153,78	118,66
1963–64	74.6 131,11	215,15	175,05	125,97	161,74	129,24
1964–65	76.2 133,92	240,70	190,05	133,26	167,32	138,21
1965–66	79.6 139,89	293,87	218,22	140,82	187,39	143,81
1966–67	80.6 141,65	299,51	248,07	—	—	—

Source: *Annuario Statistico dell'Istruzione Italiana*, Vols. IX–XX.

mental estimates tend to be inflated. The latest of these (1966–67) gave a figure of 13.4 per cent. attending university out of the 19–20 age-group. However, reworking the official estimate in conjunction with survey data I arrived at a considerably lower estimate for the same year: the percentage of the population aged between 19–26 currently registered at a university, or already having graduated, was 5.99 per cent., that is, one out of 17 persons.[10] This figure corresponds very closely to that which can be arrived at by computing the drop-out rates in cohorts of students in the years following primary school. For the period 1955–63, out of 1,000 students entering the primary school, 640 finish it; 507 enter high school; 260 gain a high school diploma; 208 enter the lycée or equivalent and 117 get the *maturità*, or equivalent secondary-school diploma; 64 (6.4 per cent.) enter the university while only 22 (2.2 per cent.) gain a degree.[11]

Such figures indicate that there is a huge potential demand for higher education. Any generalized improvement in social well-being is likely to immediately mobilize a portion of the group currently excluded and to boost the present university population. Secondly, when only six out of a hundred people attain the level of higher education and only as few as two actually get a degree, it is difficult to believe that such a tiny minority is selected on the basis of merit alone and that educational selection is not biased by social discrimination. The points at which social selectivity can be detected will be examined in turn.

(a) *Chances of entry*. Table 8.II gives the percentage of sons of selected occupational strata enrolled as first-year students, compared with the distribution of these occupational groups in the total Italian population as given by the 1961 census.

Table 8.II—*Social class and access to the university*

	% first-year students by father's occupation		*% occupation in Italian population*
Occupational stratum	(1960—61)	(1964–65)	(1961)
Professional and entrepreneur	12.1	11.4	1.4
White collar	56.1	51.2	12.7
Worker	13.2	15.3	85.9

Source: 1961 census and ISTAT, *Annuario Statistico dell'Istruzione Italiana*.

It is clear then that the chances of getting into the university and of subsequent social mobility are very scarce for lower classes in Italy, so low in fact that one is led to question how far the new republican State has actually implemented the constitutional dictate that guarantees to all 'capable and worthy persons' access to higher education, irrespective of their economic means.

(b) *Delays and attrition rates.* The analysis of the social characteristics of those entering the university tells only one part of the story: during higher education a second kind of selection takes place. In part it is connected with simple attrition and in part it relates to the choice of fields of specialization. The tendency to drop out of university is not only very high, but it is clearly related to social status. The system allows free entrance and almost limitless prolongation of studies and repetition of exams, thus making it difficult to calculate the attrition rate exactly, as delays and the *fuori corso* interfere with input-output analysis. However, a first indication of the attrition rate can be given by Table 8.III, which tells how many out of 100 students enrolled each year take a degree within the proper time interval.

Table 8.III—*Percentage of first-year student cohorts getting their degree in the prescribed number of years (cohorts starting 1960–61)*

Discipline	% graduating in time
Medicine	40.4
Sciences	20.8
Law	18.4
Humanities	9.9
Engineering	9.3
Economics	3.3
Total	12.8

Source: Guido Martinotti, op. cit., p. 112.

All in all, only about 13 per cent of a cohort of students entering the university in a given year get through in time; the rest is made up of drop-outs and *fuori corso*, that is, students who will get their degree after a considerable delay, although the proportions of the two groups are difficult to estimate. That such delays may be considerable is indicated by the fact that, on average, of those graduating in any given year one-third is composed of regular students, one-third of students who are one or two years behind, and one-third of those who are late by three years or more (although this varies according to discipline studied).[12] At a rough approximation it can be said that one out of every two students enrolled drops out of university before the end of the course. The drop-out rate, however, is not evenly distributed throughout the length of the course: there is a peak after the first year, which accounts for one-third of the entire number dropping out, and then a second peak among the *fuori corso* enrolled for a good many years. The first group is composed of those who 'can't make it' and cannot afford to go on paying university fees for more than one year. The second group, on the contrary, is mainly composed of more well-to-do students, who can delay the decision to drop out until absorbed by working life to the point where a degree is no longer needed.

(c) *Differences in social background between first-year students and degree-holders.* In any case those from a lower social background also have a higher overall drop-out rate, as it can be seen that in all the faculties the percentage of sons of workers *decreases* markedly from the group of first-year students to the group of degree recipients. Conversely, the relative weight of students coming from a higher social background *increases* considerably as one passes from first-year students to degree-holders, which indicates the advantages enjoyed by those better equipped from a social point of view. Such an attrition can be most tellingly expressed by comparing the ratio of sons of upper-class origins to those of manual backgrounds among first-year students and degree-holders in Table 8.IV.

Table 8.IV—*Ratio of sons of upper classes to sons of workers*

Medicine	1.99	2.54
Sciences	1.17	2.00
Law	1.77	2.88
Humanities	0.75	1.19
Engineering	1.89	2.19
Economy	0.51	1.47

Source: Guido Martinotti, op. cit.

It is clear that even in those 'poorer' faculties like Economics and the Humanities, where in the first year there are more sons of workers enrolled than students from the upper classes, at graduation the situation is reversed.

(d) *Selection through disciplinary channels.* The fourth important mechanism of selection operates through the channeling of students from different social backgrounds into different faculties, that is, there are disciplines which tend to attract the richer students and others which do not. The characterization of the Faculties in terms of social origins and performance of students emerges clearly from the previous table. From this it appears that while Medicine and Law were the more socially discriminatory over all, Humanities and Economics, while having a 'poorer' initial intake, were very far from immune from this practice. Indeed, in faculites which are relatively 'open' of access, like Economics, although the proportions of sons of workers remains higher among degree recipients than in all other faculties, the *change in relative* weight of the sons of workers is more drastic. One factor accounts for much of the drop-out delays, and social discrimination within the universities, namely, that some of the students work.

(e) *The Student-Worker.* A limited but increasingly large part of the student body is composed of students who are employed occupationally during the university period. Since at most of the courses given in Italian universities attendance is not compulsory, students usually have a fairly substantial amount of time for alternative activities: politics, leisure, individual study or cultural activities, and, when needed, work.

Table 8.V—*Students by occupational position (1964–65) percentage of first-year students who work*

Discipline	Full-time	Part-time	Do not work
Medicine	1.5	2.4	96.1
Engineering	2.6	4.1	93.3
Law	7.1	4.0	88.3
Sciences	7.6	3.6	88.7
Humanities	8.4	6.2	85.2
Economics	22.2	7.7	69.9
Total	11.5	5.9	82.6

Source: *Annuario Statistico dell'Istruzione Italiana*, ISTAT

Table 8.V outlines some of the major aspects of the problem. First of all, it is clear that the great majority of students do not work during the university period. This is undoubtedly a direct consequence of the relatively high social origin of university students.[13] In fact the limited number of students having a job is more an indicator of a certain bourgeois mentality that emphasizes the dependency of the youth on the family, than of a lack of need. It is interesting to note that the percentage of working students *increases* in periods of economic boom and *decreases* in slump periods, and it is therefore inversely related to actual economic need. Furthermore the percentage of working students is strictly correlated with the degree of industrialization and *per capita* income in the twenty Italian regions. This is due both to the labour market—only favouring the employment of students under certain conditions—and to the cultural outlook of the petty bourgeoisie (above all in the southern and less developed regions), which is opposed to occupational activities of sons while at the university.

Dependence of students on the family is also emphasized by the fact that a very large proportion do actually live in the family household during university studies. This group constitutes about 80 per cent. of students in Milan (against around 40 per cent. in Paris), but is not representative, as southern universities cater more for the out-of-town student.

With the expansion of student numbers and the gradual extension of higher education to the less affluent strata there is bound to be a future increase in the number of students working. However, as this phenomenon is still small in scale, what accounts for the problem of the student-worker being felt so acutely in Italy and for it having constituted one of the major issues of student protest? The reasons can be best understood by confronting the two left columns of Table 8.V, which give the percentages of students working part-time and full-time. As becomes immediately clear, the common image of a student having a part-time job to 'work himself through' the university here applies to only a very tiny minority. The majority of working students are in fact studying workers, for whom the university is an activity marginal to a fully fledged occupational life.

The typical worker-student in Italy is a person who has entered an occupational career *before* university, and who seeks a degree in order to improve his position in the occupational structure. Obviously under such circumstances the cultural value of university education is practically nil. The studying worker is obliged to bet on a low-proficiency go-as-fast-as-you-can course. Even with this approach, courses are prolonged considerably: in one of the samples I analyzed, out of 100 students with a job, 62 per cent. were of 27 years of age or more, as compared with only 3 per cent. of those not working. Furthermore, their integration into adult rather than student life is indicated by the fact that twice as many working students are married as non-workers, twice as many have one or more child, and that even when politically active, they tend to be so outside the university, with low participation rates in university politics. Such a situation can develop to the point at which the link with the university has become so thin as to break.

More importantly, even when they succeed in gaining a degree the pay-off is nil or very small, because the occupational career is already in full swing, and the point of insertion had not been made at the level of degree-holder but at a lower one. In addition to this, during the period of study this double role has certainly reflected negatively on both studies and career, subtracting energies from both. All in all, students working full time constitute the very under-privileged category of a generally privileged student body. They are lured into the university by the apparently 'open' and easy system, which permits low attendance and presents the misleading image of awarding easy degrees.

Taken in conjunction, the data presented in these sections tend to support one fairly clear image of the Italian university. The university system operates so that access to it is 'open' in the sense that there is no merit selection for entrance (as for instance in the English system); however, once within the system a tough selection process takes place which is not primarily based on merit but rather on social selectivity. In other words, the system claims to be egalitarian, but is in fact only a *laissez-faire* system, which like all other *laissez-faire* policies favours those who are stronger in social and economic terms.

The structure of academic appointments

The career structure of Italian university professors may be divided into three 'lanes', which can be followed separately and independently but are more usually taken successively, and, at least in part, separately. In addition there is an important step which is in principle outside the path of the formal career but in practice has become a vital turning point along it. This is the *libera docenza*, a degree entitling the holder to teach in a university. The three positions are respectively those of *assistente* (i.e. instructors), *incaricato* (corresponding roughly to a post as 'assistant professor', 'reader', 'lecturer' or 'chargé de cours'), and finally *ordinario* (corresponding to full professor).

The following scheme gives a general idea of the career structure.

In order to understand the problems connected with the academic profession, and the extraordinary power and prestige currently entrusted to full professors, it is necessary to examine each of these three positions and the *libera docenza*, highlighting the content of the job, the modes of recruitment, and the recruiting agency.

The formal structure

(a) *Assistente*. The *assistente* is a person assigned to a particular chair, i.e. to one specific professor, with the task of helping him.[14]

The very name of this role, emphasizing relations with the professor, instead of 'instructor'—a term that would emphasize relations with students—gives an interesting clue to its character. The *assistente* is a rag-bag of a job[15] which implies strong personal relations with an almost complete dependence on the full professor, since future career promotion rests on his support.

Ideally graduates wishing to pursue an academic career should be enrolled as *assistenti* to do their apprenticeship in an Institute, but in practice the situation is quite different. The *assistente ordinario* is an established civil servant, paid by the state,[16] and the number of vacancies made available during recent years has been constantly below the actual demand for these posts. Being a tenured post, the

ENTRY

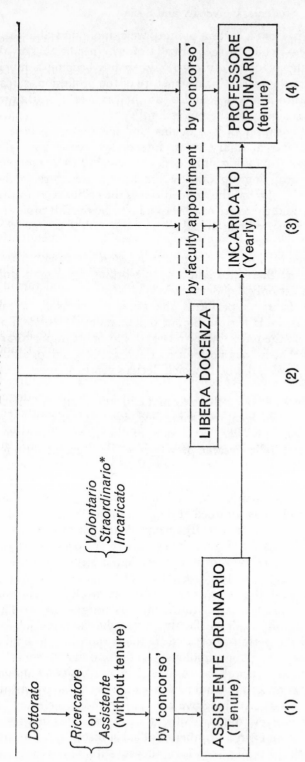

Usually the sequence is Doctorate and then 1, 2, 3, 4. (1) & (3) and (3) & (4) can be held cumulatively. (2) can be held cumulatively with all others, and is usually *required* for (3).

* In the text I do not refer specifically to marginal steps within the non-tenured role of *assistente*. These are temporary or obsolete roles.

Fɪɢ. 8.2

job of *assistente* is, from a certain point of view, more desirable than that of *incaricato*—which is theoretically of a higher level. For all these reasons the place of *assistente ordinario* has become a much coveted niche in the hierarchical structure of the profession, a real foothold for future promotion and a job that as a rule is attained after a certain seniority in the profession.[17]

Rigidity in the supply of jobs of this kind has created a host of supplementary and auxiliary roles, intended to cope with the growing needs of expanding universities. Typical of these complementary roles cropping up outside the formal structure is the *assistente volontario*, who has the same duties as the ordinary assistant, but is not paid, and therefore can be appointed by the full professor to whom he is going to be attached without any public competitive procedure.

Recently, the creation of new *assistente volontari* has been blocked by law; however, there are still 17,735 working in Italian universities as against only 8,388 *ordinari*.[18]

(b) *Incaricati*. The *Incaricato* performs the same functions as a full professor, that is, he is responsible for one or more courses.[19] The differences are in the lower salary received and, most important of all, in the fact that he has no tenure, and therefore cannot sit on the *Consiglio de Facoltà*, the body which decides yearly appointments of *incaricati*.

Anyone, even a person with no formal education but recognized as particularly knowledgeable in some field, can be given a teaching post as *incaricato*. However, possession of the *libera docenza* has become an almost indispensable prerequisite. The current ratio for all Italian universities is about three *incaricati* to one full professor.

(c) *Full professors*. At the top of the academic profession is the full professor with his 'chair'; the traditional institution of Italian academia. The chair is attained through a difficult and complex process and therefore is usually assigned to persons of great seniority.[20] It entails an extraordinary amount of prestige in the larger community, of power in the academic structure and of economic potential in the professional world.

Recruitment for full professors takes place at two levels. Nationally, the entire corporation of full professors assigns the *right* to hold a chair; locally a single faculty offers the concrete job by 'calling' one of the persons indicated by the corporation to hold a chair (or as the current terminology vividly puts it, to 'cover' a chair).[21] Whenever a vacancy occurs in a given university a national competition is set up and five full professors are elected to constitute the selection committee. These five men are themselves elected by a national constituency composed of all the full professors in a given discipline plus those from a number of allied subjects. (In the case of borderline subjects like sociology the constituency can be as large as one thousand full professors.) The elected commissioners evaluate the publications and academic qualifications of the candidates, and designate three possible 'chair-holders', in rank order. The faculty where the chair is vacant, or any other faculty, can then call one of the three designated scholars, within the following two years. The only proviso is that someone of higher ranking has the right to a job before a lower ranking candidate.

If rather cumbersome, this system seems universalistic, and it might be argued that complexity is not too high a price to pay for ensuring selection based on merit which has been ascertained with such a high degree of consensus. However, in practice, this system has given rise to one of the most sophisticated electoral machines ever. It represents one of the best examples of how the most carefully designed formal democratic procedures can be turned into particularistic practices.

(d) *Libera docenza.* The *libera docenza* is a degree given by the academic corporation through the Ministry of Education, entitling the incumbent to give a course in a university. As such the *libera docenza* is a relic of the middle ages and the system of *disputationes* (scholarly contests), or more recently from the German system of *Privatdozent*. The title can be obtained by anybody, even someone with no formal education at all, provided that he has contributed to scientific development in a given field. In current practice, it is a necessary prerequisite for the inception of a *teaching* career in a university, and in this sense it has the same functions as the Ph.D. in the Anglo-Saxon system.

It differs, however, from the Ph.D., for it is not given by a single university but by the entire academic corporation,[22] represented by a five-man commission *appointed* by the Consiglio Superiore dell'Istruzione universitaria. There are currently 17,407 *libera docenti*; of these, however, only 6,114 gave a course in 1967/68, and of the total number of *libera docenti* 11,264 are in medicine. This gives an indication of the way this title is used for extra-university purposes. Partly because of this the *libera docenza* has been under heavy criticism for many years, and has recently been abolished by a law that anticipates in part the larger reform law currently under discussion by Parliament.[23]

The dynamics of a profession

In practice the career of an Italian academic is built around the following steps: entering an Institute, gaining the patronage of a full professor, becoming an assistant, getting the *libera docenza*—the first important recognition by the corporation—obtaining a teaching post as *incaricato*, and finally becoming full professor after having 'won' a chair.

The entire profession is dominated by the very unique and enduring relationship that becomes established at the beginning of his career between the young postgraduate and a full professor. The first step is entry to an Institute, and comes about by a process which can best be described as 'hanging around'. During this period the gatekeeper is usually some senior assistant supervising the dissertation. If the work done arouses the interest of the professor he will hint that he is available to help the young scholar.

The scarcity of formal jobs available and the consequent vagueness of the role-status set of the prospective scholar are the two major structural factors that mould the relation between tbe young scholar and the *maestro*, which will be feudal in the most literal sense of the word, involving exchange of protection in return for services and loyalty. Though this kind of relation has been rightly criticized, and despite the fact that most of the young assistants will tend to object to it in principle, as to all conditions of personal dependence, most of the individuals involved will not experience it in a negative way. All in all, however, the diffusiveness and particularism of the relationship thus established will induce a very high degree of more or less conscious conformism on the part of the pupil.

The young assistant must find his way without knowing the exact delineation of his rights, and depending entirely on the good disposition of his master. Any kind of move intended to define this relation by shifting it to a more universalistic and specific plane is bound to introduce strains and to seriously jeopardize the career of the pupil.[24] During the first phase the young assistant will be encouraged to take his first steps in the 'scientific world', usually by reworking his dissertation into a fully fledged book, or by writing one or two articles to be published in scientific periodicals under the control of the *maestro*. Also the professor will have to 'settle' his assistant from the economic point of view, and in this task he will bring into play the complex network of the academic and professional enterprises in which he is involved. In the most favourable circumstances the professor will have enough power to assign a place of *assistente ordinario*, or some kind of scholarship or research job within the university structure. If not, he will find some other extramural job, varying from occasional editorial jobs to a place in a public or private concern.

Obviously the greater the power of the master, the greater the network of connections he will control, and the more chances for the assistant to find a good position. If the power of the *maestro* is limited, the assistant has a poor marginal field and is hardly able to survive the struggle for additional resources with more powerful competitors. In this case the *maestro* will not be in a position to protect his pupil in any significant way. Differences of this kind depend on the prestige of the discipline, and of the professor, and of his skills in fund-raising.

The first foothold the young assistant must gain (and correspondingly the first concrete show of the effectiveness of the professor's protection) is a job as *assistente ordinario*, which will give him a definite place in the Institute as well as a safe and durable source of financial support. Places for assistants are made available by the Ministry of Education, and their allocation—first among different universities, then among different faculties within each university, and eventually among different institutes within each faculty—reflects a distribution of resources which is definitely influenced by the distribution of power at each level. Powerful 'bosses' of large institutes in 'strong' universities will get places for assistants more frequently than others.

Once the vacancy is assigned to a single institute it is then filled through a competition national in scope, but administered by the university. Since the head of the committee which examines the candidates is the full professor to whom the assistant will be assigned, it is clear that the public form of the contest is a mere formality, because nobody without a reasonable chance of being the winner will ever dare to pose his candidature. Actually I know of no such contest where there were more than the usual three candidates—all from the same institute, of course.[25]

Here we can see a first example of what I call the particularistic universalism so typical of many aspects of the Italian academic life. What one finds surprising is not the fact that the professor will assign the job to someone who has been working in the Institute and whom he knows, appreciates and will have to work with closely for years to come. Here, of course, the main distortion, the façade of a public contest, arises from the fact that *assistente ordinario* is an established civil servant, and therefore his recruitment must be made through procedures established by the state. This, however, while it provides an explanation, does not reduce the absurdity of the situation. The scarcity of jobs available accounts for the fact that in general the assistantship does not come at the very beginning of a career. This means that for a number of years the young scholar is obliged to moonlight (do several jobs at once) to compound a plurality of sources of revenue. The salary of an assistant is very low (starting at about $250 per month), and it is not uncommon that at the time the assistantship is received the outside income is already higher than the one given by the university.

In any case, by this time the person is already involved in a net of semi-professional connections. Thus the outward orientation, which at the beginning was absolutely necessary for survival, now becomes a comfort difficult to renounce, and later on a necessary complement of the professor's power-structure, to be manipulated in turn for the next generation of young assistants. This is a typical unintended consequence of centralized bureaucratic systems. Higher salaries cannot be paid because the state's budget is always strained, but with lower salaries civil servants are driven to moonlighting.

The second important step in the academic career is the *libera docenza*. While the assistantship is something that is held in the nest of an institute, under the protecting arm of the master-professor, the *libera docenza* represents the first overture to the larger and more dangerous world of the corporation, and is taken when the candidate is considered to have produced sufficient publications.[26] This 'overture' is carefully orchestrated by the professor, who, if a serious boss, will have to be on the commission, or at least will have to have some good friends on it. Once the *docenza* is attained the young academician moves in an entirely different realm, and he has to be given an *incarico* in some university. Usually there is a pattern whereby the *incarico* is obtained in a smaller university, different from the alma mater, where he has more chance to be known by other scholars and to establish the necessary contacts that will help him to the chair. Later on in the career he can work his way back to the larger university. This territorial mobility is a very well established pattern, and gives rise to something very close to colonialism by the major universities. There are two major circuits, a northern and a southern one: the northern one gravitates around Milan and Turin, and the southern one around Naples. They overlap to some extent in Rome.[27]

This is a stage in the academic career during which Italian professors travel a lot, come to know the train schedules very well, write a second book, and while consolidating their professional prestige in and out of the university prepare themselves for the last leap forward. This comes when a chair is available and the *maestro* is ready to go into the field for an electoral campaign. Unless one is 'carried' by some professor there are very slight chances indeed of being selected for the group of three designated for the chair. As the professional committee-men are elected, the ways to success are not very different from those that may be found in most other political machines.

The *concorso* is the real testing ground where the power and prestige of the feudal lord is brought to bear. First of all he has to be located within one of the two large, though vaguely defined, parties—the 'lay' group or the 'Catholic' one. These could be considered as the larger parties, and in fact each year before the contests begin these two groups hold their caucuses where nominations are made for each chair. But probably the most important group is the faction, known under the technical name of 'school'. A school regroups on a disciplinary or university basis and includes the pressure group comprised of the close 'friends' of the full professor and 'pupils' (whom he previously helped to a chair) plus the friends of the latter. There are powerful schools in Turin, Naples, the Sicilian universities, and others.

Finally the prestige and power of the prospective commissioner is of great importance, and here is where the full potentiality of his 'baronial' power has to be brought to bear, in terms of the strength of his field (how many jobs he controls) and in terms of the alliances he has been able to establish. The campaign will develop under the form of exchange of letters, sometimes written by the professor, sometimes by a team of two or three. These will be addressed to friendly prospective voters and will state that the professor would like to be elected to such and such commission (sometimes also mentioning the intent to 'carry' such and such candidate), and solicits a vote. Finally election day comes, and in all Italian universities each professor will cast his vote for a plurality of contests, having committed himself to support candidates in several of them. During this period the prospective candidate for the chair (the one who will be 'carried') will also have to work, tapping his own independent connections and helping with the correspondence.

After the ballots are scrutinized and the given commissioner is in fact elected, there comes the second and most delicate phase of the operation, that of forming a majority on the commission. At this point there develops a very interesting kind of combinatorial game. Five commissioners, supporting a candidate each, must combine to form a majority of three in order to designate the three 'winners', or chair recipients.[28]

At the end of the long and difficult road described, the once young graduate, if he finally succeeds, has been 'carried' to a chair. At this point he will have to start the cycle again, by consolidating his power and academic prestige, and by fighting the necessary battles in order to provide the means of survival and progress for the young graduates who start working with him.

Men or structures? The problems of institutional change

Having now examined the formal structure and part of the actual workings of the academic profession it becomes apparent that in Italian universities life for a lone rider is bound to be 'nasty, brutish and short'. For the rest, life may be long but pretty brutish as well. None the less it would be preposterous to state that competition for jobs, academic nepotism, and the formation of professional cliques are the curse of Italian universities alone. Why, then, should these features be more prominent in the Italian university system? In the first place one must recognize that it is difficult to assess how 'democratic'—or rather meritocratic—a system really is. Differential distribution of power, and selection through particularistic evaluations, are the lot of all organizations, and precise measurement and comparison of the weighting of these factors in different systems are not easy. Even in Italy good scholars succeed in the career and bad ones are discarded. Outstanding cases of the contrary are the exception rather than the rule.

What can be assessed with more precision, however, is the degree of variance between the official values and goals endorsed by the formal structure of the system and the actual practices. Furthermore, it appears that it is in this very discontinuity that we can identify one of the peculiar aspects of the Italian system, namely the development of particularistic practices behind the secure screen of universalistic rules and procedures.

The entire recruitment system, for instance, based on the *concorsi*, has been devised to avoid personal biases in the selection of candidates. This end should be achieved by means of the elaborate 'democratic' or 'universalistic' procedures described above. As we have seen, however, these procedures seem to shield particularism and misjudgement on the part of individual professors.

Take for instance the notion that professors should be selected by a committee representing the entire corporation, which has practically no connection with the faculty where the professor is supposed to be appointed. In this way no incentive is provided for individual universities to better their lot. In addition, a professor sitting on the committee will not bear any of the consequences deriving from his having favoured one of his least outstanding pupils. First of all he will not have him in his faculty; on the contrary, in most cases this is the only way of getting rid of him. Secondly, although those on the inside will know it, for the public at large the candidate has been selected by the commission, not by him.

It is often said that the system would operate better if men working in it were more honest. This argument is frequently brought forward by the older professors, who claim that in the past the *concorso* system was more equitable and that professional standards prevailed over personal interest. But if this were so, it would raise exactly the point we have to explain—why have personal interests become so powerful?

The search for an explanation of this problem leads us, indirectly, to more general questions. Two major factors can be identified as important in this connection. Firstly the particular structure of decision-making within the university, and secondly, a factor I would term the 'psychology of scarcity', induced by the scarcity of resources available, which has been rendered more acute by expansion in recent years.

As we have seen, the decision-making structure of the Italian university is not characterized by control through a 'lay' body like a Board of Trustees or analogous institution. The body where all decisions about resource allocation at the faculty level are taken is the Consiglio di Facoltà, which is composed exclusively of full professors, as is the Academic Senate. Such an organizational model, while avoiding conflicts between faculty and administration so typical of many other systems, is not an efficient decision-making structure. It functions on the group-of-peers model in which the prevailing allocative pattern is by equal shares. Planning, which requires priorities, is by definition impossible, as each member is led to defend his own baliwick, and will try to stick his neck out as little as he can. Also, a system like this gives rise to chronic scarcity, as equal division, when the global resources are not abundant, usually means rationing all shareholders: and so a 'psychology of scarcity' has always dominated the Italian academic mentality. Such a system could still work passably well when the Italian university system was small and balanced in its growth, that is, before World War II. But as it began to develop, mainly under external pressures—from the input of students—the delicate equilibrium broke down.

That is why, in my opinion, the ethos of the academic profession in Italian universities has become strikingly reminiscent of the 'amoral familism' described by Banfield.[29] The one serious consequence of a system so structured is its constitutional inertia and inadaptability to change. Despite the rapid growth of the student body, the turmoil of the past two years and the changes occurring in Italian society, a legal reform of the university has been under preparation since 1962, and it is still far from finished. Therefore it may be useful to conclude this analysis by referring very briefly to the single factor which in recent years has succeeded in inducing some changes in Italian universities, namely the student movement.[30] Viewed from the standpoint of 1971 the changes introduced by the student movement are in fact much less relevant than those promised or expected in 1968. They are however substantial, not so much at the level of structural change—which has remained more or less unmodified—but at the attitudinal level, i.e. affecting precisely those aspects which no reform law could ever hope to change. Today relations between students and professors, and several other facets of university life, have assumed a form that nobody could have imagined three or four years ago. Even if the movement is now declining, there is no doubt that some of its effects in this area will last and will constitute the basis for future additional changes.

Limitations of space preclude a full analysis of the Italian student movement and of its phase of development. Perhaps one can best understand its effects on the university structure by comparing some of the major issues raised by the students in 1968 with later developments. The three major issues were (a) the struggle against professional power; (b) the *prise de conscience* of the students' role; and (c) the political organization of the movement. To describe these three aspects in detail I shall draw from an analysis I made at the time.

The first issue received the most thorough elaboration. 'The first goal of the assembly and of the demonstration we were setting up,' said the chronicler of the Turin occupation, 'was to *organize a permanent fight against the power of the academic authorities*, capable of challenging such a power. A challenge does not consist of removing the power, nor of a simple protest. It means *creating continuous difficulties in the exercise of this power*.'

In this sense, the students occupying the University of Turin accomplished unimagined progress against professorial authority. Almost without exception, the professors reacted negatively. Their reactions showed how deeply this kind of personal challenge touched them. The vision of the magnificent rector of the University of Turin lecturing, surrounded by policemen while six officers tried to convince one student to take his hat off, is almost farcical. The Turin movement was successful largely because it focused almost entirely on the question of academic authority and rejected more traditional 'political' issues. After the example of Turin, few professors in Italy dared to confront a student assembly. The second great issue—that of the student's role—was elaborated primarily by the sociology students of Trento, who saw the student as a commodity in a larger capitalist system of production. In their view, the problem was to justify the revolutionary potential of the students in largely Marxist terms. As university students were a privileged élite, it was difficult to set their action in a scheme of class politics. Indeed, the students at Turin flatly rejected any class identification with the workers, stating that 'on the basis of past experience, it is perhaps better that the "bourgeois" stay with the "bourgeois" and the workers with the workers'. But as the revolt widened, so did the desire to extend it outside the universities to achieve a closer theoretical and practical identification with the working class. Actually, this issue remained unresolved and was dealt with on a personal or local basis. The students throughout the revolt remained much more a class *für sich* than a class *an sich*, to use a definition employed by Carlo Donolo, an Italian sociologist closely involved in the student movement.

The third issue was closely connected with the preceding one: What should the movement do, and what organizational form should its leadership adopt? Even on this issue there was a rather clear-cut difference as to goals inside the university and outside of it. Inside the university, the main theme was obviously the conflict with the academic powers. The demands for increased student power ranged from a simple request for co-management to a more drastic claim of 'self-management'. A theory of so called 'structural space', a sort of student *Lebensraum*, was developed. This approach was first adopted by the architecture students in their long fight; it consisted of achieving a certain degree of power within the university and on its basis continuing student political activity and developing new lines of action. The architecture students in particular were able to secure wide areas of power. 'Structural space' has probably been the most effective of the students' political proposals. When it has been achieved, a certain amount of faculty co-operation has usually proved necessary.

For a sizeable portion of the movement, 'structural space' was a final aim, but for other groups it was only an instrument to create new militancy. The students from Trento in particular theorized in favour of this second position, claiming university unrest to be a false target, useful mainly because it can be easily created. The ensuing conflict, they claimed, was more important because it helped select new active members to be socialized and then put to work with the working class.

Thus one part of the student leadership made clear effort to orient action mainly outside the university.

In a way, this was the more militant position. At the crucial moment of the revolt, the student leadership tried to take the conflict outside the university much in the same way as the French students did a few weeks later, but with far less success. The reason for the failure remains among the unresolved issues of the Italian student movement.[31]

Looking back at these issues with the experience of the past two years we can add a fourth issue, which was less apparent at the time, or rather was considered by the student movement as merely instrumental. This is constituted by the complex of demands for greater liberalization of access to the university and for the reduction of both rigid curricula and rigorous selection. This kind of demand was considered as instrumental, and in some quarters was also criticized for its corporative character.

However, it was precisely these reasons which enhanced its potential for the mobilization of even the less politicized part of the student body. Thus the student movement returned to this issue with increasing frequency, and the climax was reached when at the University of Milan one professor was held for several hours because he refused to comply with a tacit agreement between students and the faculty over the possibility of avoiding written recording of failure in an examination.

The argument on the students' side was that since life chances have been found to be correlated with social status, any kind of merit screening is inherently a process of social discrimination. Therefore, it is agreed, exams should be rendered easier, and abolished in due course. Not surprisingly this line of attack was the one to which both the professorial body and the government yielded most completely. It obviously constituted the point of least resistance, and the students saw their opportunity. The faculty and the government perceived in it an easy way to reduce tensions within the University—by granting concessions which did not involve structural changes. Indeed the only laws the University has passed since 1968 have concerned greater liberalization of access to the university and the elimination of rigid curricula. The informal and almost unanimous shift by the faculty to easier exams and higher grades made up the remainder of the changes taking place.

During this time, however, the sound political implications contained in the students' original argument were lost along the road, and the students' pressure merely brought about the intended consequence of a debasement of the legal value of the degree. Talk about the so-called 'dequalification' of the degree and the spectre of increasing 'intellectual unemployment' began to taunt students and all persons concerned. This also coincided with the growing realization that as the number of degree-holders increases, the labour market is less and less able to absorb them at the proper occupational level. More and more 'doctors' are found working in purely routine roles in industry, marketing, public or private administration. This prompted widespread concern over the so-called 'proletarianization' of the middle classes. Thus the students find themselves caught between the need for greater democratization of access to higher education and fear of the negative consequences produced by a gap between the requirements of the labour market and university output.

Finally it must be noted that excessive concentration on this issue diverted fuel and energy away from the search for wider, structural change in the University. But another factor, more closely bound up with the internal dynamics of the student movement, also contributed to this.

The year 1968 was obviously one of unprecedented and enthusiastic participation at all levels, with the exception of the older and more conservative part of the teaching body. The pressure to introduce changes in university structure fell short of the aim, in large part because of the outward orientation soon adopted by the student movement. The student movement grew 'political' very rapidly by correctly identifying the ties between the university and the rest of society. The fear of blunting the political momentum of the protest by limiting it to university problems and the desire to take part in what then seemed a vast overall change in the wider society made the movement leave many more specific demands for changes in the university to the more moderate groups.[32]

After 1968 it is possible to detect a somewhat similar pattern in the dynamics of the movements based in several of the major centres of the revolt, Torino, Milan, Rome, Trento. The movement had been started by a militant *avant-garde* on the basis of some kind of concrete issue—teaching methods, exams, controls on faculty powers, and so on. These issues commanded a large following, constituting the majority of the student body. In general the attitude of the faculty tended to be very negative, even toward the more acceptable demands. Confronted with these refusals, the movement grew in unity and political consciousness.

At the second stage, however, some of the requests came to be accepted, especially as among the staff those more conservative members who appeared inadequate under the circumstances were put aside by the more dynamic and adaptable elements.

It is at this point that the unity of the student movement begins to break. On the right, the moderate groups tend to regard these achievements as satisfactory. On the left, the more militant groups are afraid of being trapped in a 'reformist' kind of policy and tend to radicalize the issues. Little by little, all the major university centres experienced this kind of gradual breakdown of the student movement into a series of minor factions, generally in a state of perennial conflict. At the University of Milan, where the original student movement had developed into a fully fledged political grouping, and where the movement has lasted longer than in other places, this kind of disintegration has been experienced during recent months.

If we try to take stock of the consequences that the last few years have had for the three factors characterizing the Italian university, which were referred to at the beginning of this analysis, it can be seen that student protest has affected only one. Neither the legal rigidity nor the vested interest structure has been changed in any significant way. On the other hand, access to the university and an ever-increasing growth of the student body have been facilitated. In addition, the student movement undoubtedly contributed to changing the overall cultural and attitudinal climate towards higher education.

In conclusion, and taking all these elements into consideration, it can be seen that the real strain on the university structure has yet to come, and will develop in the next two or three years when the increasing student numbers will tax not only the organizational, but also the physical resources of the university. Whether the student movement can then develop again and initiate the change will depend on several conditions, of which an important one is the general political situation of Italian society. Whatever its future development may be, it is clear that the student movement has become a political force to be reckoned with by university and society.

Notes

1. During the sixties the prevailing view, based on manpower-need forecasts made by SVIMEZ and CENSIS, held that a shortage of university-level manpower was to be expected. More recently a contrary trend pointing toward increasing 'intellectual unemployment' is being detected. See Marzio Barbagli, 'Scuola e occupazione intellettuale', *il Manifesto*, 12, 1970, pp. 51–58.
2. Among private universities the most important ones are the Catholic University, with one major seat in Milan and branches in Rome and Piacenza, the University Luigi Bocconi of Milan, a well-known business school, and the Politecnico in Milan and Turin, which are semi-public in character.
3. There are for instance smaller universities where the number of degrees given is larger than the number of first-year students enrolled, on the average. This means that these universities receive students who, failing elsewhere, enrol here for the last years and for the dissertation. See Gino Martinoli, *L'università come impresa* (La Nuova Italia, Firenze 1967).
4. See Jacques le Goff, *Les intellectuels au Moyen Age* (It. trans. Milan 1959), pp. 99–100.
5 In the majority of courses this freed students from the need to attend lectures. There are, however, cases in which attendance was needed in practice, if not in principle, in order to pass the exams in Engineering and Architecture and in some of the scientific subjects. Usually the average student in most of the faculties would attend two or three courses regularly and read the *dispensa* for the others.
6. For further details on the organization of the Italian university see Gino Martinoli, *L'università come impresa* (La Nuova Italia, Firenze 1967), and the series of studies published by the Institute Carlo Cattaneo of Bologna, A.A.V.V. *Studi sull' Università Italiana* (il Mulino, Bologna 1960).
7. *Università: L'Ipotesi Rivoluzionaria* (Marsilio, Padova 1968), p. 42.
8. Interestingly enough the increase in the number of students was not only due to draft deferments, but to a more general phenomenon, since during the first two years of the war the relative increase was steeper in the female student population.

9. This, however, is also a misleading indicator, as there are small universities with a fully fledged faculty and student numbers, and large universities with about 100,000 students, as in Rome, which have not had a comparable increase in the professorial ranks.

10. It would take too much space to reproduce here all the steps of this revised estimate: see G. Martinotti, *Gli Studenti Universitari* (Marsilio Editori, Padova 1969), Chapter 1.

11. Alberto Valentini, *Spreco di talenti e condizionamento delle famiglie italiane* (n.d., Rome).

12. For computation and sources, see *Gli Studenti Universitari*, op. cit., Ch. 3.

13. In other comparable situations a larger share of the student population add to their support during studies with a job of some sort. In France, for instance, 31 per cent. of male students and 22 per cent. of female ones have a job outside the university. More than half the males and 40 per cent. of the females add incomes from an occupational activity to other sources of support at the University. (See Pierre Bourdieu and Jean-Claude Passeron, *Les étudiants et leurs études* (Mouton, Paris 1964), p. 25.

14. Actually the role requirements of an *assistente* are rather vague. Out of a complex law of 35 articles which minutely regulates all the economic and administrative aspects of the bureaucratic life of an *assistente* only the following two lines refer to his duties: 'The *assistente* helps the professor in scientific research and in the teaching activity, with particular regard to tutorial hours.' Art. 3, par. I°, legge *18, Marzo 1958, n. 349 G.U.*, n.95, 1958, 19 Aprile.

15. A recent survey found that assistants of various categories dedicated 21.8 per cent. of their time to tutorials with students, 45.1 per cent. to personal study and research, 20.8 per cent. to professional activity within the institute, 5.9 per cent. to administrative duties, and 6.4 per cent. to contact with the professor. (See: *Gli assistenti universitari e liberi docenti in Italia*, Metron, serie C. vol. IV, Rome 1969, p. 109). These data, however, are most certainly biased in favour of study and research.

16. Except in private universities, where there are different conditions.

17. According to the survey quoted above only 18 per cent. of the *assistenti* with tenure were under 30 years of age, and the average age was 36. Op cit., p. 163.

18. Paradoxically the elimination of the *assistenti volontari* has raised additional difficulties. Formerly a young graduate willing to enter the academic profession could be given, if not a salary, at least a formal role in the academic structure. The voluntary assistantship has now been replaced by a special kind of scholarship given to young so-called 'researchers'. However, the number of these scholarships is again rather limited, and most of the aspirants to an academic career must face a period of very anxious uncertainty at the very beginning of the career. Other complementary roles are those of the *assistente incaricato* and of the *assistente straordinario*, but we do not need to go into further detail here.

19. It is possible to accumulate up to two courses. It is also possible (note 2) to hold one *incarico* with the post of assistant and of full professor. In the case of pluralism, however, the salary of the second job is reduced to about 40 per cent. Formerly it was possible for full professors to have more than one additional *incarico*, and for a long time this had been a traditional way of moonlighting for full professors. Now, however, the trend is toward limiting this procedure.

20. Full professors are established civil servants; they have tenure practically for life—that is until retirement at the age of 70, with an additional five years on full salary, but without teaching duties.

21. Interestingly enough, some of the technical jargon betrays aspects of the profession. In Italian one does not 'give' a course, one 'holds' a course. This emphasizes the fact that a course is more important in its 'job' connotation than in its 'service' meaning.

22. Originally the *libera docenza* was given locally by universities, and, since the beginning, it had the character of an academic degree coveted by local professionals outside academia. The *libera docenza* has been subsequently centralized in order to eliminate local corruption and abuses connected with the granting of it.

23. Another feature that was initially connected with the *docenza* was the practice (going back to the Middle Ages and now found more recently in the German system) of students paying professors giving courses. This apparently gave rise to abuses.

24. This explains in large part why assistants are very reluctant to engage in corporative fights against full professors. Strikes, for example, are very difficult to organize because each striker is confronted individually with the master. This obviously varies from faculty to faculty, and also in relation to the attitude of the full professor, but assistants of the more authoritarian and conservative professors have very little room to manoeuvre.

25. Three because for each contest there is one winner and two declared 'apt' (*idonei*), i.e. who can be assigned a job without further contest, should a vacancy occur within the following two years.
26. It would take too long to describe here all the antics connected with the provision that the publications must be issued one year before the exams, which gives rise to a fantastic process of books being registered before they are written, with a cover, a title, and blank pages inside.
27. See A.A.V.V. *La popolazione universitaria* (il Mulino, Bologna 1960), pp. 139–140, for statistical data on this subject.
28. Although data are lacking, it seems that during the past commissions usually decided unanimously. This now happens very seldom, if ever. No doubt this is another indication of the downgrading of the system, or better, an indicator that the 'interests' of each commissioner are much stronger. See below one proposed explanation of this development.
29. Edward C. Banfield, *The Moral Basis of a Backward Society* (Free Press, Glencoe 1958).
30. An analysis of the Italian student movement would obviously require much more space than can be devoted to it within the present framework. Literature on the subject has been very abundant, especially in the years 1968–69. For an historical overview of the student movement in Italy, see my article: 'The Positive Marginality', in Seymour Martin Lipset and Philip G. Altback (eds.), *Students in Revolt* (Houghton, Boston 1969).
31. See article quoted above, pp. 196, 198.
32. For more detail on this problem, see the survey I edited for the O.E.C.D. *Seminar on the crisis in higher education: role of the students in the academic community. Students' proposals and demands concerning renewal of higher education* (Italy, C.E.R.I./S.H.E./1969). See also the bibliography prepared on the same occasion.

9. BRITAIN

Colin Crouch

The student revolt in Britain has probably been the quietest and most restrained of the contemporary outbreaks of protest which have emerged from the student communities of most industrial societies. Unlike, for example, the French students, those in Britain have been unable to draw on a tradition of taking to the barricades: the left-wing tradition within British universities has been a predominantly intellectual one, as opposed to activist. Radicals in the current revolt have had to take their historical models from other societies rather than from their own, and have tended to take contemporary ones, such as Berkeley and Paris. In addition to the evidence of the traditional non-violence of British politics, one can search for explanations for the passivity of the British student revolt in terms of institutional variations in the universities of different societies. The characteristic smallness of the British university, the frequency of staff–student contact on a personal level, and similar factors, may be invoked in explanation. No doubt these elements have been relevant, but there is an unreality about attempts to construct total explanations on this basis. Arguments that see student revolt as a response to crowding and poor facilities are especially vulnerable; if this were an important factor then student revolt in Britain would have been virtually confined to the colleges of technology, whose conditions are far inferior to those of the universities; but in practice the very reverse has been the case.[1]

One reason for the difficulty of comparison based on such quantitative institutional data is the close inter-relationship between local university-based issues and wider political problems in any particular manifestation of protest. Second, there are differences in any occurrence of revolt between the behaviour of the small leadership group which frequently sets the tone of the event and the wider number of supporters who are needed for its success. Finally, comparison is made more difficult by the subjectivity of reactions. For example, it is not enough to talk objectively of a growth in the size of university institutions, or of restrictiveness of disciplinary rules; at least as relevant will be the way in which that growth is felt to be taking place, or the degree of freedom that students believe they ought to possess. This problem, which is of course fundamental to any comparative study, becomes particularly important with such volatile groups as contemporary students, whose attitudes tend to be, paradoxically, at once passionately held and transitory.

A more fruitful approach is to try to characterize the student revolt in terms of the issues which it selects for attention, the modes of action it adopts, the particular balance between local situation and wider politics that it achieves, and the relation of these activities to a particular ideological position. In this way one can hope to achieve some understanding of the causes and characteristics of the phenomenon, and on this basis comparison may be attempted. It is this approach which is developed below. Discussion will revolve around the following points:

1. With very few exceptions, manifestations of student protest in Britain have been short in duration, limited in scope and size, and restrained in action.

2. The protest has covered a varied but limited range of issues and, with the exception of one or two recurring themes, has tended to follow certain tides of fashion. Successive waves of protest follow a succession of issues.

3. As in other societies, the strength of a student revolt in Britain has varied with the extent to which it has been possible to relate wider political problems to the more local questions of university development. For success, the local issue has to be deeply felt, and its relation to the wider problem clear. It is characteristic of the British situation that the possibility of establishing such global-local relationships has been limited. This is one of the explanations for the restraint of British student revolt. To the extent that such activity has been successful, it has concerned itself with three broad underlying themes: authority, community, and the relationship between university and society.

4. The selection of issues which achieve any degree of success depends upon their potential for incorporation into the particular concerns of what may loosely be termed the 'new left'. It is the new left which has taken the initiative and held the lead within university protests, and it is in the universities that the new left has had its most important impact in Britain.

5. Although several different groups comprise what we term here the new left, only one point of internal division is of great importance to our discussion: that between those who belong to the avowedly Marxist tradition and those who adhere to the cult of spontaneity of the 'underground'. It is the universities which have provided the opportunity for temporary coalitions between these groups, and a student revolt will be at its strongest where this coalition appears most logically coherent.

Central issues

Protest in Britain has exhibited a recurrence of certain themes, with a tendency to follow a tidal pattern.[2] There is also considerable similarity in the type of activity displayed in the course of a protest. The first issue to gather widespread support was the search for student participation in the government of universities. This emerged as one issue among others in the first protest, at the London School of Economics and Political Science in winter 1966–67. It was then taken up by a succession of universities over the next couple of years, becoming the official policy of the National Union of Students, and finally the accepted view of both university vice-chancellors and politicians.[3, 4] As we shall see, this apparent consensus masks considerable disagreements on the implications of 'participation'.

At about the same time that participation was becoming an issue, the practice of disrupting political meetings addressed by speakers of whom students disapproved intensified. The first victims tended to be members of the Labour Government, but the focus of hostility gradually concentrated on figures of the racialist right. Probably the most important of such incidents concerned not a politician, but a scientist at the Government's Porton Down research centre where work is carried out on biological warfare. The dispute was significant, not merely because of the scope of the crisis it created within the university and the concern over biological warfare it stimulated, but because it provided an opportunity for the militant students to spell out their doctrine of intolerance for speakers of whom they disapproved.

Two final themes which have attracted recurrent interest are those of race (particularly with references to Southern Africa) and of the Vietnam War. Although several of the incidents relating to them have been external to the university itself, they have on occasions become internal. There have been attempts at staging Vietnam protests within the university, and universities have been attacked for suggested links with South Africa, Rhodesia and other supporters of racialism.

In the context of these recurrent major themes, other issues have held sway for short periods. The French événements of May 1968 were the subject of (not particularly successful) solidarity strikes and attempts at imitation. In the same month there was a massive revolt, not in the universities, but in colleges of art, questioning the content of art education. This was not, however, a 'parochial' issue since the critique of art education was related to the wider context of capitalism.[5] In June 1968 there was a limited wave of examination boycotts, again linked with a broader opposition to the concept of manipulation and categorization considered to be involved in examinations.[6] In the autumn of 1968 the increased intensity of conflict between extreme radicals and the police had multiple repercussions in Britain. The notion of the 'disruptive sit-in', which had developed in the U.S.A., was imitated by a massive but peaceable march in London, on the issue of Vietnam, which included an occupation of the London School of Economics for a weekend as a place of 'sanctuary' and medical assistance. By 1969 the level of conflict appeared to have escalated, but closer inspection suggests that in fact the left was experiencing increasing difficulty in its attempts to discover issues that would really galvanize student dissent into strong action. The above discussion gives some brief indication of the constant striving for issues; in 1969 the two major series of incidents were in fact triggered off by reactions to student unrest itself. In other words, the movement was turning back upon itself. The first issue involved a major crisis at the L.S.E. over the erection of gates by the School authorities, mainly in order to deal effectively with future sit-ins. Students tore down the gates and there followed a three-week closure of the School, the dismissal of two members of staff, court proceedings against certain staff and students, and disruptive and damaging protests. The second focus of disorder was the visit to certain universities of a select committee of the House of Commons which was investigating student unrest.

In the following academic year, 1969–70, the first signs of unrest concentrated on the question of relationships with Southern Africa, but the main burden of protest was outside the university and concerned opposition to a tour of Britain by a South African rugby team. Early in 1970, however, there was an episode of intense internal conflict following a sit-in at the University of Warwick, in the course of which students had invaded administrative offices and examined confidential files which were found to contain evidence of political information kept on staff and students. There followed sit-ins at several universities backing a demand that students should be allowed to inspect their own files.

As far as tactics are concerned, the major form of protest has been the sit-in or occupation. This does not simply involve taking over a building in order to prejudice its normal functioning: in the course of the sit-in a series of activities and discussions develop, sometimes being formally articulated as a 'free university'. A variant on the occupation is the disruptive sit-in, which involves more active steps to prevent the functioning of the university, disrupt teaching, invade offices, etc. This kind of activity has been limited, but has grown in importance since about autumn 1968. The other activities have been the march or demonstration, which essentially continues an older tradition of protest, and the disruption of speakers' meetings.

It is possible to go further than a listing of patterns, to reach certain conclusions and generalizations about the major issues and the reasons for their appearance. In making such a summary one is guided not only by the record of events, but by the analyses, written by left-wing students, of their own position and major concerns.

(i) The most frequent form of protest has remained the disruption of meetings addressed by unpopular speakers. Sometimes this appears to have happened in a general feeling of outrage at controversial figures on the extreme right, but usually there has been in the background a more developed theory of the appropriateness of such action. The rejection of 'rational argument' and the resort to direct action was a deliberate abandonment of both a form of political activity and a mode of academic behaviour in exchange for an alternative model. The notion of political debate was itself rejected; the relationship of the revolutionary student to his political enemies is not one of argument within a shared frame of reference defining the limits of legitimate action, but one of total warfare. Stopping a man from addressing a meeting may be merely a token, but tokens assume great significance for groups unable to put their substantive theory of action into practice.

(ii) Second in importance have been a varied group of protests concerned with the assertion of a particular student right, such as free speech, or a denial of certain rights to the university authority. The assertion or denial takes the form of direct action. (We are excluding for separate consideration the special cases of participation in university government and disciplinary procedures.) These protests suggest a changed attitude among students to power and authority in the university. There has been a willingness to use direct action where in an earlier period there would have been merely petition, solicitation and the passing of abusive resolutions. Similarly, there has been a growing willingness to challenge the area of operation assumed by authority and to question it, not simply in theory, but in action.

(iii) Closely related to the above, and a further important issue in protests, has been the demand for participation in university government. There has been a growing unwillingness by students to accept as legitimate a university authority that does not include their representatives. But the demand for participation is not simply for a mundane sharing in administrative decision-making, but for that type of 'participation' which signifies involvement, personal satisfaction and meaningfulness.[7] This is important in the critique of bureaucracy as an 'impersonal' form of government.

(iv) Next in prominence have been a number of protests concerned with different aspects of the relationship between the university and what are considered to be the forces of darkness in the outside world— the state (particularly its defence activities), industry, racialism. There may be concern at the role of lay governors in the university's affairs, and here the protest is not against lay governors as such but against the kind of interest normally represented by them;[8] there may be an attempt to reveal connections between the university and certain outside agencies; there may be concern at the use of the university's resources by these outside interests;[9] and there has been unrest at the apparent interference by Government and Parliament, seen as representatives of these interests. Finally, we should also place under this heading the protests concerning confidential files which were alleged to be kept by universities for the benefit of future employers.

(v) Several protests have involved resentment at university disciplinary action, usually following a protest by militants on some other issue which has led to disciplinary proceedings. This is a further case of a denial of the university authority's right to act. It also gives evidence of a willingness to use direct action as a countervailing force against the power of the disciplinary tribunal.

(vi) A further element in protest is the tendency of student revolts to become ends-in-themselves, to be used not simply to raise a protest or establish a countervailing force, but to establish an alternative structure of activity, an alternative source of legitimacy, and an alternative set of values and modes of behaviour.[10] One instance of this is the establishment of free universities as both part of and a consequence of protest. This differs somewhat from the above list of factors, which represent causes of revolt in the sense that 'cause' means source of provocation. The pursuit of protest as an end-in-itself is a 'cause' in the sense of 'motivation'.

(vii) Purely educational issues have predominated only in a few revolts, although the idea that education is in some sense polluted by capitalism is an important theme under (iv) above. Where education has figured directly it has concerned either course content[11] or examinations.[12]

(viii) Finally, while we concentrate on the critique of bureaucratic authority that emerges in a student protest, we must not assume that this is simply a protest in favour of more traditional forms. Several protests at the ancient universities have been directed against these enduring elements of tradition.

A more fruitful line of inquiry into the inspirations of student protest can be developed by discovering certain broad themes of discontent underlying this summary list. These areas are the following: authority, community and the university's relationship to the outside world. Authority as an issue figures most prominently in the new willingness of students to resort to direct action to defy constituted authorities, in the demand for participation, in the rejection of discipline and, if we consider academic as well as administrative authority, in the purely educational revolts. It also emerges in the attack on traditional authority. Traces of it may also be observed in the establishment of a counter-authority in the course of a sit-in or inauguration of a free university. The revolt does not simply attack existing authority: it establishes its own characteristic forms of expression. The elusive issue of community is seen clearly in those aspects of the demand for participation that appear to refer to personal involvement rather than the instrumental activity of decision-making. It appears again in the structure developed by the protest as an end in the course of a sit-in or free university sessions, and also figures in the critique of education articulated by the new left.

Finally, concern at the contemporary relationship between the university and the world is obviously the major factor in the group of protests that we have listed under this heading. However, it is also very much involved in the disruption of political meetings that has featured so prominently in student revolt, and also in educational critiques.

Authority, community and economy

It is through these three major themes of protest that the close relationship between university development and wider political problems which is crucial to a successful student revolt movement is articulated.

The general demand by students to be involved in the decisions made by the university authorities is limited and does not require much explanation. It can be related to the problems of increasing administrative complexity in a modern university and the concomitant decline of smaller collegiate forms, in which a notion such as formal representation on decision-making bodies has little relevance. Student unrest in Britain has followed the vast expansion in the size of a number of universities which followed the Robbins Report[13, 14] on higher education. It can also be related to the changing perspectives and expectations of young people in modern society who, for a variety of reasons, have come to expect certain powers and privileges as of right. More interesting, and far more important for a study of student revolt, is the approach of the militant students. Where such a group is involved, and this is usually the case, student demands for participation will not rest with a call for representation on decision-making bodies, although in several cases the militants have been prepared to support such proposals for a time in order to have an issue on which to unite a wide front of students.

Their own position is likely to be that students should not entangle themselves in the administrative machine and lend legitimacy to it, but should maintain their independence, and their strength, by raising demands to which it is known that the university cannot accede but which will raise student expectations and make possible the consolidation of a movement.[15] The major objective is often the creation of 'red bases' within the university, which are intended to serve as nuclei for future revolution.[16] One proposal for changing the authority structure originating on the left is for government by general assembly, that all decisions of importance in a university should be taken by a full meeting of the entire membership, including porters and cleaning staff, based on the principle of 'one man one vote'.[17] This would extend to decisions on curriculum and the appointment of academic staff. Among the ideas that inform such a proposal are the following. First, there is deep suspicion of all forms of representation, which is characteristic of the general rejection of politicians and elected officers who exercise their own judgement to secure compromises and agreements without the continuous and explicit mandate of the mass. Direct participation, for the left, has to be both universal and continuous.[18] Second, there is an attempt to achieve complete equality of participation, which involves ceasing to recognize any degrees of competence. The authority being rejected here is academic authority, in addition to that of bureaucratic hierarchy; this results from the concept of knowledge as being simply the expression of class interests.[19] Third, there is the ideal of the participating community. Finally, and more simply, the proposal is based on the kind of environment within which the student left itself flourishes, the mass meeting.

It should be clear, therefore, that the new left's rejection of university authority is rooted in a far wider critique than dissatisfaction with the pressures of change in higher education can explain. It is developed in particular from a certain view of the history of representative organizations in the labour movement. Closely allied with this is a general and crudely Marxist perspective that considers any beneficial change within individual institutions to be impossible outside the context of a general revolution. Student militants find genuine difficulty in seeing 'authority' as anything other than a vast international monolith; to distinguish, say, the Vice-Chancellor of the University of Warwick from the commander of U.S. forces in Vietnam is to make a false and probably deliberately deceptive distinction.[20]

This is the view with which the radicals analyse the problems of the university. In order to create the protests that such a view demands, it is clearly necessary to feed on a very different kind of discontent. The particular problems, blunders or abuses of an individual authority first become the source of resentment among a wide circle of students. Once the protest has begun, it is the strategy of the far left to try to relate this local concern to their global picture. The history of student revolt in Britain has to a large extent been the history of this process. In very few cases has the left managed to encourage a large number of students to adopt their total world image, and in those cases where they have succeeded it has been a temporary, transient occurrence. Authority in Britain has largely managed to avoid taking the kind of actions of extreme repression, of reliance on the forces of the state, which are necessary to reinforce this view. In addition, the kinds of issues which have emerged as sources of protest have, on the whole, not lent themselves to this kind of interpretation.

With the second focus of the student movement, that of community, we move to a different—though related—set of issues. The general complaint about 'absence of community' is raised in the context of the growth in the size of universities, the increase in the role of administrative mechanisms and bureaucratic methods, and the associated decline in the strength of shared values concomitant with the general decay of traditionalism. To some degree the problem is typical of large-scale modern organizations, but also to a certain extent it is unreal. Among modern organizations it is likely that the university strives to preserve more of what is generally understood by 'community' than will occur in, say, an industrial firm. Complaint of an absence of this elusive quality reflects perhaps as much the high expectations of the members of a university as the reality of their social relationships.

The new left also has a demand for community, and it appears to stem from awareness of a similar dissatisfaction. They complain that community has disappeared from the modern university; they claim to have restored community relationships within their own groups and within the course of their protest activities, such as sit-ins and free universities.[21] Indeed, as we have suggested above, the creation of such a community forms part of the *raison d'être* of such protests, and the image of the real university advanced by some sections of the left involves the creation of an establishment where people come to know each other as fellow members of a community. The high points of success of the British revolt have been those few occasions where a wider circle of adherents have, for a brief time, come to see participation in such a community as the resolution of many of their frustrations and dissatisfactions with the orthodox university environment.

However, it is deceptive to consider this kind of activity on the left under the heading of 'community'. A community relationship is characteristic of static, traditional institutions (or more mundanely, of the fabric of informal friendship ties that exist in any institution), and the new left is by no means advocating the re-establishment of the traditional university. The form of authority most frequently condemned by student protest corresponds most closely to the whole congeries of political and social changes in modern society which have given birth to the new left's protest, i.e. modern bureaucratic authority. Naturally, therefore, the left has tended to strike its attitudes in relation and in opposition to this type of authority. Since the language of opposition to bureaucracy and rationalized procedure tends to be couched in terms of its normal polarity—that of traditional community —a misleading impression is given. The form of social relationship in fact displayed by the new left is that of communion, not community: it is the spontaneous and deeply felt expression of untrammelled, unchannelled sentiment. It is directly countered to the rationalized and restrained behaviour of bureaucratic styles, but it is not countered to traditional community. As such, it closely relates to the left's particular critique of authority, and forms the social relationship compatible with their attitude towards authority. It relates to similar problems of change within the university; to a similar concern to go behind the forms that appear to mask bureaucratic authority in order to seek a total morality, a continuous moral critique and questioning; and to the same pessimism at the prospects of achieving objectives through 'normal' channels of rational discussion, constitutional pressure and emotive restraint.[22] Again, of course, the university is here but a special case of a wider problem. It is easier to locate such a process within a university precisely because the university is an institution which lays certain claims to being a community. It is an institution where the suffocating effects of modern economic and technological pressures can be denounced more loudly, precisely because of the university's claims to autonomy.[23]

Yet the critique itself and its associated attitudes mainly derive from the wider spheres of economy and polity where bureaucratic authority is encountered more fully. Before examining in more detail how the left reaches this critique and accommodates it within a more general framework, it is necessary to complete the picture of the different elements in the revolt by discussing the problem of the relationship between the university and the wider society.

This last point is in a way the most strongly political and Marxist of the three themes, but it is also the one which has had least success in being the focus of specific revolts. Its most important practical expression has been the conflict over confidential files being kept on students' political activities for the benefit of future employers. This is a problem which is probably of little immediate concern to the far left, as few of them are likely to seek employment from the kind of employer concerned. But the issue seems to give very real embodiment to their vision of the university in modern society: a slave to the interests of capital and state in a society in which institutions become increasingly interdependent and thus their freedom becomes increasingly mythical.[24, 25] The function of the university becomes that of training persons to fill particular posts, or of carrying out research for either the Government (mainly in defence) or industry (either on methods of producing new products or on techniques for 'managing' employees).[26]

This line of thinking merges clearly with the two previous points. Authority in the university is discredited, partly because it is seen as being hand-in-glove with these external sources of power, and partly because the special claim of an academic authority dissolves when the work of universities is felt to be directed solely to serving the interests of a corrupt and exploitative society. The restoration of expressive, local communal ties is regarded as crucial in the context of a society which is considered to be controlled increasingly by remote, centralized rational bureaucracies.

Complete though the theory may be, and sufficient as it is to explain many of the actions of the far left, it has only rarely succeeded in relating to wider discontents among students. The relationship between education and economy in Britain is very much obscured by the élite tradition of 'liberal' education, and the extent of research efforts for state and industry has reached nothing resembling the situation in, say, the U.S.A.

The new left in Britain

So far we have discussed the major themes behind the various expressions of revolt, the different relationships to them of the new left and the wider circle of discontented students who are necessary to an outbreak of protest, and the general circumstances in which these different perspectives will be able to create a temporary alliance. It remains to give some greater consideration to the new left, for it is they who have articulated every revolt of any substance, and it is in their image that the student protest movement has developed. What do we mean by the new left? What are its major characteristics? And how do these relate to the issues which we have already considered? In tackling these questions we are not concerned with the various nuances of individual writers, who have provided inspiration to the rebellion, for such subtleties are not particularly relevant for the growth of a movement. We need to understand the very broad, general themes that rest in the background, and the major formative influences on this general development in left-wing political thought.

(a) The disillusionment with Soviet communism, dramatized by the invasion of Hungary in 1956. Although there have now been several generations of men on the left who have experienced this disenchantment at some stage in their political experience, it is only in recent years that a generation has grown up with this as a fundamental element of its initial intellectual equipment, rather than as an uneasy annexe to an existing frame of reference. Communist centralized bureaucracy can take its place alongside capitalist imperialism from the outset.[27]

(b) The history of compromise that characterizes social democracy and British trade unionism, most immediately exemplified for this generation by the Labour Governments of 1964 and 1966. This traditional source of disillusionment on the left becomes intensified with the recent explicit self-identification of social democracy with the skilful management of capitalism.[28, 29]

(c) The experience of Cuba, the Chinese cultural revolution and the Vietnam war. Opposed to the disillusionment with the existing routes to socialism stands the concept of the guerrilla war of liberation. The idealized guerrilla contradicts at every point the dictates of bureaucracy. In the eyes of the left, the guerrilla band is a small, face-to-face group, voluntaristic, autonomous, non-hierarchical, flexible, working with passion for a cause in which its members believe, *and* which represents their own best ideal and material interests. The guerrilla is a virtual ideal-type of non-alienated man, and the bureaucrat conflicts with such an ideal at every one of these points.[30] It is the significance of this contrast which accounts for the Vietnam war acquiring such importance on the left.

(d) The rediscovery of the concept of alienation in early Marxist writings. If the characteristic nineteenth-century image of the industrial worker showed a poverty-stricken labourer slaving in wretched conditions, in the late twentieth century its counterpart is the worker in mass-production industry: affluent, maybe, but a slave to the rhythm of the machine and having no control over the production process of which he is but a part. Such a condition is better accommodated by Marxist writings on the spiritual deprivations of alienation than by those more concerned with material poverty. The coincidence of the recent translation of these Marxist writings with the increasing awareness of the changed industrial environment has produced a new focus of concern on the left.[31]

(e) The issue of race, within Britain, in the U.S.A., and in Southern Africa. Paradoxically, although this type of conflict is in reality most difficult to adapt to a Marxist scheme, its predominance intensifies the young radical's sense of dissociation from his own society.

(f) The left's own recent political experience in the Campaign for Nuclear Disarmament. It was through C.N.D. that the left sought to wield political influence during the latter 1950s, and their methods were essentially passive and 'demonstrative'. The reaction to the failure of such tactics leads to an advocacy of violence and to action which no longer seeks to convert or appeal, but to impel by force.[32] Thus the peaceful march becomes the confrontation with the police, the demonstrative sit-in attempts to become the disruption of the university. In this the British movement echoes the experience of the U.S.A. in a different field: the civil rights sit-down becomes the urban guerrilla campaign.

If we conflate the effect of these six major sources of influence on the new left, we find a movement which has rejected the Soviet path to a bureaucratic centralized socialism, and which sees western social democracy as having succumbed to the influence of capitalist society to the extent that, like Soviet Communism, it represents no longer the interests of the proletariat, but those of the class-ruled technocratic state. The politics of the ballot box are illusory, because in existing society no change is possible that could represent a real alternative. The impossibility of politics, and the control of economic life by a ruling class, are reflected in the impossibility of true human freedom. Men are alienated from their work in that all they may do is perform some small task in a grand structure whose design is completely beyond their control. The assembly line serves as a model for all human institutions, including the university. Finally, this class society is seen as exploiting racialism both abroad in the form of colonialism and neo-colonialism and at home in the form of hostile policies towards black racial minorities.

In stark contrast to such a bleak image stands the guerrilla and the cultural revolution, strengthened by the left's own experience of political protest. The revolution must not allow itself to be enervated by the emergence of structures or bureaucracies, but should itself exemplify the transcending of alienation. It must therefore be participative, egalitarian, unrestricted by the confine of instrumental rationalism.

These political attitudes were being vaunted in the mid-1960s by many young people who came with them to the university or developed them while studying. These students were succeeded by, and imparted their *Weltanschauung* to later generations of university entrants whose early experience has been somewhat different from that of the original agitators. These young men and women spent their adolescence in a period of Labour government in Britain; they did not even need to experience disillusionment, but came with attitudes that slipped easily into the forms of the new left. They also completed their school years at a time when student revolt had already become well publicized. Thus if the new entrants lack some of the political experiences that shaped the original character of the revolt, they compensate by arriving at the university as potential protesters.

Within the university this global stance tries to relate itself to the local issues at hand. It seeks to give shape to dissatisfaction with authority in terms of the critique of authority implied by the above analysis. It seeks to create forms of communal action in direct contrast with bureaucratic action. It seeks to expose, in the specific instance of the university, the oppression of technocratic class rule. Every university conflict can be seen, in part, as an attempt by the left to gain support for this perspective on the incidents concerned. The issues themselves are rarely created by the left, and they only rarely succeed in creating the kind of activity suggested here. But it is in those cases where they are successful that the movement has any importance.

Marxism and the cult of spontaneity

So far we have dichotomized student protest into the small groups of radicals and the wider group of potentially dissatisfied students, and diagnosed the relative failure of British student revolt as a failure to convince large numbers of the latter group that their dissatisfactions can be accommodated in the frame of reference of the former. There is, however, a further division within the left-wing groups themselves which deserves some attention and which is a further source of potential weakness.

One of the curious developments in recent left-wing philosophy is the alliance between a form of Marxism and a cult of spontaneity which bears some relation to anarchism. There is much in these two movements which is mutually exclusive. Marxism, traditionally, has been a centralizing philosophy, intensely suspicious of localized communal groupings; the cult of spontaneity, by contrast, is based on local communal action. Marxism is an essentially rationalistic doctrine, rooted in a concept of man as a rational being and seeing the progress of human history as a development of rationality; in the cult of spontaneity man is essentially emotive, and only truly lives when he 'emotes', obviously without historical direction. For Marxism the resolution of human history is governed by iron laws of historical development, men having little scope for defying them; the cult of spontaneity reaches extremes of voluntarism. Marxism sees its movement as comprising the great mass of workers; the cult is essentially small and exclusive. The Marxist is enjoined to turn his attention to the world and to organize; the cult of spontaneity drops out of human affairs and shuns organized activity.

These two groups have only been able to come together because the kind of analysis of modern society forced upon Marxism by the various historical developments discussed in the previous section has led Marxist thought away from its traditional forms and emphases.[33] Capitalism may remain at the centre of the analysis, but the stress is increasingly placed on bureaucratic capitalism and the managerial state. Existing society may still be criticized as 'irrational', in Mannheim's sense of substantive rationality; but 'functional' rationality can be seen as a major enemy, and from that springboard an excursion into the cultivation of irrationality becomes entirely possible. The aims of the revolution may ultimately be centralized and universal, but the practical task in hand consists of opposing the centralizing forces at work in the modern political economy. Laws of history may determine the course of events, but in the face of history's continued unwillingness to move in the appropriate direction, Marxism has, from Lenin through Mao, Fanon, Guevara, Debray and Cohn-Bendit, gradually developed theories of social change which have more in common with the concept of charisma than that of ineluctable historical development.

In this way Marxism has moved, in spite of itself, towards the position occupied by those whose revolt is one which has constantly recurred throughout human history: the desire to opt out of the strain of life in organized communities. These, in turn, as exemplified in such movements as that of the hippies, have come to couch their reasons for dissatisfaction increasingly in terms of a response to modern technocratic society. Thus the two movements find a meeting point, and it is where their union is strongest that the contemporary pattern of revolt has appeared most powerful, most distinctive and most successful. For such a phenomenon to occur, as it has in Paris and on a smaller scale in West Germany, the areas of consonance between the two theories, the degree of reciprocity between the two groups and the relationship between the local university concerns and the wider perspective, need to be powerful and close. In Britain this has not tended to be the case. We have considered reasons why the university–society link has failed to convince, but there has also been a failure in the relationship between the Marxists and the 'anarchists'.[34]

In part this reflects the parochial scale of the issues of the British protests and the failure of external social institutions to embroil themselves in the conflict. In part it also relates to the particular flavour of British Marxism. British Marxists have grown up alongside a vast pragmatic labour movement, and many of them have spent at least some of their political energy somewhere within that movement. This is in contrast with both the American radicals, who have had no such movement to speak of, and the left in European countries where the various left-wing traditions have characteristically exhibited a less empirical, and more ideological or philosophical, edge. The cult of spontaneity is ill-suited to the typical young university Marxist in Britain, even after Marxism has been amended in the context of current society. Usually, expatriate American students have made the running in developing the cult of spontaneity within the British protests, particularly at the L.S.E., and their success in encouraging a wider movement has been limited indeed.[35] Although a fairly wide circle of 'drop-outs' mingle in British universities, either as students or as 'non-students' (as they are meaninglessly known), these have not been prepared or able to form the focus of a non-Marxist extremist movement, as in the U.S.A. On the whole they lack the will to organize, while those on the far left with organizing talents are likely to join the Marxist wing. The British Marxists have tended to feel embarrassed about their involvement in student protest; they would be far happier leading a revolt among workers in factories and on building sites.[36] A fair proportion of the more serious revolutionaries is in fact active in a range of unofficial shop stewards' movements and the like. Their concern with the students is therefore limited, while in their attempts to create successful links with industrial workers they encounter the resistance of a different sector of British society, where the situation requires its own analysis of revolutionary failure.

Notes

1. This fact does not imply that the arguments of the student radicals have not made use of these problems of physical deprivation, see C. Harman *et al.*, 'Education, Capitalism and the Student Revolt', published by *International Socialism*, 1968, Chapter 3.
2. An extended discussion of the various events may be found in C. J. Crouch, *Student Revolt in Britain* (Bodley Head, London 1970).
3. Committee of Vice-Chancellors and Principals and National Union of Students, Joint Statement, 7 October, 1968.
4. Select Committee on Education and Science, Report, *Student Relations* (H.M.S.O. 1969), p. 153.
5. T. Nairn and J. Singh-Sandhu, 'Chaos in the Art Colleges', in A. Cockburn and R. Blackburn, *Student Power* (1969); and in *The Hornsey Affair* (Penguin, Harmondsworth 1969).
6. T. Fawthrop, *Education or Examination* (Radical Student Alliance, 1968).
7. E.g., D. Atkinson, 'The Academic Situation', in J. Nagel (ed.) *Student Power* (Merlin Press, London 1969).
8. C. Harman, *et al.*, op. cit. (note 1), Chapter 2.

9. Ibid.
10. C. J. Crouch, 'The Chiliastic Urge', *Survey* No. 69, October 1968.
11. *The Hornsey Affair*, op. cit. (note 5), Chapter 4.
12. T. Fawthrop, op. cit. (note 6).
13. Committee on Higher Education, *Report*, 1963.
14. For a discussion of some of the trends in post-Robbins development, see R. Layard and J. King, 'Expansion Since Robbins', in D. Martin (ed.) *Anarchy and Culture* (Routledge and Kegan Paul, London 1969).
15. C. Harman, op. cit. (note 1), p. 67 f.
16. See several articles on the notion of the 'red base' in *New Left Review* No. 53, 1969.
17. Manifesto of Revolutionary Socialist Students' Federation, ibid., p. 21.
18. 'A Revolutionary Student Movement', ibid., p. 43 f.
19. The clearest statement of the new left's position on existing academic traditions is to be found in the essays of R. Blackburn and P. Anderson, in Cockburn and Blackburn, op. cit., (note 5).
20. T. Fawthrop, op. cit. (note 6), pp. 65, 66.
21. Several accounts of revolts written from the perspective of the new left pay attention to this theme. Interesting examples are to be found in *The Hornsey Affair*, op. cit. (note 5), and P. Hoch and V. Schoenbach, *L.S.E.: The Natives are Restless* (Sheen and Ward, London 1969).
22. Aspects of this theme were discussed in an international context, but with some reference to Britain in L. Labedz, 'Students and Revolution', *Survey* No. 68, and in further articles in the following issue.
23. D. Martin, 'The Dissolution of the Monasteries', in Martin, op. cit.
24. D. Adelstein, 'Roots of the British Crisis', in Cockburn and Blackburn, op. cit.
25. C. Harman, op. cit., *passim*.
26. In particular attention has been concentrated on the implications of the British 'binary system' of higher education for the vocational bias of educational policy. See D. Adelstein, op. cit. (note 24).
27. The most comprehensive discussion of this theme, which, although written by an American, has been widely read by British radicals, is H. Draper, *The Two Souls of Socialism* (Independent Socialist Club of America, 1966).
28. Ibid.
29. As a further instance of this thinking, see T. Cliff and C. Barker, *Incomes Policy, Legislation and Shop Stewards* (London Industrial Shop Stewards Defence Committee, 1966).
30. R. Blackburn, in Cockburn and Blackburn, op. cit., p. 181.
31. Ibid, p. 197 f.
32. G. Stedman-Jones, 'The Meaning of Student Revolt', ibid., pp. 43, 44.
33. For an extended discussion of the changes that have taken place within Marxism, see R. Lowenthal, 'Unreason and Revolution', *Encounter*, 1969.
34. Interesting evidence of the conflict is revealed in Hoch and Schoenbach, op. cit., which is written from the perspective of the cult of spontaneity.
35. Ibid., *passim*.
36. G. Stedman-Jones, op. cit. (note 32), p. 52 f.

10. JAPAN

Toyomasa Fusé

Introduction

In the latter part of the 1960s student power has asserted itself through-out the world. Nowhere is this more true than in Japan, where student radicalism constitutes one of the main features in national politics.

The Japanese student movement has attained high visibility in post-war years in dramatic and violent activities: it captured world headlines back in 1960 when Zengakuren students successfully prevented the proposed visit of Dwight D. Eisenhower, then President of the United States, and subsequently forced the resignation of Prime Minister Kishi; again in 1968 and 1969 they shook the world by paralysing more than eighty universities in the nation with their strong-arm tactics and 'politics of confrontation'. The brush-fire of student radicalism did not spare even the University of Tokyo, the most revered citadel of higher education in Japan, which could not, as a result, admit a single fresh-man in the academic year 1969–70. The entire nation was traumatized by the virulence and violence of student revolt, and the Government of Japan enacted a highly controversial University Normalization Ordinance which facilitated speedier introduction of police riot squads on to the campus.

At a time when student radicalism is fast becoming internationalized —so much so that it almost resembles a Fifth International—a precise understanding and analysis of the student movement on a cross-cultural basis is certainly in order. This chapter will discuss student radicalism in Japan in the context of the university and society in Japan. For this purpose the history and structure of higher education in Japan will be first discussed at some length (especially for the benefit of European readers), and then the organization and types of activities of Japanese students will be analysed. Finally, in the last section of this chapter some specific hypotheses will be discussed for explaining student radicalism in Japan today in the light of available data.

History and structure of higher education in Japan

Tracing the origin of the Japanese university certainly depends upon the definition of the 'university'. In the modern sense of the word, the university is the highest institution of learning engaged in the structured and systematic *creation, transmission,* and *application* of accumulated knowledge. According to this definition, the origin of the university in Japan must be sought in the Meiji period (1868–1912), which officially launched Japan into a path of modernization and massive industrialization. Yet if the university is defined as a centre of higher learning including several specialized faculties, Japan possessed one quite early in her history. In the latter definition, the centre of higher learning for certain selected individuals destined for higher positions in government dates back to the latter part of the sixth century A.D.

By the fifth century B.C., strong and well-established kingdoms emerged in the southern and central parts of Japan. One of the most powerful kingdoms was ruled by the House of Yamato, and the present Imperial Family is regarded as a direct descendant of this house. The House of Yamato rapidly increased its power by unifying all the territories from the south to the present Tokyo area by the middle of the fourth century. Between the fourth and the sixth century, trade and commerce were established between Japan and the kingdoms on the Korean peninsula, such industrial arts as weaving, metal-work, tanning and shipbuilding were introduced, and Buddhism was imported from India through China and Korea.[1]

In 604, Imperial Prince Shotoku (573–621) issued a list of injunctions known as the Constitution of Seventeen Articles, which called for harmonious co-operation, respect for Buddhism, and faithful obedience to the Emperor. This set of injunctions was intended to set the ideals for a central government by bringing both land and people under the direct control of the Emperor. In 645, the Reform of Taika, based on the ideals of Prince Shotoku, was inaugurated by Prince Naka-no-Oye, bringing all private land into public possession, partitioning the confiscated land among the people, and dividing the country into administrative units governed by central government officials. This brought about the decline of the clan system and the emergence of a highly centralized political bureaucracy in Japan.[2]

The proclamation of Taiho Legal-Administrative Ordinance (Taiho Ritsuryo) during this period included the establishment of the *Daigaku,* or the Grand Centre of Learning, in the capital of Nara, and of a *Kokugaku* or Regional Centre of Learning in every province.[3] From available historical evidence it seems that the *Daigaku* primarily served as a training centre for future government élites. The *Daigaku* consisted of three major faculties: *Daigaku-ryo* or the Faculty of Great Learning, specializing in historiography, Chinese classics, mathematics, and law; *Tenyaku-ryo* or the Faculty of Medicine and Pharmacology; and *Yinyo-ryo* or the Faculty of Astronomy and Astrology. It did have a basic format of a university, comparable to some of the universities in Europe that emerged later. The professor was called *Hakushi* or 'learned one', and the student *Gakusei*. There were altogether 400 students in the capital university in Nara. Admission into the élite structure of the Imperial bureaucracy depended on successful graduation from the university and on passing the civil service examination.[4]

In the eighth to the tenth century further development in the institutions of higher learning was observed. During this period the former 'uji' chiefs of the Yamato Clan, who attained total hegemony of Japan by this time, converted themselves into a civil nobility centred around the Imperial Court. They staffed a centralized bureaucratic officialdom located in Heijo (or present-day Nara, built in A.D. 710) and later in Heian (or Kyoto, completed in A.D. 794). The Emperor gradually relinquished real political power to the higher court nobility such as the Fujiwara family, and the glamorous dominance of the nobility reached its peak during this period by monopolizing the fiscal and administrative function of the government. They demonstrated their ability and talent in administration, statecraft and cultural pursuits, creating a distinct aristocratic culture of Japan. The Japanese culture of this period, though greatly inspired and influenced by that of the Tang Dynasty of China, began to display its own distinct characteristics in the fields of arts and literature.[5] When the capital was moved to Kyoto, Japan witnessed one of her great periods of cultural development, and life in the capital was marked by elegance and refinement. The most noteworthy development during this period was the invention of two sets of phonetic syllables, *Hiragana* and *Katakana*, which are still in use in Japan, together with the Chinese ideographs. The adoption of these phonetic syllables gave great impetus to the growth of native Japanese literature.[6] A newly achieved aristocratic sophistication was manifested in architecture, laws, social institutions, bureaucratic structures, dress, food and court ceremonials. One of the developments of this period was a move towards establishing a number of private academies by certain noble families.

The Fujiwara family, the ruling aristocrats of the period, built *Kangaku-yin* for their offspring and relatives; this move was followed by the Tachibana family, who established *Gakukan-yin* for their relatives; and finally the Arihara family started *Shogaku-yin* for the descendants of the Imperial family as well as children of the court nobility and some military aristocracy, such as the Genji and Heiké.

The system of higher education in Japan during the periods mentioned may be summarized as follows:

1. Government University ....
    1. Daigaku (Capital University)
    2. Kokugaku (Regional University

2. Private University ....
    1. Kangakuyin (by the Fujiwara family)
    2. Shogakuyin (by the Arihara family)
    3. Gakukanyin (by the Tachibana family)

All these institutions of higher learning, however, were burnt in the great fire of A.D. 1177 in Kyoto, and they were never rebuilt. Hence, though the traditions of learning continued in Japan throughout her history, the system of higher education as on-going, well-organized centres of learning came to an end until the Tokugawa period.[7]

By the twelfth century the Samurai, who emerged during the early part of the tenth century when the effectiveness of the police and military system declined, assumed national hegemony after a series of internecine strife and civil wars. The Samurai provided the dominant way of life and salient values that permeated practically every aspect of Japanese culture. The rise of the Samurai to high prominence in Japan is one of the important characteristics of Japanese history at the end of the twelfth century.

The age of the Samurai saw the development of new religious influence in Japan, which was to have an impact on the mode of higher learning as well. New Buddhist doctrines, embodied in the Jodo-shu, Jodo-Shinshu, Zen, and Nichiren-shu, spread rapidly among the people.[8]

Because of prolonged, nation-wide internecine civil wars among the feudal military lords for more than five hundred years and the subsequent destruction of cities and urban areas in Japan between the twelfth and sixteenth centuries, the university as known in the previous aristocratic age was not revived. Instead the centre of higher learning now shifted to Buddhist monasteries, where monks and others studied Buddhist doctrines, Chinese classics and other subjects. One of the noteworthy events in the middle of the sixteenth century was the arrival of the Portuguese and the Spaniards, who introduced European culture for the first time. In their reports to their friends at home, they often referred to a 'monastic university' or 'academies' in Kyoto and Nara, indicating the continuity of learning in Japan even after the demise of the official universities.[9]

The internecine civil war that plagued Japan finally ended with the victory of Tokugawa Iyeyasu, who established the Tokugawa Shogunate Government at Edo (or present-day Tokyo) in 1603, thus marking the beginning of the 264-year-long Tokugawa period. The successive Tokugawa Shoguns maintained a rigid control over the entire nation. During this period the people were divided into four distinct social classes: Shi, Noh, Koh, and Sho (Samurai, farmer, artisan, and merchant) in vertical rank order. Despite its numerous shortcomings, the Tokugawa régime brought an unprecedented span of peaceful years to Japan. In towns manufacturing and commerce prospered, and a new culture based on the taste of the townspeople flourished. The policy of 'national seclusion', which closed Japan's doors to the outside world, brought about loss of contact with developments abroad, yet fostered the growth of indigenous culture, especially in historiography neo-Confucianism, and studies in national consciousness. Tokugawa

Japan witnessed the emergence of many prominent native scholars, and foundations were laid for the development of modern higher education as well as popular mass education.[10]

The educational system during the Tokugawa reign reflected the social stratification of its society. Each feudal lord (*Daimyo*) established a high-level academy (*Han Gakko*) in his domain for the samurai; for average citizens a *Tera Koya* (literally a 'temple school') was provided by the townsfolk. The samurai and his children were obliged to attend the Han Gakko, where they studied numerous subjects, with special emphasis on the mastery of Chinese classics and studies in national consciousness. Though the *Tera Koya* or Popular Folk School hardly qualified as a centre of higher learning, it was the only school available to the non-aristocratic average citizens. The establishment of the *Tera Koya* reflected the changing social structure of Japan during this period —i.e. the accumulated wealth of the merchants and their increasing share in the affairs of state. Hence the curricula at the Tera Koya included some Chinese classics, but greater stress was placed on learning arithmetic (necessary for trade and commerce), and the reading of well-written travelogues (reflecting the growth of highways and commerce throughout Japan). Most of the teachers at the Tera Koya were priests (who originally conducted the school at their temples), some samurai who needed extra income, and physicians. The average class consisted of 30–50 pupils; children at the age of five or six were sent to the nearest Tera Koya for three to seven years of education. It is estimated that 15,560 schools were in operation.[11]

The best known Han Gakko of all was the *Shoheikaku*, which was the forerunner of the latter-day University of Tokyo. The Shoheikaku was first started as a private, family study centre by a noted samurai-turned-scholar of the period, Hayashi Razan, but it was later transformed into the official Shogunate University for selected samurai as well as talented citizens.

Towards the latter part of the Tokugawa period European imperialism reached its peak in Asia, and Japan could no longer rest in her self-imposed national seclusion. After the visit by the United States Commodore Mathew Perry, the Shogunate was forced to conclude and sign the Treaty of Commerce and Amity with the United States, which was followed by similar treaties with other European powers. In proportion to the degree of contact with the West, there emerged an acute need for translation and introduction of Western learning to Japan. In reponse to this need, the Shogunate established the *Hansho Chosho* or Bureau of Translation. It was later renamed *Yosho Chosho*, or Bureau for the Study of Western Books, and finally came to be called *Kaiseijo* (Centre for Development and Enlightenment), on the eve of the Meiji Restoration. It is to be noted that both Shoheikaku and Kaiseijo laid the foundation for the first modern university in Japan, the University of Tokyo.[12]

The sudden contact with foreign countries aroused a spirit of intense nationalism among many Japanese and spurred political movements to overthrow the Tokugawa Shogunate. As a result of the rallying cries of the nationalists, the last Tokugawa Shogun resigned and supreme authority was restored to the Imperial Throne.

With the resignation of the last Shogun began the colourful Meiji period (1868–1912), which transformed feudal Japan into a modern nation-state. The nation under Emperor Meiji (1852–1911) set out to accomplish the task of catching up with the advanced countries of the West. Importing Western knowledge and technology, the Meiji government initiated a series of reforms and changes in Japan: the Constitution was promulgated, the Parliament opened, civil and criminal laws codified, railways constructed, a modern banking system inaugurated, electric lighting and telephones introduced. However, one of the most important changes wrought after the Meiji Restoration was the introduction of a modern educational system in Japan.[13]

There are roughly six periods in the development of higher education in Japan, from the Meiji Era, through the Taisho period (1912–25) to the Showa Era (1925–), which will be discussed below.

(1) First Period: 1868–71

When the Meiji government was formed in 1868 after the bloody civil war which put an end to the 264-year rule of the Tokugawa family, there were three major institutions of higher learning inherited from the Shogunate: *Shoheizaka Gakumonjo* (or *Shoheikaku*), specializing in historiography, law, mathematics, and Chinese classics; *Kaiseijo* (Centre for Development and Enlightenment) which was concerned with translation and introduction of Western scholarship; and *Igakusho*, the Medical College, with a strong emphasis on classical Oriental medicine as well as Dutch medical science. The Meiji government wasted no time in restoring these existing schools to their former status and immediately embarked upon developing and improving them.

Thus in December 1869, the *Daigaku* (University) was officially created in Tokyo on the former foundations of the Shoheikaku; the Kaiseijo was renamed *Daigaku-Nanko* (Southern Branch University), and the Igakusho came to be called *Daigaku-Toko* (Eastern Branch University). It is generally believed that the inauguration of the Daigaku in 1869 marks the true beginning of the present-day University of Tokyo.

The University thus created was not only an institution of higher learning, but also a governmental administrative organization in the absence of a Ministry of Education. The curricula of the universities included such subjects as Pedagogy, Law, Medicine, Science and Humanities, clearly reflecting the influence of European educational systems. The first period in the annals of Japanese higher education came to an end with the establishment in 1871 of the Ministry of Education, thereby transferring the administrative function of the university and of higher education in general to the government. Despite definite attempts on the part of some nationalists to reintroduce emphases on Kokugaku, Kohgaku, Kangaku, and other traditional, nationalistic studies (which are all admixtures of Confucianism, neo-Confucianism and indigenous ideologies), the university in Japan irrevocably drifted toward Western-style learning.[14]

(2) *Second Period:* 1871–77

In 1872 the new Education Act was promulgated, introducing for the first time in Japan's history a unified concept of popular education at all levels. Accordingly elementary schools were set up throughout Japan and the concept of the educational district was introduced: there were eight university districts; each district was further divided into 32 middle school districts, and each middle school district was then divided into 210 elementary school districts.[15] It is important to note that the principle of the 'ladder system' was adopted, in which a person was enabled to climb up the ladder of the educational system one step at a time. Yet in reality what Japan adopted was a 'dual ladder system' in which there were two separate channels of education, one for the élite and the other for the masses.

The establishment of higher education was not limited to Tokyo alone; medical colleges were started in many prefectures and other specialized colleges were also established. Of the latter category, the most famous are the *Gakunosha* or Agricultural College, *Shoho Koshujo*, or Centre for Commercial Studies (the forerunner of present-day Hitotsubashi University, renowned for economics), and Sapporo Agricultural College set up by William S. Clark from Massachusetts Agricultural College, which produced many outstanding leaders for Japan.[16]

(3) *Third Period:* 1877–86

On 12 April 1877 the University of Tokyo was officially inaugurated by combining the Tokyo Kaisei Gakko and Tokyo Medical College. Then the university added the faculties of Law, Science, Literature, and came to occupy the most hallowed place in higher education in Japan. Its eminence is evidence by the fact that of the total educational budget of 1880, the University of Tokyo received almost 40 per cent. of the sum.

In addition to the University of Tokyo, some of the other outstanding universities were also organized during this period as Japan saw the development of private universities. Since the University of Tokyo was a government-sponsored élite university geared primarily to educating future government officials, some leading Japanese citizens started to establish private universities based upon Western ideals. Yukichi Fukuzawa and Shigenobu Okuma, for instance, were enlightened and inspired by Western ideals of democracy and egalitarianism during their study abroad, and they took a lead in the movements for civil rights and called for constitutional government in the early Meiji period. Thus Fukuzawa took it upon himself to start Keio University and Okuma Waseda University in 1882. Keio University had a utilitarian slant and trained leaders in business, while Waseda University was geared to political economy, journalism and literature. Before Japan's massive industrialization the most prestigious positions available to university graduates were in the government and army. Thus the divided market—training for government primarily at the University of Tokyo, business at Keio, and politics and journalism at Waseda—produced little conflict among the graduates of the three schools.[17] The move for private universities gained momentum and saw the establishment of following institutions: Tokyo Hogakusha, a predecessor of Hosei University; Meiji Horitsu Gakko, the latter-day Meiji University; Tokyo Shoko Gakko, the prototype of the Tokyo Institute of Technology; and Igirisu Horitsu Gakko, the forerunner of Chuo University. By 1886, therefore, the basic foundations for modern higher education in Japan were firmly laid.

(4) *Fourth Period:* 1886–1918

In 1885 the Cabinet System was instituted in Japan, and Mori Arinori was appointed the first Minister of Education. The leaders of Meiji Japan, and Mori Arinori in particular, regarded Humboldt and the Prussian educational system as their model, differentiating between the 'indoctrination' function of primary education and the 'creative' role of the universities in fostering research and training leaders. The initial educational ordinances drawn up by Mori Arinori were explicitly concerned with such distinctions.

> He believed that primary education, by being based on the doctrines of Japanese nationalism and militarism, would help teach the people to be loyal to the state while they were still in the formative period of their lives. But he also believed that if education were limited to the primary level, leaders could not be produced with sufficient grasp of science and technology to contribute to the prosperity of the nation. He was therefore convinced that, in both research and training, universities and professional schools should assume the task of preparing such leaders and that sufficient and appropriate freedom should be allowed for this purpose. . . .[18]

Thus educational reform was carried out under the aegis of Mori Arinori, and on 1 March 1886 the first Imperial University Act was issued, whereby the University of Tokyo was renamed the Imperial University of Tokyo. According to the blueprint of Mori, the Imperial

University was to perform two major functions: to provide a graduate school for advanced research, and to offer undergraduate teaching in several faculties. Moreover, the function and aims of the university were required at all times to be consonant with the objectives of the state. Thus elements of nationalism were fused with a highly instrumental view of the university as a tool for the furtherance of national objectives. In response to nationalism, which was mounting in Japan, most of the foreign teachers were replaced by Japanese nationals as they returned from their training abroad; at the same time new emphases on nationalism and national consciousness were implemented by the introduction of such subjects as Japanese jurisprudence, national history, Japanese language and literature, and courses in Oriental philosophy together with European philosophy. Though there was much European influence on the Japanese universities, there emerged some basic differences as well during this period. For instance, most Japanese imperial universities had already introduced departments of engineering and agriculture (much like their American counterparts), whereas these departments were conspicuously absent in French and German universities. This period witnessed the emergence of some other government-sponsored universities: Kyoto Imperial University in 1897; toward the end of the Meiji period (1868–1912) the Imperial Universities of Tohoku and Kyushu were established; and in 1918, the Agricultural College within Tohoku Imperial University was separated from the latter and became Hokkaido Imperial University.[19]

(5) *Fifth Period:* 1918–45

During the period 1868–1918, Japan rose from a feudal background to the status of a first-class economic and political power. Following the end of World War I, Japan's industrial structure successfully attained a transition from light to heavy industry. If the Meiji period was Japan's 'Take-off', by 1938 Japan terminated her 'drive to maturity' and entered into the stage of 'high mass consumption', anticipating her plunge into the post-industrial stage in the 1960s.[20]

Because of this industrial and economic maturity of Japan, demands for university graduates increased enormously. One of the noteworthy educational reforms during this period was the introduction of the *Koto Gakko*, or Higher School, which covers the first two years of university education, with a strong emphasis on general education. Thus the Higher School was a mid-way station between the middle school and the university, training potential students for the Imperial Universities. To most prefectural, municipal and private universities were attached Preparatory Schools (called Yoka in Japan), fulfilling the same function as the Higher School for the Imperial universities. The Higher School during this period set the tone and style of intellectual life for many pre-university students by stressing the importance of religion, philosophy, and literature, self-rule in the dormitory and a spirit of liberalism. The numbers of students, enrolled in preparatory schools and other institutions of higher learning in Japan are shown in Table 10.I.[21]

Table 10.I—*Student enrolment in Institutions of Higher Learning*

	Institutions of Higher Learning				Student Enrolment		
year	national	public	private	total	depts.	other*	total
1890	1			1	635	677	1,312
1900	2			2	2,364	876	3,240
1910	3			3	5,514	1,725	7,239
1920	6	2	8	16	11,175	10,740	21,915
1930	17	5	24	46	41,292	28,313	69,605
1940	19	2	26	47	50,356	31,643	81,999

From: Tokyo Daigaku Shuppansha, *Nippon no Daigaku* (Universities in Japan: University of Tokyo Press, Tokyo 1968), p. 55.

* 'other' includes students enrolled in Yoka (prep schools), Higher Schools, Teachers' Colleges and other specialized colleges.

As mentioned earlier, this period was one of Japan's growing industrial maturity and military expansionism, creating many difficulties in the social, economic and political life of the nation in the mid-twenties. These difficulties were further aggravated by the Great Depression of 1929, which put the army into a position of national leadership. The short-lived Taisho Democracy, in which party politics flourished, was eventually replaced by the military-fascist régime which came to dominate the entire country. In line with the militarism and ultra-nationalistic policies of the new fascist government, stringent control and regimentation were introduced over every aspect of Japanese life, especially over the universities, where a spirit of freedom and liberalism had persisted. During this period, therefore, many progressive, liberal, and left-wing professors were chased out of their university posts, and a blanket of silence covered the life of the university and the nation as a whole. Though natural sciences were encouraged and even expanded, as they helped the military fascists in their expansionist objectives, many social sciences such as Sociology were either reduced considerably or disappeared entirely from the curriculum.[22]

(6) *Sixth Period:* 1945—

Japan's crushing defeat in 1945 brought about major social-institutional changes in every aspect of national life. Education likewise underwent various reforms. Acting on the recommendations of the Education Mission of the United States, the government of Japan adopted a new '6-3-3-4' system: six years of compulsory elementary-school education, three years of compulsory junior high school, three years of optional senior high-school training, and finally four years of university (and then on to graduate school). Numerous junior colleges, modelled on U.S. counterparts, were created throughout the country as an intermediate institution between senior high school and university. For the first time in the country's history, the principle of co-education was introduced at all levels of education, opening the door of higher education to men and women alike.[23]

In 1947, the Civil Information and Education Section of the G.H.Q. (the General Headquarters for the Allied Occupation Forces) made a recommendation for the reorganization of Japanese universities on the model of American state universities. Though the plan met with stiff resistance from the educational establishment in Japan, the status of all the universities in Japan changed from that of the former Imperial University status to that of the four-year *Shinsei Daigaku* (New University). Accordingly, former Imperial universities and other national universities were reorganized, and former Higher Schools, teachers' colleges, and technical-specialized colleges were either elevated to the status of university or absorbed into existing universities supported by prefectural or municipal governments rather than the central government in Tokyo. Most of the specialized colleges that were not promoted to the status of the university were transformed into junior colleges. Thus educational decentralization was established, resulting in at least one university in every prefecture; and Japan further accelerated the process of transition from élite education to mass education, which had already started in the fifth period mentioned earlier.[24] The extent of accessibility to higher education (including junior colleges and universities) in Japan is shown in the following tables.

Table 10.II—*Number of colleges and universities and student enrolment in 1947*

Type of school	number	number of students		total
		men	women	
University	49	87,657	266	87,923
Higher School	39	29,205	30	29,235
Yoka (Univ. Prep School)	62	39,312	187	39,499
Specialized College	368	186,202	45,151	231,353
Teachers' College	140	55,395	26,662	82,057
total	658	397,771	72,296	470,067

Source: Tokyo Daigaku Shuppankai, *Nippon no Daigaku*, op. cit., p. 59.

By 1950 new junior colleges and universities went into operation. Their breakdown is as follows:

Table 10.III—*Growth of junior colleges and student enrolment*

	Junior College			Students		
Year	national	public	private	total	men	women	total
1950	0	17	132	149	9,220	5,878	15,098
1965	28	40	301	369	37,175	110,388	147,563

Source: ibid., p. 60.

Table 10.IV—*The number of universities and student enrolment: 1950–68*

	University			Students		
Year	national	public	private	total	men	women	total
1950	70	26	105	201	207,599	17,324	224,923
1955	72	34	122	228	458,274	65,081	523,355
1960	72	33	140	245	540,455	85,966	626,421
1965	73	35	209	317	785,437	152,119	937,556
1968	75	35	267	377	957,205	203,220	1,160,425

Source: for data for 1950–65, *Nippon no Daigaku*, ibid., p. 60; for data for
1968, Yano Tsuneta Kinenkai (eds.), *Nippon Kokusei Zué* (Japan
Statistical Yearbook: Kosuseisha, Tokyo 1969), p. 479.

In May 1968 the total number of junior colleges reached 451. Hence,
as Tables 10.III and IV show, there are altogether 828 junior colleges
and universities in Japan, with a total student enrolment of more than
1,500,000. In terms of the college population, 19.4 per cent. are going
on to some sort of post-secondary education, the highest rate of higher
education in the world except for that of the United States. In order to
fully appreciate the remarkable progress in the availability of higher
education in Japan today, this figure must be compared with the percentage of youth going on to the Middle School in 1935 (18.5 per cent.),
which indicates that the rate of access to post-secondary higher education today is better than the rate of access to secondary school thirty-five
years ago.[25]

The student movement before World War II

The history of the student movement in Japan dates back to the
Meiji-Taisho periods, roughly from 1874–1918, followed by perhaps
one of the most turbulent periods in Japan's recent history, 1918–45.

There were sporadic student movements after 1874, when the Civil
Rights Movement (Jiyu-Minken Undo), demanding free speech, a free
press, the Constitution, Parliament and universal suffrage, was mounted
in Meiji Japan. But an organized student movement emerged only

after 1918. Many influential organizations were born in 1918, the year when the Bolshevik Revolution shook the world and the ideologies of liberal-democracy, socialism, anarcho-syndicalism and communism poured into Japan, leaving a deep imprint on the Japanese intellectuals and workers. Class conflict and tension were sharpened in response to the rapid development of capitalism, industrialism, and urbanism in Japan during World War I.[26]

The student movement after World War I was directed to the following issues: (1) the campaign to rescue hungry Russians, which led to the formation of *Gakusei Rengo* (Federation of Students) in 1922; (2) opposition to the introduction of military training into Japanese universities in 1923, when the government tried to employ surplus army officers there: this resulted in the creation of the National Student Union against Military Training in 1923; (3) organizing of Shakai Kagaku Kenkyu Kai (Society for the Study of Social Science) and the Student Settlement Movement in 1924; (4) underground activities against the policy of the Military-Fascist complex in Japan after the passage of the notorious *Chian Ijiho* (Public Security Maintenance Law), which literally decimated radical activists throughout the 1930s.[27]

The disorder following the Great Earthquake of 1923 in Tokyo provided the government with an excuse for the massive suppression of radicals, culminating in the passage of the Public Security Maintenance Law in 1925. It subjected all progressives and dissenters to terrorism at the hands of the military and the dreaded Tokko Keisatsu (Japan's Thought-Control Police). In the light of mounting oppression and fascism in Japan, it is not difficult to understand why the student movement adopted such ruses as the theoretical study of revolutionary ideologies under the guise of the Society for the Study of Social Science, or the more humanitarian and less political approach of the Student Settlement Movement, in order to survive the constant surveillance of the long arm of the law.[28] Yet the student movement was by no means stamped out, but kept up its resistance to the increasingly fascist-oriented policy at the time, as shown in Table 10.V.[29]

Table 10.V—*Student riots and number of students arrested*

	1925	1926	1927	1928	1929	1930	1931	Total
Number of school riots	15	7	13	75	117	223	395	845
Number of students arrested	45	—	29	120	292	950	1,119	2,555

When Japan moved her troops into Manchuria in 1931, what little vestige of party politics there was came to a virtual end, and thereafter all progressive-liberal movements were totally silenced. The shattering defeat of Japan in 1945 emancipated the nation from the repressive political order, and there came a nation-wide development of political concerns and movements, including student organizations.

The student movement after World War II: Emergence of Zengakuren

The Japanese student movement attained its organizational structure and prowess with the emergence of Zengakuren (an abbreviation of Zen-Nippon Gakusei Jichikai So-rengo, or National Federation of Student-Government Associations). It was organized on 18 September 1948, with affiliated units in 168 national, 31 municipal, and 61 private universities, with an estimated membership of about 300,000 in the total student population of approximately 400,000.[30] Accepting Communist leadership, it had as its first chairman Akio Iwai, then a member of the Japan Communist Party (J.C.P.). The agreement adopted at the founding convention in Tokyo read as follows:[31]

> Zengakuren, with the objectives of realizing all justifiable demands of all students by democratic methods and of contributing to the foundation of a democratic Japan through movements for restoring education, shall emphasize the following programs: (1) security and improvement of student life, and equal opportunities for education; (2) defense of academic freedom and national culture; (3) thorough democratization of educational administration; (4) security of right of autonomy of faculties; (5) unification and enlargement of student fronts; (6) defense of peace and democracy; (7) support of all other kinds of movements necessary for realizing the federation's objectives.

There are ten regional Gakurens (Regional Federation of Student-Government Associations) and three special Gakurens. Zengakuren, then, is a national federation of these thirteen Gakurens. These regional Gakurens represent the following regions (which do not necessarily coincide with the administrative units of the local government prefectures): (1) Hokkaido Gakuren, (2) Tohoku Gakuren, (3) Kita Shin-etsu Gakuren, (4) Kanto Gakuren, (5) Tokyo Metropolitan Gakuren, (6) Tokai Gakuren, (7) Kansai Gakuren, (8) Chugoku Gakuren, (9) Shikoku Gakuren, and (10) Kyushu Gakuren. These ten regional Gakurens are joined by three special Gakurens: (1) Igakuren (Medical Student Federation), (2) Yagakuren (Federation of Night-School Students), and (3) Shigakuren (Federation of Private University Students). Zengakuren affiliational structure is shown in Figure 10.1.[32]

Of 1.5 million students attending 828 universities and colleges in Japan in 1968, approximately 71 per cent. have student self-government associations, with at least 700,000 members affiliated with Zengakuren.[33]

The internal organizational structure of Zengakuren is an extremely complicated one, reflecting the Japanese penchant for organizational hierarchy, and it was modelled after that of the Japan Communist Party. Its organizational structure is shown in Figure 10.2.

There are two important organs within Zengakuren as an organization: the Executive Committee and the Secretariat. The Executive Committees are decision-making organs and the Secretariat is the organization that carries on day-to-day business and implements the decisions of the Executive Committee and the Zengakuren Congress. The Central Secretariat, perhaps the most important organ of all, has the following eight bureaus: (1) student welfare bureau, (2) information and propagation bureau, (3) organization bureau, (4) finance bureau, (5) bureau of educational problems, (6) bureau of night school problems, (7) bureau of medical school problems, and (8) international bureau.

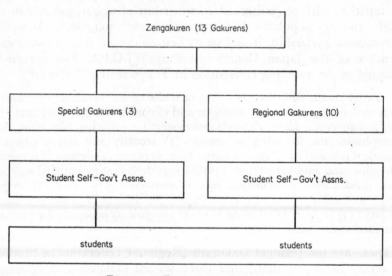

FIG. 10.1.—ZENGAKUREN AFFILIATIONS

The General Secretary works as chairman of the Conference of Secretaries. Positions of the Secretariats must be filled by the votes of the Congress of the Central Committee.[34] The General Secretary represents the Zengakuren Secretariat, and the President of Zengakuren the Zengakuren Central Executive Committee. The President also serves as chairman of the Central Committee. He has to hold two major conferences, the Zengakuren Congress and the Central Committee, when a quorum of over one-third of Zengakuren membership may request a meeting of either committee. At the same time, the Congress or the Central Committee has a right to dismiss all of the officers of the organization, if one of the two legislative organs obtains a majority vote requesting such an action.[35]

Zengakuren has undergone considerable changes since its inception in 1948. There developed within Zengakuren an increasing trend towards defying the Communist Party and asserting its own viewpoint. Early in the 1950s Zengakuren was already divided into two main factions: the Mainstream Faction (Shuryu-ha) and Anti-Mainstream Faction (Han Shuryu-ha), both of which competed for the hegemony of Zengakuren. The Mainstream Faction, centred around the University of Tokyo and Waseda University, espoused anti-Americanism

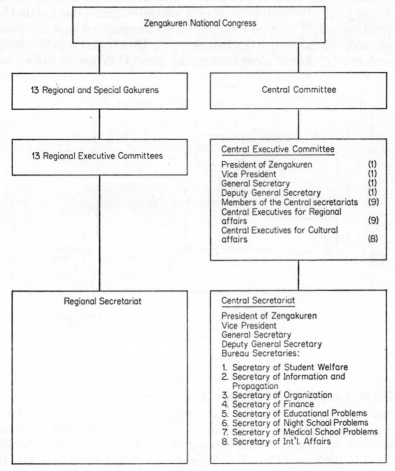

FIG. 10.2.—THE ORGANIZATIONAL STRUCTURE OF ZENGAKUREN

and anti-Stalinism; its ideology was so radical and thoroughgoing that it was dismissed from the Communist Party later on. The Anti-Mainstream Faction advocated the theory of 'two-step revolution', i.e., that revolution should proceed from moderate parliamentary socialism to communism. Following the Sixth National Consultative Conference in July, 1955, the Japan Communist Party denounced the tactics of Zengakuren as 'irresponsible left-wing adventurism'. Fluctuations and events within the Communist world such as Khrushchev's criticisms of Stalinism (February 1956), the Hungarian uprising (October 1956), and mounting evidence of tension between the U.S.S.R. and the People's Republic of China in 1958, all contributed to the erosion of the monolithic grip of the Soviet Union and further induced a split among Marxists around the world.

On 1 June 1958, immediately after the so-called Yoyogi Incident,[36] the Mainstream Faction completely and irrevocably severed its ties with the J.C.P. Following the bloody struggle against the Japan–U.S. Mutual Security Treaty in 1960 (for which Zengakuren captured world headlines), the movement fell into disarray. Thus it split into four major groupings: (1) *Minsei* Zengakuren, the pro-J.C.P. group, which was

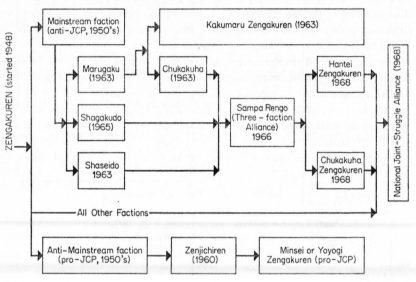

Fig. 10.3

officially formed by the former Anti-Mainstream Faction in Zenga-kuren in 1964; (2) the anti-J.C.P. groups are divided into three major sections—*Kakumaru* Zengakuren (Revolutionary Marxist Faction), organized in 1963, *Hantei* Zengakuren (Anti-Imperialist Faction) created in 1968, and *Chukakuha* Zengakuren (Main-Core Faction), also started in 1968.[37] With the exception of the pro-J.C.P. *Minsei* Zenga-kuren and *Kakumaru* group, all other factions were strategically united in the National Alliance for Joint Struggle (*Zenkyoto*) in 1968. The evolution of Zengakuren is shown in Figure 10.3.

The students who have been capturing the headlines in Japan, therefore, are the far-out radicals in the anti-J.C.P. factions. They totally reject tactical retreat, political compromises or tentative negotia-tions. They seem to be driven by a chiliastic belief that their sacrifice will eventually trigger off a revolutionary blast all over Japan. From their viewpoint, the Japan Communist Party (J.C.P.) is a reactionary group. They regard themselves as the 'vanguard of the revolutionary force', and plan to destroy the existing socio-political structure. Because they are a vanguard, they believe they are destined for defeat. The Communist Party in turn denounces them by alleging that their reckless adventurism is playing into the hands of the system. But such criticism only fuels their militancy and hostility to the existing left-wing political parties and drives them to even more violent tactics to demonstrate their contempt of the 'moderate liberals'. So intense is the rivalry and so deep is the schism among these student groups today that they seem to agree only on one point—i.e., that the Socialist and Communist Parties are opportunist, deserters from the true revolutionary cause, and must, therefore, be rejected. On every other point there is sharp disagreement. But at the core of the disagreement is the irresistible desire to occupy the hallowed place as the vanguard of the revolution. The result is a race for salience and visibility that can only be attained by being more militant than the other factions. It is this factional rivalry within the student movement today that has been one of the causes of escalated violence, characteristic of Japanese student radicalism in the late 1960s. Thus the students battled not only with the police but also against the other factions: the pro-J.C.P. group against anti-J.C.P. groups, and the anti-J.C.P. factions against each other.[38] The current strength of major Zengakuren factions is shown in Table 10.VI below.

Table 10.VI—(as May 1968)

	Faction	Number of affiliate universities	Total membership	Activist	Number of the mobilizable
		%	%	%	%
Minsei (pro-J.C.P.)		156 (61.9)	460,900 (55.2)	11,900 (61.0)	38,300 (54.7)
Anti-J.C.P. groups	Kakumaru	16 (6.4)	66,100 (8.0)	1,800 (9.2)	3,400 (4.8)
	Chukakuha	25 (9.9)	67,800 (8.1)	2,000 (10.3)	6,400 (9.2)
	Hantei	38 (15.1)	154,800 (18.5)	2,800 (14.3)	8,300 (11.9)
	Other	17 (6.7)	85,300 (10.2)	1,000 (5.2)	13,600 (19.4)
	total	252 (100)	834,900 (100)	19,500 (100)	70,000 (100)

Source: rearranged from data in *Asahi Nenkan* (Asahi Yearbook),[25] *Asahi Shimbun*, 1969, op. cit., p. 546.

Painfully aware of such divisions and fragmentation, major Zengakuren factions (with the exception of the pro-Communist *Minsei* group and the anti-J.C.P. *Kakumaru*) finally arranged a pragmatic alliance in their joint struggle against the power structure, resulting in the National Joint-Struggle Alliance (Zenkyoto Rengo) in 1968. It is further predicted that fierce confrontation will continue between the police and the radical students, and between the pro-Communist faction and the anti-J.C.P. factions of Zengakuren, especially in 1970 when the Japan-U.S. Mutual Security Pact comes up for review.

Student revolt and the type of issues involved

The main activities of Zengakuren students from the past to the present
can be classified into two major categories of issues involved: specific
campus issues, and those geared to national-international issues.[39]

(1) National-International Issues

Since its inception in 1948, Zengakuren has been strongly tied at first
to the Japan Communist Party, and then to far-out left-wing ideologies.
The emergence of Zengakuren somehow coincides with the beginning
of the Cold War and its accelerating intensification. It is no wonder,
then, that it became deeply involved with national and international
issues with a strong commitment to the left. Fragmenting intra-mural
battles among the Zengakuren factions described earlier also mirror
the emergence of a multiplicity of orientations within the Communist
camp. Because of limited space, a very brief list of national-international
issues that involved Zengakuren students will be given.[40]

Table 10.VII—*Major issues involved, 1950–69*

Major Issue	Year	Description
Opposition to the Red Purge	1949 through the early 1950s	U.S. occupation forces ordered the dismissal of 'Communist' and left-wing radicals from campuses
Opposition to Peace Treaty for Japan	1948–52	Zengakuren insisted that a multi-lateral treaty, including U.S.S.R. and Mainland China, must be signed
U.S.–Japan Military Security Treaty	1950s	Japan was thereby obliged to provide the U.S. with land–air–sea bases as treaty obligations
Rearmament of Japan	1950s	Creation of so-called Self-Defence Forces (land–air–sea)
Opposition to Nuclear Testing	1950s to 1962	Zengakuren opposed nuclear testing by major powers
Opposition to the U.S.–Japan Security Treaty	1950s to 1960, and 1970	Opposition continues through 1970 against the renewal of the Treaty
Return of Okinawa	1960s to 1970	Return of Okinawa with nuclear weapons stripped

(2) Campus Issues

Table 10.VIII—*Major campus issues, 1968*

School	Description of Issues
Tokyo University[41]	Opposition to the intern system
Nihon University[42]	Misappropriation of university funds

School	*Description of Issues*
Tokyo University of Education[43]	Opposition to planned relocation of campus
Chuo University[44]	Tuition fees increase
Hosei University	Protest against police invasion
Jochi University	Protest against police invasion
Kansai Gakuyin University	Tuition fees increase
Shibaura Polytechnic Institute	Tuition fees increase
Tohoku Gakuyin University	Tuition fees increase
Rissho University	Tuition fees increase
Toyo University	Relocation of campus
Niigata University	Relocation of campus
Tokyo Medical–Dental University	Intern system
Komazawa University	Repeal of student punishment—campus democracy
Kanto Gakuyin University	Campus democratization
Osaka University	Repeal of student punishment—campus democracy
Kanagawa University	Campus democratization
Kyoto University	Against physician registration system
Hiroshima University	Against physician registration system, and revocation of student scholarships
Waseda University	Demand for changes in election of rector
Doshisha University	Democratization of election of rector
Fukushima University	Demand for resignation of rector
Toyama University	Teacher shortage and demand for change in personnel policies
Akita University	Against changes in the curriculum of the Education Department
Keio University	Borrowing of U.S. Army-financed money
Tokyo University for Foreign Languages	Against construction of new dormitories
Kanazawa University	Against dormitory policies
Chita University	Student management of dormitories and student union
Kagoshima University	Against academic–industrial tie-up
Shiga University	Teacher shortage in classroom

Source: T. Fusé, 'Student Radicalism . . .', op. cit.,[37] pp. 330–332; Asahi Shimbunsha, *Asahi Nenkan*, op. cit.,[25] p. 544.

Discussion: Aetiology of student radicalism

In the aetiology of student movements there are two basic factors: *predisposing* and *precipitating* variables. The latter refer to specific, concrete issues or incidents that are discernible and trigger off student protest, which may develop into massive revolts and movements at times quite unrelated to the original issue or incident that precipitated the crisis. Earlier on this chapter listed a number of such precipitating causes. The former, the *predisposing* factors, on the other hand, are those variables, less visible and more subtle, that are the necessary, accumulated conditions in which the triggering mechanism can take place. In this section, then, some theoretical analyses of the factors in student radicalism will be discussed in the light of some available empirical data.[45]

(1) Erosion of Legitimation

A political system is legitimate when people consider it to be the proper and desirable way to run the country. As such, legitimation means power is justified by the community's socio-cultural values, and governing is freed from primary reliance on the naked exercise of force.[46] Any political order is dependent on the stability of power and authority, and, therefore, must eventually develop some form of quasi-moral justification for the cold reality of 'unequal distribution of power' and exercise thereof.

One of the major characteristics of student radicalism in the present decade seems to be the tendency among radical students to reject both *the symbol and agent of legitimation*,[47] creating a virtually revolutionary rather than reformist situation. The four basic modes of response to a socio-political situation are shown in a paradigm in Figure 10.4.

FIG. 10.4.—MODES OF RESPONSE TO SOCIO-POLITICAL SYSTEM.

		acceptance of legitimation	
		High	Low
perceived need for restructuring of socio-political power arrangements in society	High	Reformist Movement (liberals)	Revolutionary Movement (radicals)
	Low	Conservatism (conservatives)	Retreatism (religious sects, etc.)

Reformist Movement: when students accept the symbol of legitimation and also perceive a need for changes in the socio-political system, they are likely to be 'liberals' and join a reformist movement, employing the institutionalized means of dissent and opposition. This is by and large the form of dissent and reformism in liberal-democratic systems.

Conservatism: when the symbol of legitimacy is accepted and the need for social-political reform is not perceived, students are likely to be bent on the preservation of the *status quo* and join a conservative movement.

Revolutionary Movement: in this case, students *question* and then *reject* the symbol of legitimation; when such rejection is coupled with a high perception of a need for basic socio-political changes, it is most likely to turn into a *radical movement of either Right or Left.* Today's left-wing radicalism among students is best characterized by this model.

Retreatism: when students reject the symbol of legitimation as irrelevant, and at the same time do not perceive the need for socio-political change, they are most likely to 'opt out' from this society in various ways, such as joining a religious sect or Hippie community, etc.

In Japan the symbol of legitimation has been the Imperial system and the Emperor himself. The new Japanese Constitution of 1947 proclaims the Emperor to be the 'symbol of the unity of the Japanese nation'. Yet one of the recent surveys on students' attitudes towards the Emperor and the Imperial system revealed that a sizeable portion of Japan's young students either do not accept this symbol of legitimation or are indifferent to it:[48]

Question: What do you think of the presence of the Emperor in Japan's political system?

1. We should have it 46.9%
2. We should not have it 23.8
3. I don't care one way or the other 26.2
4. Don't know 3.1

_____

100.0%

Question: How do you feel towards the Emperor and his family?

1. Have feelings of respect 5.0%
2. Feel close to him 24.4
3. Don't feel anything 60.1
4. Feel antagonism 7.7
5. Feel strong hatred 1.3
6. Don't know 1.5

_____

100.0%

In reference to the first question on the students' attitude toward the presence of the Imperial system, 50 per cent. of them were either indifferent or did not wish to have it. As for the second question, to gauge their feeling toward the Emperor and his family, 69 per cent. of the respondents felt either totally indifferent or hostile.

Students' confidence in the *agent* of legitimation also seems to be pretty low. Another poll taken recently at Waseda University in Tokyo to find out the favourite political leaders among students revealed that Prime Minister Eisaku Sato and the Socialist Party Chairman, Seiichi Katsumata, failed to make even the bottom of the popularity test.[49] Since these survey results were an indication of the attitudes of students at large, one could assume that the reaction of radical students in Japan to the question of legitimation would be much more negative.

(2) Problems of the University
High concentration of students in metropolis. In the history of the Japanese student movement, most radical revolts have taken place at prestigious

universities located in big industrial metropolises such as Tokyo. In recent years student radicalism has spread far and wide, from Hokkaido University in the north to Kyushu University in the south; yet major student revolts are still waged largely in Tokyo, where most of the bright students come and where most of the leading universities are located; where organizations such as labour unions are powerful; where social problems are highly visible.[50] Unlike capitals in the United States or Canada, where they are located in smaller cities, Japan's capital, Tokyo, is the uncontested centre of political administration, economy, commerce and education in the nation. Hence the radical student movement that aims at challenging the seat of power tends to operate in Tokyo, and the high concentration of universities and students in the capital certainly helps the growth of student movements, as shown in Table 10.IX.

Table 10.IX—*Distribution of universities and students in Japan (1967)*

	Number of universities	Number of students	Percentage of students
Tokyo	102	540,392	46.6%
Osaka	32	110,854	9.6
Aichi Prefecture	24	65,359	5.6
Hyogo Prefecture	24	40,350	3.5
Kyoto	21	81,657	7.0
Fukuoka Prefecture	18	50,391	4.3
Kanagawa Prefecture	13	29,044	2.5
Other	135	242,378	20.9
total	369	1,160,425	100.0%

Source: *Nippon Kokusei Zué* (Japan Statistical Yearbook), op. cit., p. 482. This means that more than 63.2 per cent. of all university students are concentrated in three cities in Japan: Tokyo, Osaka and Kyoto; and more than 42 per cent. of all universities are located in these three cities.

'Quality of Education' and the University in Japan. The Japanese university, once revered by students and public alike, has been under severe criticisms since the end of World War II, when Japan witnessed a mushrooming of universities and colleges all over the country based upon U.S.-inspired 'reforms', which gave priority to the form of the university rather than to the substance and quality of life in the university. In short, today, Japan also faces the negative phenomena of the 'multiversity'. The emergence of the multiversity is perhaps an unavoidable result of the increasing population, the rising numbers of young people going on to higher education, the increase in national

wealth and standard of living, and the advance in science and technology. In other words, the multiversity is one of the results of a 'post-industrial society'. As such it is usually characterized by such tendencies as the increasing bureaucratization of the university, the greater stress on science and technology, and the operation of the university as a service and 'profit-making' organization much like a modern industrial corporation.[51]

If the multiversity is big in size, it hardly offers quality education to the students. The over-crowded classrooms, incompetent lectures, total indifference to the problems of students (the American-style adviser system is utterly lacking in most universities in Japan), chronic shortage of teachers and in budgets,—all these contribute to the accumulated frustration of the students.[52] The qualitative 'backwardness' of Japanese universities is attested by the fact that Japan's expenditure for higher education is one of the lowest of advanced industrial nations of the world, as shown in Table 10.X:

Table 10.X—*Educational Expenditure for Higher Education*

Country	% in terms of national income	% in terms of education budget	Expenditure per student: Japan = 100
Japan (1962)	0.6%	11.5%	100
United States (1962)	1.1	20.7	264
Great Britain (1961)	0.7	16.4	314
West Germany (1961)	0.9	18.3	240
Soviet Union (1962)	0.8	16.4	116

Source: Ministry of Education, Government of Japan, *The Level of Education in Japan* (Monbusho, Tokyo 1964).

Another sign of the inferior quality of education in the universities has been the tendency on the part of Japanese universities to accommodate more students into law and humanities faculties, as it is easier to build more and more of such faculties which require no laboratories and equipment. This is especially true of most private universities in Japan, which prefer to increase student enrolment in humanities, law and social sciences as the easiest source of revenue. It has been observed, then, that a large proportion of student radicals come from law and humanities rather than science and engineering. The distribution of degree subjects in various countries is shown in Table 10.XI.

From 'élite education' to 'mass education'. Ralph Turner classifies social mobility into two types: *sponsored* mobility and *contest* mobility. In the former the established élite select candidates and aspirants for vacant positions and social mobility is granted 'from above', whereas in the latter the aspirants for mobility compete among themselves. Hence for the former the purpose of education tends to be the accumulation of

235

cultural enrichment as a general background before entry into the élite positions, and recognition is given by and large to 'moral success' and cultural achievement. The educational system in a sponsored-mobility-oriented society tends to be a 'dual-ladder system', i.e., one for the masses and the other for the élites. Contest mobility operates in a society where education is regarded as primarily pragmatic, and instrumental for material and economic success rather than intrinsic moral success or cultural embellishment; hence in such a case education is characterized by a 'single-ladder system' which everyone tries to

Table 10.XI—*International comparison of degree subjects*

Country	Science and engineering	Education and home economics	Law, social science and humanities
Japan (1964)	30.5%	12.9%	56.6%
U.S.A. (1964–65)	16.1	27.6	56.3
Britain (1964–65)	55.3	—	44.7
France (1965)	53.6	—	46.4
West Germany (1963)	46.9	—	53.1
Soviet Union (1965)	62.8	24.2	13.0

Source: Tokyo Daigaku Shuppankai, *Nippon no Daigaku*, op. cit.,[3] p. 106. The distribution has not changed much in 1969. See, Asahi Shimbunsha, *Asahi Nenkan*, op. cit.,[25] p. 549.

climb to the top. Elite education tends to sustain and solidify existing social values, whereas mass education is likely to contribute to social change.[53]

As mentioned earlier in this chapter, Japan's higher education has made a transition from élite to mass education over the years, and now ranks second in the world in terms of the numbers of young people going on to higher education. Further growth in contest mobility and an increasing challenge to well-established social values in society may therefore be expected. The rate of the college-age youth going on to higher education is shown in Table 10.XII:

Table 10.XII—*International comparison of access to higher education*

Country	A		B		Rate of increase $\dfrac{A-B}{B} \times 100$
Japan	1963	15.7%	1958	10.9%	44%
U.S.A.	1963	38.1	1958	33.6	13
Great Britain	1962	8.4	1957	6.9	22
West Germany	1961	6.5	1956	4.5	44
France	1962	12.1	1957	8.6	41

Source: Ministry of Education, *Wagakuni no Kyoiku Suijun* ('Educational Level of Japan': Monbusho, Tokyo 1968).

(3) Status-Deprivation as a source of radicalism

It has been argued that class cleavages will decrease as income is distributed more equally among the population and that subsequently conflict politics will be replaced by consensus and bargaining politics.[54] Yet a glance at the political scene around the world is enough to convince anyone of the fallacy of this argument, as conflict politics, especially involving students, are on the ascendant.

Political cleavage, then, does not seem to be based solely on class antagonism, but at times on status deprivation and power struggle among status-groups. In other words, even if the distribution of wealth does not present a major problem, people may still fight over the distribution of status and power. Indeed, the distribution of status and power has become a crucial problem in most of the affluent post-industrial societies, of which Japan is an important example.

The decline of ideology should not be confused with the decline of division. When Max Weber and Robert Michels examined the socio-political conditions of a bureaucratized society, they both postulated that the basic problems of modern politics are not so much the competition between capitalism and socialism as that between political bureaucracy and individual freedom, whether or not a particular society is capitalist or socialist. In a time of diffused egalitarianism, 'participatory democracy' (distribution of power) at all levels of the socio-political process will be sought by an increasingly larger part of the population, but in particular by intellectuals, who are usually more sensitized to status-deprivation than others.[55]

Students' sense of status-deprivation may be further accentuated by the fact that in consensus-model societies, including all the highly industrialized societies of Europe and America as well as Japan, the political system tends to be less attentive to the problems of people who exist outside the loyalties, values, and identification of the great mass of voters, precisely because these people lack well-defined bargaining power, as a result of low status or deprivation of status (as in the case of students), poor organization, or isolation. Somehow, students in general, and also the urban poor, seem to fit into this category, a fact which may explain their propensity to rely on violent, extra-institutional means of attaining their objectives.

(4) Demographic-Ecological Factors

As long as there have been parents and children (or elders and youths), there have always been confrontations between the authority of age and the challenge of youth. Lately the clashes have become more direct and intense. Such factors as the differential rate of socialization between the generations, youthful 'idealism' versus adult 'realism', and the like, certainly contribute to the conflict between generations. But one other factor seems to be the sheer number of young people. The growth of a separate teenage subculture and the rise of mass campus groupings

have given youth the power to question the legitimacy of adult authority
and to directly attack its institutions.[56] By 1970, 70 per cent. of the
eligible Japanese voters will be below forty-three—in other words, those
born in the Showa period (since 1925). If Japan is still governed then
by the hopes, ideas, commitments, and values of the remaining 30 per
cent., the generational and political conflict can only deepen.

Students, furthermore, in contrast to workers, are not well organized
and are not represented by a permanent corps of leaders. The rapid
turnover of membership in the student body means that no student is
a permanent, entrenched bureaucrat within an organization with a
stake in the system. The restraints that often prevent members of
organizations from revolting do not, therefore, operate on students.

Students not only have common interests and experiences: society
also isolates them as a special group different from the general population. By definition, students are all of a kind, living apart from the rest
of the occupational community. This ecological segregation of students
within a limited geographical area, bringing together many young men
and women of similar socio-economic background, stratified by age
and sex, temporarily suspended from the occupational community, in
which the non-students of similar age fully participate in life through
marriage, jobs and spending, and isolating them for a few years in a
self-contained 'ghetto' called the university, certainly contributes to
student restlessness and frustrations.

Conclusion

In the preceding pages the origins of the Japanese university have been
traced, and the system of higher education in Japan discussed. In the
last section of this chapter some hypotheses were suggested and analysed
in terms of some available secondary data. In concluding this chapter,
the writer ventures some predictions on the future development of
student movements in Japan.

(1) In the foreseeable future, student movements in Japan are likely
to become more radicalized and be involved in intensified conflicts,
because of the mass nature of higher education and the ideology of
student radicals. Any issue peculiar to a particular academic institution
(e.g., tuition increase, campus relocation, etc.) would be linked to
broader national–international *political* issues. University issues are
considered by radical students to be the logical, unavoidable outcome
of the reactionary capitalist system and of the well-devised 'imperialist
plots'. As Michiya Shimbori points out,[57]

> According to this logic, any trivial issue must be interpreted in a broader
> context—from the perspective of an evaluation of the social and political
> order, or even the state of international politics. Since this logic is un-
> familiar to and cannot be accepted by the majority of students, the leaders

must use every issue that is clearly relevant to the campus situation as a starting point in the process of 'educating' the majority into an 'enlightened and awakened' perspective. Accordingly, the student movement must continue to struggle until the present power structure comes to an end.

(2) In the wake of left-wing radicalism among several factions of Zengakuren, there is a move among the right-wing students to organize themselves as a counter-force, further accentuating the right–left polarization in Japanese student movements. There are now several extreme-right student organizations, which are preparing to battle with left-wing factions of Zengakuren. The student movement in Japan, therefore, may shift eventually from intra-mural fights among the left-wing radicals to a confrontation between the rightist and leftist students. In the wake of mounting hostility to the left-wing students in Japan among the general public, the Japanese political pendulum may swing towards ultra-conservatism.[58]

(3) Campus-based student revolts will no doubt continue for some time, as most Japanese universities are uniquely vulnerable to student militancy. They have created thus far a deep fissure (perhaps too wide to be repaired) by the years of imperious disdain on the part of the authorities for the students and indeed for the faculty. This fissure is further deepened by the sobering reality that so many university faculty members have been educated and trained for handling figures, numbers and symbols, and the quantitative aspects of our life. They are often unable to deal with qualitative aspects of life, and to provide an 'education for life' rather than a 'training for a career'; nor can they deal with aspirations, feelings and highly individualized ideals which transcend socially agreed norms. Students in 1970, in Japan as well as elsewhere, have refused to merely regurgitate what society feeds them. They refuse, institutionally prescribed norms and try to create individually generated values, rejecting in the process anything that looks dogmatic, authoritarian and unauthentic to them. They seem to aim at the further spreading of democracy at all levels of society—including the university —so as to broaden the social base of participation in the decision-making process of the university and, indeed, of the nation. In short, they seem to demand 'participatory democracy'. Short of drastic and thorough restructuralization of the Japanese university, student radicalism would not diminish.[59]

(4) Despite its radical-sounding slogans, the opposition Japan Socialist Party has been merely pursuing its partisan ends, and even the Japan Communist Party is busy cultivating its own ground in the student movement. On this basis, there can be instances of mutual accommodation between the conservative government and opposition.[60] The tragedy is that in the well-organized bureaucratic society of Japan there is no third choice available between being an 'organization man' and being a drop-out. As for the university administrators, there are only two types in Japan: one type consists of mild liberals, and the

other of those ultra-rightists who try to browbeat newsmen who show even one iota of sympathy for the students. This second type is so aloof from the university as to be unable to view the matter except from the angle of political control. It is not difficult to understand why student radicalism may continue under such circumstances in the university and in the nation as a whole.

It is the nature of the young to question, to protest, to change the present and to shape the future. It is their nature to shock and shake the established order. And it ought to be the role of the university, which teaches the young to think critically, to provide a platform for a continuing criticism of the university and society. Eventually the university may have to be an active agent of change in the process of modernizing and humanizing society. If students do not stir things up and protest, then the university and society will be the victims of complacency and the prisoners of anachronism. Perhaps out of all this chaos today will emerge a new vision of the university and society. Perhaps historians of tomorrow may rightly designate the students of today as creative agents of change, who shook the very foundation of our archaic universities into making an important step towards the creation of a modern university and more humane society.

Notes

1. Abé Makoto, Nagashima Fukutaro, and Inouyé Kaoru (eds.), *Nyumon Nipponshi*, (Introduction to Japanese History: Yoshikawa Kobunkan, Tokyo 1969), pp. 21–43.
2. Iyénaga Saburo and Kuroba Kiyotaka, *Shinko Nipponshi* (New History of Japan: Sanseido, Tokyo 1968), pp. 27–45.
3. Momo Hiroyuki, 'Nippon no Daigaku no Rekishi' (History of the Japanese University), in Tokyo Daigaku Shuppansha (ed.), *Nippon no Daigaku* (Tokyo Daigaku Shuppansha, Tokyo 1968), p. 5.
4. Ibid., pp. 5–8.
5. Ishida Ichiro (ed.), *Nippon Bunkashi Gairon* (General Outline of Japanese Cultural History: Yoshikawa Kobunkan, Tokyo 1967), pp. 137–206.
6. Ibid., pp. 155–171; Abé Makoto, *et al.*, *Nymon Nipponshi*, op. cit. (note 1), pp. 92–150. By using Chinese ideographs the Japanese began to write verses that had been handed down verbally from ancient times. *Kojiki* (the Chronicle of Ancient Times), the oldest existing history of Japan, *Nihonshoki* (the Chronicles of Japan), and *Man'yoshu* (Collection of Myriad Leaves), the oldest anthology of Waka poems, were written during this period. As for the Japanese phonetic syllabaries, they gave great impetus to the growth of Japanese literature. Literary talents found expression in the so-called *Monogatari* or tales, instead of in the mythologies and legends as before; and such works as *Ise Monogatari* (Tale of Ise), *Takétori Monogatari* (Tale of the Bamboo-cutter), *Makura-no-Soshi* (The Pillow Book), and finally *Genji Monogatari* (Tale of Genji), which is still judged one of the greatest novels of world literature and widely read in the Western world.
7. Abé Makoto, *et al.*, *Nymon Nipponshi*, op. cit. (note 1), pp. 117–121.
8. Ishida Ichiro (ed.), *Nippon Bunkashi Gairon*, op. cit. (note 5), pp. 241–258.
9. Momo Hiroyuki, 'History of the Japanese University', op. cit. (note 3), pp. 14–16. In comparison to the university in the previous period, the academy in the monastery stressed tutorial situation considerably. For curricula, they adopted Chinese classics, rhetoric, medicine, astrology and Buddhist doctrines. Among the Portuguese who came to Japan was a Spanish missionary, Francisco Xavier. In his correspondence with friends in Spain, he stated that there was a 'university' in Kyoto and five colleges. It is generally

considered that he was referring to the five Zen monastery-academies of the time (Zenshu Gozan).

10. Sir George B. Sansom, *Japan: A Short Cultural History* (New York: Appleton-Century-Crofts, Inc., 1962), pp. 441–463; Abé Makoto, *et al.*, *Nuymon Nipponshi*, op. cit., pp. 401–414; Ishida Ichiro, *Nippon Bunkashi Gairon*, op. cit., pp. 367–415.

11. Karasawa Tomitaro, 'Nippon no Kyoiku Hyakunen' (History of Education in Japan in the last 100 Years), in *Gendai Kyokyo Hyaka Jiten* (Akatsuki Tosho Kabushiki Kaisha, Tokyo 1968), pp. 453–454.

12. Tokyo Daigaku Shuppankai, *Nippon no Daigaku*, op. cit. (note 3), pp. 16–19.

13. Ibid.

14. Naka Arata, 'Nippon no Daigaku no Rekishi' (History of Education since Meiji in Japan), in Tokyo Daigaku Shuppansha, *Nippon no Daigaku*, op. cit., pp. 21–32.

15. The educational system in the Tokugawa period was a typical 'dual-ladder system'—i.e., one for the élite and the other for the masses. But the Unified Education Act at least envisaged a 'single-ladder system', which was in many ways even more advanced than that of any European country at the time. Though the plan was a remarkable blueprint for mass education, theory was not really translated into practice and was abandoned in 1880.

16. Naka Arata and Mochida Eiichi, *Gakko Seido* (Educational System in Japan), (Daiichi Hoki Shuppan Kabushiki Kaisha, Tokyo 1968), pp. 14–15.

17. Michiya Shimbori, 'The Sociology of a Student Movement: A Japanese Case Study', *Daedalus*, Vol. 97, No. 1 (Winter 1968), p. 204.

18. Nagai Michio, 'The Development of Intellectuals in the Meiji and Taisho Periods', *Journal of Social and Political Ideas in Japan*, Vol. II (April 1964), No. 1, p. 29.

19. Naka Arata and Mochida Eiichi, *Gakko Seido*, op. cit., pp. 237–249.

20. Walt. W. Rostow, *Stages of Economic Growth* (Harvard University Press, Cambridge, Mass. 1960), p. 59.

21. Naka Arata, 'Nippon no Daigaku no Rekishi', in *Nippon no Daigaku*, op. cit., p. 55.

22. Tetsu Nakamura, *Seijishi* (Political History of Japan: Toyo Keizai Shinposha, Tokyo 1967), pp. 187–249; Abé Makoto, *et al.*, *Nyumon Nipponshi*, op. cit. (note 1), pp. 471–532; Iyénaga Saburo, *et al.*, *Shinko Nipponshi*, op. cit. (note 2), pp. 479–555.

23. Miyahara Seiichi, *Kyoikushi* (History of Education in Japan: Toyo Keizai Shinposha, Tokyo 1967), pp. 323–340.

24. Naka Arata and Mochida Eiichi, *Gakko Seido*, op. cit. (note 16), pp. 253–259.

25. Asahi Shimbunsha, *Asahi Nenkan* (The Asahi Yearbook of Japan: Asahi Shimbunsha, Tokyo 1969), p. 541.

26. Michiya Shimbori, 'Comparison Between Pre- and Post-War Student Movements in Japan', *Sociology of Education*, Vol. 37, No. 1 (Fall, 1963), p. 64.

27. Ibid., pp. 64–67.

28. Ibid., pp. 66–67.

29. Adapted from S. Takakuwa, *Nihon Gakusei Undo-shi* (History of Student Movements in Japan: Tokyo 1955), p. 156. A lot of surveys of the participant students by the Ministry of Education and other offices during the second stage are available. Cited in Michiya Shimbori, 'The Sociology of a Student Movement . . .', op. cit. (note 17), p. 217.

30. Shakai Mondai Kenkyu-kai, *Zengakuren Kakuha* 'Zengakuren Factions': Shakai Mondai Kenkyu-kai, Tokyo 1969), pp. 20–24.

31. Michiya Shimbori, 'The Sociology of a Student Movement . . .', op. cit. (note 17), p. 219.

32. Shintaro Yazaki, 'A View on the Recent Japanese Student Movement', mimeographed (International Bureau, Central Secretariat, Zengakuren, Tokyo 1965), pp. 3–4.

33. The Ministry of Education, Government of Japan, 6 January 1968, reported in the *Japan Times Weekly*, 15 January 1968.

34. Shintaro Yazaki, op. cit., pp. 5–8.

35. One of the major problems that faced Zengakuren later was the ambiguity of the power relationship between the Central Secretariat functions under the leadership and directives of the Central Executive Committee, which in turn is accountable to the Central Committee and the Zengakuren National Congress. Ever since the 1960 struggle against the Japan–U.S. Military Security Treaty, however, the Central Secretariat assumed a much more crucial role than the Central Executive Committee. Indeed, the Secretariat declared itself independent of the Executive Committee. It is not too difficult to understand this shift of power within the Zengakuren organization. In fact, during the 1960 crisis, the administrative function of the central Executive Committee, which directs the

Central Secretariat, virtually ceased to exist, when almost all the Executive Committee members were arrested by the police. Out of this crisis emerged the independent and relatively powerful Central Secretariat as the chief organ that can guarantee the function and continuity of the national organization.

36. On 1 June 1958, the National Conference of Zengakuren Representatives was held at the Communist Party Headquarters in Yoyogi section of Tokyo, at which the Zengakuren representatives passed a resolution demanding for the resignation of all members of the Central Committee. To add insult to injury, Zengakuren students physically manhandled staff members of the Japan Communist Party, which thereupon summarily expelled the students. Thus after this incident, the Mainstream Faction of Zengakuren was to all intents and purposes severed from the Japan Communist Party.

37. Toyomasa Fusé, 'Student Radicalism in Japan: A Cultural Revolution?' *Comparative Education Review*, Vol. XIII, No. 3 (October 1969), pp. 327–330.

38. Ibid., p. 329. What must be remembered here, however, is the fact that there emerged recently a multiplicity of right-wing student groups with the aim of defending the present socio-economic arrangements of power as well as of combating the left-wing Zengakuren factions. Because of their relative weakness at present, discussion of their activities has been omitted in this chapter. Interested readers are referred to Shakai Mondai Kenkyu-kai, *Zengakuren Kakuha* (Zengakuren Factions), op. cit. (note 30), pp. 189–226, 229, 230.

39. Michiya Shimbori divides the types of issues into three categories: intra-mural, inter-mural and extra-mural. Yet this writer believes it is much too difficult to separate national from international issues, as they are both intricately related to each other. See Michiya Shimbori, 'The Sociology of a Student Movement', op. cit. (note 17), p. 221.

40. For a detailed analysis, see Toyomasa Fusé, 'Student Radicalism in Japan', op. cit. (note 37), pp. 332–334. Some of the salient issues in 1968 were as follows: (1) In January 1968, in the U.S. Sasebo naval base in north-western Kyushu, the militant Sampa Rengo students (Three Factions Alliance), armed with helmets, shields and poles, clashed with armed riot police, called out from various parts of western Japan to defend the base. The students, along with members of the J.C.P. and unions, opposed the port-call of the U.S. nuclear-powered aircraft-carrier *Enterprise*. While the union members and the pro-J.C.P. Zengakuren students limited themselves to more or less orderly street demonstrations, the Sampa Rengo students clashed head-on with the police. There ensued four days of bloody battles, with 62 students arrested and 200 injured. (2) In February 1968, Zengakuren students joined local farmers opposing land sequestration for construction of the new Tokyo International Airport in Chiba Prefecture—an unusual alliance of radical students and otherwise conservative farmers. (3) In October 1968, and again in 1969, fierce battles took place between students and riot police in down-town Tokyo. The anti-J.C.P. faction students and some peace organizations staged a massive, nation-wide 'International Anti-War Unified Action Day' demonstration; more than 6,000 students and 8,000 members of peace organizations rallied at 30 places in 18 prefectures. Students were joined later by 800,000 workers to demonstrate against the war in Vietnam in 600 Japanese towns. Thousands of anti-war demonstrators captured a major Tokyo railway station at Shinjuku, set part of it on fire, and staged massive demonstrations at the Japanese Defence Department compounds. They battled with police in surrounding streets through the early hours, and this resulted in the invocation of the Anti-Subversive Activities Control Act.

Today from Tohoku University in the north to Kyushu University in the south, nearly three score of universities in Japan have been embroiled in student disputes of some kind or another, with academic activities at a virtual standstill. The tactics used by radical students have become even more violent, and some far-out groups have started mobilizing para-military armed squads in the struggle. Faced with such student confrontation politics and disruptions, Prime Minister Sato hardened his stance on student radicals, and his security authorities have been giving some serious thought to resorting to the law against illegal assembly with dangerous weapons, and invoking the Anti-Subversive Activities Control Act to deal with the Sampa Rengo students and other radical factions. Finally, in the summer of 1969, the Parliament of Japan, after a stormy session, forced through the controversial University Normalization Bill, according to which the Ministry of Education can directly intervene in university disputes and is authorized to wipe any university out of existence if it is not capable of settling disputes and student revolts after a specified time.

41. What has really stunned the nation is the fact that student unrest did not even spare the

Japan

University of Tokyo, the most renowned of all national universities, where most of the nation's Prime Ministers have been educated. It has been facing the worst crisis in its 91-year history: most classes have been closed since mid-June and it is feared that about 7,000 or about one-half of the total number of students may be automatically disqualified from advancing to the next academic year owing to lack of class attendance. The critical situation had its origin in a quite unlikely issue—the revised Medical Practitioner's Law, which was debated by the Parliament and became law on 10 May 1968. Yet the law triggered off student revolts at nearly twenty medical colleges across the country. At first glance, there seems to be nothing for the medical students to grumble about in the revised law, which came into being in an attempt to meet some of their complaints about the unpaid internship system under the old law. Under the Clinical Training System of the revised law, medical college graduates can become accredited physicians by passing the state examination before receiving clinical training. The successful examinee is then recommended to take a two-year clinical course with a monthly salary of between 15,000–20,000 yen, depending on the training institution with which he is affiliated. This period roughly corresponds to the former internship. When the new system was made known, students and interns at medical colleges across the nation expressed dissatisfaction, claiming that the new system provided a way for university hospitals to secure the services of young doctors at low salaries. The medical students and interns at the university asked the Dean of the University to give them a large share in formulating the clinical training curriculum and also to accept a student-intern 'joint struggle council', a request which was rejected by the Dean and the faculty. This more or less abstract dispute suddenly developed into a down-to-earth struggle with the university authorities when on 12 March the Dean punished one researcher, four interns and twelve medical students for their part in an alleged case of violence that occurred earlier. Then the students went on strike, and with the help of activists from other faculties forced the cancellation of the commencement ceremony scheduled on 28 March by blockading the entrances to Yasuda Auditorium. At first most of the other students were relatively unconcerned, and many blamed the medical students for disrupting important functions of the university for their own benefit. But the whole campus rallied to their cause when Rector Okochi called in the riot police on the morning of 17 June to evict more than fifty activists who, two days earlier, had occupied the university's administration offices. Students argued that the intrusion of the riot police infringed the autonomy and the traditional extra-territoriality of the campus and demanded an apology from the Rector. Starting with those in the Faculty of Letters on 25 June, the students went on strike. The University finally capitulated, and on 10 August, the Dean of the Faculty of Medicine and the Director of Tokyo University Hospital resigned, followed by the Rector himself in November. Repercussions of this incident at the nation's most celebrated university were far-reaching. The University of Tokyo did not admit a single freshman for the academic year 1969–70; and applications for the university, usually the largest number in all Japan, dropped considerably in February 1970, indicating some loss of prestige among the applicants.

42. At Nihon University in Tokyo, with the largest student enrolment in Japan, a scandal broke out over the misappropriation by university officials of part of the university funds, totalling two billion yen, and tax evasion. Students demanded a complete investigation of the affair and student participation in the ways and means of appropriating the university funds and budget. For days furious battles were waged on campus between critical students and pro-administration student athletes. Finally, the riot police were called in to quell the disputes. In the aftermath, students staged a 'kangaroo court' and engaged in 'collective bargaining' with university officials. The affair ended with the resignation of the university president and other officials.

43. At Tokyo University of Education, dissident literature students continue to oppose the planned move of the overcrowded university to the country-side. Their reason for objecting to the relocation of the site was that the plan was unilaterally mapped out by the university administration and the Ministry of Education without consulting the students.

44. A major incident occurred at Chuo University in January 1968, when the university announced a tuition increase plan. The administration explained that this was necessary for private universities, that the changing nature of the economic situation in Japan justified the increase and that money was needed for the improvement of research and education. Students countered by saying that the improvement of research and education

would only serve the ends of capitalists, who need college graduates equipped with necessary technological skills. Thus students started boycotting classes and barricaded the main buildings on the campus, making it impossible to conduct mid-term exams. The university gave in to the students, and made a major concession by promising postponement of the increase (which was originally to come into effect on 1 April 1968) for a year. But the students, led by the Sampa Rengo, would not accept the concession and demanded a total scrapping of tuition increase. On 23 February, President Tatsuo Inouyé told a press conference that the university board of directors had decided on the total withdrawal of a tuition rise averaging 36.2 per cent., and that he would resign shortly after the entrance examinations were conducted in the spring.

45. For detailed discussion of the aetiology of student radicalism, see Toyomasa Fusé, 'Student Radicalism in Japan: A Cultural Revolution?', *Comparative Education Review*, Vol. XIII, No. 3 (October 1969), pp. 334–342.

46. Max Weber, *The Theory of Social and Economic Organization* (The Free Press, Glencoe, Illinois 1947), p. 294.

47. Legitimation can be divided into two component parts in polity: the *symbol* of legitimation and the *agent* of legitimation. The former refers to symbols of political consensus such as a generally accepted constitution and/or traditional monarchy; the latter refers to the political executives in government. In stable democracies, the agent of legitimation is not essential to the continuity and function of a polity. Hence the transition to a new agent of legitimation is effected within the accepted rules of political process guaranteeing the peaceful transition of power. In unstable democracies or non-democratic societies, the symbol and agent of legitimation are fused: thus the constitution is treated as merely the latest revolutionary manifesto or as the personal manifesto of the charismatic leader. In such a political system, every political crisis is a 'constitutional crisis', precipitating the removal of the agent of legitimation as well as resulting in the scrapping of the constitution itself. For details, see T. Fusé, 'Student Radicalism . . .', op. cit. (note 45), p. 334.

48. Though this is a study of student attitudes in only one university in Tokyo, it can still give us some idea of student sentiment in Japan toward the Emperor. Meiji University, where this survey was taken, is a well-known conservative institution. So the results from more liberal universities in Japan could lend even greater support to the implications of this study. The survey was conducted by Zenmei Yoshida and David A. Titus, both on the staff at Meiji University, Tokyo, among 1,280 students in 1967. More than 99.6 per cent. of the questionnaires were returned. See, *Meiji Daigaku Shimbun* (The Meiji University Daily, 4 April 1967), p. 4.

49. 'Kennedy Myth and Japan's Youth', *Japan Times Weekly* (Tokyo, 2 December 1967), p. 7.

50. Michiya Shimbori, 'Comparison between Pre-war and Post-war Student Movements in Japan', op. cit. (note 26), p. 68.

51. Ralph H. Turner, in A. H. Halsey, *et al.*, *Economic Development and Education* (Organization for Economic Co-operation and Development, Paris 1964), Hiroo Suzuki, *Gakusei Undo* (The Student Movement: Fukumura Shuppan, Tokyo 1968), p. 11.

52. One of the surveys made in Japan reveals negative views toward the Japanese university, not only among students and professors, but also among a wide spectrum of the national population. See T. Fusé, 'Student Radicalism . . .' op. cit. (note 37), p. 337, Table 1.

53. Ralph Turner, op. cit. (note 51).

54. Daniel Bell, *The End of Ideology* (The Free Press, Glencoe, Illinois 1962); Seymour Martin Lipset, *Political Man* (Heinemann, London 1960). Talcott Parsons perhaps best exemplifies this attitude in the following quote: 'In general . . . the management of cleavage is accomplished by subordinating conflicts on the political level to some higher overarching attitudes of solidarity, whether these attitudes be the norms associated with the 'rules of the democratic game' or the belief that there exists within the society a supra-party solidarity based upon non-partizan criteria . . .'. See Talcott Parsons, Eugene Burdick and Arthur Brodbeck (eds.), *American Voting Behavior* (The Free Press, Glencoe, Illinois 1959), p. 92.

55. Finally it must be remembered that the decline of *objective* deprivation—i.e., low income, malnutrition, unemployment, etc.—does not automatically reduce the potential tension of society, because so long as men are differentially evaluated and rewarded in status, power and prestige, they will certainly feel *subjectively* deprived, and this provides further fuel for igniting the fire of conflict and cleavage. See S. M. Lipset, *Political Man*, op. cit.,

pp. 28–29, 407–409. The importance of status cleavage rather than economic cleavage has been treated increasingly in sociological research in recent years. The best example is Gerhard Lenski, *The Religious Factor* (Doubleday, Garden City, New York 1960). Another example is the cultural and linguistic cleavage between French Canadians and English Canadians in Quebec.

56. Some 6.5 million college students finished the academic year in 1968 in the United States. And like labour and the black Americans, students today constitute a new twentieth-century power bloc by their sheer numbers. See David Riesman and Christopher Jencks, *The Academic Revolution* (Doubleday, Garden City, New York 1968).

57. Michiya Shimbori, 'The Sociology of a Student Movement . . .', op. cit. (note 17), p. 209.

58. Most of these rightist student organizations are called *Minzokuha* (Nationalist Faction) and advocate the normalization of university life and reawakening of the nationalist spirit among the students. Soka Gakkai, an offshoot of the Nichiren Buddhist sect in Japan, has organized its own Zengakuren with strong religious overtones. For details, see *Zengakuren Kakuha*, op. cit. (note 30); and *Chosa Geppo* (Monthly Research Report: Prime Minister's Office, Tokyo, November 1969), pp. 1–43.

59. Kazuo Kuroda, 'The Student Opposition', *Japan Times Weekly*, 9 March 1969. Madame Han Suyin, the noted historian-novelist, has pointed out the similarities between student radicalism today and the philosophy of Mao Tse-Tung as expressed in the Great Cultural Revolution:

'A cultural revolution implies the restructuring of attitudes, customs and ways of thought. Seen as such, it is a true revolution in its total sense. Far from considering China's cultural revolution an isolated event which only affects China, it has to be considered within the context of the world as a whole. It is a measure by which we can begin to view the past and the present in a new light. Its main feature is a mass participation in toto, at all levels. We must compare what is going on in China today to what has been happening in other countries, including Asia, Europe and even America. Such youth movements around the world must be assessed in the context of a world-wide cultural revolution.'—Dr Han Suyin, Beaty Lectures, McGill University, Montreal, Canada, 22 October 1968.

60. Kazuo Kuroda, 'The Student Opposition', op. cit. (note 59), p. 4.

11. U.S.A.*

Martin Trow

Autonomous and popular functions of American higher education

If we consider American higher education today with any degree of detachment, we are struck by a paradox. On the one hand, the system seems to be in serious trouble and perhaps even in crisis. Almost all major universities and many others as well have been the scene of student disturbances and even insurrections. Events at Berkeley and Columbia, at Harvard and San Francisco State, have become national news; on many other campuses militant blacks and whites and dissident faculty confront their university's authority with bold demands, threats, strikes, and sit-ins. On the other hand, if looked at from another perspective, and especially from a European perspective, American higher education is successful and thriving, and, indeed, provides the model for educational reformers in almost every European country. American research and scholarship make contributions to every field of learning and dominate many. U.S. applied science and technology are the envy of the world: as Servan-Schreiber has observed, the Americans have worked out 'a close association between business, universities, and the government which has never been perfected nor successful in any European country'. American universities are deeply involved in the life of society and contribute much to the efforts to solve its problems— from social medicine to the inner city. And finally, this sprawling system of some 2,500 colleges and universities enrols over 40 per cent. of the age grade, and over 50 per cent. of all high-school graduates, and these proportions are steadily rising.[1] In some large states like California, where roughly 80 per cent. of high-school graduates go on to some form of higher education, the system of mass higher education begins to be very nearly universal. Whatever one's assessment of these figures and their implications, they must be counted a considerable achievement.

But there must be irony in a celebration of the triumphs of American higher education just at present, when scarcely a day goes by without another report of a confrontation or disruption on a campus. There is perhaps more profit in considering its difficulties. I believe these, of

* This contribution first appeared as 'Reflections on the Transition from Mass to Universal Higher Education' *Daedalus*, Vol 99, No 1.

which student unrest is only the most visible, can be better understood in light of the heightened tension between the autonomous and the popular functions of American colleges and universities, arising out of the movement from mass toward universal higher education.

American colleges and universities, almost from their beginnings, have performed these two sets of functions. The distinction is between those activities and purposes that the university defines for itself and those that it takes on in response to external needs and demands. The autonomous functions are intrinsic to the conception of the university and the academic role as these have evolved in Europe and America over the past 150 years, and are now shared with universities all over the world. The popular functions, most broadly developed in the United States, are best seen as services to other institutions of the society. The line between them is not hard and fast; ultimately, it can be argued, all university activities are in some sense responsive to societal interests. But the distinction is a useful one, perhaps most clearly to Europeans whose universities until recently have largely confined themselves to their traditional and autonomous functions and have resisted accepting tasks set for them by other parts of the society or the population at large.

At the heart of the traditional university is its commitment to the transmission of high culture, the possession of which has been thought to make men truly civilized. This was really the only function that Cardinal Newman and more recently Robert Hutchins have thought appropriate to the university. Closely related to this, and certainly central to our conception of liberal education, is the shaping of mind and character: the cultivation of aesthetic sensibilities, broad human sympathies, and the capacity for critical and independent judgement. The second autonomous function of the American university is the creation of new knowledge through 'pure' scholarship and basic scientific research. Third is the selection, formation, and certification of élite groups: the learned professions, the higher civil service, the politicians, and (though less in Britain than in the United States and in Europe) the commercial and industrial leadership.[2] These functions involve values and standards that are institutionalized in the universities and élite private colleges, and are maintained by them autonomously and even in resistance to popular demands and sentiments.

The popular functions fall into two general categories. First, there is a commitment on the part of the American system as a whole to provide places somewhere for as many students as can be encouraged to continue their education beyond high school. For a very long time it has been believed in this country that talented youth of humble origins should go to college. But the extension of these expectations to all young men and women—that is, the transformation of a privilege into a right for all—dates no further back than World War II. In part, this notion is a reflection of the erosion of the legitimacy of class cultures and of the growing feeling in every industrial society, but most markedly in the

United States, that it is right and proper for all men to claim the possession of the high culture of their own societies.[3] In school and through the mass media, ordinary people are encouraged to send their children to college to share in the high culture, for its own sake as well as for its instrumental value in gaining entrance to the old and emerging élite occupations. Higher education is assuming an increasingly important role in placing people in the occupational structure and, thus, in determining their adult class positions and life chances. Social mobility across generations now commonly takes the form of providing children with more education than their parents had, and the achievement of near-universal secondary education in America by World War II has provided the platform for the development of mass higher education since then. The tremendous growth of occupations demanding some form of higher education both reflects and further stimulates the increase in college and university enrolments. All this shows itself in yet another way, as a marked rise in the educational standard of the whole population. Throughout the class structure, already fully in the upper-middle but increasingly so in the lower-middle and working classes, 'going to college' comes to be seen as not just appropriate for people of wealth or extraordinary talent or ambition, but as possible and desirable for youngsters of quite ordinary talent and ambition, and increasingly for people with little of either.[4] We are now seeing what was a privilege that became a right transformed into something very near to an obligation for growing numbers of young men and women.

If one popular function is the provision of mass higher education for nearly everybody who applies for it, the second is the provision of useful knowledge and service to nearly every group and institution that want it. The service orientation of American higher education is too well known to need discussion. But the demands on the universities for such service are increasing all the time. In part, they reflect the growth of the knowledge base created by the scientific explosion of the past few decades. Not only is much of this new knowledge of potential applied to industry, agriculture, the military, the health professions, and so on, but also new areas of national life are coming to be seen as users of knowledge created in the university. We may know more about how to increase corn production than how to educate black children in our urban slums, but it is likely that the universities will shortly be as deeply involved in efforts to solve our urban and racial problems as ever they were in agriculture.

The academic division of labour

How has American higher education been able to fulfil both its autonomous and its popular functions? Put differently, what have been the institutional mechanisms through which the colleges and universities have been able to contribute to the transmission and creation of knowledge, and also serve the variety of other demands the society has made on them?

The chief such mechanism has been the division of labour between and within institutions. A very large number of American colleges are essentially single-function institutions, either autonomous or popular. Swarthmore College, Haverford, and Reed are essentially preparatory colleges for graduate and professional schools. Their faculty staff for the most part are men who have taken a Ph.D. in distinguished universities, but who prefer a career in a teaching college rather than in a big university. In addition, there are the élite private universities which are highly selective in admissions and which subordinate service to basic research and the transmission of high culture.

By contrast, a very large number of American colleges are essentially service institutions. The roughly two hundred teachers' colleges, the many small, weak, denominational colleges, the less ambitious engineering schools, the over eight hundred junior colleges—these are serving primarily vocational ends, preparing youngsters from relatively modest backgrounds for technical, semi-professional, and other white-collar jobs.

There is another group of institutions—most notably the big state universities—which performs the autonomous and popular functions within the same institution. On the one hand, these institutions, along with the state colleges and junior colleges, have taken the brunt of the enormous expansion in enrolments in recent decades. They are centres for community service of every kind; they train the teachers, the social workers, the probation officers, the market researchers, and the myriad other new and semi-professionals required by this service-oriented post-industrial society. On the other hand, they are also centres of scholarship and basic research, and contribute to the advancement of knowledge in every academic subject. Moreover, they offer, in their undergraduate colleges of letters and sciences, the full range of academic subjects, some of which centre on the transmission of high culture and are concerned less with public service than with the cultivation of sensibility and independence of judgement, a sense of the past, of the uniqueness of the individual, of the varied forms of human experience and expression—in brief, all the desired outcomes of liberal education.

Within such universities, the popular and autonomous functions are insulated from one another in various ways that serve to protect the highly vulnerable autonomous functions of liberal education and basic research and scholarship from the direct impact of the larger society, whose demands for vocational training, certification, service, and the like are reflected and met in the popular functions of universities. These insulations take various forms of a division of labour within the university. There is a division of labour between departments, as for example between a department of English or history and a department of education. There is a division of labour in the relatively unselective universities between the undergraduate and graduate schools, the former given over largely to mass higher education in the service of social mobility and occupational placement, entertainment, and custodial care, while the graduate departments in the same institutions are often able to maintain a climate in which scholarship and scientific research can be done to the highest standards. There is a familiar, though far from clear cut, division of labour, between graduate departments and professional schools. Among the faculty staff there is a division of labour, within many departments, between scientists and consultants, scholars and journalists, teachers and entertainers. More dangerously, there is a division of labour between regular faculty members and a variety of fringe or marginal teachers—teaching assistants, visitors, and lecturers—who in some schools carry a disproportionate load of the mass teaching. Within the administration there is a division of labour between the dean of faculty and graduate dean, and the dean of students. And among the students there is a marked separation between the 'collegiate' and 'vocational' sub-cultures on the one hand, and academically or intellectually oriented sub-cultures on the other.

Despite the strains that have developed around these divisions of function between and within American colleges and universities, they have worked surprisingly well, surprising especially to observers in European universities who have opposed the encroachment of popular functions on the universities as incompatible with their traditional commitments to increasing knowledge, transmitting the high culture, and shaping the character of the élite strata. American higher education, as a system, has been able to do these things and *also* to give a post-secondary education, often within the very same institutions, to millions of students, while serving every institution of society, every agency of government.

The enormous expansion of American higher education, both in its numbers and its range of activities, is putting great strains on these insulating mechanisms and thus is threatening the autonomous functions of the university.[5] The expansion of the university is involving it more directly in controversial issues and is therefore increasing the number and range of significant publics in the larger society that are attentive to what goes on in the university. This in turn is causing severe problems for boards of trustees and regents, and for over-all government of universities and protection of their autonomy. These problems are reflected on the campus, in the growing politicization both of the faculty and the student body (which also has other sources). The intrusion of politics on to the campus has many consequences, among them the threat to the procedures by which these institutions govern themselves. At the same time, the growth in enrolments brings to the campus large numbers of students who do not accept the authority of the institution's traditional leadership to define the form and content of higher education: some of these are disaffected middle-class whites, while increasing numbers are militant blacks. The progressive politicization of the campus threatens most the intellectual activities that require the suspension of commitment and an attitude of scepticism towards all received truth and conventional wisdoms. The central question for the American university is whether its indefinitely expanding popular functions are compatible with the survival of its autonomous functions of disinterested inquiry, whether in the classroom or through research and scholarship.

Governing boards and their changing publics

The role of trustees in American higher education is a peculiar one. They are, by law, the ultimate authority over these corporate bodies: they own the physical resources of the institution; they select its chief administrative officers; they possess the formal authority that is exercised by delegation by the administrative officers and faculty alike. And yet two parallel tendencies have been at work in recent decades to reduce the actual importance of the trustees. On the one hand, more and more power has been drained away from the trustees with the growth of major alternative sources of funds for academic programmes over which the trustees have, in fact, had little or no control; and on the other, administrators and faculty have come increasingly to assert that powers that have over time been delegated to them are theirs by right. The growth of the contract-grant system has enormously increased the power of the faculty in relation to administration as well as to trustees; and the tight competitive market for academic men, together with institutional ambitions for prestige in the academic league standings, have insured that trustees rarely exercise control over the funds granted to research professors. Trustees have been relatively ineffective in controlling even capital expansion, one remaining bastion of their power, when funds for new buildings come to support new research programmes for which professors and administrators have jointly applied. Moreover, administrators are increasingly turning to outside funding agencies, especially to foundations, to support new academic programmes, to set up experimental colleges, or to bring more minority-group students on campus. And again, trustees are really not consulted about these matters. External sources of funds mark a major diminution of the trustees' power to shape the character or guide the direction of 'their' institution.

Secondly, the broad encompassing concept of 'academic freedom' has meant that both administrators and faculty members come to feel that the powers they exercise over instruction, admissions, appointments, the internal allocation of resources, and even, increasingly, the physical design of the campus are all theirs by right. Some of the forces that have led to the extension and deepening of the concept of academic freedom have had to do with the enormous influence of the most distinguished American universities as models for all the others. Characteristically, it is in the most distinguished universities that the academic community has gained the widest autonomy, the broadest control over its own conditions of life and work. Many lesser institutions have come to see faculty power and institutional autonomy as a mark of institutional distinction, to be pursued as part of the strategy of institutional mobility to which so much of the energies and thought of academic men is devoted. The power of the faculties in the most distinguished universities flows precisely from their academic distinction, through the familiar academic transmutation of prestige into power. The faculties of weaker institutions see the relation, but endeavour to turn the causal connection on its head: they mean to gain the power and transmute it into prestige, for their institutions directly and themselves indirectly. Whatever its justification, the growth of faculty power has meant a diminution of the power of trustees and regents.

Boards of trustees traditionally have looked in two directions: inwardly to the government and direction of their universities; outwardly, to the groups and interests which provide the support for, and make claims for services on, the university. On the one hand, as I have suggested, trustees have been losing power over their own institutions: many things are done and funded behind their backs, so to speak. At the same time (and this applies more to public than to private universities), their constituencies and their relation to their constituencies have been changing. Boards have traditionally dealt with very specific 'relevant publics': legislative committees, wealthy donors, alumni organizations. In the leading universities, their job has been to get support from these publics while resisting inappropriate interference. And in this task trustees of public universities have not been so different from those of private universities: in most of their relationships, they have been dealing with people very much like themselves—in many cases graduates of the same state university, men of similar sentiments and values and prejudices. These relations could be, for the most part, cosy and private. Under these circumstances some of the leading state universities, such as the University of California, could until recently imagine themselves to be private universities operating largely on public funds, in a relationship to public authorities not unlike that of the British universities.

Today, the constituencies, the relevant publics, of state universities are much wider, more heterogeneous, and less familiar. In part, the growth of relevant publics has accompanied the simultaneous expansion of the universities and of their functions. For example, eleven years ago the University of California consisted of two major campuses, three small undergraduate colleges, and a medical school, with a total enrolment of about forty thousand, operating on a state budget of a little over one hundred million dollars. Today the university consists of nine campuses with over a hundred thousand students and a state budget of over three hundred million dollars, with nearly as much again from outside sources. The student body and faculty are not only bigger, but more heterogeneous, reflecting a variety of interests, many of which touch directly on sensitive and controversial issues. The schools of agriculture still do research on more fruitful crops and more effective pest control, but other students and faculty members are active in support of the movement to organize migratory farm workers; the schools of education still produce school-teachers and administrators, but also provide expert advice to school boards embarked on programmes of total integration, while other faculty staff testify in defence of black militants and invite Black Panthers to give lectures on campus; administrative officers still define and defend academic criteria for admissions, while their colleagues press for the admission of larger numbers of minority-group students outside the ordinary procedures. And California, like many other universities, is now embarking on a major commitment to the solution of urban problems that inevitably will involve it in the most intense and passionate political controversies.

As a result of the expansion of the public universities, both in numbers and in the range of their activities, more and more people have come to take an interest in them and to feel that they have views on them that ought to be heard. In some uncertain sense, the constituency of the University of California, for example, has become the population of the state. But it is out of just this uncertainty about the nature and composition of the university's relevant publics that the Regents' anxieties arise. As the constituency of the trustees has grown, it has become less distinct. It is unclear just who the relevant publics are to which the Regents should attend. Moreover, with the disruption of the old cosy relations between the Regents and specific limited publics, they can no longer know their constituents' minds by consulting with them or by reading their own. And as the Regents lose touch with their constituents, so also they come to be less well known and trusted by their new constituents. To this new mass public, they are not people one can telephone or one has talked to; they are merely a remote part of the apparatus of government—the powerful people who need to be pressured. And some unrepresentative part of the anonymous public begins to write letters complaining about the university, and the Regents, for want of a genuine relation to these new publics, begin to read them and become anxious and worried. One important difference between the older specific and differentiated publics and the emerging mass undifferentiated public is that the former reflect specific interests that can be met, or compromised with, or educated, or resisted. A mass public, by contrast, does not have interests so much as fears and angers—what it communicates to the trustees is, 'Why can't you clean up that mess at the university—all those demonstrating students and unpatriotic faculty?'

These two tendencies—the trustees' sense of a loss of control over 'their' university and the emergence of a mass public of uncertain size and composition and temper with whom the trustees have no clear representative or communicating relationship—can undermine a board's conceptions of who they are and what their role is, and generate in them anger and anxiety. And out of that fear and anger, trustees appear to be more inclined to intervene directly in the academic life of the university: its curriculum, faculty appointments, and student discipline. In California, where these developments are far advanced, these interventions are creating a serious crisis of authority within the university—what might be called a constitutional crisis—centring on who actually controls the curriculum and appointments of staff, which is not yet resolved. If it is not resolved, or if it leads to bitter struggles between the faculty and administrators and the Regents, or between the university and the state government, then the university's capacity to sustain a climate of intellectual excellence will be gravely threatened, and its ability to perform all its functions, but most especially its functions as an international centre of learning, will be seriously weakened.

California is in many ways a populist democracy. The governor and legislature discuss and revise the university's annual operating budget in an atmosphere increasingly directly political and responsive to popular sentiments and indignation; and the whole electorate votes directly on proposed bond issues that are required for capital expansion. The Board of Regents, the majority of whose members are appointed to sixteen-year terms, was conceived precisely as a buffer between the university and popular or political pressures, to protect the necessary freedom of the university to explore issues and engage in educational innovations that might not have popular support at any given moment. But the board appears increasingly unable to perform that function. Instead of defending the university to its external publics, it begins to function as a conduit of popular sentiment and pressure on the university. And this, as I have suggested, places all the functions of the university in grave jeopardy.

But the problems I have been discussing are not confined to public state universities and populist societies. The emergence of a mass undifferentiated and angry public indeed poses a special threat to public universities. But the more general pattern in which university expansion creates new and easily neglected bodies of constituencies can be illustrated in the events at Columbia University two years ago. As Walter Metzger has noted, the physical expansion of Columbia, situated right at the edge of Harlem, made of that community a highly relevant and attentive public. Over many years Columbia has been expanding its operations into areas and buildings from which minority-group people have 'necessarily' been evicted. But its board of trustees, and unfortunately also its administration, had not begun to see that Harlem was at least as relevant to Columbia's fate as were its alumni, its wealthy donors, and the great foundations. And it was the representatives of the black community, within the university as students, who precipitated the crisis that was then exploited by white radicals and greatly exacerbated by undisciplined police action.

Many of the popular functions of the universities in the past—mass education and public service—have indeed been popular in the other sense of the word and have gained the support or indifference of the general public. But it seems inescapable that the university in the future will be involved much more frequently in highly controversial issues and actions for which mass support cannot always be gained. The expansion of the universities, both in size and function, means that we will be living in an environment increasingly sensitive to what the university does, and especially to what it does that has direct effects outside the university. It is not generally recognized how much the university's freedom and autonomy were a function of popular indifference and of the management of special interest groups outside the arena of popular politics. But for various reasons the society is less and less indifferent, at the same time as trustees and regents are less able to perform their traditional function of defending the university through the forms of élite politics. And this is especially clear in the university's relations to the racial revolution.

Black studies and black students

Almost every major college or university in the country is trying, in one way or another, to contribute to the enormous social movement that goes by the name of the 'racial revolution'. The first and most common response of universities is to increase the proportion of black students in their student bodies; the second is to develop programmes or departments or colleges of black or ethnic studies; the third is to increase their commitment to the solution of urban problems.

The way a university responds to each of these challenges conditions the way it will or can respond to the others. How it goes about recruiting minority-group students heavily affects the character of a programme or department of black or ethnic studies, and that in turn affects the ways in which an institution can try to approach a wider variety of urban problems. Moreover, how a university deals with all three of these programmes will greatly influence how well its autonomous functions—of liberal education and basic research and scholarship—survive the current waves of populist sentiment and pressure.

But much of the discussion surrounding the need to increase the numbers of black students and staff in American colleges and universities has focused on the mechanisms of black recruitment and the organization of a black curriculum. There has been little discussion of the characteristics and attitudes of black students and of differences among them. But the success of all these efforts may depend greatly on what black students in universities want from the institutions and the extent to which their hopes and desires are compatible with their basic values and processes.

We can usefully distinguish four positions among black students in colleges and universities today:

1. The revolutionaries, represented by but not confined to the Black Panthers, whose attention and energies are focused primarily on the black ghettos and the larger society, and who see the university chiefly as a base of operations and a pool of resources for revolutionary organization.

2. The radicals, who focus more on the university, but see it in its present form as a racist institution and in need of fundamental reorganization as a part of the radical transformation of society. They reject existing forms of university organization and government: the way it selects its faculty, admits students, defines its curriculum, and awards credits and degrees. They demand 'open enrolment', the abolition of 'white' standards for appointments, admissions, and performance, and the full commitment of the institution, or a major part of it, to the racial revolution. They are likely to be separatists, demanding autonomous departments of black studies and special provisions for the recruitment and housing of black students. They differ from the revolutionaries chiefly in being less ideological, less interested in a world revolution along Maoist lines, and more in transforming the university. They are prepared to disrupt the university, to damage its buildings and close its classes, and indeed to destroy it, if necessary, to reconstruct it as an institution devoted to 'the welfare of the people'. Their hostility to the 'racist' university as it exists is so great that they doubt that there is anything useful they can learn from it.

3. The militants, who also focus their attention on the university, but who accept, with some reservations, its basic character as a centre for the creation and transmission of knowledge and values through free and objective inquiry. They push hard, however, in an active and organized way for a larger role for blacks in the university, both in numbers of students and faculty and in resources devoted to their special interests and problems. They may support departments or programmes of black studies, but are prepared to see these integrated into the structure of the university, conforming (again with some reservations) to its academic norms and standards. They are prepared to demonstrate forcefully, but not (deliberately) in ways that threaten to destroy a university that they wish to reform. Most importantly, they differ from the radicals in having a greater interest in gaining an education for themselves in the university.

4. The moderates, who are largely committed to gaining skills and knowledge and training for careers in a multi-racial society. These people often support the demands of the militants, but draw back from confrontations and disruptions, and are little interested in, and indeed may oppose, separatist forms of education represented by departments of black studies. These students are often strongly committed to taking their skills back into the larger black community, where they may in fact be highly militant in relation to the white society and its institutions.

Individual students often straddle or combine two of these positions, shifting tone and emphasis on different issues and in different circumstances. Moreover, individuals will often use the rhetoric and arguments of one position while acting more consistently with another. In the general inflation of rhetoric, black militants often sound like radicals, making sweeping condemnations and demands when in fact their intention is to increase the numbers of black students and to gain somewhat larger resources for them in their institutions. Similarly, often under pressure and out of fear, moderates may sound like militants, expressing support for demonstrations when in fact they want nothing so much as to be allowed to get on with their studies. But this inflation of rhetoric is not merely a personal or group tactic; it has consequences for individuals and institutions. Students are captured by their own rhetoric, committed to positions and actions they may not have intended; the institution and the larger community often respond to the words and not the intentions, adopting either more submissive or more intransigent positions than are appropriate.

The inflation of black rhetoric, coupled with certain illusions and misconceptions among white faculty members and administrators, serves to obscure the actual character of black students on any given campus and the real distribution of sentiments and interests among them. The distortion is usually towards an exaggeration of the importance and influence of the radical and revolutionary blacks, as compared with the moderate and militant reformers. A case in point is provided by the events surrounding the strike called by the Third World Liberation Front at Berkeley during the winter of 1968–69 in support of demands for an autonomous department of ethnic studies. The leadership of this organization and of its black component, the Afro-American Student Union, was predominantly radical. It had the support of black and white revolutionaries and also of many militants, though some of these opposed the more violent and destructive forms the strike took. It may be useful to sketch the background and context of this damaging strike.

At Berkeley, as at numbers of other major universities, the decision was made several years ago to increase the number of minority students in the student body. This was to be done both by encouraging black and Mexican-American students who qualified for admission in the ordinary way to apply to Berkeley and also by recruiting others whose high-school records did not make them admissible through the ordinary procedures, but who might be admitted under a special rule which allows 2 (now 4) per cent. of the student body to be admitted outside the ordinary admissions criteria of the university. At Berkeley an 'Educational Opportunity Program' was set up in 1966 to encourage youngsters from ethnic minorities to attend the university, and specifically to admit some of them under this special 2, now 4, per cent. rule. The first director of this programme, acting under the Chancellor's authority, was a man of great energy and commitment who developed relations with many of the black communities in the Bay Area and began to increase the numbers of students coming to Berkeley from those communities. In autumn, 1966, the Berkeley E.O.P. recruited and enrolled 130 students; in 1967, the number doubled to about 260, and in 1968 it doubled again. By January 1969 there were over 800 E.O.P. students at Berkeley, with the number still growing. His successor has continued this policy with similar energy and devotion. As a result of the efforts of this and other programmes, and of the ordinary processes of admissions, there were in 1968–69 some 1,200 black students at Berkeley.

I do not believe that anyone ever made a decision about the nature or characteristics of the black students to be recruited to Berkeley. The assumption was that the numbers were small and ought to be larger for many reasons, and that the way to do this was to go into the black neighbourhoods and recruit students from substantially all-black high schools. Indeed, the Chancellor himself held the view that the university had a special responsibility to the most deprived black students. Increasing numbers of these youngsters have been going on to junior colleges, but, in his view, the university was richer and more powerful than these, and thus carried a larger responsibility to just those youngsters from the most handicapped and deprived backgrounds.

The resulting relationship between Berkeley and its growing numbers of minority students is conditioned by three factors: first, the characteristics of the minority students themselves, especially the values and attitudes that they bring with them to the university; second, the attitudes towards and perceptions of the minority students held by the faculty and especially by the administrators; and third, certain characteristics of the campus itself.

First, the black students recruited to Berkeley by and large have been militant and radical, clearly much more so than the black community as a whole. It may be that they reflect the attitudes of the average minority-group students of college age. It seems equally likely that there is a self-recruitment of more militant and radical blacks to the university, and a special interest in them on the part of the administrative officers who have headed the special programme. There is, I think, a widely held belief that radicalism and militancy among young blacks is itself a sign of special energy and intelligence and, indeed, of potential leadership qualities. The youngsters with these characteristics recruited to the campus have brought their values with them and are indeed shaping the continued recruitment of black students to Berkeley.

Second, the romantic view of black militancy by white faculty members and administrators is itself a factor of great importance in the present situation. It arises in part out of a generalized sense of guilt among liberal white men about the situation of Negroes in America— a sense that indeed blacks ought to be very angry, and that to be very angry and to express that anger in militant and radical forms are evidence of a certain freedom from older cultural constraints and a mark of being among the leaders of the emerging black community in America.

There is also the sheer ignorance of most white people regarding the distribution of attitudes and values among the black population, as a result of which young militant blacks are taken to be far more representative of their race than they in fact are. It was a source of great surprise and some embarrassment to members of the university community to discover that over 90 per cent. of black voters across the country voted for Hubert Humphrey in 1968, and that in California the Peace and Freedom Party, which carried the most radical and revolutionary racial slogans on its banners, gained very little support, even in the black ghettos.

The attitudes I am describing have affected the recruitment of black students to Berkeley and have exaggerated the significance of the black militants among the black students on the campus. For example, it was widely assumed that the Afro-American Student Union did, in fact, represent the black students on the Berkeley campus and express their views. It was also widely assumed that all black and other minority-group students supported the strike of the Third World Liberation Front during the winter quarter of 1969, and in their relations with the minority students on the campus the administration carefully dealt with the Third World Liberation Front as their legitimate leadership. But no one really knew how representative that body was, nor indeed how many black and minority-group students did not support the strike and even continued to attend class in the face of considerable fear and intimidation during the strike. There has been, in general, a marked indifference in the university to the moderate or moderate-militant black and minority-group students, an indifference that in some cases has bordered on contempt.

There are two elements in this that are worth pointing to. The first is the invisibility of the Negro, which Ralph Ellison wrote about in his penetrating novel some years ago. In the university, both faculty and administrators are still inclined to deal with black students as group members, imputing to them a variety of characteristics and attitudes that reflect the guilt and wishes and assumptions of the whites themselves. The black students themselves, as individuals with unique characteristics, are largely invisible. It is in many ways more convenient to assimilate them to an Afro-American Student Union or Third World Liberation Front, where they comprise another political force which has to be accommodated in the university and with which one can negotiate and deal. Whatever the difficulties of that, it is still less difficult than to confront black students as people in all their uniqueness and individuality, differing sharply among themselves in their attitudes and orientation to the university.

In addition, there is the powerful ideological weapon of 'Uncle Tomism'. Uncle Tom, as an epithet, is assigned by radical and revolutionary blacks to any blacks less militant than they. It is a way of dismissing and discrediting the views of those who are still committed to an interracial and integrated society, and who do not in all cases support violent or other militant tactics. The term is reserved especially for moderate black students who want to use the university in traditional ways—to gain an education and increase their skills and opportunities in their future careers. Ironically, the university has accepted the black militants' definition of the non-militant Negro as an Uncle Tom, and has paid little attention to the interests of the very considerable number of black and other minority-group students who have not supported the Third World Liberation Front. This is, I think, in part because of the romantic apotheosis of black militancy among white liberal academics that I spoke of earlier, and in part because the militants can cause more trouble and are more powerful than the non-militants, who by the very fact of their not being organized can be safely ignored. And indeed they are ignored.

The black students recruited recently to the campus have brought their own values and culture with them. Many of them have had painful experiences throughout their school careers and have found schools and teachers unrewarding and punishing. They arrive at Berkeley and often begin to have the same kinds of unhappy and unsuccessful experiences in class that they have had before. Some very quickly cease going to class altogether, and for many the university, which so far as they can see is just another punishing kind of school which offers them little personal reward or psychological support, becomes the object of enormous anger and resentment. Berkeley, unlike some private and residential institutions, has never paid a great deal of attention to the emotional lives of its students, nor has it made any special effort to socialize them to the campus community. Nor has it been greatly concerned with the extent to which students hold the values which are essential to teaching and learning in the university. The university has traditionally concerned itself with the purely cognitive aspects of the student's life, and allowed his social and emotional life and moral development to take care of itself, or to find a home in the extra-curricular forms of collegiate life. This was never very satisfactory, but it was not disastrous so long as the university recruited largely middle- and upper-middle-class students who already shared many of the views of themselves and the university that their teachers did, and whose attitudes, if not strictly academic, were at least not hostile to the university as it existed. These assumptions cannot be made about young militant blacks from the urban ghettos of the Bay Area,[6] but still nothing much has been done to socialize minority-group students to the university world after they are admitted. Indeed, even to suggest such an attempt is often seen as encouraging them to betray their identifications with their own ethnic communities.

Currently almost the whole of the attention of the university in this area is directed to problems of the curriculum and the organization of black studies. The issues have been autonomy, the recruitment of the faculty, the role of students in decision-making, and so forth. Those who have seen the report of the Harvard committee on black studies (the Rosovsky Report) will remember that the question of black studies there was embedded in a matrix of concern for the individual student and his sense of belonging, concerns that grew out of an awareness of his loneliness and anxieties on the campus. As much was said about the necessity for a black student union and for the integration of black students into the residential houses as about the curriculum of the black studies programme.[7] In the Rosovsky Report, we see a sensitivity to the black student as an individual with special difficulties in adjusting to a university community. At Berkeley, as at many large public universities, there is no tradition for this kind of concern; instead, it deals with black students as an organized political force and bargains with them about the forms of a college of ethnic studies. The absence of a concern for the individual and his adjustment to the campus will have the most profound consequences for the relation between the university and minority-group students.

The decision at Berkeley to proceed with a College of Ethnic Studies will have consequences for the university, I suspect, as a source of continuing conflict and turmoil. It will also have consequences for the university's new broad commitment to urban problems. The proposed College of Ethnic Studies, at Berkeley as elsewhere, has in my view less to do with education than with politics. Some of the leaders of the Third World Liberation Front who are centrally involved in the creation of the new college see it primarily as a base for political action in the black ghettos and for the training of revolutionary cadres for the future. The real target, for them, is not the university, which is only incidental or instrumental, but rather the black community itself, which gave the bulk of its votes in the last election to Hubert Humphrey. For the radical and revolutionary Third World leaders, that is the real challenge—it is their brothers in the community who must be reached and shown the true nature of a racist society and the true nature of their own interests. And the disputes over the college, not all of which are yet resolved, have not centred on its academic character or curriculum, but on its degree of autonomy, its freedom from the ordinary constraints of the university, which might inhibit its primary mission in the black community.

Chancellor Roger Heyns was aware of the problem. In a statement to the Academic Senate at Berkeley, in which he reaffirmed the necessity for the continued application of ordinary university procedures to the new college, he observed:

> I have a protective view about the proposition that the unit should engage in community service. I assume this does not mean service which is useful in the teaching and learning process as in field work or internships—to which there can be no objections. But I am very wary of any unit of the university becoming an instrument of community action.
>
> If the academic community chooses to use the University or any part of it as a base of political action, if it tries to identify the University with its causes, and mobilize the prestige and the resources of the University to goals which it chooses, then it has made the University an important piece of political real estate. And it will follow, inevitably, that others, outside the University, will then regard its control and management as important goals which *they select*.[8]

These are good and strong words. But I think they are illusory. I do not believe the Chancellor will be able to control events after the college has been established. The new college emerges out of a strike marked by many acts of violence and vandalism which the Chancellor himself has enumerated; it will grow and develop under the threat of renewed strikes and violence. The campus is desperate for peace; its faculty committees and its administration will be very reluctant to disrupt fragile agreements and ambiguous understandings by denying the college what it wants, especially if the college is prepared to get what it wants through regular university procedures. I believe the procedures will be defended (though they, too, have been attacked by faculty groups); but they can be operated with enough flexibility to demonstrate that they need not be 'obstructive'. My doubts on this score apply to staffing, curriculum, and admissions, but also, in the present context, to the college's role in the community. An active role in the ethnic communities is absolutely central to the concerns of many Third World faculty and students. The notion that their college will not be allowed to be 'an instrument of community action', in the Chancellor's words, is, I believe, quite unrealistic. The further assumption—that such activity will not involve organizing and educating people and groups in that community for political action, but will be merely field work in connection with some course of study—is equally illusory. And, indeed, many of the Third World leaders and their supporters affirm in the strongest terms that the university should change its relation to the community, and precisely be an instrument for change in it. They point to the fact that the public land grant universities have long accepted their role as agents of social change, and merely demand that they broaden their conception of that role and of the forms of change it can effect in the community. The power of this strong tradition in American higher education, coupled with the moral and political power of the militant black movement itself, will make it extremely difficult for the Chancellor, or university presidents elsewhere, to try to prevent directly political activities in the community based in the new colleges of black or ethnic studies.

What are the consequences for the universities' new broad entry into the field of urban problems? The question is almost rhetorical. American universities have had some experience of service in public areas which involve political controversy. But surely the problems in this regard are likely to be greater in the area of urban affairs than in agriculture or medicine. The heart of the matter is whether the university can find a way to approach urban problems without being transformed into a political weapon or arena. I believe it can if the university can remember and respect its own unique qualities as a centre for basic inquiry and rational discussion of issues, as a source of new ideas and critical examination of existing policy and practice, and as a training ground for the variety of professions and semi-professions whose skills are in such short supply in the areas of urban problems. At best the university cannot avoid being drawn into areas of controversy, and its autonomy will be further strained by the appearance, if not the reality, of partisanship. Facts are, or quickly become, political weapons, and reports and recommendations, however firmly based on facts, have a tendency to support one position in a debate and not others. But if there is a continued concern for the quality of the knowledge base, a dedication to the effort to illuminate issues and to increase the number and variety of policy options, a scrupulous attention to negative evidence, and a sensitive avoidance of technocratic contempt for the ordinary political processes, then the university may indeed survive its most ambitious programme of service to the community.

But these are just the qualities that one can hope for, but not assume, in a college of ethnic studies. Some of its founders *know* what the problems are and know what must be done. 'Enough of this endless study and discussion,' they say. 'After a hundred or two hundred or three hundred years of it, let us now do what needs to be done.' However justified this may be for a radical political programme, it cannot but complicate the university's broad involvement in the problems of the city, with which it will inevitably be associated in the public mind. As a result, it seems likely to me that the university will come to be seen as the source of direct and radical intervention in the politics of the minority communities themselves. The reaction to political action based in the university, as Chancellor Heyns observed, will be political reaction from the community and the state.

I have suggested that some of the problems at Berkeley have had their roots in the casual and almost unnoticed decision to increase the numbers of minority-group students by recruiting youngsters through special admission directly from the ghetto high schools. This decision has shaped succeeding events at Berkeley, including the strike and the ensuing proposals for a college of ethnic studies. But given a commitment to increase the numbers of minority students on campus, a commitment almost unanimously supported throughout the university, is there any alternative to the way Berkeley went about it? Was all this not inevitable, an inevitability embodying, as I have heard said, a kind of cosmic justice which visits on the university an appropriate suffering for its decades of neglect of the minority groups in the population? I do not believe it was inevitable, nor do I see a divine spirit at work in our current travail. I think there is another way to increase our service to minority groups in the state and nation—and that is by helping to strengthen and expand the strata of black and other minority-group professionals and semi-professionals: teachers, lawyers, engineers, social workers, probation officers, professors, scientists, researchers, students of urban problems. Education in the freshman and sophomore years, after all, is not the strength of Berkeley, nor of many other big state universities; on the whole, it is done badly, and what success is achieved is with students who come already motivated and well-educated, who can use the resources of the university in the service of their own self-education. Youngsters from local black high schools need much more than that. But the state universities are ill-equipped to give them the kinds of counselling and personal attention and patient concern that they need and deserve. Ironically such universities are much closer to being able to provide this kind of education to juniors and seniors and graduate and professional students. And there, I think, is their special opportunity. The university can recognize and accept its unique qualities as a centre for advanced undergraduate, graduate, and professional training, and for scholarship and research, and not use a programme of special admissions to compete unreflectively with junior colleges and state colleges for youngsters just out of high school. It might, instead, come to be seen as a place where the minority-group draughtsman and technician could return to school to become an engineer; the school aide, a teacher; the teacher, a trained administrator or educational specialist; the advanced undergraduate or graduate, a scientist or academic man. This would mean not a smaller, but a different commitment. It is true that many graduate departments and schools are also making special efforts at recruiting minority-group students. But what is required is a much fuller commitment by the university in this direction. For example, it may mean that it has to find ways of being more hospitable to older undergraduates with broken academic careers, and to use the special admissions programmes for the man of thirty-five who left college ten or fifteen years ago, who does not meet the ordinary criteria for admission to the university, but who needs additional training to go beyond his dead-end white-collar job. And such people might need to be sought out—in industry and politics, the civil service and community poverty programmes and schools—with as much energy and initiative as now goes into looking for youngsters to come as freshmen. It may well be that one way to organize the education of many of them would be in a school of urban studies.

All this implies an effort to broaden and strengthen the black middle class. But somehow middle-class Negroes have a bad name among white academics—indeed, the name is Uncle Tom—and we have come to identify leadership in the minority community with radical militancy. That is not, I think, a service either to the minority communities or to the university.

The question, of course, is not whether public universities should or should not enrol more minority-group students, or develop programmes of studies centring on their history and culture and experience and problems, or commit more of their resources and energies to such programmes. There are many good reasons, moral and intellectual and pragmatic, for making these commitments. The question is the form such programmes of special recruitment, ethnic studies, and the like should take; or, more precisely, what criteria we should use in making those decisions—decisions we are in danger of making either unreflectively, as with recruitment, or in direct response to confrontation as a way of gaining peace, as with ethnic studies. The answers lie in a clearer sense of the kinds of programmes that are compatible with one's conception of the university. And here, of course, we come to what may be irreducible value preferences. In so far as one sees the university as merely a political instrument, functioning at present chiefly to arm and legitimate a racist and utterly corrupt society, then indeed one need not worry overmuch about its survival; one may want to use it, or seize it, or, failing that, to unmask and then smash it. But if one sees the university as a vulnerable institution that in some respects can stand apart from politics and society and provide an arena for the critical examination of all views of man and society, then the survival of this function in the university is a matter of some consequence for the way in which the university performs its other, more directly service functions.

'Compulsory' higher education

The growth of American higher education and the powerful wave of popular sentiment that accompanies that growth are affecting its relations to its environment, with trustees and regents, at the point of greatest strain. But the same forces, both within and outside the universities, are affecting the internal fabric of the universities: the character of their undergraduates and graduate students and faculty members, and their processes of government. It begins to appear as if the expansion of American higher education, in numbers and functions, is transforming it from a system of mass higher education into one that will bear responsibility for nearly all of the college-age population—that is, into a system of universal higher education. That development, clear in trends and projections, is obscured by the fact that currently only about half of all high-school graduates across the country go directly from high school to some form of higher education. But in the upper-middle classes and in states like California, the proportion of youngsters going on to some form of post-secondary education is already over 80 per cent. For youngsters in those places and strata, universal higher education is here: nearly everybody they know goes on to college. And these strata and areas are growing inexorably. Many of the difficulties now being experienced by American colleges and universities reflect the strains of this transformation from mass to universal higher education.

In the recent past, attendance in the American system of mass higher education was voluntary—a privilege that had in some places become a right, but not yet for many an obligation. Whether seen as a privilege, as in certain selective, mostly private, institutions, or as a right, in unselective, mostly public, institutions, voluntary attendance carried with it an implicit acceptance of the character and purposes of the institution as defined by 'the authorities'. The authority of trustees or administrators or faculty to define the nature of the education and its requirements could be evaded, but was rarely challenged by students. With few exceptions students played little or no part in the government of the institution.

The growth of enrolments and the movement towards universal higher education has made enrolment in college increasingly obligatory for many students, and their presence there increasingly 'involuntary'. In this respect, in some strata and places colleges begin to resemble elementary and secondary schools, where it has long been recognized that compulsory attendance increases problems of student motivation, boredom, and the maintenance of order. The coercions on college students take several forms. The most visible in recent years has been the draft, which has locked many young men into college who might otherwise be doing something else. But other pressures will outlive the reform or abolition of the draft: the unquestioned expectations of family and friends and the consequent sense of shame in not meeting those expectations; the scarcity of attractive alternatives for youngsters of eighteen and nineteen without college experience;[9] the strong and largely realistic anticipation that without some college credits they will be disqualified from most of the attractive and rewarding jobs in the society as adults. As more and more college-age youngsters go on to college, not to be or to have been a college student becomes increasingly a lasting stigma, a mark of some special failing of mind or character and a grave handicap in all the activities and pursuits of adult life.

The net effect of these forces and conditions is to make college attendance for many students almost involuntary, a result of external pressures and constraints some of which do not even have the legitimacy of parental authority behind them. The result is that there are large numbers of students who really do not want to be in college, have not entered into willing contact with it, and do not accept the values or legitimacy of the institution.

In the past, the relative accessibility of higher education brought large numbers of students to American colleges and universities who had little interest in learning for its own sake, but who had strong ambitions to rise in the world and wanted the degree and sometimes the skills that would help them better their status. We are now seeing large numbers from more affluent homes who similarly enter college without much interest in bookish study, but who also are less interested in vocational preparation or social mobility—who either have little ambition for a middle-class career, or else take it completely for granted, or, as in many cases, both. These students also differ from the members of the old 'collegiate culture' who took refuge from the higher learning in the 'gentleman's C' and the distractions of college sport and social life. But these students, already securely lodged in the middle and upper-middle classes, were not inclined to challenge any authority, especially when the institution made its own relaxed compromises with their styles and evasions. For the members of the old collegiate culture, as for the vocationally oriented and the serious students with an interest in academic work, a willing contract with the college of their choice was implicit and, for the most part, honoured.[10]

The entry of large numbers of 'involuntary' students introduces into the university considerable resentment and hostility directed, among other things, to its conceptions of achievement and ambition. There have always been large numbers of people, in this as in other societies, whose ambitions were modest or who felt that the human price of striving and ambition was not worth the problematic gain. But these views are represented more strongly in the university today, where they assert their legitimacy in ways the institution seems peculiarly unable to counter. Part of the attack is on the *ends* of ambition, and takes the form of rejection of academic institutions and programmes that threaten to fit people for jobs and careers in a 'sick society'. Part of the complaint is that academic or intellectual work is *intrinsically* dehumanizing, separating people from one another, destroying their human qualities, authenticity, and so forth. This sentiment sometimes takes the form: 'Look, stop trying to put us on your treadmill; your own lives are spent running around doing pointless things. We just want to look at the flowers and love one another.' This point of view, in its pure form, is clearly incompatible with any kind of consistent goal-directed effort. But many students, under the constraints to be enrolled in college, hold views close to this while continuing to attend classes and earn credits.

Such students pose a special problem for the university. They are not only bored and resentful at having to be in college, but they are also quite vulnerable to the anti-rational or politically radical doctrines currently available in the university—and especially to those that explain and justify their distaste for formal academic work and their reluctance to get caught up in the patterns of striving and achievement.

There is no doubt that many student complaints have real objects— bad teaching, faculty indifference, and the impersonal people-processing of the big universities.[11] But it is sobering to learn that much the same anger is expressed by students in the most varied kinds of colleges and universities—in small liberal arts colleges as in multiversities, in innovative and permissive colleges as in conservative and traditional ones. Where does all the anger come from? Surely some of it comes from forcing youngsters into college who have no interest in bookish study, at least at this point in their lives. There may be other things for them to do now, and perhaps better times for them to be exposed to the disciplines and pleasures of formal study.

Problems of graduate education: a new breed

There are interesting parallels between developments in undergraduate and graduate schools. The rapid expansion of higher education, along with other developments in the larger society, has also brought into faculties and into departments young men whose commitments to academic values are weak or ambivalent. In part, this is because increasing numbers of students are entering graduate school who have little interest in the discipline and for whom graduate school is a chance to continue their liberal education, sometimes under more favourable conditions. There is visible among an increasing number of graduate students (and some of the ablest) a sharp recoil from professional training and, indeed, a rejection of that ambition to achieve distinction in one's field that has always been assumed to be a chief motive of the best graduate students, as of their teachers. For these students any ambition or striving, even for a successful academic or scientific career, involves the loss of personal authenticity and human qualities, and in social terms is a sell-out to a basically corrupt and sick society. In these respects, it resembles the rejection of ambition and fear of success that are even more widespread among undergraduates. These new graduate students also reflect the enormous growth of higher education and of affluence that allows undergraduate interests to be pursued in graduate and professional schools. They cannot be said to be involuntary students, even in the metaphorical sense in which I have referred to a class of undergraduates. But in so far as their interests and motives are at odds with the purposes of graduate training and the values and expectations of the faculty, tensions and resentments develop among them that are not unlike those we find among the reluctant undergraduates.[12] For these students, graduate study has certain attractions that are quite independent of the department's central function of providing professional training for scholars and college teachers. The university is a pleasant, stimulating, and protected environment that affords the students the leisure to read in areas that interest them and, in a sense, to pursue the liberal education that many feel they did not really gain as undergraduates. It also provides the necessary conditions for the political activities in which some are involved.

Some of these students do in fact drop out of graduate work, especially from departments in vertebrate disciplines that have rigorous professional standards and do not allow themselves to be used as extensions of undergraduate liberal arts colleges. In many other departments, especially in the humanities and social sciences, professional training has always been tempered by the encouragement of the continued general intellectual growth of the graduate students. And, in some, the discipline and the faculty itself are divided on the relative importance of technical training, on one hand, and a broad general education and familiarity with the literature of other fields of study, on the other. This reflects an older struggle within universities between gentlemanly, aristocratic attitudes towards learning and the conception of the discipline as a body of knowledge that grows by patient systematic inquiry, employing the technical apparatus of scholarly and scientific research. The disdain for 'narrow technical studies' or professional training, as well as for the kinds of research that lead to a successful academic career, is common both to the gentlemanly conception of the university and to these graduate students, who would be horrified to be accused of behaving like gentlemen or aristocrats. (And indeed in other respects they do not resemble these older models.) Many professors of sociology and English, of history and anthropology, would argue that it is precisely the combination of professional skills and broad learning that is the best preparation for a life of scholarship and future work of high distinction. So the students of whom I am speaking often find encouragement from their teachers for studies that in their teachers' eyes are an appropriate part of their professional training, but to the student represent more accurately a rejection of the discipline and of the scholarly or scientific career.

The irony, of course, is that some of these students do in fact 'succeed' in their graduate studies, sometimes with the help and sponsorship of faculty members who are themselves least in sympathy with the dominant professional and research orientations of their fields and departments. These students are rarely the most brilliant in their class (that usually requires a serious professional orientation as well as a general interest in ideas), but they are often very able and can meet the sometimes modest professional requirements of their department without too great an effort. They frequently also hold teaching assistantships (though rarely research assistantships). And in some departments a very large part of undergraduate education is carried by T.A.s, many of whom are deeply hostile to their own departments and to the subject as it is taught there. In the sections of large undergraduate lecture courses that they teach, such T.A.s can effectively sabotage the design of the course, developing alliances with undergraduates who are similarly hostile to the institution in which they are studying. Increasingly these T.A.s, led or protected by sympathetic (often junior) faculty members, in fact create their own courses, which are explicitly designed to counteract the 'conservative establishment' courses offered by the rest of the university. These courses, which as they multiply develop into a kind of shadow university, provide an academic base for dissident and politically active undergraduates.

Some of these students eventually pass their qualifying exams and, for want of an alternative, proceed on to college or university teaching, with or without a dissertation in hand. And some join the ever-expanding university departments, in many cases with their own values —their sharp and painful ambivalence toward success and an academic career, their hostility to the discipline as a cumulative body of learning, to research, and to the organization of the academic departments, curriculum, and university—unchanged.

From another perspective these students and junior colleagues reflect a failure of graduate departments to socialize their students effectively or to gain from them a commitment to their purposes and values and conceptions of the discipline and the university. This is in part due to the values these students hold on entry to graduate school, values which are reinforced by currently fashionable cultural and political ideologies and sentiments, and by their peers. It also reflects the loss of confidence of the faculty in its own values and its inability or reluctance to communicate them with conviction. Perhaps most important, these departments are no longer (if they ever were) normative communities. And that, in turn, reflects the growth of the departments, the increasing specialization of knowledge, and the privatizing centrifugal pulls of research (as compared with the centripetal force of teaching and of curriculum design). The core values of a department may still be assumed, but they are not continuously reasserted, redefined, and reinforced by men coming together and acting around them. The breakdown of a department as a moral community reflects these centrifugal forces, and then in turn reacts back on and contributes to them. Academic men are even less likely to interact around the shared work of a department when they discover deep divisions among them about the central purposes and conceptions of the subject and department. All this has marked consequences for each discipline, but it also contributes to the general weakening of academic authority and of the ability of graduate departments to socialize their graduate students to a common conception of the academic and scholarly role.

In short, there is steady recruitment of people to college and uni-

versity faculties who are deeply hostile to the central values and functions of the department and institution they join. They are seen
increasingly at scholarly conventions and as supporters or leaders of
student demonstrations. They are seen in growing numbers on departmental and university committees, where the old assumptions regarding
the shared unspoken values of academic men, cutting across disciplinary
lines, can no longer be sustained. And where these shared values are
no longer shared, whether because of political students or dissident
faculty, the old forms of university government by discussion and
consensus begin to break down. The consequence is the steady politicization of government at every level and in every arena, attended
by the withdrawal of men whose sense of obligation to university service
does not extend to polemical politics.

The management of internal conflict

This leads me to the impact of external pressures and student activism
on the internal government and climate of universities. A number of
forces work to limit the extent and intensity of disputes within the
university; these forces tend to mute disputes and press towards compromise and accommodation between differing points of view. One of
these is the broad acceptance of the legitimacy of the multiple functions
of the university. The practical effect of this conception of the university
as multiversity is to remove from dispute the sharpest and fundamentally
irreconcilable issues; disputes then can take the form of arguments
about the relative emphasis to be given to different views or the relative
support to be allocated to different programmes. And even these disputes are further diluted in situations in which there is secular growth
or expansion throughout the university, and where disputes then
become merely questions of priority and time.

Disputes are also softened by a general agreement to conduct them
within the regular academic and administrative machinery—the system
of committees and meetings through which major universities govern
themselves. They are still further softened by the institutional (and
often also the geographical) insulation of conflicting views. For example,
the humanistic scholars are typically centred in a university's college
of letters and sciences, or its equivalent; the service orientations in the
professional schools and some of the graduate departments. Historians
and engineers may have different conceptions of the primary functions
of the university, but they rarely have occasion to confront each other
in argument.

Conflict between different conceptions of the university is also
minimized by making the department, rather than a college or the
university, the unit of effective educational decision. The departments,
or most of them, are more homogeneous than the faculty as a whole,
and they have their own strong mechanisms for compromise and

accommodation, not least of which is to minimize the number and importance of issues involving collective decisions, allowing the privatization of intellectual life, a withdrawal to one's own classroom and research. On the graduate level, the university *is* for all practical purposes the aggregation of departments and professional schools, their satellite research centres and institutes, and the supporting infrastructure of libraries, labs, buildings, and administrative help. The departments effectively govern their own appointments and promotion of staff (subject to certain review procedures by extra departmental committees), admit their own graduate students, and organize their instruction. On the undergraduate level (I am speaking here of the central liberal arts college), there is, of course, the necessity to organize some structure of education that is not confined to a single department. The form this takes at many institutions is a set of distribution requirements—so many units required in fields outside one's major, so many in a major field, the remainder in electives. This system, whatever its failings as education, has the substantial virtue of reducing the amount of academic decision-making that is necessary. This reduces the occasions for conflict involving educational values and philosophies, thus letting men get on with their own work. What we see there is a spirit of *laissez-faire*, within broad administrative constraints set by limitations of space, time, staff, and other resources, that mirrors the broader philosophy of the multiversity as a whole.[13]

This pattern may be seen as an institutional response to the problem of combining post-secondary education for large numbers of students of the most diverse character with the highest standards of scholarly and scientific work. But the events of the past few years have revealed basic weaknesses in the system, which are in a sense the defects of its virtues. One of these is the lack of a central, widely shared sense of the nature of the institution, and a weakness in its capacity to gain the loyalties and devotion of its participants. This means that the institution operates on a relatively thin margin of error. Closely related to this is its tendency to generate both among students and faculty somewhat diffuse resentments, feelings of frustration and alienation from an institution which provides services and facilities, but which seems singularly remote from the concerns of individuals, responsive only to pressures and problems that are organized and communicated through the regular channels, and not always even to those. It is this kind of institution, marked by weak faculty loyalties, vague resentments, and complex administrative arrangements that is showing itself to be highly vulnerable to political attacks from without and within.

These attacks have consequences other than the disruptive demonstrations and sit-ins that are most widely publicized. The attacks, whether from a governor or a radical student group, work to politicize a campus, to polarize a faculty, and to force its members to make choices in an atmosphere of passion and partisanship. The differences that crystallize around the issues I have been describing differ from the ordinary issues of academic politics: for one thing, they involve the students more directly; for another, they are more stable, more closely linked to deep-rooted values and conceptions of the nature of the institution. Moreover, at many of the leading universities they are being institutionalized in the form of faculty caucuses and parties, which will persist as permanent elements in the governmental process, further contributing to the polarization of faculties out of which they arise. Perhaps most importantly, these tendencies threaten to disrupt the informal processes of consultation, negotiation, and compromise, among and between faculty members and administrators, by which universities are ordinarily governed. And they threaten to break through all the devices for softening conflict that I was describing.

In their place are put forward two powerful democratic models for the government of institutions. One is the model of representative democracy, complete with the party system and judicial review. The other is the model of direct democracy in the self-governing small community. Both models, as well as a combination of the two involving the formalization of the governmental process in addition to the provision of a high degree of participatory democracy, have been advocated for the university. Such systems would require a relatively high and continuous level of faculty involvement in the issues and instruments of university government, as well as a basic decision regarding the extent of citizenship—that is, the role of the students in the decision-making machinery. And, indeed, both of these issues have been raised in a recent student–faculty report on university government at Berkeley, which calls for a high level of participation by both faculty and students in units of government at every level, from the campus as a whole down to the individual departments.[14]

Many arguments can be made against such a proposal—its cumbersomeness; the impermanence of the students (they do not have to live very long with the consequences of their decisions on a campus); their incompetence to decide certain matters; and so forth. But, in my own view, more important than any of these is the absolute level of political activity and involvement required of teachers and students under these arrangements. The casual and rather informal methods by which faculty members and administrators govern a campus may have many failings, most clearly visible to those who are not part of such a government. But their chief virtue is that they have allowed students and teachers to get on with their work of teaching and learning. Some students and faculty members who want to radically transform the universities are at least consistent in wanting to change the form of government by making the process itself a central part and focus of a university education. But liberal education, scholarship, and research are not inherently political activities, even when they take politics as their subject. And they are threatened by a highly politicized environment, both by its partisanship and demand for loyalties and commitments, and also by its distractions, its encroachments on one's time and energies. The reactions of academic men who are not much interested in university government is usually to withdraw their attention and let others govern. But this works only if those others, who *are* interested in politics, share the faculty's basic values and are concerned to create and protect an environment in which the old functions of teaching and research can go on without distraction or intimidation. That is an unlikely outcome of any arrangement that makes its own government a central activity of the university, insures that all disputes pass through its formal machinery, and brings students and faculty members with a passion for politics to the centre of the governing process. But that is the direction of much student and faculty sentiment at the moment, and of 'reforms' on many campuses.

The demand for participatory democracy by those who see it as an instrument for radical change in the university involves a paradox that makes it suspect. Genuine participatory democracy, as those who have seen it at work in university departments or New England town meetings know, is an inherently conservative form of political organization. In these bodies there is a strong pressure for consensual decisions, arising largely out of the potential divisiveness of disputes unmediated by any representative machinery. The anticipation that one is going to have to continue to live and associate with one's colleagues or neighbours outside the political arena is a powerful inhibitor of actions or changes which some of them object to strongly.

But the forms of participatory democracy can be a vehicle for radical action when they involve large aggregates of people who do not comprise a genuine community, and whose relations with one another are not diffuse and continuous, but segmental and fleeting. Under these circumstances, participatory democracy becomes plebiscitary democracy, manipulated by small groups of activists who speak in the name of the passive masses. (And the demand for constant participation insures the passivity of most students and faculty members, who have other things to do than govern themselves.) For a university government based on the forms of participatory democracy to be used for radical change, it must be captured and manipulated by political activists. The conditions making for this kind of manipulation grow as activist groups among faculty members and students gain in strength, tactical experience, and ideological fervour. These conditions are also strengthened by persistent and, in some universities, highly successful attacks on the legitimacy of existing forms of university government.

The quest for legitimacy

It is widely recognized that events over the past decade, perhaps coinciding with other more fundamental and long-range developments in the society, have greatly weakened the legitimacy of institutional authority. The loss of authority and of confidence in that authority is nowhere more evident than in American colleges and universities. The constant attacks on the universities for their 'irrelevance', their neglect of students, their 'institutional racism', their implication in the war in Vietnam and in the 'military-industrial complex' have deeply shaken the belief of many academic men in their own moral and intellectual authority. Many academic men no longer really believe they have a right to define a curriculum for their students or to set standards of performance, much less to prescribe the modes of thought and feeling appropriate to 'an educated man'. Indeed, the very notion that there are qualities of mind and sensibility to be gained from experience in a college or university is often treated with amusement or contempt, as merely a reactionary expression of middle-class prejudices.

This crisis of confidence is at the heart of the crisis of university government. One common response in universities is to try to re-establish the legitimacy of institutional authority not on the older grounds of wisdom, technical competence, or certification, but on newer grounds of responsiveness to democratic political processes. And this coincides with demands from the student left for 'more responsive machinery of government which will reflect the interests and sentiments of all the members of the university community', including, most particularly, the student body. And everywhere reforms and changes are under way to increase the role of students in university government—not merely in areas of traditional 'student affairs', but directly within the faculty and departmental committees that deal with such matters as the curriculum, faculty recruitment, and student admissions. But this has not been done only to gain the perspectives and advice of students on academic issues. That could be done by co-opting students who are especially highly qualified or interested in a given area, and who would be likely to make the most thoughtful and helpful contribution to discussions. Changes currently proposed or being made reflect a greater interest in strengthening the legitimacy of academic decisions than in improving their quality. And that has meant borrowing the legitimacy of student government—its legitimacy as a democratically elected body—by assigning to it the authority for selecting the student representatives on academic committees. This effort by university authorities to borrow legitimacy helps to account for the exaggerated importance that they attach to all organized groups, and for their relative indifference to the majority of unorganized students, black and white.

One consequence, of course, is to increase greatly the political component in academic decisions; for the student governments in major American universities are primarily political, not academic bodies. Their leading officers are now often nominated by political groups and parties, representing more or less elaborately articulated positions on general academic-political issues, and they are elected after heated and well-organized campaigns. To be nominated and elected, these students must themselves be highly political men who give to student politics a large part of their time and energy. They are consequently not likely to be students who are most deeply involved in their studies—in nineteenth-century history or solid state physics, for example—and in this important respect they are less likely to share the values and perspectives of the academic men whose committees they join. Moreover, on those committees they see themselves as representing constituencies with attitudes and interests, and this, coupled with the continuing fear of every student politician of being outflanked on the left, makes their position highly resistant, if not impervious, to change through reasoned argument in the ordinary give-and-take of committee discussion. By contrast, faculty members on committees are more likely to represent no one but themselves, and therefore can change their minds or views without concern for a constituency or for charges of 'selling out'. This may change with the institutionalization of parties and causes in the faculty, and that would similarly increase the purely political component of academic decisions.

In most discussions about student representation in university government two assumptions are made: first, that the student representatives do, in fact, reflect 'student' views and perspectives; and, second, that while these may differ in certain respects from those of faculty members and administrators (properly reflecting the special experience and age of students), they will arise out of fundamentally common values and conceptions of the university. Students are seen, in these discussions, as junior colleagues or apprentices in a common enterprise of teaching and learning. There is no doubt that many students do, in fact, have the character of junior colleagues, equally concerned from their own special perspectives with an environment in which teaching and learning can most fruitfully be carried on. And faculty members who have served on committees with able and serious students know just how valuable their perspectives can be on many issues, and how important they can be as a corrective to the administrative considerations and research orientations most strongly represented on those committees. But not all students are, in fact, junior colleagues: some are indifferent time-servers, and still others are hostile antagonists. The nature of the political process surrounding student government in large universities these days makes it likely that student leaders will be far more political and almost certainly more radical than the average student. Moreover, they are likely to be more dogmatic and doctrinaire in rhetoric and action in their official positions than they might be in private. Nor can we safely assume that the leaders of student governments will share basic commitments to learning, scholarship, and academic freedom with the faculty members.[15]

Universities are fragile and vulnerable to disruption; in the face of bitter attacks, academic men and administrators lack confidence in

their own authority and want to borrow that of elected student representatives. Both these facts help explain why academic men so rarely
criticize student representatives and so commonly make them the
objective of fulsome flattery. But by making student government the
source of student representatives on faculty and administrative committees, universities may be shredding the very delicate procedures by
which they govern themselves, procedures which depend on mutual
trust, shared values, rational discussion, civility, and discretion. In so
far as important academic committees become arenas for ideological
confrontation, short-run political manoeuvres, and immediate exposure
to publicity, they cannot function. Under these circumstances, serious
scholars and students would refuse to serve on such committees,[16] and
university government would be carried by political students, the
minority of academic men who enjoy polemical politics, and the hapless
administrators who have no choice.[17]

Where next?

The growth of numbers, functions, and political pressures within
universities takes many forms and has many consequences. I have
touched on only a few of those which I believe are especially serious
threats to the university's core functions of liberal education, scholarship, and basic research. I have not spoken of the crisis in undergraduate education arising out of the complete collapse of any generally
shared conception of what students ought to learn; nor of the role of
teaching assistants in the big state universities, who carry a great part
of the undergraduate teaching, who begin to see themselves as exploited
employees, and organize in trade unions. Nor have I done more than
touch on the changing character of American undergraduates, on the
boredom of some and the apparently unquenchable anger of others,
and on the meaning of their demands for 'a relevant curriculum'.
Merely to point to these issues is to affirm that I do not judge the state
of American universities by the conventional measures of success that I
mentioned in my opening sentences. But I cannot close without at least
acknowledging the most pressing question of all: given the inexorable
movement towards universal higher education in this country, what is
likely to happen? How will American colleges and universities respond
to the enormous strains and dislocations already visible within
them?

I can see a number of possibilities, some of which have already begun
to emerge.

Progressively more repressive sanctions by public and private
authorities may be enacted against disruptions in the universities and
colleges and against people and activities perceived as 'radical' or
'subversive'. These sanctions, if carried very far, are likely to bring
teachers and students into direct confrontation with the state or the

governing bodies, and result in further disturbances and loss of autonomy, morale, and a measure of academic freedom.[18]

There may be an acceleration of the movement of academic men, especially research scholars in the natural and physical and social sciences, out of the universities and into various public and private research centres which are (or seem to be) better protected against attacks from left or right. Certainly there are models for the separation of teaching and research in the Continental and Soviet systems of higher education. Although this shift would run sharply against strongly held conceptions of the academic career in the United States, it is likely to be present as one alternative for many academic men in the event of a deepening crisis in the university.

The system may develop an even sharper and more effectively insulated differentiation of character and function within and among institutions. Some universities may self-consciously commit themselves to the primacy of disinterested inquiry in research and teaching, and select students, staff, and service missions with that primary criterion in mind. Parts of other institutions—departments, schools, research centres—may attempt to do the same. It is problematic, and will surely be variable, how effectively universities or parts of universities will be able to insulate themselves against the powerful populist forces afoot in higher education.[19]

There may evolve alternative forms of undergraduate education, breaking radically with the bookish and academic traditions that still link even the more 'innovative' efforts at 'relevance' with the high literary and scientific cultures. Much of the demand for 'relevance' on the part of undergraduates is a revolt against formal learning and a wish to be involved immediately and directly in society and its problems and opportunities. It is no use telling such students they should not be in college, but in the world and at work; the meaning of universal higher education is that these students have little choice but to be in some college, and that our system of higher education 'owns' the years from eighteen to perhaps twenty or twenty-two of most of our youth. What may, perhaps must, emerge are various forms of non-academic learning and service, organized by colleges and universities, allowing youngsters to define themselves as college students, earning credits for 'degrees' and certificates, but off the campuses and free from classrooms, library, and laboratory disciplines. I believe we must reduce the involuntariness of college attendance for many who do not want to study, if the college and universities are to survive in a recognizable form for those who do. The creation of non-academic forms of 'higher education' off campus may be the most important innovation on the agenda for our colleges and universities.[20]

Finally, a word on the great state university. It is a matter of continual amazement that an institution so deeply involved in public service in so many ways has been able to preserve its autonomy and its critical and scholarly and research functions. The question is whether its new commitments to public service, on campus and off, will seriously endanger that autonomy and the disinterested and critical intellectual life that it allows. One very tentative answer is: that depends on *how* it performs these new services. The issue is very much in doubt. But if the autonomous functions of the great state universities are threatened and then crippled by the political pressures arising out of their commitments to service, then these functions, at their highest levels of performance, will be confined to the private universities or forced outside the university altogether. And if that happens, something very precious—the presence within institutions of popular democracy of the highest standards of intellectual life—will have been lost in America.

Notes

1. *A Fact Book on Higher Education* (American Council on Education, Washington, D.C. 1969), p. 9048.
2. And in Europe, the preparation of teachers for the selective secondary schools where the children of those élites are educated and prepared for their own accession to élite status.
3. This is now as much a scientific as a literary culture.
4. For discussion of the forces associated with the growth of mass higher education in the United States, see Martin Trow, 'The Democratization of Higher Education in America', *European Journal of Sociology*, Vol. 3, No. 2 (1962).
5. This essay will focus on the problems of the great American 'multiversities', public and private.
6. Nor can it be made about many white undergraduates today. On this, see below, on 'compulsory' higher education.
7. *Report of the Faculty Committee on African and Afro-American Studies*, Faculty of Arts and Sciences, Harvard University (January 1969). The programme of black studies recommended by the Rosovsky Committee and accepted by the Harvard faculty has been greatly modified under pressure, and is no longer a model for Berkeley or the country.
8. *Campus Report* (University of California, Berkeley), Vol. 3, No. 10 (March 6 1969). Italics his.
9. And, of course, the 'attractiveness of alternatives' is also defined by social norms held by family and friends.
10. The contracts and mutual understandings, of course, differed enormously for the great variety of students and the almost equally great variety of institutions.
11. Indeed, one function of political action on campus for many students is to introduce them to other students with similar values and attitudes, and to the pleasures of belonging to a community of like-minded people working together in a common task with common ideals and purposes. The euphoria in evidence in some demonstrations and sit-ins (for example, the occupation of Stanford's Applied Electronics Laboratory in the spring of 1969) is some indication of the deep intrinsic rewards for participants in political activism around issues whose moral content seems to be absolutely clear and simple. It is important that this kind of communal life and action does not seem to be possible within the framework of the university itself; it is difficult and dangerous *outside* the university (for example, in communes or community action programmes); it is relatively easy and highly rewarding *inside* but *against* the university.
12. Of course, for undergraduates and graduate students alike who are locked into school by the draft, the term 'involuntary' is not all metaphorical.
13. For a fuller discussion of the triumph of *laissez-faire* over general education in American universities, see Martin Trow, 'Bell, Book and Berkeley', *The American Behavioral Scientist* (May–June 1968).
14. *The Culture of the University: Governance and Education*, Report of the Study Commission on

University Governance (University of California: Berkeley, 15 January 1968). See also my 'Conceptions of the University', *American Behavioral Scientist* (May–June 1969).

15. An example of academic discussion (cant is perhaps too strong a word) on this issue is the following from the pen of the Chancellor of the Minnesota State College System: 'Let us admit that, despite differences in age, experience, maturity, and background, our students should be viewed as colleagues-in-learning who must be actively and meaningfully involved in shaping all of the institutions of the campus—its curriculum, faculty, social life, administration, learning resources—its total image.' G. Theodore Mitau, 'Needed: Peacemakers and Social Engineers', *A.A.U.P. Bulletin* (Summer 1969), p. 157.

    This statement shares with many others on this theme these characteristics: (a) it imputes to all students the qualities of 'a colleague in learning' possessed by only some; (b) it recommends a larger role for students in college and university government without specifying either the forms, mechanisms, or possible limits of their participation, or anticipating the probable consequences for the institution; (c) it encourages students to make unlimited demands on the faculty which, if not met in full, will surely increase student feelings of frustration and anger.

16. There is already a noticeable withdrawal of participation by academic men from those areas of the university government which are most exposed to student attack. The withdrawal thus far is largely due to changes in the style of 'debate', and to a distaste for threats and personal abuse in the gutter language sometimes employed by radical students to whom ordinary civility and rational discourse are contemptible middle-class evasions.

17. I am speaking here chiefly of undergraduates and campus-wide government. In the graduate departments and professional schools, a strong case can be made for participation of graduate students in at least some departmental decisions. But what kind of participation, in what kinds of decisions, will properly vary from department to department (depending on its size, the character of its students, and other factors), and should not be governed by any institution-wide formula or policy.

18. Continued campus disturbances may have even more serious consequences for the political climate of the larger society.

19. I suspect that, in the foreseeable future, institution-wide policies and standards in most multiversities will work more to dilute than to defend scholarship and academic freedom. Under great pressures, university administrators will be tempted to take popular positions on academic issues. For example, one of the few issues on which the New Left and the far Right agree is that an overemphasis on research embodied in the doctrine of 'publish or perish' is the prime enemy of good teaching in our big universities. University presidents can come out squarely on the side of virtue by instructing academic committees to give greater weight to 'teaching effectiveness' in the appointment and promotion of faculty members. Some will go a step further and instruct these committees that this is the appropriate place for student evaluations to enter the appointment and promotion procedures.

    'Effective teaching' is notoriously hard to assess or even to define. In the present political climate, to stress it further in the assessment of faculty staff is to put even more pressure on teachers to seek the approval of their students, with subtle but serious implications for academic freedom and the fate of certain controversial subjects. A serious move toward the improvement of undergraduate teaching in the big public universities might start with an improvement in the ratio of teachers to students, which in turn would allow the institution to reduce the very large role of graduate teaching assistants in the undergraduate courses. But that would be expensive, and not nearly so popular.

20. We should also be able to increase the amount and legitimacy *within* the university of 'expressive' activities—painting, music, the dance, the performing arts generally—for students prepared to submit themselves to these demanding, though less bookish, disciplines.

    For another approach, the Swedes are just beginning to discuss the idea of an 'education bank', under which all citizens would have a commitment from the state for one or two years of further (higher) education, which they can take at any time during their lives if they choose to leave school during or on completion of their secondary schooling. The Swedes will very shortly also be bringing nearly all their youth to the point of university entrance; they anticipate mass but not universal higher education. An 'education bank' would increase the voluntariness of university entrance and deserves consideration in the American context.